10-17-79

Studies and surveys
in comparative education

A series prepared by the
International Bureau of Education, Geneva

Titles in the IBE Studies and surveys in comparative education series

Wastage in education: a world problem
A statistical study of wastage at school
Initiatives in education
Constructive education for children

Constructive education for children

By W. D. Wall, B.A., Ph.D.

Professor of the Psychology of Education; Head, Department of Child Development and the Psychology of Education, Institute of Education, University of London.

Foreword by Jean Piaget.

Harrap, London
The Unesco Press, Paris

First published in 1975 by
George G. Harrap & Co. Ltd
182–184 High Holborn, London WC1V 7AX and
The Unesco Press
Place de Fontenoy, 75700 Paris

ISBN 92-3-101195-2 (limpbound)
ISBN 92-3-101196-0 (hardbound)

Printed and bound in Great Britain by
Redwood Burn Limited, Trowbridge & Esher

Preface

The first version of this work was written by Professor Wall under the title *Education and mental health* and published by Unesco and Harrap in 1955; it summarized the results of the Regional Conference on Education and the Mental Health of Children in Europe, which was organized by Unesco in Paris in 1952.

Due to its widespread success—it was translated into several languages and reprinted many times—to the growth of knowledge in the field of child development in the last two decades and to the fact that many problems latent in the 1950s now have a critical significance for all educators, Professor Wall was invited by the Secretariat to undertake a complete revision of his book. The vastness of the subject and the complexity of the problems to be treated led to the decision to divide the work into two volumes. The first volume, *Constructive education for children,* deals with the first ten years of a child's life and the second, *Constructive education for adolescents,* with the years of puberty and adolescence. In view of the role of the International Bureau of Education as Unesco's centre for comparative education, which undertakes studies designed to assist Member States develop and reform their education systems, it was also decided that these works should be published in its series *Studies and surveys in comparative education.*

In this volume the author first analyses the roots and directions of contemporary social change—which seems fundamentally different in its nature from the changes of the past—and derives a series of questions to which education has to find practical answers and a concept of mental health defined not as adjustment but as dynamic adjustability. In the light of present knowledge of the dynamics of child development, he reviews the role of the family, of pre-school institutions and of the first five years or so of compulsory schooling with two ends in mind: to identify and eliminate unnecessary deprivations and stresses; and to search for means—in terms of social organization, child-rearing styles and pedagogic methods—which will increase the ability to tolerate and use the anxiety inherent in rapid change and also to develop the intellect as a flexibly creative means of dealing with open-ended problems.

This involves an analysis of the research literature concerned for example with the early development of competence, the nature of a heuristic environment, differentiated concepts of cultural deprivation, cultural difference and cultural disorganization, equality of opportunity, compensatory education, nursery schools and playgroups and the like. There follows a detailed discussion of the aims of primary education as they may be derived from philosophical, sociological and psychological analyses and as they may be embodied in school climates, discipline and education method. Concepts like reading readiness, school readiness, active methods, grouping, setting and streaming are reviewed in their practical and psychological contexts. A chapter is devoted to such special problems of the primary school as the general difficulty of meeting individual differences, dullness, failure, immigrant and migrant groups, maladjustments, the exceptionally able child, and examinations and selection. A final chapter draws a general conclusion concerning the growth development and education of the pre-pubertal child and sets the scene for the second volume, which will deal with adolescence and secondary education.

While Professor Wall has based his work largely on European research and practice he does throughout point out the analogies between problems in different national and regional contexts. It is for this reason that many of the original references to scientific works of the thirties and and of the immediate post-war era have been preserved. In some cases they are still the standard sources; in most, it is because they may be more relevant than contemporary sources (which are also cited) to the circumstances of the less developed regions of Europe and of the Third World. It is therefore hoped that the book, though not necessarily expressing the opinions of Unesco, may have particular value for readers in developing countries.

Finally, the Secretariat records its sincere recognition of the extensive knowledge, experience and devotion that Professor Wall has brought to his task and the hope that this book will prove valuable not only to the educator and child psychologist but also to the parent, administrator, guidance worker and youth leader, who can contribute so much to the healthy mental development of the child.

Contents

E. Selective and open systems: predictive and competitive examinations.
F. Conclusion: constructive mental health in the primary school. Further reading.

Pre-adolescent children; something more than adjustment; the effect of failure; independence and autonomy; the integrity of the primary stage; emotional and social education; a constructive role for the teacher; creativity and dynamic adjustability; genius; fostering creativeness; school as a provocative environment. Further reading.

All our lives long, every day and every hour, we are engaged in the process of accommodating our changed and unchanged selves to changed and unchanged surroundings; living, in fact, is nothing else than this process of accommodation; when we fail in it a little we are stupid, when we fail flagrantly we are mad, when we suspend it temporarily we sleep, when we give up the attempt altogether we die. In quiet, uneventful lives the changes internal and external are so small that there is little or no strain in the process of fusion and accommodation; in other lives there is great strain, but there is also great fusing and accommodating power; in others great strain with little accommodating power. A life will be successful or not according as the power of accommodation is equal to or unequal to the strain of fusing and adjusting internal and external changes.

The trouble is that in the end we shall be driven to admit the unity of the universe so completely as to be compelled to deny that there is either an external or an internal, but must see everything both as external and internal at one and the same time, subject and object—external and internal—being unified as much as everything else. This will knock our whole system over, but then every system has got to be knocked over by something.

Much the best way out of this difficulty is to go in for separation between internal and external—subject and object—when we find this convenient, and unity between the same when we find unity convenient. This is illogical, but extremes are alone logical, and they are always absurd; the mean is alone practicable and it is always illogical. It is faith and not logic which is the supreme arbiter. They say all roads lead to Rome, and all philosophies that I have ever seen lead ultimately either to some gross absurdity, or else to the conclusion already more than once insisted on in these pages, that the just shall live by faith, that is to say that sensible people will get through life by rule of thumb as they may interpret it most conveniently without asking too many questions for conscience' sake. Take any fact, and reason upon it to the bitter end, and it will ere long lead to this as the only refuge from some palpable folly.

The Way of All Flesh, by SAMUEL BUTLER

Foreword

In my preface to the first edition of *Education and Mental Health* (1955) I concentrated on the central idea, proposed by Professor Wall, that the harmonious development of the individual, from an intellectual, emotional and social point of view, is being threatened constantly today by the crumbling of collective values—the aftermath of two world wars fought, principally, in Europe; and that the solutions to these problems are to be found in a re-examination of educational methods in the light of our current knowledge of child psychology.

Or to express the above in more concrete terms: the idea put forward throughout this book is that mental development is a continuous process —one can hardly look back far enough or disregard the earliest causes of imbalance in one's life if one is to achieve, ultimately, 'broadening of the personality' and 'co-operation', the dual objectives of education.

With social adaptability and international understanding as their ultimate goal, the author and other experts invited to the regional conference in 1955 were not afraid to carry their researches back to earliest childhood. They were rightly convinced that internal conflicts, arising either at nursery school or in the family as a result of wrong methods or misunderstanding on the part of adults, tend to have a greater effect than is generally imagined upon the subsequent development of the child. And thus these expert researchers studied in detail the essential problem of co-ordination between school and family.

Of course their analyses and findings are still valid, but profound social changes, already emerging in the 1950s, have since become more apparent: the fundamental role which education has to play today is both a clearer one and also a more difficult one. The education system is no longer simply an adjunct to modern life, with the school playing a supporting role to the family. Mankind has undergone such changes that education cannot afford to restrict itself merely to transmitting knowledge and values: more than ever before it must aim to create personalities of greater adaptability, who are capable of transforming their societies.

However, our ever-expanding knowledge of the mental development of children in relation to their physical and social environment leads us to ask some basic questions about the role of the school, its teaching methods, teacher training, and education in general. (See our essays on 'Psychology and Pedagogy', and 'Where is Education Going?')

There would not be sufficient space in the scope of a single volume to re-examine the current problems of the education and mental health of children and adolescents; nor would there be space to relate these permanent problems to those raised by the social, educational and political changes which have occurred since the 1950s. This new work is presented, therefore, in two volumes.

Constructive Education for Children concentrates on the first decade of life. Before coming to discuss this period, the author analyses changes in Western culture and economic and political problems which must be resolved before the year 2000—bearing in mind the consequences such changes would have on the mental and emotional development of children. After seeking to identify those values which should be maintained in spite of the difficulties and privations imposed by modern society on children and parents, the author tries to channel our knowledge of child development towards a 'working definition' of educational aims. He puts particular stress not only on family and pre-school education but also on the formative aspects of 'background' and teaching methods.

In his second volume, *Constructive Education for Adolescents*, Professor Wall will consider the development of knowledge and of emotions in adolescents, and the problems which new situations raise for youth today. Our pluralistic society forces young people to make far more decisions and judgments of great difficulty than a more stable and uniform society was called upon to make in earlier generations. This is why it is necessary to develop and improve education in schools and ancillary services (in particular teacher training), rather than to abandon the school as an institution, as is forecast by some people.

Professor Wall and his collaborators must be congratulated for their constant and untiring efforts to overcome the increasingly complicated problems of education; and for their courage and optimism in seeking out possible solutions.

JEAN PIAGET

Acknowledgements

In preparing for this new version, it would have been ideal to call together a conference similar to the one of 1952, augmented by experts from the developing world. This was not possible. However, comments and criticisms on the original and suggestions for new themes and material were invited from individuals all over the world and from the non-governmental organizations which collaborated in the original activity. In addition, many men and women having special knowledge, and from a variety of countries, have given of their time and expertise to comment on and criticize each new chapter as it has been drafted. Former colleagues in Unesco, with their unrivalled experience of the World's problems, have been most generously helpful, particularly the staff of the International Bureau of Education, in conjunction with whom the writer has prepared an annotated bibliography on education and mental health[1] which is a companion to this work.

It is impossible to detail in any precise way what each has done—particularly since many have been right through the manuscript in its various stages, commenting almost page by page, whilst others have been more closely concerned with particular chapters dealing with subjects on which they are acknowledged specialists.

The following international non-governmental organizations either designated individuals who could be helpful, made direct comments and suggestions or sent highly relevant literature of their own: many of them in fact doing all three:

> Centre d'Observation et de Réadaptation Accélerée
> International Catholic Movement for Intellectual Cultural Affairs
> International Paediatric Association
> International Union for Child Welfare
> World Confederation of Organizations of the Teaching Profession
> World Union of Organizations for the Safeguard of Youth

In addition, in the course of writing I received general or detailed comments on specific topics or criticisms of particular chapters from:

> Professor Hans Aebli, Abteilung pädagogische Psychologie Universität Bern
>
> Dr. André Berge, Directeur du Centre psychopédagogique de l'Académie de Paris, Neuilly
>
> Father Henri Bissonnier, Commission médico-pédagogique et psycho-sociale, Bureau international catholique de l'enfance, Paris

Professor G. M. Carstairs, University Department of Psychiatry, Edinburgh

Mr. H. Houghton, Redhill, Surrey

Mr. A. Isambert, formerly Président du Conseil d'administration, Fédération international des ecoles de parents et d'éducateurs, Paris

Professor R. S. Peters, Professor of Philosophy of Education, University of London Institute of Education, London

Professor J. Tizard, Research Professor of Child Development, University of London Institute of Education, London

Seven colleagues and friends have given help of a kind the generosity and richness of which it is difficult to acknowledge without hyperbole. Miss M. Brearley (formerly Principal of the Froebel Institute College of Education, Roehampton), Mr. H. L. Elvin (formerly Director of the University of London Institute of Education), Dr. F. Congy (Chef du Service de l'enseignement, Centre international de l'enfance, Paris), Professor F. Hotyat (formerly pro-recteur, et président de l'Institut supérieur de pédagogie, Centre universitaire de l'etat, Mons), Professor Denis Lawton (Curriculum Studies Department, University of London Institute of Education) and Dr. N. P. Masse (Directeur des enseignements, Centre international de l'enfance, Paris) have read all or a very substantial part of the manuscript in its early drafts, have commented critically upon it and have drawn my attention to innumerable references and topics which have greatly enriched the text—and have certainly corrected or helped me avoid some major faults of emphasis or interpretation. To Dr. M. Denis-Prinzhorn of the Ecole de psychologie et des sciences de l'éducation, Université de Genève, I am particularly indebted. Not only has she read and commented upon the original drafts, but she has seen most of the many revisions as well as giving invaluable help with bibliographical data.

A word too should be said about the intelligent and good humoured assistance given by Mrs. Jeannette Cash and Miss Vanessa Shenton. The typing, retyping and typing again of drafts, the checking of the accuracy of titles in languages not their own, the deciphering of handwriting which I am forced to admit as not being of the clearest and their occcasional commonsense comments of the 'ordinary reader' have made an essential contribution.

The wealth of help, comment and criticism I have received has given an immensely valuable additional dimension to the work; but it remains, perhaps inevitably, imperfect. For its faults, errors of emphasis and omissions the writer is alone responsible. The theme is vast and its importance, I believe, crucial. There are no doubt many blind spots and there are certainly topics which are too superficially treated or important omissions; there are probably errors of inference or of fact. The book, in its present two volume form, is long, even over-ambitious. However, the widespread use of the first version encourages the thought that an overview of the present kind provides at least an introduction to some of the most important themes in education as a constructive activity and that each reader—parent, teacher, administrator, responsible voter— will take from it what he needs, using the bibliographies and references as means of going deeper and more thoroughly into his own special problems.

W.D.W.

Burnham, Bucks., 1973

NOTES

Wall, W. D. Education and mental health. *Educational documentation and information* (Geneva, Unesco: IBE), 47th year, no. 188-199, 1973.

Introduction

Many problems which were latent in the immediate post-war period have since emerged to a crucial prominence and are engaging the attention of educators all over the world. Our knowledge of child development has grown and our perceptions of the ways in which increasingly complex environments interact with the growth of ability and personality have become more acute—we see the ways of change but not so clearly the ways of controlling and directing them. Many of the desirable but remote ideals of the middle 1950s are now seen to be urgent essentials to the survival of a humane and democratic society. Equality of opportunity, the capacity to make autonomous moral choices, a command of the knowledge and skills required not only to solve the immediate problems of personal life but to participate in decisions about man's whole future—these and many others of a like kind have been proclaimed for centuries as the aims of education; we now know that they have to become more than the orotund prefatory phrases of school programmes. They have to be made precise, worked out in concrete educational methods and be embodied in institutions.

We see this, too, in a context of the relative failure of education to achieve what it has set out to do. Increased and increasing investment, far-reaching 'reforms' of structure and of curricula have been accompanied apparently by widespread increases in social and personal disturbance. The attempts to assist, through education, the countries of the developing world to raise the standards and quality of life for their citizens have been disappointing. Initial optimism has given way to an increasing sensitivity to the failures of education to live up to the high and idealistic hopes entertained for it, an increasingly anguished search for causes, and a certain pessimism about the value of formal education as a means of changing individuals and their societies.

Not surprisingly, schools and their teachers have come under bitter attack and the manifold ills of society have been laid at their door. There are those who clamour to abolish them altogether, to 'de-school society' in the name of egalitarianism and relevance. Nor has that other great educator, the family, escaped censure. Pointing to the weakness and uncertainties of parents, the ways in which affection can stifle or neglect destroy, ardent reformers propose to break it down and 'liberate' children from it. In such, and even more shrill, proposals there is more than a note of panic; and all too often, openly or implicitly, the reforms advocated seem motivated as much by exclusive and authoritarian political convictions as they are by care for the right of an individual to such an initiation into his culture as will set him free to examine the assumptions on which it is based.

The stance adopted in this book is evolutionary, not revolutionary. The view taken of mental health is wide—many would say too wide to have full significance, and difficult to distinguish from other meanings of education. Even education itself is considered as embracing not only the formal institutions but the family, the community and its media. No apology or defence is made for this wholistic and global view. It is the writer's belief that, because the school is an artificial institution with trained men and women to staff it, it is a social instrument which, if we find out how to use it sensitively and intelligently, can do more than palliate or prevent mis- or maladjustments arising in the lives of children from causes outside its walls. We must find the means and the methods by which schools can not only, within their traditional framework, positively and constructively educate their pupils, but whereby they can call into collaboration the other and even more powerful educators in the home and in the community. Only if school, home and society accept, respect and understand each other's responsibilities can we hope to prepare present and future generations for a world the nature of which we cannot foresee. This implies not only that we understand how to use the formal educational institutions to complement, extend and if necessary to compensate for the work of other educators, like the family and the media of communication and entertainment, but also that those professionally concerned with education must win the confidence and cooperation of the family and the community to work together in the education of the young. We must, in fact, 'en-school' society.

The next thirty or forty years seem likely to confront mankind with problems and decisions, the magnitude and consequences of which have little precedent in our experience. Children now at school and the generations which succeed them will have to be better educated, more able to control their passions and their aggressiveness, more able to deal with tensions within and between countries than any group of their ancestors. This will demand knowledge, a high degree of intellectual skill and insight, a genuine psychological security and the capacity dynamically to adjust and to continue to adjust to change.

We know something of the irrational elements that underlie international and national tensions, violence of all kinds and communal conflicts. Families, schools, communities, nation states are aggregates of individuals and ultimately their capacity to live harmoniously depends upon the stability and lack of markedly 'neurotic' features in at least a majority of those who make them up. Economic and social reasons for strife, problems of living space, of food supply, of personal or economic survival have always existed; and there is no reason to suppose that they will cease to do so or even become less severe—rather the reverse. The increasing complexity of the groups in which civilized man lives in it-self makes for a more fragile stability and disturbances are likely to be more far reaching in their effects. But how such problems are dealt with —by force, by fight, by flight or by compromise and negotiation—is very much a function of the psychology of those who deal with them. We must be concerned with the removal of external and objective causes of anxiety, injustices and reasons for tension. We must also devise the political and social machinery and institutionalized ways of behaving which enable us to deal constructively with conflicts of all kinds. How-ever, as experience shows, neither the removal of objective causes for strife, nor the existence of satisfactory democratic institutions are suffi-cient in themselves. If there are substantial societies or groups within society whose anxiety is pathological, they will seek objects or groups on which to fasten their fears and such can always be found; they will look for security in beliefs and loyalties which render them hostile to other groups and block the paths to a peaceful resolution of conflict.

The human being is very much the product of the education, formal and informal, which his society provides for him. Hence if men and women are to understand and shape the changes in their society, it is to the whole education of the young that we must look at least for the prevention of damaging and ultimately socially dangerous maladjust-ments. More hopefully we must view it as a means constructively to form human personalities whose insight into and mastery of their own nature makes them able to shape a future for themselves and their children which takes full advantage of what the world has to offer.

Mental health like physical health is thus much more than an absense of disease or maladjustment. One at least of its aspects is freedom from fears, anxieties and insecurities which have no rational cause. Coupled with this is the knowledge of what to do to free oneself from a real threat. Frustration, fear, anxiety and the like are not in themselves bad : they may constitute the necessary stimuli which tone the individual or the group for action; but it is crucial that groups or individuals are equipped with the means of meeting them rationally and of effectively reducing them without harm to the self or to others. Similarly, aggres-sion is a potent and necessary spring of human action; the problem is not to suppress it but to deflect it from interpersonal and intergroup violence or strife, to socialize its expression and turn it towards constructive ends.

Mankind has rubbed along for a million or more years without a global disaster, though there have been increasingly frequent local disasters of growing magnitude. The two world wars of this century left scarcely anyone untouched. There are those who think we may again narrowly escape without taking too much thought or too many positive decisions. However the signs accumulate that doomsday may be round the corner.[1] Even to the optimist, it looks as though the race between education and disaster is quickening.

In what follows it is suggested that the psychological climates in which children and young people all over the world are growing up have profoundly changed over the past century and it is a change different in many of its features from the great changes of the past. To some very considerable extent too it seems that man's nature may also be changing as a consequence. This process of environmental change, of change in the climate of ideas and in the balance of human personality seems to hold considerable threats of prejudice to normal harmonious growth in the rising generations of children—by depriving them of certain essential experiences and exposing them to major uncertainties. On the other hand, it also seems to hold out great promise[2] partly because materially there are many things we can afford to do if we have the will and partly because our knowledge of human psychology and of the precise ways in which the child fathers the man is growing daily. Such promise is only likely to be realized if, through education in its widest sense, we can develop a sufficiency of men and women whose social and political wisdom will enable them to grasp the opportunities of technology, use them to provide enough for all, and restore the non-material elements of man's existence.[3] Even this will fail unless the bulk of the participants in what is becoming a closely interrelated and interdependent series of societies throughout the world are themselves capable of a continuing and dynamic adjustment, of bringing about change, of taking part actively in controlling it, and of making the ultimately moral choices on which the quality of the future depends. This means no less than a rational attempt to alter human personality in positive ways through education.

Some will categorically and pessimistically condemn such an attempt, referring to the ancient wisdom that 'you can't change human nature'. In the sense that human nature consists of a biologically determined equipment of reflexes, unorganized drives, some complex maturational patterns all dependent upon a complicated neurological mechanism which permits the development of abstract conceptual thought and speech, this contains a form of truth. It also seems to be true that some dispositions, male aggressiveness for example, and some would say greed and acquisitiveness, are difficult indeed to eradicate—*naturam expelles furca, tamen usque recurret.* There are many touches of nature, good and bad, that seem to make the whole past and present world kin.

Yet in all that we think of as particularly human—in character, in personality, in the content of consciousness, in attitudes and ideals, in ideologies and in patterns of behaviour—nurture is probably at least as important as nature.

The course of history demonstrates moreover that human mental and physical environments do change in important ways, sometimes swiftly and dramatically, often through the agency of man himself. It seems at least likely, in the light of our knowledge, that massive changes in environment, particularly if they are rapid and pervasive, will bring about corresponding changes in thought and behaviour. What seems then to be important is to examine such changes in the recent past and to look more closely at what is going on at present. From such an analysis we can hope to perceive the directions of development, something of the problems which it produces and ways in which we may intervene educationally to shape the future of our society.

Because education is an applied activity and because it has ends which are involved with choices of values, such an analysis cannot be neutral. The endeavour is nonetheless made to show that while certain broad aims or values—tolerance, respect for others, willingness to accept a democratic rather than an authoritarian style of interpersonal and intergroup relationships and the like—are regarded as essential, there are many forms in which these can be acceptably embodied and that cultural pluralism, the acceptance of the value of difference, is in itself worthy of cultivation if we are all to profit from the rich and inherent diversity of human beings.

Further, in this large context, we are brought to view mental health as something which goes well beyond the absence of neurosis or maladjustment; and even beyond what we have considered hitherto to be the minimal aims of education. If indeed the future of our society is to be shaped in democratic ways, very many of the participants must have a developed ability to make conscious choices based upon rational grounds and to look beyond personal or even sectional interests to considerations which deeply concern mankind, its future and the quality of life for all who inhabit this planet. Education, then, and particularly the school's part in it, must be regarded as a constructive process aimed not merely at personal development but at the creation of the psychological condition in individuals which will permit the human community really to control its destiny rather than leave it to the free play of irrational or at least only partly rational processes, to various forms of interacting egotisms and selfish interests.

This is no easy business, particularly when we try to translate it into the task of imperfect parents and their growing families or imperfect teachers confronted by thirty or forty pupils—children or adolescents. Those who educate have not only to prevent things from going wrong and to remedy deficiencies and difficulties; they have to shape human personality in some quite conscious and definite ways—and that in a society which subscribes now to no coherent system of morality and values.

Much of what follows, particularly in Chapters II and III will be sadly familiar ground to many readers and to some it will seem a rather hurried treatment of vast problems. But the attempt to draw together at least the more important strands of growth and change seems essential to provide the background against which the major argument of this book is developed. Whatever terms we use—'mental health', 'constructive education'—the argument is that, in our present and future dilemmas, education cannot be regarded simply as a means of adapting an individual to his society, as a straightforward initiation to a slowly evolving culture, as a means of preventing inequalities and maladjustment—though it may partake of all these; it has to be seen as a consciously and deliberately used instrument which, if we succeed, will enable man to control his own nature and the psychological environment he creates for himself. Perhaps the biggest change we have to recognize is this change in the function of education; and the biggest difficulty that of helping the educators (parents, teachers, the communicators of the mass media) to undertake a positive role without slipping on the one hand into anarchistic irresponsibility and on the other into forms of indoctrination.

FURTHER READING

Clark, B. R. *Educating the expert society.* San Francisco, Chandler, 1962.
Cowen, E. L.; Gardner, E. A.; Zax, M., eds. *Emergent approaches to mental health problems.* New York, Appleton Century, 1967.
Lobrot, M. *Les effets de l'éducation.* Paris, Les Editions sociales françaises, 1971.
Müller, J. *Ländliche Schul—und Bildungspolitik.* The rural school and educational policies. Schwelm i. Westf., Schule und Nation, 1965.
Saiyidain, K. G. *Man in the new world.* London, Asia Publishing House, 1964.
Silver, H. *The concept of popular education.* London, MacGibbon & Kee, 1965.
Sutherland, J. D., ed. *Towards community mental health.* London, Tavistock Publications, 1971.

NOTES

1. Meadows, D. H., *et al. The limits to growth* (Club of Rome). London, Potomac Associates, Earth Island Ltd., 1972.
2. But see: Roszac, T. *The making of a counter culture.* London, Faber, 1970. Roszac's counter culture reflects technology as dehumanizing—as do certain other powerful marginal groups today.
3. Reich, C. A. *The greening of America.* New York, Random House, 1970. Gabor, D. *The mature society.* London, Secker & Warburg, 1972.

Chapter one

Origins of change in the nineteenth century[1]

CONTINUITY AND DISCONTINUITY

Contemporary Western man is a very different being from his ancestors who roamed the plains and forests of Europe before the dawn of recorded civilization, from those who built the Romanesque and Gothic churches and cathedrals, and from the men of the Renaissance.

There are passions and thoughts from the past that stir us still and a certain continuity of emotion is recorded in history and literature:

> But have you wine and music still,
> And statues and a bright-eyed love,
> And foolish thoughts of good and ill,
> And prayers to them who sit above?[2]

Some at least of this continuity is, however, illusory. The essence of great art is that it is re-interpreted from age to age. We project into it our own different meanings. It is most unlikely for example that the Bible means to us what it means to its first translators; or to them, what it meant to its authors; and try as we will we can hardly recapture the mood of the first audiences that saw *Macbeth, L'Avare* or *Nathan der Weise*. Still less can Western man respond to the ancient poetry of the East as its first hearers did.

For the most part, human nature changes slowly and imperceptibly, but a careful reading of history and literature indicates that there are some periods when what amounts to a mutation of consciousness and personality takes place at least in a substantial minority. The economic, social and political climate in which men live changes so fundamentally that a culture or a nation sets a new course. Such changes are, as a rule, more striking in retrospect. Their effects were spread over many genera-tions in such a way that the profound adjustments in human personality, thought, emotion and action, though possibly striking for individuals,

9

have collectively taken place relatively slowly and without apparently too great a tension and strain. Certain proportionately small groups of individuals separated geographically or temporally may betray a new restlessness or a new way of approach; but usually such changes have first affected a restricted social or intellectual élite and have filtered down through generations at sufficient intervals to allow accommodation to take place without great and universal social upheaval.

THE RENAISSANCE

The Renaissance was one such change. It took several centuries to work out and just as in Shakespeare and Montaigne or in Chaucer and Boccacio—separated as they were by nearly two centuries—we find medieval as well as renaissance elements and outlooks, so in the culture in which each lived we find the same mingling. 'In social history . . .' writes Trevelyan, 'we find in every period several different kinds of social and economic organization going on simultaneously in the same country, the same shire and the same town. . . . In everything, the old overlaps the new—in religion, in thought, in family custom. There is never any clear cut; there is no single moment when all Englishmen adopt new ways of life and thought.'[3] The psychologist would add to this statement that each human personality has the same mixture of consistent and inconsistent elements and will itself reflect the differing elements of the society by which it has been conditioned. He would also add that because of the co-existence in an apparently unified culture of very different personalities and social structures, while a particular cast of personality may dominate and represent the mode, survivals, previsions and sports will also exist to contradict it.

THE INDUSTRIAL REVOLUTION

A second and more abrupt transition, for which the slow working out of the impulses of the Renaissance paved the way, was what might be called the 'steam power and transport' phase of the Industrial Revolution, which affected the countries of Europe differently in detail with some being later than others to feel its impact. From the point of view of the climate in which children grew up, we may draw attention to the immense and rapid increase in the total population,[4] the violent sprawling urbanization and the feeling abroad that there were no limits to the creation of wealth. More and more children grew up in towns. The towns themselves largely lost their ancient character of small, socially mixed communities, and became populous agglomerations with increasing segregation of the social groups. For almost the first time in history the way was open, apparently, to a general and rapid social mobility—upward and downward. Soldiers of fortune, courtesans and merchants had, in all history, been able to move upward in at least a limited way to fortune and rank; the service of the church and the embryonic civil service of the king had also allowed able recruits from the lower social classes to climb, though their security was always somewhat dependent upon noble or royal favour. The expanding home and overseas markets of the nineteenth century, the growth in the techniques of mass produc- tion, the discovery of the ways in which demand may be created by advertisement, made it possible for many more individuals to make, in their life-time, large fortunes which were not dependent upon the favour of any of the traditional holders of power.

Nevertheless, for the majority of people in Europe, the nineteenth century was not particularly revolutionary. It certainly was not revolu- tionary elsewhere, even though the period of colonial expansion brought many ancient cultures under the domination of the West and opened up Africa to trade. Overtly in Europe and elsewhere the social order re- mained as it had been in its main assumptions founded upon religion and most men stayed in the station to which it had pleased God to call them; public morality was similarly sanctioned and—however harsh it might have been in many instances—provided a coherent framework within which the overwhelming majority of children and adolescents grew up.

England, probably because of its earlier start and the importance of non-conformity, felt the impact of change more violently than else- where, and reacted with vigorous social change. The sons of those whose accumulated fortunes allowed them to overleap many social barriers were provided for by the new public schools inspired by Arnold's reforms and were trained in self-discipline, religious principle and leadership. They provided the educated recruits to the expanding civil and military ser- vices necessitated by the growth of industry and of empire; but at the same time, they and their less fortunate brothers and sisters were in- doctrinated with a social-religious ethos which right up to the outbreak of the First World War, successfully maintained—with occasional signs that all was not for the best in the best of all possible worlds[5]—the ap- pearance of a stable, self-confident and optimistic society.[6]

In the whole of Western Europe, and particularly in the towns, the over-all change in the social and psychological climate from one genera- tion to the other was more marked and rapid than similar changes before. The conflict and the clash of generations to which it led forms the theme of many novels. It is not without significance either, that, apart from a few isolated instances due to special individual circumstances, there is very little mention in literature[7] of the struggles, problems and disturb- ances of adolescence as a general phenomenon until the middle and late nineteenth century. From the second phase of the Romantic movement— and particularly in the poetry of Keats, Shelley, Byron, Lamartine and de Vigny—it becomes a dominant theme; it had been preceded by the beginnings of what became by the mid-century a major literature about children and for children, some of it reformist and humanitarian,[8] some of it moral and moralizing as well,[9] some of it deeply concerned with the psychological implications of environment and of adult attitudes and actions for subsequent character.[10] So, too, a general preoccupation with education as a major instrument of social policy began in Europe in the mid-nineteenth century[11] and by the end of the century (1898) the first society for the study of child psychology was founded in London, followed shortly by a similar society in Paris.

THE ROOTS OF CONTEMPORARY CHANGE

Three currents of thought which rose to the surface in the West in the nineteenth century are of far-reaching importance to our understanding of to-day. Darwin's theory of evolution, announced in 1859, was a major blow at the certainties and dogmas of organized religion. Doubt and rationalism increasingly reinforced the agnosticism of science and tended to break up the alliance of political parties with conformist and non-conformist religious beliefs. At the same time, evolutionary theory gave immense impetus and a new framework of hypotheses to all the biological sciences. It was probably not without its influence on the work of Marx and Engels; it certainly was one of the contributory currents which swept rapidly into oblivion the idea that the social order was fundamentally divine in origin and hence could not be radically changed. By implication it attacked the roots of the subconscious beliefs on which society had hitherto been founded and seemed to give objective basis to the philosophies bequeathed by the French Revolution.

The second great shock, whose effects were not fully felt, in England at all events, until after the First World War—although some at least of the thinking was implicit in the writings of Sully and McDougall well before that—was given by the popularization of the works of Sigmund Freud.[12] Apart altogether from the truth or otherwise of the doctrines expounded and the accuracy with which they were disseminated, three main ideas enunciated by Freud have deeply influenced contemporary life and thought—the notion of psychic determinism which seemed to undermine the basis of most philosophical and religious controversies about free will and predestination; the stress on unconscious and subconscious mentation, which seemed to give the *coup de grâce* to notions that human problems could be solved solely by the use of human reason; and the ascription to the sex drive of the principal place in the determination of normal and abnormal behaviour which, with its accompanying doctrine of the evils wrought by repression, seemed to attack the very sources of nineteenth century morality.

The third major current of thought and one highly provocative of change arose from the work of Karl Marx.[13] His dialectical materialism constituted a direct attack upon current idealistic and dualistic philosophies which, he held, supported the interests of the ruling classes. His economic doctrine struck at the basis of nineteenth century industrial society by making manifest (and condemning) the difference between the wages paid and the surplus value in capitalist systems, and suggesting the political remedy of Communism. Until 1917 most revolutions and major shifts of economic and political power had taken place within the ruling groups. Marx, followed by Lenin, preached the dictatorship of the proletariat and common ownership of the means of production and exchange. This revolution was intended to be a radical change in the power structure that had hitherto universally held.

Each of these in its way proved a powerful ferment and prepared, over the second half of the nineteenth century, the changes of which we are feeling the accumulating impact today and which have rippled out over the world. It is, however, of great importance to recognize that these ideas struck in a way without historical precedent in terms of Western man's view of himself in his society, in his relation to himself and his world, and opened the way for the technological exploitation of the conquest of nature; the Reformation altered man's idea of himself in relation to God; the nineteenth and early twentieth century called in question the whole structure of Western society and most of the beliefs, the value systems and the formal and institutional relationships on which it was based—and this at a time when the material and psychological environment was itself undergoing massive and pervasive change.

Many other factors and ferments in the world of nineteenth and early twentieth century Europe could be pointed to as contributing to the alterations in the whole socio-psychological environment in which children and adolescents grew up, particularly towards the end of the last century and in the first decade of this.

Two main points should be made however. The first of these is the suggestion that the second phase of the Industrial Revolution in Europe wrought changes in human personality and in society comparable only to those brought about earlier by the Renaissance. The second is that the rate of change in the West in the last half of the nineteenth century and the first decades of this—and the corresponding strains and tensions put on individuals, sub-groups and society itself—were immeasurably greater than at any earlier epoch. The majority of men and women adjusted to and digested these strains and changes, but a substantial minority did not; the public life and the literature of the period is testimony to the personal problems and conflicts which arose.

FURTHER READING

Appelbaum, R. P. *Theories of social change.* London, Markham, 1970.
Gotesky, R.; Laszlo, E., eds. *Evolution—revolution.* London, Gordon & Breach, 1971.

NOTES

1. Much of what follows in the whole of this part is based on an earlier work of the present writer: *Child of our times.* London, National Children's Homes, 1958.
2. James Elroy Flecker: 'To a poet a thousand years hence'.
3. Trevelyan, G. M. *English social history—Chaucer to Queen Victoria.* London, Longmans Green, 1947.
4. Though, of course, the essentials of change began much earlier, between 1801 and 1851 the population of England rose from nearly 9 millions to nearly 18 millions; by 1901 it was over 32 millions. In the process of urbanization there were two very important contributory factors—the enclosure of common lands culminating in the Enclosures Act of 1845 which broke up the traditional village communities, and the immense increase in the import of cheaper foreign wheat from about 1875 onwards. By 1901, only 23 per cent of the population was rural. In the same period the population of Europe grew from 187 millions in 1800, to 266 millions in 1850 and to 401 millions in 1900.
5. English literature is full of such signs—from novels like *Mary Barton* (1848), by Mrs. Gaskell, with its fierce class consciousness and emphasis on the lack of sympathy between employers and employees, to *Jude the obscure* (1896), a novel of the frustration of an able young man denied educational opportunity. Arnold Bennett, writing much later of course, depicts the atmosphere of the sudden rise to prosperity and equally sudden fall in many of his 'Five Towns' novels. Chartism (1837–48), the rise of the Trade Union Movement and of radical socialism as enshrined in Morris's *The dream of John Ball* (1888) and *News from nowhere* (1891), the attack on established religion and the accompanying hypocrisy of the whole social system in *Erewhon* (1872) are others. There was of course, too, a considerable underground pornographic literature (see: Marcus, S. *The other Victorians.* London, Weidenfeld & Nicholson, 1966) which provided the mirror image of morality.
6. As Trevelyan points out (*English social history,* Op. cit., p. 484), following Clapham from 1820 onwards the purchasing power of wages rose and, after the Great Exhibition of 1851, there was an even greater rise.
7. But see: Kiell, N. K. *The universal experience of adolescence.* London, University of London Press, 1971. Most of Kiell's references are nineteenth century or later and the earlier ones concern for the most part either superior social groups or specific circumstances. On this subject see Volume II, Chapter 3.
8. Cf. the many portraits of the misery of children in the books of Dickens, the work of Robert Owen, and the agitation of Robert Peel the Elder for State control of factory conditions. Many of the early poems of Wordsworth, as well as the 'Prelude' begun in 1799, are highly sensitive portrayals of

childhood experiences. Maria Edgeworth (1767–1849) was much earlier of course and her *Parents assistant* (1796–1801) and other books depicted childhood in a realistic way.

9. For example Kingsley, *The water babies*.

10. *The way of all flesh*, though not published until 1903, after Butler's death, is a remarkable summary of many of the psychological features of nineteenth century life and in particular of the effects of social mobility and of the effects on children of their parents' beliefs and ambitions.

11. Cf. Herbert Spencer and later Durkeim. See also: Tempels, P. *L'instruction du peuple* (1864), which led among other things to the establishment of the *Ligue de l'enseignement*. Universal and compulsory education was earlier, at least as a proposal, elsewhere: in Prussia (Education Law 1717); in certain American states; the notion was written into the Calvin's Ecclesiastical State of Geneva (1542); and in Scotland (Act of Discipline 1598).

12. *Psycho-pathology of everyday life, 1904/Three Essays on the theory of sexuality,* 1905/First International Psychoanalytic Congress, 1908.

13. *Das Kapital.* Vol. I. 1867.

Chapter two

The psycho-social background to contemporary western personality

There are many strands in the processes of change which are taking place all over the world; and some of them have their roots well outside and independent of the European tradition. But a principal phenomenon of our time is that the intellectual ferment of nineteenth and twentieth century Europe has been highly influential in all kinds of change and development elsewhere. Moreover many phenomena which we, somewhat ethnocentrically, call 'Europeanization' or 'Americanization' are in fact responses to the growth of similar conditions rather than the direct effects of cultural contagion. Furthermore, as ideas and aspirations become disseminated they interact with indigenous beliefs, deeply seated customs and folkways which colour change but rarely halt it. In one very real sense the developed countries and particularly the most affluent, are a comparatively long way into a future which ultimately one may expect to embrace the world; what is happening to us therefore has prophetic implications for the rest of mankind.

Europe after the First World War was dramatically different from what is was at the turn of the century. The four years of conflict precipitated intellectual and emotional events so rapidly in almost every country of Europe that 1914-18 seems a natural divide, cutting off the past so abruptly from the twenties and thirties that it seemed to have swept any lingering nineteenth century certainties completely away.

The Second World War greatly accelerated the process. The society which has been emerging since at least the mid-century in Europe and North America seems so profoundly different even from that of the inter-war years that it is difficult to reconstruct the certainties by which even our fathers and grandfathers lived. One is tempted to speak as though what we now experience were a mutant, brought about by the wars themselves, but, as we have seen, the roots of our present changes and dilemmas go back into history. In certain respects what has been and is happening is that change has precipitated to a critical point at which an accumulating series of scientific and technological leaps is confronting us with human dilemmas, which to the cold observer seem completely novel and lacking in any useful precedent.

PROMULGATION OF CHANGE

In some ways the most dramatic change is in the mechanisms by which change itself is p omulgated. Certainly until the arrival of mass literacy in Europe and the popular Press, cultural change, the dissemination of new ideas and life styles was mediated by élites. Even to the mid-nineteenth century it is doubtful whether the audience for any book constituted much more than 10 per cent of the population who because of their education were the least suggestible and by and large the more experienced and older groups. The rise of the popular Press based on an increasing literate readership did much to extend this base towards the end of the nineteenth century and in the first half of this, but the popular newspaper scarcely touched the pre-adolescent or the very large number of the not very well educated.

Nor was there much direct international contact. Even with the coming of steam transport, travel remained the privilege of the few and the notion of seeing other men and other climes was largely conceived of in strictly European terms. In the colonial era armies went further abroad and there were the great emigrations from Europe to America. But these were little different in kind from earlier colonization and travel and the travellers tended to be enshrined in their sense of cultural superiority: such travel in any case did not deeply affect the majority of people. Awareness of what was happening elsewhere, until the coming of the telegraph and radio telephony, was slight and information long in coming. There were small trans-national groups sharing a common life-style and often speaking a common language—for example the early humanists with their common tongue of Latin or the eighteenth and nine-teenth century aristocracy communicating in French. These tended to be centred on Europe and even on Western Europe.

We now live in what McLuhan[1] calls, aptly in some respects, 'the global village'. The motor car and the aeroplane have paradoxically enlarged living space and made the world smaller and in closer contact. Holidays with pay and cheap package tours have brought for many European and North American social groups the possibility of visiting parts of the world which were formerly accessible only to the rich or the adventurous. This has particularly affected the young whose taste for wandering to far places can be relatively easily indulged with a tent, a second-hand van and comparatively little money.

News flies across the globe in minutes rather than days or weeks. Communication by the printed word, even when this is popular and illustrated journalism (which characterized mass communication in the first three decades of the twentieth century), implies a certain minimal element of literacy[2] and a certain maturity. Newspapers, even illustrated ones, are less immediate in their effects than oral speech or visual presentation and require rather more interpretive effort from the reader. The radio—and particularly the transistor radio—conveys news through speech to a much wider audience and skilfully used can overleap the barriers of illiteracy. Thus the nomad on his camel can overhear the conversation of astronauts on the moon and receive instant news from all corners of the world. Even more direct is visual presentation; first the cinema and now the television show other ways of life, other views, opinions and happenings in instant and realistic actuality without necessarily involving the use of words at all. Just as economically and socially in a developing country now, highly westernized groups in towns can be seen to coexist with medieval peasantry, so all men can be aware of the immense material and cultural gradients which exist between countries.

In many ways visual imagery is the most primitive form of expression and communication and, as the mechanism of dreams tell us, can be profoundly symbolic. Both verbal and pictorial communication can be manipulated, of course, and presentation is inevitably selective. What seems to be important is that—even more than speech transmitted by radio—television communicates directly to all, both at a cognitive level and unconsciously. In this sense it is powerfully educative and is likely to be most powerful with the most suggestible—children,[3] young people, the relatively uneducated. Because it may appeal particularly to the unconscious it may have influences in ways exceedingly difficult to detect or control. The appetite of the media for news—and news frequently means disaster, accident, crime, conflict, aggression or the trivial aberrations of human nature—inevitably leads to a search for interesting items—a spotlight on the underside of life. This phenomenon of 'instant news' constitutes, in cybernetic terms, a feed-back loop which, even if it is not manipulated for political ends, tends to present the world to itself in a selective and probably distorted way.[4] Because of the high cost of all forms of news service and particularly of television, huge subventions either from the State or from industry via advertising are essential, and this raises the problem of at least covert censorship and manipulation, not necessarily in the direction of maintaining a high quality of comment or presentation.

It is easy to take a conspiratorial view of the mass media and particularly of commercial television, but doubtful whether this is supported by fact in most cases. What seems to be important is that it tends to feed back and intensify the *status quo* in a highly simplified form while at the same time ensuring rapid and on the whole uncritical dissemination of novelties of thought, expression or behaviour. It is difficult, too, within the limits imposed by space, time and immediate intelligibility, to present a nuanced and balanced view of any important question.[5]

INVERSION OF THE MECHANISM OF CHANGE

From our point of view the crucial difference with the past lies in the inversion of the ways by which change is communicated. The élites of age, experience and education are likely to be less suggestible and by and large to make a more discriminating use of the visual media; they are likely to fit what they see within an organized and thought out matrix of knowledge and experience which they have built up from other sources. It was just such élites who in the past were in the forefront of change, interpreting, digesting and passing it on, as it were, so that the manners and views of the ruling group of yesterday became the general climate of the morrow. Now communication is direct and its impact more potent and rapid. The interpretive 'élites', if one can call them such, tend to be journalists, broadcasting personalities or propagandists of one kind or another concerned as much to arouse and maintain interest and curiosity as with a balanced presentation of life as it is. The younger, more suggestible and less educated are those most likely to be directly and profoundly exposed to and influenced by the visual media. Change is thus mediated as much or more by them as by élites of any kind. The teacher in front of a class, a reasonably educated parent talking with a child, may in a sense be living in the past; the content of their con-sciousness will be so considerably different that they may be completely out of touch. A generation gap and to some extent a gap in consciousness between the most and the least educated has of course always existed in Western society. What is being suggested is that this gap has not only widened but fundamentally changed in its nature. The young and more suggestible can be further forward into the future than their elders and the former educated élites.

AFFLUENCE AND THE ATTITUDES IT ENGENDERS

This is the context within which profound qualitative changes are going on in other fundamental aspects of life and thought in the developed countries of the West. Until comparatively recently in Western Europe and North America (and still of course over more than half of the world) the available resources of food, goods, shelter and services were less than sufficient to guarantee for all the essentials of a life free from real want, hunger and ill-health. It is now true that—if it thinks only of itself and solves the problems of an equitable distribution—any Western society can guarantee these minimum essentials to all its citizens. What is more, the productivity of industry is such that more goods are made by the West than can be consumed in the ordinary processes of a full and healthy life.

In situations of scarcity, conservation and self-restraint are virtues. Conversely, when everyone is convinced that rising production is essential, consumption must be encouraged, even to the point of conspicuous expenditure and waste.[6] Hence the enormous activity of the advertising industry, the elaborate packing, the planned obsolescence.

RISING ASPIRATIONS

This has important psychological corrolaries. Right up to comparatively recent times, the appropriate attitudes, for most people, were those of aspirations restrained within fairly narrow limits, the idea of being reconciled to one's lot. Men laboured to provide for today and if possible to put a little by for the morrow. It was virtuous to be contented with one's lot and not to strive excessively to change it. The position of the few 'haves' (who shared in general the ethic of accumulation for the future and development of capital), was supported by a general doctrine of resignation for the many, by the idea that poverty, suffering and renunciation patiently borne in this life laid up treasure hereafter, and that it was easier for a camel to go through the eye of a needle than for a rich man to get to heaven. For most people possessions were comparatively few and in general utilitarian; they tended to be handed carefully on from generation to generation; waste was a sin. In two-thirds of the world gross general insufficiency still dominates thought and behaviour; but the affluence of the West is more clearly perceived by the developing countries and many, especially the young, see the increasing differences between peoples as a cruel injustice.

Not only advertising but the whole general climate of our times incites to high and rising aspirations; in health, in housing, in education, in security but also in possessions and in material standards of living. The idea that one should enjoy today and pay tomorrow is the reverse of the Protestant ethic. It is important to realize that this is subtly different from the value put on success by effort, the idea of working to be able to pay one's way and of the guilt implied by poverty which marked the nineteenth century. Even our notion of poverty has changed. It is regarded not as the failure of the individual but the failure of the community and its organization, and internationally as a failure of the affluent countries to assist the less fortunate parts of the world. Many goods, services and conditions of life which were a luxury of privilege are now regarded as minimum essentials which should be guaranteed by social means; the current aspiration is that the 'good life' (whatever that may mean) is a general human right which it is the duty of society to provide for all. To some extent conversely, affluence which seems to owe its rise to a greedy exploitation of the world's resources, and to the profit motive which puts gain before the humane and non-materialistic values, leads to the development, particularly among the young, of a counter culture.[7]

AUTHORITARIANISM

This is bound up with other changes, notably with changes in our notions of social class, in the structure of authority and of attitudes towards it. With only minor exceptions all societies in the past and most societies in the world at present have been or are essentially authoritarian and socially stratified in their organization. This hierarchic structure was pervasive and still is outside the West. Families usually were dominated by the father whose rights in law and religion over his wife and children were more or less absolute: 'he made for God and she for God in him' pretty fairly sets out both the relationship and its divine sanction. Within this, of course, limited forms of matriarchy were possible and in some countries or within some social groups there were clear divisions of responsibility between the mother and the father—though rarely on any basis of equality. The structure of authority (and of privilege) in the State (and in such institutions as the school, the factory, the farm, the army) tended to reflect this.[8] Democracy where it existed in eighteenth- and even in most of nineteenth-century Europe tended to mean the election of alternative oligarchies, and even then by a franchise restricted to a property owning group. Full manhood franchise without property qualifications did not come in England until 1918.[9] Women gained full electoral equality with men in England only in 1932, in Belgium in 1947 and in Switzerland in 1971.

Law and morality were largely coincident and both sanctioned by the authority of religion. At their best such societies in Europe were 'paternalistic' in a good and responsible sense, the authority of the ruling groups being exercised within a framework that took note of the interests of the ruled, of the same kind as that of a wise father for his children. Indeed the attitude for example of officers in the army, of the Church and of enlightened employers was reflected in the actual words or imagery which were used—'*mon enfant*', the shepherd and his sheep and 'my people'.

This authoritarian and paternalistic structure was in general supported by the class system, by the beliefs which sanctioned it and where it existed by a highly differentiated and selective education system. Though it was always possible, and particularly in times of disturbance or of military or mercantile expansion, for individuals to be socially mobile and for new classes to arise, like the mercantile middle classes of the eighteenth century and earlier, and the entrepreneurs of the nineteenth and twentieth centuries, social mobility did not so markedly characterize most societies previous to the present. New social groups in any case took their place in an existing ascending hierarchy.

The social order was maintained by the belief that it was divinely ordained and that there were genetic and other inherent differences between groups. Birth determined status, and even the recruitment to the middle classes of nineteenth-century Europe by education was a slow process rarely achieved in any full sense in one lifetime—'it takes three generations to make a gentleman' was an article of faith at least up to the First World War. It was believed that superior social groups had a natural talent for leadership and a right to exercise authority, as had certain liberal professions like medicine and the Church.

UNIVERSAL COMPULSORY EDUCATION

All this has now radically altered. To some extent this may be attributed to the effects of universal compulsory education and its extension through all kinds of communication; hence it is connected with the inversion of the processes of change referred to earlier. Since the turn of the century in Europe all children have had some schooling and the length of the compulsory period has been steadily raised from five to ten or more years. Broadly this has had three effects, revolutionizing the whole social structure, particularly in Northern Europe and the United Kingdom but, less rapidly, elsewhere as well. Educational stimulus has certainly raised the level of available or functional intelligence; educated men and women can reason out more difficult problems, control technically more advanced apparatus, articulate problems more clearly.

Perhaps even more important than any other effect, however, is the immense increase in social mobility which resulted from the expansion and extension of secondary and higher education. The Jude of the 1920s and onwards does not need to remain obscure. Place and position won in the remote past by favour and by arms, in the nineteenth century by business acumen, is now open theoretically[10] to all who can exploit their intellectual capabilities.

Because the secondary school and university traditions in parts of Europe and particularly in England are a blend of Renaissance and nineteenth-century concepts of the humanist ('gentlemen', *honnete homme*) and are associated with 'middle classness', this has meant, for many since 1918, that they have had to abandon in adolescence the social group into which they were born, and move more or less uneasily into another.[11]

DECLINE OF RELIGION

The third group of factors is less tangible but its effects are at least as pervasive and difficult to evaluate. Reference has already been made to the impact of Darwinism, Marxism and the doctrines of Freud on nineteenth- and early twentieth-century thought, and in particular to their effect coupled with the immense advance of science on religious belief.[12] At least until the turn of the present century, religion as the ultimate sanction of morality, of the social order and the alliance between worldly success and the pursuit of the divine will, were deeply a part of the conscious and unconscious thought of the majority of people in Europe. Even nineteenth-century rationalism and agnosticism were of the nature of a protest against religion rather than an abandonment of it.[13]

The last decades have seen, particularly in England but in varying degrees in Europe, many religious revivals; but they have also seen steadily an increase, not so much in rationalism or agnosticism, as in indifference to organized religions of all kinds. The currency of the musical banks of *Erewhon* is no longer generally exchanged even formally. In large parts of northern Europe, in spite of the public respect paid to religion, in spite of the legal tolerance for religious teaching in sectors of the education system, we see the steady growth of a largely non-religious society. Even where, as in the Catholic countries of southern Europe, the Church retains its hold on education, the position of religion and religious education is ambiguous in the minds of many adults. Sanctions for a moral code are becoming political, social and ethical, legal and pragmatic, rather than doctrinal, dogmatic or even generally spiritual or religious.

Over large parts of Eastern Europe, Marxism-Leninism has become an ideology and operates rather like an organized State religion. Elsewhere it exists as an idealistic alternative to other forms of belief and non-belief. It is, however, profoundly different from most traditional religions in that its morality does not appeal to spiritual ideas or the notion of an insubstantial god, and its conception of man in society is derived from economic and social analysis according to dialectical materialism. Basically it believes that the manipulation and regulation of society itself to eradicate interpersonal and intergroup exploitation will bring about the perfection of man. In this system guilt is projected into the class war or is transformed to shame, a matter of not conforming to notions of the common good. It is an other-directed rather than an individual and personal concept.[14]

THE NEED OF BELIEF

A system of belief in which much is taken on trust, and particularly belief in powers beyond the self, seems to be a human need. We see all around us religious revivals, imported and esoteric religions or mystical philosophies like Zen Buddhism; all over Europe, even in advanced societies, there is a revival of superstition and witchcraft;[15] even non-spiritual systems of political thought tend very quickly to take on irrational elements and betray the psychological marks of religion. A fairly uniform and shared system of belief is supportive for very many as a way out of the uncertainty and anxiety of doubt. If it sanctions a social order and rests on a coherent explanatory system,[16] it provides an easily comprehensive rationale for morality, for the acceptance of higher authority and for the comforting attitude that, since others know best, one should be resigned. What we are confronted with now in the West is a confusion of beliefs and non-beliefs, coupled with a rather vague acceptance of the notion that there is only one life to live, that man must perfect himself by his own efforts and that evil and suffering are determined by social causes and are not the result of some mysterious divine order. Even for those who reject indifference or unbelief, there remains the agonizing choice of religions, and of political and social creeds of varying degrees of spirituality.

Many religions, and particularly, of course, those deriving from the Judao-Christian tradition which has dominated Europe and North America, accentuate the notion of personal responsibility, the individual conscience, the considerable element of free will in the choice of right and wrong. They embody and use the idea of guilt as a means of personal and social control. Dynamic psychology in its more or less garbled and simplified form has, however, deeply undermined notions of guilt and responsibility. Free will is a very different concept in the context of psychological determinism, just as it is if we accept the Marxist analysis of capitalism and the notion of evil as a product of the class system.

Psychologically, acceptance of authority, religious morality and guilt—especially in the more puritanical religions—were often associated. If, however, all one's moral defects can be attributed to early experiences and if even virtues are determined by amoral and unconscious elements from the same source, then choice of good and ill is no simple matter: it may even be impossible. Guilt and responsibility are both diminished; they are certainly suspect. Child-rearing patterns in the West have been deeply affected by this, particularly by the ways in which psychodynamic ideas have been interpreted by the popularisers. Parents have become uncertain of their tasks and hypersensitive to their influence on their children for good or ill. Notions like those of A. S. Neil[17] have called profoundly into question even the benevolent authority of parents and of parent substitutes like teachers.

This is not to say that the concepts of dynamic psychology are untrue nor that their influence has been mainly evil: far from it. Our child-rearing practices, our educational systems, our understanding of psychosis and neurosis and of the roots of crime and our treatment of the mentally sick and criminal have immensely gained in humanity. But it remains true that secure, comprehensible and effective attitudes concerning authority, responsibility and guilt are increasingly hard for the individual to come by: and that humanity has been given an array of good reasons for not adhering to any prescriptive system of virtue. Morality has become a highly personal thing, a matter of individual choice and to some extent even suspect in itself. It is not a code of accepted rules; it has to be a game that you make up as you go along.

The effect of this is to remove a major element of certainty and to leave the individual to find for himself a philosophy and a rule of life. It naturally increases anxiety and displaces, if it does not actually increase the possibility of, psychological conflict. It also removes a simple and unquestionable explanatory principle of why the established order is good and right and its morality true; it rejects the basis upon which resignation and acceptance can be justified as well as sweetened. Paradoxically too it tends to elevate the individual conscience to the position of final arbiter. In a very real sense man has turned from the idea that if the individual is right with himself and with God, society will take care of itself, to the much more perplexing notion that a good society depends upon the regulation, by law and by organization, of the tendency of individuals and subgroups to exploit others to their own advantage. For the school and the home, it proposes an extremely difficult task—that of equipping children and adolescents with the power to make and adhere to moral judgements without the support of a set of predetermined rules and beliefs.

AN ANTI-AUTHORITARIAN SOCIETY?

Ours, as a result of this and of other changes, is a society where more and more people are confused in their notions of and attitudes towards authority. In some respects it is anti-authoritarian and, by a confusion between authority and authoritarianism, there are substantial groups who reject authority of any kind, political, familial, religious or social. As a society we have not reached any general agreement on the need for authority nor have we developed a genuine concept of democratic consent to put in place of the concepts of the nineteenth century. Powerful groups reject even the best aspects of responsible paternalism, regarding it as creating a hierarchic and condescending relationship or leading to

the worst forms of capitalistic exploitation. The manifest inequalities between individuals, between classes, between nations, are regarded by
many as entirely man-made, the result either of blind forces of interest
and greed or of an élitist social conspiracy by those who for centuries
have manipulated the system to protect their own advantages and privileges. There is suspicion of the authority of the parent over his children
and of the teacher over his pupils. Because we have not yet come to any
concensus about authority nor developed the subtle concepts which
would underlie social discipline in a genuinely free democratic society,
the roles of parents, teachers, the police, management and labour are at
present ambiguous. They present the growing child and adolescent with
a confused and confusing picture and with no clear guide as to what to
think or how to behave in the manifold situations of life. Such as it is,
authority tends to be personal. It has to be earned in each new situation,
and the school particularly but also the family face the dilemma in its
most acute form.

EGALITARIANISM

The problem of authority is connected and interacts with another strand
in the tissue of change. The notion that 'a man's a man for a' that . . .'
and that the 'rank is but the guinea stamp' is an old one—at least as old
as Christianity: but in practice there has always been a distinction between 'equality in the sight of God' and the apparently divinely sanctioned inequalities of the social order. Modern societies are moving
towards an egalitarianism based upon a confusion of the notion of equal
worth as a human being with the very different notion that *all* the inequalities we see around us are factitious, the products of chance or of a
'wicked social and economic system'. There is sufficient truth in these
ideas to give them great power when they are associated with rising
aspirations and the fantasies that accompany them. For example, much
of the difference in learning ability among children probably derives
from social rather than genetic factors, as do the differences between
'races'. But it is more difficult to attribute all differences and disadvantages exclusively and simply to favourable or unfavourable circumstances. Still less easy is it to see how they may be quickly eradicated.

However, in a context of belief in social and psychological determinism, egalitarian notions clearly lead many to attribute their lack
of success in life, and any failure to fulfil their wishes, to factors external
to themselves. Authority and privilege are attacked without the distinctions being made between a freely consented authority and an arbitrarily
imposed one, between privileges necessary to the discharge of responsibility and those which are the unjustified apanage of a particular social
group.

EMANCIPATION OF WOMEN

A special aspect of egalitarianism is the progressive emancipation of women, which is of importance because it affects directly the structure and behaviour of the family and because it introduces an element of conflict into social and emotional life which had not been there before. The emancipation of women in Europe and North America was a relatively lengthy process historically and is not yet fully complete. It has yet to begin in any real way in many other parts of the world. However, in between the two wars its effects combined with profound economic changes became very noticeable. Middle class and upper middle class families became less and less able to obtain or pay for servants and the burden of domesticity and of the upbringing of children has fallen more and more exclusively on the mothers. In its turn this has affected parental roles, and not merely in middle class families. Fathers as well as mothers have a share in domestic and child-rearing duties; and parents now generally come into much closer contact with their children, a process accelerated by a marked decrease in the size of houses, the splitting of many larger houses into maisonettes and the building of small flats.

On the other hand it has become the accepted and general thing for women to work at least before marriage; and many continue to do so afterwards. Of course women have always worked inside and outside the home and the economy of rural communities depended upon female labour as much as upon male. The nineteenth-century factories and sweat shops employed very many women and 'home work' was also fairly general. The rural employment of women, however, did not necessarily take them away from their children, nor did home work. By and large too it did not greatly influence the role and status of the father. Although the proportion of mothers at work in nineteenth-century England may not have been much lower than at present, at least in urban centres, it was certainly differently distributed socially and affected those social classes where, by and large—even in the slums of large towns—there was sufficient community feeling for children to be cared for by friends and relations in the absence of their mothers, or where the 'little mother' of a large family served a sometimes harsh but frequently effective apprenticeship to maternity by caring for younger brothers and sisters. This is still the norm in many developing countries where the extended family and the tribe provide a secure framework for the young child, and where the emancipation of women has scarcely begun.

Emancipation has had other consequences much more difficult to elucidate. Equality of opportunity and of status was, and still is, often confused with similarity of function and identity of capacity. Indeed in many cases, the invasion of 'men's jobs' by women was valuable, in others less so. The roles of a man as a wage earner, as an authority figure, as a citizen and so on, in our society were, and still are, relatively well defined; the specifically feminine roles are much less clearly so. After thirty years or more of complete female suffrage in England, and general acceptance of emancipation, there is a basic conflict between the image of 'femininity' and the allied notions of courtesy and chivalry on the one hand and the claim to equality on the other. For very many adolescent girls and young women this takes the form of a conflict between the desire for sociosexual approval, the hallmark of acceptability given by marriage, domesticity, and maternity, and the desire for economic and personal independence conferred by a career or a job. In the structure and tone of many women's organizations can still be traced the militant feminism of half a century or more ago. In a few professions and jobs, a distinctive feminine contribution is recognized and regarded as equal to, but different from, that of men; in some there is apparently equal access but a tendency to prefer men; and in most either an exclusively male or female choice coupled often with a status and salary differential. Moreover, the increased political and economic power of women and their slight but quantitatively considerable preponderance, have led to advertising campaigns, open and indirect, to win their custom. Only too often these play upon the idea that domesticity is a dull, unrewarded grind, that 'a woman's work is never done' and that in some way she has to score off her husband and trap him into a share of the domestic chores. In contrast are the notion of attractiveness to the male and the invitation to dominance in political, intellectual and other fields. Only rarely is a serious attempt made to help adolescent girls or mature women to see clearly and realistically the part which they can play in social and economic life by developing fully a specifically feminine contribution complementary to that of men. More recently a movement, calling itself 'Women's Liberation',[18] is gaining ground, aimed, it almost seems, at a repudiation even of those differences which have a manifest biological base—at least in so far as they affect social attitudes and employment opportunities.

The psychological reasons for many of the phenomena suggested above probably lie too deep for easy elucidation. But we may draw attention to two points: first, that the last half-century has brought about an unprecedented change in the role of women in Western countries, which affects their whole social status but particularly the way in which they discharge their tasks as wives and mothers. Secondly, adolescent girls are confronted with a confused and contradictory picture of what society expects a woman to be.[19] Within the Western family, particularly the urban educated family, the mother-father role difference is becoming more and more blurred, with reverberations on the ways in which children learn and internalize their sex roles and attitudes to a bisexual world. An increasing sexual freedom supported by easier and more certain contraception, greater tolerance of illegitimacy and abortion and a considerable conflict between old moral standards, feelings of uncertainty and guilt and newer more 'emancipated' views of the relations between sensuality, sexuality and love have considerably complicated the task of reaching mature adult attitudes.

ROLE CONFUSION

There are two other connected phenomena, which may have profound significance because they affect the ways in which young children and adolescents learn to relate to the hierarchies of adult life and to the authority of the community—the decline of manifest social and occupational role differentiation and a decrease in social distance. The authority and privilege structures of the past were supported, as they still are in tribal communities, by clearly defined social roles usually manifest in distinctions of dress, speech, behaviour and life style. Between social groups, and between age groups, there was a certain, sometimes very marked social distance. The doctor, judge, schoolmaster, lord, butcher, baker and candlestick maker were clearly distinguishable by their dress and manners. Class differences too were overtly marked, often by physical characteristics allied to differences in nutrition, hygiene, education and the like.

Within the family and in general in all social classes the parental roles were clear and many unquestioned signs indicated status differences —for example, 'father's chair'. To children and adolescents the social and status hierarchy was manifest and intelligible. Fairly stylized expectations were set up—just as they are in societies which are not westernized. In contrast, differences of status and role in our present advanced societies tend less and less to be manifested by style of dress or even by overt styles of life, behaviour and speech. There are a few dress distinctions left in England, for example, except for uniforms associated with functions like the postman or policeman or the cleric; but outside business hours the butcher, the skilled workman, the schoolmaster, the bank clerk and the doctor are indistinguishable in appearance. They tend to live in similar houses, to drive similar cars and although they may pursue leisure activities which are different, the differences are more likely to be related to personal tastes or financial circumstances than inevitably to social group or social origins.

These changes are accompanied by another and more subtle one. In primitive and agrarian societies as well as in the slums of the industrial revolution, parents and children lived in close physical proximity sharing the available housing space. The European upper middle classes tended to separate parents and children in a variety of ways and this norm generalized itself quite widely toward the end of the nineteenth century and the first decades of this in urban Europe. Rising standards also mean more space generally in homes and in Europe now the separation of children from their parents for sleeping and often for private play is increasingly widespread, particularly in towns and suburbs.[20] In tribal and primitive societies in general and still in very many rural and urban working class groups, there were very clear distinctions between adults and children marked out by rules, forms of address, particular privilege and the like. Thus although physical distance may have been and still is minimal, what we might call the hierarchic distance was marked; and it was even more so in the middle classes of the nineteenth century and the period before the First World War. These distances were reflected in the community both in terms of social class and in terms of occupational role; they indicated certain forms of dependence and underlined a system of authority.

Now within the European family, and particularly in the Anglo-Saxon world, parents and children whether working or middle class share more nearly equally the physical and psychological life space of the home.[21] In terms of social distance they are close, much closer than ever before. Few middle class families now can afford resident help and even the *au pair* is nearer to a family guest than to a paid servant. Children are highly regarded, parents tend to spend more time with them. They are no longer 'seen and not heard' but, from a comparatively early age, are mixed in family affairs and treated even in otherwise working class families more nearly as equals with equal rights. In some families this extends to a drive for early independence or a complete withdrawal of adult control. At the same time, clubs, churches and similar neighbourhood groups have declined in their influence; the family has become more home centred.

Again the change reflects and is reflected in society; role differences and hierarchies are much less apparent and on the whole are rejected where they exist. They are not as a matter of course marked by signs of overt respect or by styles of address (though elements of formality linger). This does not mean that we are less conscious of social distinctions; it seems rather to be that we are less sure of how to handle them and somewhat ashamed to recognize them. The 'prestige symbol' has taken the place of position assured by hereditary social class; and figures in the news, particularly pop artists, politicians and to some extent business men are concerned to build up an 'image'.

AN ANTI-HYPOCRITICAL SOCIETY

What is of importance from the point of view of children whose growth towards identity is much influenced by the models offered first by parents and increasingly by others in their environment, is that, along with the diminution or concealment of a rank or authority hierarchy, has gone an abandonment of what we might call the 'conspiracy of hypocrisy'. Between classes, even within the respectable working class, as between adults and children there used to be a kind of tacit agreement to keep up a facade of virtue and perfection. 'Not in front of the servants' . . . 'not in front of the children' were current middle class phrases; 'not going native' was important to colonial occupiers; and even for working class families keeping up appearances both in front of the children and in the eyes of the neighbours was important. The peccadillos of public figures were discretely hidden from the general gaze unless their flagrancy called into operation a public mechanism of rejection from the social class or group. When groups were clearly separated this was relatively easy; similarly parents, teachers and other adults could be presented in black and white terms. In a society like ours with its egalitarian propensities, its greater physical mixing and proximity, pretences are more difficult to maintain. We may go further. Just as ours is at present a confusedly anti-authoritarian rather than a genuinely democratic society so it is an anti-hypocritical or even cynical rather than a sincere or honest one. For example, it is only partly because of the laws of libel that we do not savagely attack public figures in the manner of Rowlandson, which in itself implies a kind of inverted respect. Attention tends to be focused on showing that the great and the eminent share with 'us' the weaknesses, the flecks and the flaws, that they are really no different and certainly not superior. The corollary is that they are where they are by luck, or smartness, not by any inherent superiority.

Similarly children tend to be much mixed with the private lives of their parents and to see that their idols have feet of clay. This kind of 'debunking' mixed with the relativist view of moral codes makes it difficult for young children to find the security of a black and white system of rules out of which the more nuanced adult ethic can develop. It makes even reasonable parental authority or the necessary discipline of a school very difficult to maintain.

GEOGRAPHICAL AND SOCIAL MOBILITY

All this clearly has a bearing upon the kind of notion of community, of social and moral roles and upon the ideas of himself and his family in relation to them which a child builds up. For very many the situation is further complicated by geographical and social mobility. The communities of the past, even those which grew out of the rush to the towns, tended to be fairly stable. Children were born and lived in the same house, the same quarter of a town, the same village, the same slum at least until adolescence and most stayed there for the whole of their lives.

A recent study in England[22] suggests that by the age of 7, 64 per cent of children had moved at least once and a third of these had moved out of range of their immediate friends; some 27 per cent had moved more than once, and around 6 per cent four or more times. A study twelve years earlier[23] gave rather lower figures but suggested that 12 per cent of a national sample had moved more than 20 miles by the age of 11 years.

This particular aspect of the phenomenon of change varies considerably from country to country. It seems to be at its most marked in the United States, Scandinavia and Britain. But in other countries, notably for example in France, major changes in agriculture are now accentuating the migration to the towns.[24] In the Western democracies, this tends to be a development of the pattern of urbanization which began long before. In many parts of the developing world—in Africa for example or in parts of Latin America—it is fairly recent and of startling rapidity, exhibiting in very clear form the socio-psychological phenomena which are more subtly displayed in Europe.[25] We might also draw attention to the growing number of migrant workers, many of them accompanied by wives and children, in Western Europe. For the most part these migrants do not intend to settle in the country in which they are working but to return to their native land. The number in Europe working in three heavy industries (1971) is estimated at approximately a quarter of a million (of whom 70,000 come from developing or poor countries around the Mediterranean basin).[26] Thus workers of a nationality different from that of the country where they are employed form one-fifth of the work force. Many European countries too, particularly the United Kingdom, have substantial populations of permanent immigrants.[27] Whether in developed or developing countries, mobility seems likely to provoke change, to demand adjustments and to increase stress for parents and children alike. Inevitably many of a child's relationships outside his immediate family are disrupted. If the family itself is socially mobile[28] a change of town removes the known and familiar supports and checks from the family; furthermore it permits and even invites quite considerable change in behaviour and in the way the family lives, in what is or is not acceptable in speech, dress, tastes, possessions and even in overt moral codes. Those families which are not highly privileged may in the new community meet with prejudice and rejection; and even where this is not so, suffer from considerable stress and anxiety, economic and social, at least in the early stages of settling down.

THE NOTION OF COMMUNITY

Increasing population densities also have their effects. One research indicates that in very small communities (population 500-1,400) children between 6 and 11 are likely to know about a quarter of the 120-150 families in their immediate vicinity, they will know something of the occupation of about 20 adults; but children in communities of 30,000 (which are still small by the standards of most industrialized countries) tend to know only about six of the nearest families, and something of the occupations of only seven or so adults. The children from very small communities have a considerably more restricted choice of settings but, not surprisingly, they take an active part in what is going on much more frequently.[29] Most European communities are much bigger than 30,000. Indeed more than half the children in the United Kingdom live in towns of 50,000 or more and 45 per cent of the French population lives in 6 per cent of the communes into which France is divided; many towns and their bidonville surburbs in Africa, or in Latin America are even more highly populous. Again it is of interest to note that, in some circumstances, slum dwellers, who have created some sort of community, tend to like their neglected neighbourhoods, whilst dwellers in public housing tend to dislike theirs perhaps because the public housing estates have been created whilst the slums have grown.[30] The extensive rehousing programmes and building of new satellite towns and suburbs which have been carried out in recent years in most European countries have certainly provided a better physical environment but have not necessarily improved the psychological climate for the families and their children—at least for the first generation.

The great suburban housing estates from which most of the workers commute daily to the big cities in fact provide very incomplete community experiences for the children left behind in the care of women. What is more they tend to deprive children of resources of exploration, experiment and danger which the environment of a village or small market town provided more or less accidentally because of its implantation in the countryside and its relation to the productive activities which brought it into being.

There are obviously large differences from culture to culture and, within cultures, from one set of circumstances to another. But the trends to urban concentration, to industrialization which takes work out of the sight (and participation) of children, to physical and social mobility and to a lack of clear-cut role differentiation and similar changes, appear to be fairly general. There is an increasing isolation of the individual or the small nuclear family group. Even in developing countries where family and tribal structures remain strong, the westernized individual tends towards a more isolated life and his family becomes more and more cut off from the generality of families, especially if the children attend private schools on the Western model. Partly because of the nature of work and partly too because although complex, modern communities are neither complete nor perceptibly coherent, it is difficult to avoid feelings of alienation. From the present viewpoint what is significant is that increasingly large proportions of children all over the world are growing up in physical, social and emotional circumstances which are different from those on which most of our knowledge of the dynamics of child development is based. In view of the steady increase in the world population which is taking place and the trends towards industrialization in the developing countries, it is to be expected that these changes will be intensified and generalized.

GUIDANCE

Changes, too, are occurring in what might be called the structures of guidance. Typically in a community with an overt hierarchic or socially stratified structure, power of various kinds is wielded by identifiable individuals, the squire, the chief, the policeman, the elders, the owner of a small factory, the farmer, the priest. The sources of advice, consolation, help and discipline are manifest; and there are well-worn customs by which relations are regulated. In agricultural communities and in small rural towns these customs are associated with the cycle of the seasons as well as with a system of beliefs and can be 'explained' intelligibly. The child in an extended family in Africa, or even in the large families which were characteristic of the nineteenth- and early twentieth-century European rural and small urban groups, was rarely dependent solely upon his immediate parents and siblings. Nor were his parents unsupported by other and related adults. Thus although relatively free within their environment, children tended to participate in adult work and when at play to be in the presence of adults who knew them, whom they knew and who would intervene in their lives—protectively or punitively. Grandparents, mothers, aunts and uncles were near enough to be sources of advice and help to young parents and, since change was relatively slow, their authority tended not to be greatly challenged—though of course there were generation frictions. The priest, the doctor, the schoolmaster lived where they worked, were known and in general respected as authorities even outside their immediate professional competence; the squire and the employer had apparent and real power and the priest was believed to have; they could effectively intervene and change the course of life. These sources of guidance and power were by no means always beneficent, and the situation was not ideal. But they were a clear part of the local structure, they were intelligible and to some extent manipulable. Even as late as the 1930s in England and much later in the stable rural areas of Europe, this state of affairs continued.

The modern suburb or housing estate which have become more and more characteristic of Europe since the decades between the wars tend to have a population relatively homogeneous in age and closely similar in economic circumstances. Many of those who are there are recent arrivals and a high proportion will not live in the same house or district for much more than five or ten years. The extended family if it exists at all tends to be split up not only by distance but by social mobility. It certainly no longer represents an entity based on possessions; and with a common educational and social background. Educational opportunity and the greater mobility of labour, particularly the increase in service occupations, and the rise of new professions and occupations have exerted a considerable divisive effect. The norm in the West is in fact the nuclear family, a relatively small cell of two parents and two or three children. Outside his immediate circle a child is relatively unknown. Even the policeman and the teacher no longer live in the areas of their work; employers and employment may be even more distant. The influence of the Church is certainly not undivided and has on the whole declined. The possession of land for the most part is no longer the major source of power and influence; hence the big landowner is rarely the main local leader, even if he still exists as a private individual rather than some sort of commercial enterprise. Mobility and education have tended to separate the generations and to produce kaleidoscopic agglomerations of individuals rather than articulated communities.

From the growing child's point of view two things are important. Any notion of community which he may have will not be a clearly articulated system of roles and relationships. He can perceive himself as part of a small family group or as part of a form or class in school. He does not see himself as a member of a varied and reasonably complete human group whose participants and whose work and property knit together. He may be part of a smaller partial neighbourhood community gathered round a church or community centre; but for much of his time in the streets, parks and even in the fields he is a stranger among strangers.[31] The adults he sees have no clear function and only exceptionally intervene in his life; they are figures in the background.

What is perhaps of even more importance to child and adult alike is that whereas in small stable and articulated communities the group of adults in their several ways and more or less casually, exercised authority and guidance over children and each other, the larger and more diffuse groups of Western urban and suburban living have developed institutional and professional services. The social worker, the district nurse, the marriage guidance counsellor, the vocational guidance officer have replaced the village schoolmaster, the doctor, the clergyman and the squire's wife. Books on baby and child care, radio and televised advice on child rearing have taken the place of grandma. Moreover much of the help in times of need and distress which depended upon the community or upon a paternalistic and generous concern for others, is now bureaucratized and, although given as a right by the State, more frequently and usually more generously than in the past, is seen not as a gesture of human solidarity but as an impersonal (and often humiliating) piece of officialdom.[32]

A CHANGED BASIS OF WORKING LIFE

This diffuseness and lack of structure which is becoming characteristic of Western communities is reflected in the way in which the high production and high consumption stage of industrialization affects the whole basis of the working life of men and women. Whatever political or economic form it takes, it inevitably seems to lead to concentrations of capital equipment and power too great to be controlled by one man or even by a small group intimately acquainted with each other. Private enterprise capitalism, and state capitalism, whether it be socialist or communist, all tend to centralization of power in corporate form. Even at the top, individual responsibility is diminished; decision-making is the work of increasingly large numbers of administrators and technologists, many of whom never see each other face to face, and no one of whom takes a fully comprehensible share in the responsibility for success or failure. Lower down the line as products become more complex and industrial processes more split up and simplified, fewer and fewer workers can conceive even a partial whole, let alone the ramifications of the organization which pays their wages. Inevitably, the feeling of involvement in the finished product, of responsibility for it, and of pride in being part at least of a comprehensible process diminishes.

The security of belonging to a firm, of being needed and valuable, of having a personal craft or contribution to make, of having some responsibility, is denied to increasingly large proportions of the working population. Indeed, only in a few skilled and semi-skilled jobs employing diminishing proportions of the working population does it remain. Farmers, market gardeners, the small retail traders, the back-street garages and repair shops and the declining number of very small manufacturing industries may still offer some satisfaction and intrinsic involvement with work. The professions too—especially those which are salaried—provide the possibilities of vocational satisfactions in the work itself, rather than in the rewards which allow escape from it at regular intervals. But for most people now it is not surprising that 'job satisfaction' and 'vocational adjustment'—two significantly contemporary terms—depend much more on material conditions of pay, hours of work, peripheral advantages like social clubs, insurance, group holidays and welfare of various kinds, upon 'social status value' and upon immediate incidental relationships at factory or office than upon any intrinsic satisfaction in identification with the firm, in the work itself or in its value as a service to the community. Nor is work seen to be, as it is in subsistence economies, essential to survival.[33]

DIFFERENT STAGES: A COMMON TREND

There are many other aspects of contemporary change which, in varying degrees, have directly affected the climate in which children and adolescents grow up; and which, for some at least, deeply colour their awareness of themselves. The analysis just given is inevitably summary and incomplete. The elements of change in consciousness, in life styles and their relative importance differ from country to country in Europe and the North American continent; and they differ from group to group and even from family to family within any one country. Across the world too the differences are even greater and in some ways seem to increase rather than diminish—particularly in such things as material conditions, and the structures and sanctions of authority in a particular culture and within the typical family.

Political and social systems vary in how far they present or appear to present, in public life, in private life, in the media and in education a unique model of the desirable citizen, a unified concept of man, sanctioned by a political or religious creed. They vary in their attitudes to dissent, their tolerance of a wide variety of personal style and of individual difference. However, most are in some ways affected by change; and in very many the present educated middle class groups are increasing proportionately to the rest[34] and are becoming 'Americanized' or 'Westernized'—that is to say beginning to undergo the same kinds of change as are now pervasive in Europe. Indeed much of what we have been talking about is only made possible by the increasing affluence of post-industrial societies and by urbanization. In developing countries which are far from affluent there is none the less the kind of urbanization which characterized the Industrial Revolution; some groups are becoming affluent and modern communications are arousing high material aspirations. Education, particularly, is bringing about considerable stresses between the old and the new within families.[35]

FURTHER READING

Bullock, A., ed. *The twentieth century.* London, Thames & Hudson, 1971.
Gabor, D. *The mature society.* London, Secker & Warburg. 1972.
McClelland, D. C. *The achieving society.* Princeton, Van Nostrand, 1961.
Open University. *Stability, change and conflict.* Bletchley, 1971.
Winslow, R. W. *Society in transition.* New York, Free Press, 1971.

NOTES

1. McLuhan, M.; Fiore, Q. *The medium is the massage*. London, Allen Lane, 1967.
2. More than a third (34.3 per cent) of all adults in the world cannot read even now. The number is growing as education lags behind population growth, even though the proportion is declining (*The Guardian* (London), 6 September 1971).
3. 'The process of increasing the range of perception by means of such media as film and television, without providing adequate means of interpreting and understanding, must be anti-educational.' Lawton, D.; Campbell, J.; Buskitt, V. *Social studies, 8–13*. London, Evans/Methuen Educational, 1971 (Schools Council W.P. 39). See also: Schramm, W. *The effects of television on children and adolescents*. Paris, Unesco, 1964.
4. Boorstin, D. *The image*. London, Weidenfeld & Nicholson, 1962 [especially chapters I and VI].
5. See for example the analysis by F. R. Gannon (*The British press and Germany 1936–39*. Oxford, Oxford University Press, 1971) of the way the newspapers in England treated the rise of National Socialism in Germany in the 1930s.
6. See for example: Packard, V. *The waste makers*. London, Penguin, 1970.
7. See: Roszac, T. *The making of a counter culture*. London, Faber, 1970.
8. This is something of a simplification applicable particularly to the developing societies of Europe. In many other societies, it was rather the family, the village or the tribe which ultimately exercised an enveloping authority and responsibility—as for example in Japan where the first loyalty is to the family and ultimately to the village group. Across the world there are immense variations in the settings and relationships within which authority is exercised over children and adults by the micro-society in which they grow. These differences tend to be reflected in social institutions determining not so much their form—which may change under outside influences as when a country adopts 'democratic' practices and attempts parliamentary government—as the ways in which people behave within them. The one party 'democracies' of Africa, or the enterprise-based trade unions of Japan, are cases in point.
9. The Representation of the People Act 1918. Nonetheless, 'From 1885 the U.K. had a system of fairly widespread male franchise, limited however by a year's residence qualification and some other restrictions'. Butler, D.; Freeman, J. *British political facts 1900–1968*. 3rd ed. London, Macmillan, 1969.
10. Even now, however, proportionately more children from middle class and upper middle class homes are recruited to grammar schools, lycées and gymnasia and universities in Europe (see for example: Floud, J.; Halsey, A. H.; Martin, F. M. *Social class and educational opportunity*. London, Heinemann, 1956. See also: Chapter 9 of this work). But between 1902 and 1920 in England the percentage of children from lower economic strata in academic schools and universities steadily increased; the scholarship scheme after the war greatly accelerated this and the 1944 Act pushed the process much further. Elsewhere in Europe the process began more slowly but similar reforms in the structure of education took place in the Europe of the late forties and fifties. Since about 1960 there has been a strong move

towards comprehensive secondary education, particularly in Sweden and since 1965 in the United Kingdom and elsewhere. In Belgium, for example, the proportion of children in secondary education is high but from the age of 12 it is divided between two types of institution—the one the academic school, the other vocational. Since 1968, there has been a progressive change to a more comprehensive system (*enseignement rénové*) with three cycles, each of two years: *cycle d'observation, cycle d'orientation,* and *cycle de détermination.* In all countries the population of university students has increased markedly and changed somewhat in social composition. It is how-ever still far from true to say that the old differentiating influences of social class have been eliminated and that universal schooling has brought about a full democratization of education (see: Little, A.; Westergaard, J. The trend of class differentials in educational opportunity in England and Wales. *British journal of sociology* (London), 1964, p. 301). See also Chapter 9. Recent analyses (OECD, 1971) of the social composition show that the per-centage of university populations recruited from social classes I and II are considerably higher than those recruited from classes III, IV and V. In absolute numbers, however, students from lower middle class and working class homes have considerably increased. Moreover, many children of middle class parents have grandparents of working class origins—which suggests that upward mobility in terms of the ability fully to take advantage of educational opportunity takes more than one generation (see also: Kelsall, R. K.; Kelsall, H. M. *Social disadvantage and educational opportunity.* New York, Holt, Rinehart & Winston, 1972). The position in developing countries is very different. For example a study made in Montevideo (Uruguay) in 1947 (Grompone, A. M. Problemas sociales de la ensenanza secondaria, cited by Havighurst, R. J. *Psicología social de la adolescencia.* 2nd ed. Wash-ington D.C., Unión Pan Americana, 1969), gives the proportion of working class children in the second secondary cycle as 7.6 per cent compared with 3.4 per cent from managerial groups and landed proprietors, 20 per cent from professional and 25 per cent from State and private white collar employees.

11. See for example: Jackson, B. *Education and the working class.* London, Routledge & Kegan Paul, 1964. / Dale, R. R.; Griffith, S. *Down stream: failure in the grammar school.* London, Routledge & Kegan Paul, 1965. This tendency is strikingly more marked in England than in countries such as France where the tradition of the lycée and of the university is Napoleonic, even Revolutionary, and where the schism between State and religion has tended to accentuate intellectual discipline at the expense of education of the personality. The American education system is different again and in living memory was, and still to some extent is, aimed at 'Americanization' of the culturally heterogeneous groups of immigrants.

12. It is of interest that both Marx and Freud regarded religion as an illusion, and that Darwin was violently resisted by the Fundamentalists.

13. Bradlaugh insisted on conformity to the morality of his day, he 'preached' and even had a hymn book.

14. On the whole topic of the failure of contemporary ideologies see: Macintyre, A. *Against the self images of the age.* London, Duckworth, 1971.

15. Burger, P. L. *A rumour of angels.* London, Penguin, 1971.

16. For an interesting if somewhat impressionistic analysis of the effects of uniformity of belief on an education system, see: Bronfenbrenner, U. *Two worlds of childhood—U.S. and U.S.S.R.* London, Allen & Unwin, 1971. Communist societies, it should be pointed out, largely because they retain a

firmly authoritarian structure, a firm Marxist-Leninist belief with a clearer and more uniform idea of man in society and a consequential moral code, provide for a majority at any rate a much easier moral environment: by and large political belief, law and morality are coherent; the choices are limited; and anxiety diminished—just as they tended to be in the eighteenth and nineteenth century religious states. The same could be said, *mutatis mutandis,* for a Catholic society enshrined in a Catholic State.

17. Neil, A. S. *The problem parent.* London, Jenkins. 1932. / Idem. *The free child.* London, Jenkins, 1953.

18. See for example: Greer, G. *The female eunuch.* London, MacGibbon & Kee, 1970. / Figes, E. *Patriarchal attitudes.* London, Panther, 1972. / Miller, R. *Sexual politics.* New York, Doubleday, 1970. But for a less polemical (and more balanced and factual study), see: Sulleval, E. *Woman, society and change.* London, Weidenfeld & Nicholson, 1971.

19. In some countries, Sweden, for example, deliberate attempts are being made in schools to reshape the traditional sex-roles: 'the new teaching plan demands an active contradiction of traditional sex-role concepts' and this is embodied even in early reading primers where father is shown in an apron serving tea, or where father stays home while mother goes out to work. See: Choate, R. Eroding sex-roles stereotypes. *The Times educational supplement.* (London), 12 May 1972.

20. It is interesting to note that contemporary European definitions of over-crowding—$1\frac{1}{2}$ persons per habitable room—would have been considered laughable by all but the privileged few in the eighteenth and nineteenth centuries, and still would be by the inhabitants of more than half the world.

21. See Chapter 6 'The role of the family in mental health'.

22. Davie, R.; Butler, N.; Goldstein, H. *From birth to seven.* London, Longman, 1972.

23. Douglas, J. W. B. *The home and the school.* London, MacGibbon & Kee, 1964.

24. In the eight years from 1954 to 1962 the number of towns in France with a population of more than 50,000 rose from 53 to 83. In 1965 about one-third of the population were in towns, a further one-third in suburbs and one-third rural. Of the French population 62 per cent is thus in towns and suburbs compared to 75 per cent in West Germany and 80 per cent in Britain (Halls, W. D. *Society, schools and progress in France.* Oxford, Pergamon, 1965).

25. For example in Puerto Rico (Hansen, M. ed. *Social change and public policy—a seminar at the University of Puerto Rico, 20–24 February, 1967.* Rio Piedras, Social Science Research Centre, 1968), 44.2 per cent of the predominantly rural population had become urbanized by 1960 and by 1968 the San Juan Metropolitan area had grown from a population of 200,000 to 700,000 in the space of a few years. The effects of such dramatic changes on the family structure, on the child's security and the consequent upsurge of maladjustment and delinquency are now well documented. See also: Paul-Pont, I.; Bonnal, M. J. *The living conditions of the child in urban environments in Africa.* Paris, Centre international de l'enfance, 1965 [especially chapter IV].

26. Communauté européenne du charbon et de l'acier; Communauté économique européene; Communauté européene de l'energie automique. *Exposé sur l'evolution sociale dans la Communauté en 1971.* Bruxelles; Luxembourg, 1972.

27. Estimated in the United Kingdom at over 2 million. Immigrants tend to

show a higher proportion of paranoid psychotic illnesses, and their children present considerable learning difficulties in schools. See: Bagley, C. Migration, race and mental health. *Race* (London), vol. 9, pt. 3, 1968.

28. R. J. Havighurst (op. cit, Footnote 10) points to the rise of middle classes in Latin America since 1950 and a change in their nature and composition. For example the percentage of upwardly mobile families in Brazil (1957) is 40 compared with 33 per cent in the U.S.A. and 27 per cent in the United Kingdom.

29. Wright, H. F. Urban space as seen by the child. *Courrier: revue médico-sociale de l'enfance* (Paris, International Children's Centre), Vol. XXI, Sept.–Oct., 1971, p. 485–495. [Contribution to the Seminar on the Child in the City, Paris, November 1970.]

30. Hollinshead, A. B.; Rogler, L. H. Attitudes towards slums and public housing in Puerto Rico. In: Duhl, L. J., ed. *The urban condition: people and policy in the metropolis.* New York, Basic Books, 1963.

31. In the inner rings of large cities, where large and poor families tend to live, there are many direct physical hazards to inevitably unsupervised children. See the study of 56 problem families reported by: Wilson, H.; Herbert, G. Hazards of environment. *New society* (London), 8 June 1972.

32. It is of interest to note that informal 'networks' now tend to develop, particularly among adolescents and young adults with little overt structure and with communication based upon word of mouth. Such networks are often powerful sources of mutual aid.

33. See the European Community report cited above (note 26): 12 per cent of the working force is employed in agriculture, 45 per cent in industry and 43 per cent in services; but the differences between countries are very wide— 20 per cent are employed in agriculture in Italy as compared with 8 per cent in Germany and 6 per cent in Belgium.

34. See the figures on 'social mobility' quoted from Havighurst (note 28).

35. See for example: Laye, C. *The African child.* London, Collins, 1956.

Chapter three

The next thirty years

MAJOR DECISIONS

These influences and processes will certainly continue to affect our own lives and those of our immediate descendants directly and indirectly. But we have by no means reached a position of stasis; and there are many problems affecting the physical and psychological environment which have been in the background certainly since the first half of this century but which have now crossed the threshold of startling urgency. Their pressure seems likely to affect human thinking and behaviour at least as much as anything hitherto and to demand even more profound change. The children entering their primary schools in the last quarter of this century will be adult by the year 2000, the second millennium A.D. Men approached A.D. 1000 thinking that it would bring the end of the world; the crisis turned out to be unreal. Increasingly many fear now that the next thirty years may be genuinely doom laden; there seems little doubt that they will be critical and the decisions of the next decades seem perched upon the edge of disaster.[1]

Currently public anxiety seems to be concentrated largely upon the energy crisis, environmental pollution and upon the feeding of the hungry world. There is little doubt that these are major problems requiring ultimately more than local or national decisions. Even in the absence of fundamental discovery in the natural sciences, the technological development of what we know already could, peacefully applied, radically and rapidly solve many of the problems of pollution and probably in a decade or more provide a sufficiency for the majority of human beings who have neither enough nor the right kind of food.

The problems and choices of the next decades do not in fact seem to be so much scientific and technological as moral, ethical and political. Indeed it is argued that the principal impetus to change even over the past century has not in fact been scientific discovery as such; but the response of technology to need or greed, feeding, stimulating and changing public demand. This has happened in largely unplanned ways in response to a market economy and a philosophy of *laisez-faire*.

42

Moreover, until the turn of this century most advances in technology and scientific knowledge were within the general intellectual grasp, at least of the better educated, and seemed therefore susceptible to understanding and control—even though the control which was exercised was not one related to clearly stated political principles. The massive substitution of steam power for natural and muscular power, for example, was imaginatively comprehensible by the majority of mankind[2] and some legislative restraints were put upon its exploitation. Modern physics, chemistry, electronics and biology and their manifold applications tend to overwhelm the mind of all but the ablest. It is even more difficult to see what restraints could and should be put upon them without either losing their benefits or allowing them to affect our lives or environment adversely. In some respects we are back in the magical world of medieval man fearfully regarding the inexplicable powers of nature, but with the difference of knowing that they can be controlled but not by us—and we fear they won't be by anyone.

This mystifying complexity has two consequences. Few decisions can now be arrived at by a consideration of the data derived from any one science. The application of any major technological advance, political or economic change, involves social and psychological considerations and choices which imply judgements of value about such things as 'happiness', 'good'. We have thus arrived at a dilemma which outstrips the powers of analysis and judgement of most people. The complex knowledge which delimits the areas of choice is in the possession of the few and is by its nature arcane and not generally available. It is obviously susceptible to selective presentation whether consciously or otherwise. More important, the syntheses and predictions which we need cut right across the conventional disciplinary boundaries and demand a capacity to understand and weigh data and inference of very disparate kinds. We are in the situation where notions of simple cause corresponding to simple effect must give way to probabilistic thinking because the matters with which we deal are so highly complex.[3] Up to a point this is not new, but there are two differences now. In smaller and more isolated societies, errors of judgement, though sometimes serious in their consequences for the society, were usually confined in their effects and more or less self-regulating. Moreover man's control over and impact upon his environment was limited, both geographically and in its possible consequences for good or ill. Now, to take only banal examples, a 'dirty' atomic explosion can leave traces of strontium in the bones of children many thousands of miles away and in communities which had no share in the making of the decision to explode it; and the discharge of crude oil tars into the sea, apart from fouling the beaches of the world, now accounts in some places for about 20 per cent by bulk of the plankton supply. Currently there is concern about lead-polluted dust in cities as a possible cause of biochemical changes in children.

Crucially, however, the problem comes back to the commonplace observation, which is neither less true nor less urgent for being commonplace, that technological advance has outstripped man's power to understand it and to control his own nature. In any decision and most dramatically in those which have far reaching consequences for the future, there are two main elements. The cold appraisal of facts, of the permissible inferences from them and the varying degrees of probability with which the outcomes of particular choices can be predicted. This aspect can probably be greatly improved by the use of computer science and by improving our ability to allow for all kinds of human bias in the collection of data, in inference and in the determination of the questions to be put to the data. Improvement here, important as it is, merely reduces the chance or irrational elements and in one aspect only, of decision making. The act of choice itself cannot be determined in this way. Within the possibilities and their probabilistic outcomes, choice is concerned with 'goods', with judgements of value, with in fact political and social philosophies; and these too have irrational elements which are ill understood. In this very important sense society is free to choose its own path of technical change according to the values which people hold or develop.[4]

DISTRUST OF SCIENCE

Considerations such as these account for the current general anxiety about, even distrust of, science and technology. Suddenly we seem to have passed a threshold and become aware that, although perhaps neutral in fact, science and the gifts it brings when allied to certain impulses in man's nature or when left to the free play of national and sectional interests tend not to Utopia but to nightmare. Man finds himself confronted not so much with the high endeavour of wresting nature's secrets from her and harnessing them for the enrichment of life, but with the far more difficult and subtle problem of understanding, and above all, disciplining his own nature. He has to develop concepts of man in society which will enable human groups, probably even larger than those we know at present, to live together on this planet without destroying each other or so irreparably damaging the environment that life, in a way undreamed of by Hobbes, becomes 'nasty, brutish, and short'.[5]

A vague general compassion and goodwill will not tide us harmlessly over such changes and it does not seem reasonable to hope that, as in the past, humanity will escape by the skin of its teeth, by luck rather than conscious control. Something must occur and soon, to arrest many current trends in the West. Unless this happens by cataclysm, it will have to come about by drastic changes in our personal and social values.[6] Indeed the historian Toynbee suggests that unless such conscious control is exercised, the most probable development is not annihilation by world wars but 'the establishment of a dictatorial world state in the style of the Akkadian, Persian, Roman and Chinese Empires . . . imposed on the majority by a ruthless, efficient and fanatical minority, inspired by some ideology or religion. And I guess mankind will acquiesce in a harsh Leninian kind of dictatorship as a lesser evil than self-extermination or than a continuing anarchy which could end only in self destruction'.[7]

MAN'S IDEA OF HIMSELF

Whatever the details of projections of population, conservation or wastage of resources, technological development and social organization may be, one thing is apparently quite certain. Our children and grandchildren will be confronted with a continuous demand to make quite profound modifications in how and where they live, in life styles and ways of thinking and behaving. Certainly they will have very frequently to learn new skills, and not just of a vocational type. If ours becomes a society in which increased leisure is an economic necessity, then an even more fundamental attitudinal change will be necessary.[8] Beyond even this lies a profound modification in our concepts of 'political maturity', responsible 'involvement' and 'democracy'.

These changes, important as they are, are but facets of something far more fundamentally affecting man's idea of himself, the structure of his motivations and his view of the human condition. We are aware how previous periods of change have been prepared for and have been accompanied by changes in value systems, in the climate of thought and in personality. Weber[9] has pointed out and carefully documented the interaction between such things as the rise of the Protestant ethic and the development of an entrepreneurial and capitalistic middle class. More recently McClelland[10] has produced evidence to suggest that periods of economic and technological expansion are preceded by an increase in the number of individuals with high achievement motivation and, in folk tales and other literary forms, of themes of achievement. For the more recent and better documented periods of history, he has been able to show an association between achievement motivation and other aspects of value structures and personality. This study is the more impressive since it covers a number of historical periods, including the flowering of Ancient Greece, and a number of widely separated countries from Japan to the U.S.A. Technical advance itself strengthens some values whilst weakening others—for example it leads people to value leisure and place less stress on hard work.[11] From many sources now we have accumulating evidence to suggest that patterns of child rearing, the emotional and intellectual content of cultures, and the form which education takes, interact—sometimes very rapidly but usually in the course of a generation or two—with economic, technological and even climatic change to modify societies and the values to which they adhere. In some ways too the irrational elements underlying change are seen to be more significant than the overtly rational.

Paradoxically just as the decay of the religious explanation of society and its sanction for law and morality have in fact put the individual face to face with his conscience and responsibility and as awareness of the defects of our systems and the environmental dangers confronting us grows, some at least of the changes in political and industrial organization seem to be affecting personality in a contrary way. Reisman[12] suggested in 1950 that the image held of himself by man is altering profoundly. The nineteenth-century European model was that of a person whose life and attitudes were directed by an inner conscience which enabled him to stand out against the crowd for what he thought right; a man whose prosperity was founded upon saving money and building up resources and who had a private inner life. This image is still cherished by Western European man. However, Reisman claims that for increasing numbers in North American society (and in Europe), this 'inner directed' image is giving way to an 'other-directed one'. Other-directed personalities are more sensitive to group pressures, to the desire for conformity, to advertising in all its forms and to 'human relations techniques' than they are to conscience or 'inner-direction'. To such persons, acceptance by others, conformity, good fellowship, openness of mind and the absence of secrets, even of personal reticence, are virtues; non-conformity, privacy, and independence of thought outside certain very rigidly defined limits are suspect.

This change he suggests is due to a number of trends in society, notably that rising standards of living depend upon mass production and standardization of products and production of this kind depends for success upon high consumption, much of which must be wasteful in the sense that articles must be discarded before they are worn out. Advertising and propaganda are necessary to maintain this high consumption and they in turn—because of the basic standardization of the products to be sold—must insist on conformity, on keeping up with the Joneses. On the other hand, industries tend to get larger and larger and to eliminate competition between themselves by agreement. Hence rugged non-conformist individualism no longer has a place and no one man can dominate an enterprise. Good industrial relationships become important and, since work itself has little intrinsic capacity to satisfy, the marginal satisfactions of being on good terms with workmates and colleagues become of cardinal importance. Techniques of group dynamics, sociometric techniques, popularity polls and the like, are held to be symptoms of the same trend and, by their action, to intensify it.[13]

CHOICE

Such a thesis is difficult to prove conclusively, but whatever one may think of it, there is little doubt that some of the causes and some of the manifestations of which Reisman speaks are indeed apparent; and that they tend, in contrast to the developed Protestant ethic, to reduce the individual's willingness to sustain a personal moral choice if necessary against current opinion.

The irony of this situation lies in the fact that whereas advertising directs attention to choices which at best are marginal, the open, free and pluralistic society into which we are moving presents everyone, and particularly the young, with genuinely critical moral, economic, philosophic and political choices, the very dimensions of which are not fully known or understood.

It is no surprise therefore that anxious aggressive bewilderment or opting out are common responses. 'Inner direction', the force of conscience and of principle, religious or social, does not seem to count for much except in the intimacy of personal relationships; in work or even in political life either apathy or sensible conformity are more acceptable and easier than the thorny conscience and the stress of individual decision. For many, especially for the young, opting out and developing an anti-society, seems to be the only appropriate response. It may well be that affluence and its accompaniments necessarily favour 'other-directed' types of personality both inside and outside the 'system', as the answer to a situation which, if faced in its stark reality, leads to intolerably agonizing choices. One must, however, ask whether crude responses of fight or flight are the only alternatives; and whether one cannot through education maintain the power to make responsible and enlightened moral choices within a framework that uses human aggressiveness to constructive ends.

FURTHER READING

Barrett, J.; Louw, M., eds. *International aspects of overpopulation*. London, Macmillan, 1972.

Gotesky, R.; Laszlo, E., eds. *Human dignity: this century and the next*. London, Gordon & Breach, 1971.

Havighurst, R. J., ed. *Metropolitanism. Its challenge to education*. Chicago, University of Chicago Press, 1968.

Leach, G., ed. *The great doom debate.* London, Observer Ltd., 1972.
Maddox, J. *The doomsday syndrome.* London, Macmillan, 1972.
Medawar, P. B. *The hope of progress.* London, Methuen, 1972.
Mesthene, E. G. *The Harvard University Programme on Technology and Society 1964-1972: a final review.* Cambridge, Mass., Harvard Information Office, 1972.
Polunin, N., ed. *The environmental future.* London, Macmillan, 1972.
Toynbee, A. *Surviving the future.* Oxford, Oxford University Press, 1971.

NOTES

1.	A simple extrapolation, for example, of current trends in productivity, in the use of resources, in accumulating pollution of the atmosphere, in population growth, suggests that by the turn of the century some decisions involving a level of international co-operation at present quite unprecedented will have to have been taken if the adults of the second millennium are in their turn to have sufficient freedom of choice to avert disaster. One should recall that, for example, the most optimistic assumption that we can make at present about population increase is that there will be a world population at the turn of the century of 6,000 million or more. If, as seems by no means unreasonable, the then population wishes generally to live at half only of the American standard of the 1950s (and still well below that currently obtaining in Western Europe), a sixteen-fold rise in production will be necessary as well as major shifts of resources from the 'haves' to the 'have nots'. This growth would enormously increase the rate of use of such resources as metals, fossil fuels (by 40–45 times) leading to the exhaustion of some in a matter of years. The implication of this is that, if significant economic development of this magnitude is to take place then the present technological base of our civilization will have to change to synthetics even more rapidly and radically than in the past century it changed from agriculture to industry. Such a change would have to be more abrupt and therefore more far reaching in its impact on life than the first Industrial Revolution. (Villard, H. H. The need for technological change. In: Morse, D.; Warner, A. W., eds. *Technological innovation and society.* New York; London, Columbia University Press, 1966. / Kahn, H.; Weiner, A. J. *The year 2000.* London, Collier-Macmillan, 1968. / Meadows, D. H., *et. al. The limits to growth.* London, Angus & Robertson, 1972. / Picht, K. *Reflexions au bord du gouffre.* Paris, Laffont, 1971.) It does however seem probable that the tone of many prophecies is exaggeratedly alarmist—or at least is interpreted popularly in rather more absolute ways than the authors intend. There is, it is argued, much room for choice and, in choices concerning the environment, technology properly used is an immensely important ally. The danger of extreme statements is that they may lead to an outright rejection even of beneficial technology (Maddox, J. *The doomsday syndrome.* London, Macmillan, 1972).
2.	Even by Doughty's Sheik (*Travels in Arabia Deserta.* London, Cape, 1936).
3.	A good example is the siting in a highly developed and overpopulated country of a new international airport. The balance of environmental, economic, individual and technical considerations is difficult to assess, and the 'general good' of the community at risk is interpretable only in the final analysis by what is understood by 'the quality of life'.

4. See: Mesthene E. G. *Harvard University Programme on Technology and Society, 1964–1972*. Cambridge, Mass., Harvard Information Office, 1972. See also the review of the report in: *New society* (London), 12 June 1972.
5. Already in 1959, in a letter to the *New statesman*, Julian Huxley put it in a nutshell: 'In general we must consider the relation between quantity of population and quality of life, and must take account of all kinds of resources, not only food resources but resources of space, enjoyment, education and fulfilment. Excessive numbers and population density impinge upon the quality of human life and curtail the realization of many of its desirable possibilities such as health, human dignity, active employment, and sense of individual significance. They are producing water shortages, traffic congestion, and cities far beyond optimum size for efficiency and beyond optimum scale for truly human living. Above all they promote over-organization and regimentation and reduce the area of human freedom.' Bertrand Russell even earlier was discussing the difficulties created for the individual by the increasing complexity and centralization of society. (*Education and the social order*. London, Allen & Unwin, 1932).
6. It is being urgently suggested (for example, see: Mansholt, S. Note for the Members of the Commission. Text of a letter sent to Mr. Malfatti. CAB/II/145/72-E, Brussels, 9 February 1972) that the West should abandon its philosophy of continuous growth in productivity and concentrate upon improving the quality of life. This might imply, however, an abandonment of the Third World to its fate unless the countries of the West undertook very considerable political and economic changes both in restraining their own growth and directing human and material resources to help developing countries to reach a sufficient level of productivity to sustain a fully human existence for their people. Others argue that while technology determines the general directions of change, values determine which technologies will be developed and applied, and thus the specific form changes will take (see: Mesthene, E. G. Op. cit.). See also: Leach, G. Spaceship Earth. *The Observer* (London), 8 August 1971; and the United Nations Conference on the Human Environment held in Stockholm.
7. Toynbee, A. *Surviving the future*. Oxford, Oxford University Press, 1971. P. B. Medawar is more optimistic. He reminds us that while human beings have a history of half a million years, it is only during the past 500 that they have begun to be biologically successful and, because we are mere beginners, we may hope to improve: 'To deride the hope of progress is the ultimate futility, the last word in poverty of spirit and meanness of mind.' (*The hope of progress*. London, Methuen, 1972).
8. de Grazia, S. *Of time, work and leisure*. New York, The Twentieth Century Fund, 1962 [especially Chapter I and Chapter X]. George Picht (Scientific Counsellor to the German Government) in an interview with *L'Express* (Paris) (no 1049, 16–22 aout 1971), puts it succinctly: 'Dans les prochaines décennies, une pression grandissante sollicitera, dans tous les pays de la Terre, les capacités et le rendement extrême de toutes les couches de la societé. La mobilité sera beaucoup trop faible pour désigner la révolution permanente qui pourrait s'emparer de nos conditions de vie: concurrence acharnée, accélération de changements qui mineront toute stabilité sociale. . . . Le pregrès technique entraînera une fluctuation constante des forces productives, et un appel de plus en plus pressant aux capacités intellectuelles.'
9. Weber, M. *The Protestant ethic and the spirit of capitalism*. London, Allen & Unwin, 1930.
10. McClelland, D. C. *The achieving society*. Princeton, Van Nostrand, 1961.

C

11. Mesthene, E. G. Op. cit.
12. Reisman, D. *The lonely crowd.* New Haven, Yale University Press, 1950.
13. It will be noted that both 'inner directedness' and 'other-directedness' can take many forms and have different ethical contents. In many respects the tribal African and the rural Japanese are 'other-directed' since they depend upon the tribe, village or family and are more susceptible to shame and social pressure than to guilt. Similarly certain religions, e.g. Buddhism, imply withdrawal into contemplation and rejection of materialistic social demands; they are 'inner-directed' in a different way.

Chapter four

The containment and socialization of aggression

TENSION AND AGGRESSION

The spread of the twentieth-century technological revolution to parts of the world which have not experienced the slow preparation which preceded the industrial growth of Europe, has increased tensions everywhere. This is true for individuals, for groups within nations and in international life. The key problem which must be solved is now evident to all—how may we live together internationally without self-destruction? and this in a period when, for all men and women everywhere, the whole climate of thought and life is changing so rapidly as to augment feelings of insecurity and put great strain on human capacity to adapt and grow with the times, let alone undertake the conscious and fundamental changes suggested earlier.

In one very real sense, culture may be interpreted in terms rather of how far it provides security and controls human aggression than, as the Freudians see it, of how it regulates sex impulses.[1] The search for security through achievement, esteem and love, and the search for formulae and patterns of behaviour which turn aggression outward, use it constructively and protect others from its consequences, are two interpretative factors which help to explain the growth of many social structures. The committee system within which members may only speak to each other through the chairman, the displaced aggression of a suit at law, the forms and presuppositions of parliamentary democracy with its attempt to reconcile representation with responsible and effective leadership, the formulae of exaggerated politeness within which it is possible socially to be extremely rude, and the immediate reaction in some cultures of public opinion against losing one's temper or raising one's voice, as well as the privileged occasions, usually in sport, when direct expression of aggression, even in the form of violence, is permitted —all these lend colour to the idea.

The nineteenth century, with many imperfections, saw in much of

51

Europe and North America the Christian-humanist idea of the sanctity of the individual because he is human embodied in law and in public life. This notion which is still dominant in Europe fused with Anglo-Saxon (and ultimately Icelandic) notions of collective responsibility, lies at the foundation of democracy, as we understand it, of government by consent, of elected representation and the responsibilities of leadership, of equality before the law and of the protection of the weak and of the underprivileged.

THE SEARCH FOR SECURITY

The search for security is a basic one, from very earliest years; and it is related to aggression. Many of the checks and safeguards of society are designed to meet threats to individual or to group security and serve the purpose of making violent and crudely aggressive defence reactions unnecessary. On the other hand, aggressiveness which does not overtly threaten the security of others or which is sublimated to constructive ends like scientific discovery, the building of a business or some other organization, the overcoming of material difficulties, is in many of our societies a socially sanctioned, indeed admired, way of restoring or maintaining the security/insecurity balance; peaceful inter-personal and inter-group competition with the loyalty and muted hostility which it involves is encouraged and even when it leads to some excess or even to certain forms of direct expression, tends to be tolerated.

No society, and few individuals or groups, have attained that level of balanced development and maturity at which aggression is always and invariably deflected from the threat of interpersonal or intergroup violence. This is as much as to say that we have not yet solved the twin problems of bringing up children and adolescents in such a way that they feel themselves unthreatened by human beings within their own group or by groups which are different from themselves, and that of canalizing rather than repressing aggression, by turning it to concrete problems in the external world. There are indeed many signs that the feelings of rejection and alienation experienced by considerable groups in modern societies erupt increasingly in intercommunal conflict, vandalism, violence against the property symbols of society and riots directed against society's symbols of order.

Almost every advance we have made in the containment of direct aggression has had behind it (at least in its early stages) the sanction of force, it has harnessed the aggressiveness of a group which would feel its own stability threatened if one of its members stepped too far out of line. Nineteenth- or twentieth-century liberal-humanism recognized this and formulated many of the regulations in codified and in conventionally accepted form which are the basis of what we know as the democratic way of life.

However, it is not often realized how much this development was, and still is, dependent upon a combination of circumstances which could radically change. In a very real sense the coherence of a group depends upon the level of security of its individual participants. If the group is threatened from without it may become more cohesive but more intolerant of deviation in its members. The violence of a group reaction against a particular individual deviation is likely to be proportional to the fear in each group member of impulses within himself to similar deviations. We can readily see examples of both of these tendencies at work during war time. Increasingly we see it in the attitudes of particular sections or groups in a community against others; religious and ethnic differences are particularly liable to precipitate such violence; but so are differences of age group and of social class.[2]

PANIC

If, however, the external pressure is very great and there is a direct threat to individual survival, such as starvation, then the group may disrupt in panic. Habits—especially habits of almost automatic response to threatening situations, a practised knowing what to do—and beliefs, especially those which are deeply held and appeal to religious ideals, sanctions, and rewards, may be very powerful factors in holding groups together when otherwise they would disrupt under external threat. Both of these, habit and belief, are vital to what is generally known as morale, and a breakdown in either usually precipitates some kind of crisis. This is, of course, well understood by the practitioners of psychological warfare, and by those who seek to disintegrate strong personalities by breaking up the habitual coherence of the world of the senses, and of the more or less consistent predictions we make of the behaviour of others. They are no less well understood by those who wish to exploit latent but often genuine sources of tension within otherwise peaceful communities.

LIBERAL HUMANISM—THE UNIVERSAL DECLARATION OF HUMAN RIGHTS

The past fifty years have seen developments of immense importance in man's attempts to contain aggression. Although during this period religious beliefs of the traditional Christian kind, and their organized manifestations, have markedly declined in their hold upon daily life in the West and the religious reason for acting morally is no longer for very many people in many countries the main one, attempts have been made, internationally, in the Covenant of the League of Nations, in the United

Nations itself and particularly in the Universal Declaration of Human Rights, to embody the ethical code of liberal-humanism in international form. This latter has not been signed by all nations as a covenant and even if it were it could, in the last resort, only be maintained internationally by force similar to that behind secular law in most countries. Such a force does not exist and without some kind of international police strong enough to hold national armies in check it is unlikely to.

This is as much as to say that laws of the liberal-humanist kind in the international field cannot be much in advance of the attitudes and beliefs of most of those nations who live under them, though their existence may lead a growing number of people to accept them as a guide to behaviour. To a very large extent the same is true of national law and custom. Unless they correspond to a deeply consenting attitude in a majority, they cannot be maintained by force—at least in a democracy. Many of the forms of law-abiding behaviour of modern man and many of his attitudes are, in fact, in part habit patterns first induced by social and legal sanctions against other patterns of behaviour. In general, as children, we learn to behave in an acceptable way before we internalize as attitudes and principles the moral basis which supports that behaviour and extends it to more complex fields. International behaviour is not in fact individual but collective, and only the beginnings of ways of behaving have been laid down, and these are for the most part too remote to be readily perceived by individuals as related to their own attitudes and habits.

The alternative may be the imposition of law by a minority disposing of overwhelming force, an alternative which, in the past, has led either to tyranny or to revolt and is unlikely, under contemporary conditions, to lead to an enlightened rule of law.[3] Paradoxically, therefore, the Universal Declaration of Human Rights can only be enforced when its enforcement is rendered possible by the fact that a sufficient majority of people in sufficient countries have deeply rooted attitudes leading to the determination to maintain these ideals, cost what it may to particular nations, and when, moreover, collective behaviour patterns have developed, as well as techniques for the solution of international problems, less cumbersome and equivocal than those of traditional diplomacy. Neither of these two broad circumstances can arise unless the real and external causes of difficulty—population pressure, large economic differences and the like—are reduced to manageable proportions, if not entirely abolished. Internationally as well as nationally such an idea implies not only the machinery of negotiation, but the habits of thought and forms of collective behaviour rooted in a belief in their efficacy and in the value of what they aim to preserve. This is the key problem. Government by consent is essential to any society, national or international, which wishes to preserve the sanctity of the individual; in turn this implies that a majority of its participants accept, emotionally as well as intellectually, the right of others to different opinions and ways of life.

BELIEF AND DOUBT

Belief, however, especially a system of belief which clearly sanctions particular decisions and imposes collective habits of response in the form of a moral law, is a double-edged weapon. It is a powerful factor in social cohesiveness and in the buttressing of individual security. But it is the nature of the belief which determines the ends which will be sought. There is indeed a strong human tendency to seek for the support which faith gives. The decay of organized religions in the West—apart altogether from the fact that for many people this has withdrawn the spiritual sanction for the liberal ethical code—has removed an essential defence, leaving many hungry for faith and for an authority external to themselves, against which to rebel mildly and in submission to which they may find security, tranquillity, and peace from the need to make difficult decisions. Provisional belief rather than conviction, the acceptance of the notion that 'truth' may be personal and many-sided, the dynamic tolerance of true agnosticism which accepts that doubt is an essential background to action and that conviction may be a bad master, are psychologically very difficult attitudes to develop in education and for adults to maintain in the face of threat. Such a state of mind depends upon a complex of knowledge, trained capacity to think analytically and critically, and a solidly based emotional maturity. It depends too on the ability to control such fundamental impulses as fear. Doubt is threatening—conviction reassuring; and conviction shared by a group all subscribing to the same views provides a refuge for the individual, who will, with relief, relinquish the liberty of doubt and tolerance for that freedom from anxiety which conformity and its preordained patterns of behaviour and attitude will give.' When to this we add the reflection that insecurity is probably the basic psychological state, beginning in the child's earliest experiences of frustration and anxiety, and that security is only painfully and slowly acquired, if at all, in the course of growth and education, then we are ready to understand that whereas a given religion may decline in its hold upon people, the need for belief and for a shared faith may well remain. When there are no great external threats, or when material gains lull broader anxieties, this need may remain dormant and we have the situation of passive unbelief—a broad acceptance of institutionalized religion without active participation, belief, or agnosticism. When the threat to the individual or to his group moves nearer, we have religious revival, or the search for new religions.

AN AGE OF FAITH

Hence it is not liberal agnosticism, as was hoped by some nineteenth-century philosophers, that has filled the gap left by the decline of organized religions and which provides the energy ultimately to uphold the rule of law. The twentieth century has so far been indeed as much an age of faith as the middle ages; but many of its new 'religions' have taken the form of authoritarian political systems with ethical and moral contents different from those of Christianity or of the other great international religions of the world.

At this stage it should perhaps be said that faith and belief are, in themselves, neither good nor bad, and what has been said above should not be construed as an attack upon religion. What is being argued here is that the tendency towards faith and belief is the natural psychological outcome of the basic insecurity/security structure of the human being. Furthermore, the less fundamentally secure the individual, the more likely is he to look for an authoritarian form of belief—whether religious or political—and the more readily does he move from faith to fanaticism. The aggressive drives of the personality seek sanction from belief, as well as give force to it. If this turns inwards we have the self-tormenting, masochistic, 'intropunitive'[5] individual; if it turns outwards we have the kind of person who, given a lead and the safety of numbers, readily becomes the persecutor and tormentor of others, finding in attack the best means of meeting the threat which his underlying anxiety perceives in the existence of those who do not belong to his group or believe as he does. The paranoia of Hitler's Germany, the grandeur of its claims to world leadership, and its roots in the deep depression and unemployment of the 1920s are an excellent example. It is not without significance either that when a political system becomes in effect a State religion, it turns to the persecution of other religions within its borders, whether these religions are organized and international or whether they are 'heresies', 'deviationism' or simply other ways of life which have a different ethic of human relationships.

What has just been said, though broadly true at least in contemporary circumstances, needs some qualification, particularly in individual cases and with particular religions. We should note first that systems which are behaviourally speaking 'religious' need have no 'supernatural' content—indeed the overtly political ones often do not though they may have god-like figures. Belief is only one aspect of the matter, the ethical or moral content of a belief is another, and a third is the forms of behaviour which are sanctioned by it. Thus it is possible for secure individuals or groups to cherish beliefs, part of the contents of which preach intolerance of other viewpoints and prescribe persecutory forms of behaviour as a duty. On the other hand, as the history of Christianity bears witness, individuals and groups have ignored the basic moral prescription of love for others and turned to persecution. With this qualification, we may therefore suggest that the predominant security/insecurity balance in the society and in its leading individuals will do much to determine manifestations; and a group in power can, for a time at all events, through fear, through the enforcement of conformity, induce those who do not feel strongly either way to remain at least quiescent; conversely a positive attitude of tolerance will minimize intolerant and persecutory behaviour in the group—provided that there is no great external threat. Truly liberal attitudes can in fact only flourish when internal personal psychological security and real defences against external threat are prepotent over real or imagined fear; and when substantial portions of the group have learned, through their education, the ways by which they can judge situations and act in them by a rational appeal to moral princip'es which they have themselves freely and understandingly developed.

THE MODERN CONFLICT

The essential conflict of modern times, then is that between liberalism defined in these ways and 'religion', taken in the sense of belief which feels itself threatened if others do not agree or believe something different. Such a liberalism is by no means incompatible with faith or with religion although perhaps in its most liberal form it tends to agnosticism. In concrete terms the conflict is between those who say with Montaigne: 'I do not rank any opinions so high that I would index or roast all who oppose them',[6] and those who in effect say: 'Mine is the truth. Those who are not for me are against me. If you are in error then for your own good and the good of others, you must be converted—forcibly if necessary—or purged, eliminated or liquidated'.[7]

This is of course an age old conflict. Hitherto, only groups of people in exceptionally favoured economic and geographical circumstances or even isolated individuals like Montaigne have been able to hold to liberal tenets, even partially, and threats of attack have only too frequently brought out an underlying fanaticism. Until recently, however, some parts of the world at least have been free enough at all times to preserve and develop liberal ideas. The danger now is, as Orwell sees in his *1984*, that the large concentrations of population and economic power of the superstates are so intimately and constantly in contact that there is a continual threat both real and imaginary: and the circumstances are so complex as to defy ordinary powers of analysis and understanding.

In its simplest terms, the contemporary problem of survival is as

c*

follows: human aggression is most likely to take the form of inter-personal, intergroup or international hostility where the individual, group or nation feels itself threatened. The Universal Declaration of Human Rights and the Charter of the United Nations are the embodiment of liberal thought about the value of man *per se* and the sanctity of exist-ence. No physical, military or economic power exists or probably can exist to sanction and enforce these against the will even of a substantial minority of nations. Only therefore if there is a widespread conviction of the importance of negotiation, compromise and respect for the rights of others, prepotent over fear and anxiety, can we escape either enslave-ment or destruction.

Such an attitude or conviction will be the product of education and experience: it may be motivated and reinforced by religious faith or by an agnostic philosophy; but it cannot stand against the continuously besetting anxieties and threats, real and imagined, which seem a per-manent part of life in the world, unless it is rooted in personalities who can accept themselves as they are, whose aggression is directed against things and circumstances rather than against themselves or others, and who feel themselves to be fundamentally safe in the world.

Moreover, and this is the real crux for education, if such a convic-tion has been built up by indoctrination rather than won by a process of rational accession through knowledge and experience, it may well prove fragile in extreme circumstances or some of its tenets formulated in terms of learned behaviour become, with the passage of time and change, out-moded. An authoritarian style of education in school or in the family, however humane and benevolent it may be, tends to indoctrinate; a more open and questioning style, supported by a genuine authority which initiates and helps the individual through questioning and exploration to understand, though more difficult, seems likely in the long run to pro-duce a genuinely liberal personality.

THE INTERACTION OF MATERIAL AND PSYCHOLOGICAL FACTORS

This is the psychological side of the picture. On the other, there are two conditions of almost equal importance. The material and economic incitements to anxiety and fear have to be reduced and where possible eliminated. As we have suggested however, it looks as though population and economic pressures are likely rather to rise than to diminish. Inter-nationally, as we have done nationally, we have to develop behavioural techniques which enable aggression to emerge in non-violent ways, and wherever possible, constructively. The United Nations Organization to some extent meets both of these problems but with inadequate financial resources for the first and, for the second, a not fully adequate emancipa-tion from the behavioural patterns of the old power diplomacy. It has scarcely yet been permitted to begin upon such problems as the global use of resources, an equitable distribution of wealth or the planning of a kind. The 1972 Stockholm Conference on the human environment is a beginning and has resulted in some agreement; but it is noticeable that some nations were absent and that there was a marked conflict of interest and a crisis of confidence between the industrially developed and the developing nations. Subsequent conferences (1974) on food and population have shown similar cleavages.

It is no part of the purpose of this chapter to discuss, except incidentally, the organization of international or indeed of national life; nor to examine the desirable external forms of behaviour which interact with human psychology which it is our purpose to discuss. What however must be emphasized is that to regard human relationships, collective or individual, as exclusively determined by economics, institutionalized social systems, externally imposed frameworks of law, custom, procedure or behaviour, is as erroneous as it is to regard them as solely the product of internal needs, drives, anxieties, securities and insecurities. Behaviour influences thought and attitudes; thought and attitude affect behaviour. The removal of causes of difficulty does not necessarily remove the psychological tendency to seek for difficulties, but it is an essential factor in their solution. Removal of the causes or incitements to personal, group or international insecurities or hostilities will not necessarily prevent aggression or the threat of it; but we cannot develop the kind of dynamic adjustments which are essential, nor the will to peace, until at least the major external real and unreal threats have been removed.

Basically, however, conditions or events are important mainly because of their repercussions on and interaction with human psychology, with personality in all its aspects and manifestations. There are physical and mental conditions to which even the most fully developed and balanced personalities cannot adapt; there are conceivably others in which adaptation is possible even for the most delicately balanced. The problem we have to face is how to construct a society which can accept the great cultural and psychological diversity of mankind, which can use what one might call 'creative nonconformity' and thus can bring about change locally, nationally and internationally without destruction or the wasteful ineffectiveness of revolution. To match this, much higher proportions of men and women than at present must in varied ways consonant with their different cultural values and goals be able effectively to adjust to changing circumstances, to maintain a degree of happiness and psychological comfort, with, nevertheless, sufficient anxiety and discontent to keep them active in the pursuit of constructive change.

A society in rapid evolution demands of its participants a very high measure of this capacity to accept and adjust to fundamental alterations affecting all aspects of life. Enforced and dramatic changes in the nature of a man's work, for example, are threatening and productive of anxiety. They tend to provoke defensive and rigid attitudes. The difficulties inherent in dense urban populations induce tensions which augment fatigue and even neurosis. The great moral and political issues now arising confront individuals and groups with decisions which they are ill-equipped to take or even to understand. Hence one most important criterion of mental health is the ability continually to make adjustments not without strain or stress—these are inevitable and to a degree healthy—but without being overwhelmed by them and driven into maladaptive responses or the search for an external saviour. In its turn this implies a basic security which permits risk-taking, a flexibility which allows one to change one's mind and habits, a background of knowledge and a capacity to acquire, analyse and understand the objective facts which define novel situations. In effect this means a freedom to continue to learn, a freedom which is partly emotional and partly a matter of trained intelligence. If any form of participatory democracy is to survive, the individual must be able to relate to his society and to subgroups within it in terms of moral choices, adjusting his personal needs to general goods in the light of knowledge; and this he cannot do once and for all but will be called upon to do continually whilst coping effectively with the concomitant struggle, tension and anxiety.

FURTHER READING

Bourcier, A. *La nouvelle éducation morale.* Paris, Les Editions sociales françaises, 1966.

Eibl-Eibesfeldt, I. *Love and hate: on the natural history of basic behaviour patterns.* London, Methuen, 1971.

Hacker, F. *Aggression—die Brutalisierung der modernen Welt.* Aggression—the brutalization of the modern world. Wien; München; Zürich; Molden, 1971.

Jones, N. B. *Ethological studies of child behaviour.* Cambridge, Cambridge University Press, 1972.

Laing, R. D.; Cooper, D. G. *Reason and violence: a decade of Sartres' philosophy, 1950-60.* 2nd edn. London, Tavistock, 1971.

Williams, L. *Challenge to survival.* London, Deutsch, 1971.

NOTES

1. Even orthodox Freudians seem now to be turning their attention to aggression as a major human problem in its own right rather than as an offshoot of sexuality. See proceedings of the Int. Psych. An. Congress, Vienna, 1971.

2. F. Hacker (*Aggression—die Brutalisierung der modernen Welt*. Wien; Müchen; Zürich, Molden, 1971) suggests that the ways in which societies and individuals use and control aggression are based on conscious or unconscious strategies; and proposes a social board of control to resolve aggessive situations.

3. See Chapter 3, pp. 44–45.

4. Orwell puts this very powerfully in the second half of *Animal farm* where beliefs are reduced to simple slogans: 'Four legs good; two legs bad'. See also the kinds of graffitti spawned by student sit-ins, especially those of May 1968 in Paris (Besançon, J., ed. *Les murs ont la parole*. Paris, Tchou, 1968). Very many are of the kind into which the reader can project what he likes, using them to reinforce his own half-formulated needs. They tend like the 'thoughts' of some revolutionaries to be bold simple statements which cut through nuanced thought and speak directly to the emotions. In a broad sense they are 'poetic' rather than factual or scientific statements, though they are often stated as such. It is worth noting that 'radicals', 'anarchists' and other similar groups which reject current beliefs in fact find their support in systems of counter belief involving an equally or even more rigid conformity.

5. Flugel, J. C. *The psycho-analytic study of the family*. London, Hogarth Press, 1921 (reprinted 1948) (The international psycho-analytic library, no. 3).

6. 'Après tout, c'est mettre ses conjectures à bien haut pris que d'en faire cuire un homme tout vif.' *Essais*. III, 11.

7. One sometimes finds that men and women of liberal views (to say nothing of radicals) are in fact inclined to persecute in the name of freedom. This is not surprising when one considers the basic difference between the content of a belief (which may be liberal) and an attitude to belief in general.

Chapter five

Education, mental hygiene and the level of human functioning

INTELLIGENCE IS NOT ENOUGH

The great questions are how do we achieve such a capacity for dynamic adjustment, and whether indeed this is possible, in all or at least a substantial majority of our populations, and how this is to be reconciled with cultural pluralism, or even with the cultivation of human diversity. We may remark that, as societies become more complex, the demands made on human intelligence in any case increase. In simple societies one can adjust and survive with a few skills, a little knowledge and minimal intelligence—particularly when such societies, as most were, are ruled by an oligarchic élite. Even if we accept as a rough guide current rather partial notions of intelligence, it is evident that at one end an increasing proportion of people find that the demands made upon them by daily life outstrip their capacity to learn and change, and at the other there are few indeed who can fully grasp the great problems of our time. We are thus concerned to raise the level of human functioning in general and to find ways effectively to solve problems the complexity of which outstrips the individual mind. In their turn these imply a structure of values which have not simply been acquired by indoctrination but have developed and continue to develop by processes which, because they are as rational as possible, permit change and evolution in the individual's idea of himself and of the community.

Neither task is entirely hopeless. No individual unaided could have conceptualized and solved all the intellectual problems involved in putting man into space. In fact the successes of Soviet and American technology in this field provide a paradigm for that combination of man in co-operative groups and thinking machines which is probably the model for the future. But it should be pointed out that this is easiest to realize when the goal is largely free of ethical or moral correlates and when the subordinate decisions are strictly scientific or technological. Real human dilemmas are not in general like this. Economic and social problems, for example, at all points involve judgements of relative good not determinable by strictly scientific means; and the task is to separate for thought and combine for judgement the possible with the desirable at all levels in objectively dispassionate ways.

It is in this sense that 'intelligence' is not enough. It is possible to have, for example, a highly trained scientific intelligence in association with deeply rooted prejudices or rigidities which prevent its functioning objectively outside the laboratory, even in scientific controversy. Still more, the very intensiveness and adequacy of a given training or education may produce mental rigidities which forbid the mind to look impartially at certain hypotheses. Resistances to new scientific discoveries are of this kind, a kind of *odium theologicum* which owes more to passion than to thought.[1]

Thus three things seem important: the cultivation of the kind of flexibility of thought which leaves the mind alert to novel combinations and new hypotheses; the capacity to be aware of and to discount prejudice, particularly one's own; and certain positive attitudes or values, which while not rigidly unchanging, are none the less firm. Implied too is the ability to be aware that scientific inference and moral judgement are different dimensions of thought with rather different skills and strategies involved, each of which requires training and the decision as to what to do is usually in the end a function of both.

In one very real sense what is being described is a high form of human character in which intelligence and emotion are in harmonious synthesis; and the individual is capable of moral autonomy because he is either free from unconsciously determined drives or armed with the means to prevent them distorting his judgement and his ability to entertain alternatives. But it is more than this. One could be balanced in this way and yet lack the training and the education which provide the intellectual tools for analysis, synthesis, creation and judgement; and at each level both knowledge and sheer intellectual capacity are essential.[2]

Hence there is another aspect to the task. It is true that without vision the people perish; but a genuine democracy cannot survive on a brilliant élite alone. Universal free and compulsory education, whilst it has produced many novel problems, has had one remarkable effect. Just as improved general nutritional standards have in this century increased the average height and weight of western populations without producing an increase in giants, so the exposure of an entire population to schooling seems to have raised the general average level of what we might call 'operational intelligence', and it has done much to increase the stock of information, to equip people to learn more and to reduce prejudice. A generally educated population can solve more, and more complex, problems than an uneducated one; it can be more productive of material wealth and it can be more widely open to a more varied and rich culture.

CRITICISMS OF THE SCHOOL

However, no one can claim that the schooling which we have is fully effective. We have become aware, for example, that equality of educational opportunity is not achieved by providing the same kinds of schools for all children. There are groups—and considerable ones—in our populations who cannot adequately profit from what is offered for reasons which lie outside the control of the school. Thus, even in the relatively highly developed societies of the West, there seems to be a pool of human ability which does not achieve its full potential. Moreover the education system, while it raises average levels, tends none the less to increase differences between those who profit most from it and those who profit least. What is perhaps equally if not more important is the series of questions which one can and should raise about the quality, direction and effectiveness of education.

The criticisms come from two directions which, though related, are in some respects different; both will be dealt with at greater length later. The first concerns the formal education system, those aspects of knowledge, those forms of mental functioning and those values which it appears to foster or to neglect. The second concerns the nature of the educational process, how far it fosters the kind of dynamic adjustment of which we have been speaking, and how far the climates of educational institutions, the systems of authority, the sanctions and rewards, the expectations which are set up, favour or threaten the growth of stable, secure and effective personalities.

Those concerned with the sociology of education have been quick to point out that curricula, particularly, and general aims tend to reflect the choices of particular social groups and that the organization of knowledge is related to the distribution of power in society. Education has operated as a means of social mobility and increasingly does so, but by its nature, it is suggested, it is selective as much by its definitions of knowledge as by the nature of the institutions themselves in which it is given.[3] On the other hand, philosophers insist that there are at least two criteria which must be applied: one concerns such aspects of development as autonomy, creativeness and integrity, and the other is educational—an all-round awareness based upon knowledge. It is contended that so far as the first is concerned, schools tend to indoctrinate rather than encourage creative independence; that the second criterion is not fully met by the conventional curriculum which tends to stress certain areas of knowledge (mathematics, science, history and the like) and omit such things as an educated awareness of self and others, training in moral judgement and philosophical understanding.' It is further contended that although of course the two are closely inter-related, it is possible to be 'excellent' by the first criterion but to be lacking in breadth of understanding by the second—one can be an excellent and developed human being without being an educated one and of course one can be educated without necessarily displaying ex-cellence in development. Schools and other educational institutions only imperfectly if at all ensure excellence of development and genuine breadth of understanding.

These two lines of thought, the sociological and the philosophical, are not necessarily incompatible. Neither precisely prescribes the con-tent of education nor does either define, except in broad senses open to considerable variation in detail, its aims. In their complementary ways they provide the framework of analysis and thought within which we can think about education as a process whereby human personality and character are shaped both by the ways in which the school treats its pupils and by the public modes of experience which it offers as a series of deliberate cultural choices.

However, we know that, in practice, with whatever ends in mind a school may be organized, it will do both more and less than its pro-ponents intend. Moreover not all pupils will be affected in the same ways; nor will they all come to the school with the same tendencies, capacities, prior experiences and the like. There are practices—for ex-ample, streaming by ability or grouping for particular aspects of work—which in some circumstances may be helpful and in others may provide adverse tensions for individuals or groups. There are forms of discipline necessary at one stage of growth which provoke dependence or revolt at another. Some children bring with them conflicts arising outside the school but which must be resolved before learning can take place. In short, there are individual psychological dimensions which escape the broad theoretical frameworks of sociologist and philosopher but which may do much to determine the mental health of growing children and adolescents.

EDUCATIONAL AIMS

If we are to avoid the waste of human ability which still marks our system, and if we are to produce a healthy participant society able to meet and solve the kinds of problems which loom in front of us, we have none the less to be very clear about our educational aims. Under-lying the educational changes, experiments and reforms of the past decades lies recognition that the task of the school has considerably changed in the past fifty years, and that the old formulae and attitudes do not match up to current needs. Some, both in the nineteenth century and more recently, see education as having a primarily economic value. They may wish to shape curricula strictly in terms of the needs of industry and the manifest utility of the skills and knowledge demanded by vocations.[5] Although there has always been a vocational element in education and there is no essential conflict between vocational and other aims, strictly economic concerns are insufficient. More and more consciously, we see the education system as a series of institutions which reflect and thus perpetuate and shape the entire social group in which they exist. Like their philosophic predecessors in revolutionary France of the eighteenth century, the nineteenth- and early twentieth-century reformers hoped that, through formal education alone, they could remould the world to their heart's desire. We are more cautious and perhaps more pessimistic. We know that a good part of a child's education takes place in the early years long before he passes the doorway of the school and that all experience which he undergoes outside as well as inside the classroom, for good or for ill, shapes his attitudes and his personality. We know too that because of this, and because of the invincible individuality enshrined in every child, the claims which may be made for the school as an isolated social instrument may have to be more modest. We are increasingly aware that there are alternative cultures and powerful informal educational influences which may conflict with the school and with the home; and that somehow the school must reconcile itself to them.

Nevertheless the school is the only social institution which we have created which is in contact with all children and their families over a very important decade or more of the child's growth. It is society's formal instrument for moulding the young, for transmitting the cultural heritage, for inculcating those values, ideals and modes of behaviour on which both the continuity and the evolution of humanity depend. It is likely, for the majority of children, to be the only place in which they will acquire an insight into and some control over those public modes of experience which provide the intellectual tools and the knowledge by which as adolescents and adults they may hope to be able to take a responsible and enlightened part in the social and political choices which will shape our destiny.

STABLE CULTURES

This mission was apparently easier to fulfil when the schools existed only for a limited group selected in some special way—by social caste, by intellectual level, by religious or by political belief. Then school, home and community presented to that privileged minority which was educated, a united and coherent scheme of values, and the task of each was clearly defined. In relatively stable societies which are changing slowly or in privileged social groups, education at home, in the tribe, in small communities and in schools can be and normally is both coherent and conservative. It tends to confine itself to the transmission of an agreed body of traditional knowledge and wisdom, to the inculcation of accepted cultural norms, and it is concordant with a generally accepted concept of man in his society. By and large, it tends to indoctrinate and socialize rather than to stress independence, creativity and diversity. Moreover, since homes and educational institutions tend to complement each other, working towards the same generally agreed ends, it has a powerfully cohesive effect. The choices in front of the individual being at best limited, most usually determined by where he was born, his place in the social hierarchy and what is available in his immediate vicinity, there is little need to ensure more than a reasonable adjustment.

UNCERTAINTIES AND CHOICES

While some contemporary societies still seek to maintain a monolithic concept of man and a universal set of values, many of the materially highly advanced ones tend to be open, pluralistic and mobile—and increasingly so. The families into which a high and growing proportion of European and North American children—and of children of Western educated parents in developing countries—are born, will themselves be subject to change and to confusion, their values increasingly relativistic, their authority structures unsure. Parents who themselves are uncertain find it difficult to give clear meaning to events. If they have disengaged themselves into a vague distrust of 'them' or an equally vague condemnation of the 'system', or if they feel the impotent helplessness of the urban poor, they can provide little help to children and adolescents struggling to understand the world into which they are moving. Nor can they be greatly supportive to the school. They and other adults are likely to be unsure in their handling and uncertain in their attitudes to education; generation differences in what is to be expected from a child may be marked; and a child will be aware of great variation in discipline and expectations between his own home, those of his friends and what is presented to him at school. In highly organized urban environments, even in a salubrious suburb, there may be no provision for safe, unsupervised and spontaneous play, for the experience of a complete and orderly community, for the security which comes of knowing that you are known and that others care for your welfare. The school may be the only place where a coherent group experience is available to child or adolescent, where he can get some essential forms of play and where he can learn to care and to be cared for in non-dependent ways. As they grow, children and adolescents become tantalizingly aware that no aspect of their life is predetermined, almost everything depends upon an agonizing range of choice. There *seem* to be no limits to what one may become, to what one may believe, to what life style one may adopt. But the key to choice escapes them; and frustration may become intense. For them the school may provide the only disinterested source of guidance which is available, since even parents themselves are unclear.

However similar uncertainties affect the school and its teachers. No substantial or general concordance between the aims and values of the home and those which underlie the teachers' own work can be counted on. Nor can they assume that their pupils' general emotional development will be such that most of them are free from serious disturbance in their basic security and can therefore turn their energies to learning. Even the traditional tasks of instruction are more difficult than they were; but in fact education—and notably the school itself—is called upon to undertake a positive, some would say. a psycho-therapeutic role with an increasing proportion of children who, by the very circumstances of their lives, are deprived of experiences on which emotional stability and intellectual growth depend.

The mixed and developing cultures of Europe and the highly open and pluralistic societies which are emerging, the belief in democracy and equality, and the concept of education for all, have thus thrown on the schools a task, the immense complexity and importance of which is not always clearly realized by teachers and parents, by administrators or philosophers.

An equipment of basic skills coupled with a body of systematic knowledge—even if it is fully acquired—is no longer, if it ever was, a sufficient supplement to the work of the immediate family. Moreover, however much in our theory and philosophy we may attempt to isolate the task of the school as one of a purely intellectual discipline and formation, we cannot escape the fundamentally emotional aspect of all learning. Children learn, not always consciously, from what is omitted as well as from what is taught, from the pedagogic method, and from the ways used to evoke effort. They react to the implicit as well as to the explicit values of their schools and to some extent incorporate them into their growing personalities. Thus even an apparently neutral stance is in fact the taking up of a position.

LACK OF AGREEMENT ON AIMS

We are not agreed upon the content or the aims of education. Most schools exist in more or less of a void, reflecting roughly the values of the world outside their walls, emphasizing roughly what accumulated experience and tradition assert to be valuable, and avoiding too definite an expression of what contribution they should bring to the growth of their pupils. As an avoidance of indoctrination this may have merits; yet the absence ot clear guidance for growing children and adolescents may present them with grave problems of anxiety if the society in which they live also presents them with problems to which there are no solutions, with situations for which there are no accepted techniques of behaviour, and with moral crises before which the adult world itself is perplexed, anxious and undecided. If the child's own home provides a stable, confident environment, all may be well for a time and the school may continue without a declared or implied philosophic or moral aim. Many educators would affirm that much more depends upon the spirit and atmosphere of the school, the latent curriculum, as it is sometimes called, than upon any declared philosophy or system of belief. It is indeed arguable that many degrees and kinds of belief and unbelief should be presented to the child during his education so that, by the free play of differences, he may be led to reflect and choose for himself without the risk of indoctrination. This however is a situation markedly different from one of indecison; and if the school merely reflects the indecision of the home and of the surrounding world we have an atmosphere of grave anxiety for the child, the seed-bed of emotional difficulty and a most serious menace to mental health.[6]

THE SCHOOL AS A THERAPEUTIC AND CONSTRUCTIVE ENVIRONMENT[7]

A school may, however, for many of its pupils ensure a reasonably healthy development of the intellect and personality, in the sense that it produces no unnecessary strains, induces no maladjustments and provides a harmonious atmosphere, and still fail in two important respects. The first of these is the most obvious and though very far from easy, in some ways the least difficult to provide for. Many children and adolescents come to school with severe maladjustments, difficulties in learning or deprivations of experience which, even in a good and efficient school will not disappear by the simple process of being in class. Increasingly the deficiencies and disharmonies of the home and out-of-school environment frustrate, for many children, the possibilities of learning. We have therefore to find ways not only of preventing difficulties of development and maladjustments arising within the school itself but of increasing and developing the remedial and compensatory aspects of formal education.

We have to find out how to use educational method in its widest sense quite deliberately and purposefully to raise the level of intellectual functioning where it has been depressed by the environment and to cure or prevent anomalies of growth, unproductive tensions, unobjective anxieties, prejudices and neuroses.

Unless we succeed in doing this we shall deny many children and adolescents the right of full participation in their society; and frustrate for them the second major and overriding aim of education. Schools can no longer be conservative or even mainly remedial. The education which we give must be dynamically constructive and prospective, equipping the individual with the skills, concepts and knowledge necessary to move forward into the unpredictable, to meet the anxiety inherent in change, without becoming defensively rigid or panic stricken, with sufficient genuine autonomy and knowledge critically to examine and integrate the new, and with the security and the intellectual skills necessary to continue to learn and adjust. In addition, education is overtly concerned with attitudes, towards the self and others, and with judgements which have been consciously made on broad moral issues and which have become integrated as motives to act. Thus in a real sense, education is guidance in choice of what to be, what to know and what to become; its aim is to help the individual to determine what kind of person he wishes to be, to construct a chosen identity.

It must, too, equip the young with the means of seeking and finding appropriate leadership and of using it in democratic ways. Mannheim[8] pointed out long ago that political power and leadership can now more readily be concentrated in the hands of a few and perpetuate itself against the wishes of the ruled because of the much closer interdependence of modern society and because technology fosters centralization. By skilful use of social and psychological techniques a leader or leader group can be built up to appear to embody the fears, aspirations and values of a nation; and once accepted can in fact rule unchecked by public opinion. Indeed creeds, beliefs and behaviour can be superimposed which do not correspond with the real nature of the citizen. The major modern problem is that of passing from the relatively unorganized small groups of a *laissez-faire* society to a centralized or at least planned society without falling into dictatorship. Mannheim[8] argues that the defence of democratic liberty is largely a function of the values consciously accepted by the society and that these arise partly from personal striving and partly from social pressures. This again underlines the vital importance of personal autonomy and integrity, and of an educated intelligence which is critical without being merely contra-suggestible, and which is creative rather than conservative.

DYNAMIC ADJUSTABILITY—THE STRATEGIC ROLE OF THE
SCHOOL

In more personal terms, we are speaking of what might be called
dynamic adjustability. It is a concept which, incomplete as it may be,
has emotional and psychological reference and implies a concern for
the education of ways of feeling much in the way that a psychotherapist
would view it. But it has more than a strictly emotional reference; it
implies a command of knowledge and the power to acquire more, as
well as a trained cognitive capacity which includes what is called creativity[9] in its intellectual aspects. Finally it has an integrating ethical
or moral component based not upon unexamined beliefs or convictions
but upon a developed understanding of self and others and coherent
principles which have been deliberately acquired.

Because they are charged to educate and because they are manipulable and artificial communities with broadly normative aims, schools
are strategically placed to attempt to foster this—even though at present
many seem ill equipped to do so both in their ethos and in the training
of their teachers. There are implications for curriculum in terms of
the relevance of the knowledge provided and how far it fosters the
variety of modes of thought, experience and feeling which we see to be
necessary. But the implications are even more marked for pedagogic
method, the organizational climate, the kinds and quality of interpersonal relationships—in short for the varieties of learning which schools
offer. For example, if genuinely creative thinking, which is involved in
the power constructively to solve novel problems, is to be developed,
stress will have to be laid upon the utilization of acquired knowledge
in new ways rather than mainly upon its reproduction. Critical skills
will tend to be developed as tests of the efficacy of proferred solutions,
rather than as exercises in finding faults. Similarly we shall be concerned with the combination and synthesis of lines of thought deriving
from different areas and kinds of knowledge as much as, or more than,
with isolated disciplines.

The ability to form satisfying relations with others, certainly in
situations which go outside the immediate and familiar, does not come
by chance. In relationships between the sexes, in potentially conflictual
situations between groups of different races, social background or interest, a vague general and unanalysed good will is not likely to be sufficient. Formally and informally in school and out, it is increasingly
necessary to educate children to understand, emotionally as well as
intellectually, how and why others act and feel as they do, to set this in
a framework of acceptable forms of behaviour and of what might be
called an empathic comprehension of ethical principles.

In a very real sense (and perhaps the most important) the apparent separation in many of our education systems between on the one hand the development of moral character and personality, which tends to be left to the home or glided over, and on the other the cognitive, intellectual growth of a human being as the product of more formal education, is dangerously artificial. There are few situations in life from which the emotional aspects can be abstracted and the mind operate as a purely intellectual instrument. In almost all that we do and certainly in most decisions of any consequence, affective and cognitive elements are inextricably intertwined with motivations, some of them below the threshold of consciousness. Hence education has to be concerned deeply with the *balance* between the development of personality, moral nature and capacity for dynamic adjustments and the education of the mind as an instrument for the analysis of experience, for continued learning and for creating and testing new solutions for problems. In this sense education is concerned to enable the individual to make rational analyses, suggest rational solutions or choices first and then to test them in terms of his beliefs, moral principles and convictions, rather than in effect to decide emotionally and use his intelligence to provide a rationalization of his prejudice. We may go further and assert that education needs (and teachers should be trained to give) a dynamic emotional and therapeutic dimension.[10]

MENTAL HYGIENE AND EDUCATION; THE GENERATION AND
CONTROL OF CHANGE

We must be on our guard, too, against any concept of education or definition of mental health which tends to be uniquely conservative, or which aims at inducing a perfect adaptation of the individual to his society. It seems to be clear, from earlier chapters, that ours is not and is not likely to be a static society but one changing increasingly rapidly and profoundly. The problem then of mental health and education is not that of adjustment but that of enabling the individual dynamically to participate in satisfactory and satisfying ways in his society whilst providing him with the means (intellectual and emotional) of constructive criticism, of generating and controlling change. In their different ways the conservative and the revolutionary, those who oppose change utterly and those who wish to destroy all that has been achieved in favour of unique, idealistic but untried solutions, are equally unadjusted. One is tempted to say that each is responding to deep-rooted insecurities with which they cannot cope adequately, in part because they command neither the intellectual nor the emotional dispositions to view situations objectively and to perceive that human problems have relative and multiple rather than unique and absolute solutions. The insecurity and challenge inherent in social evolution demands those who are able to test solutions objectively, being willing to change if they are proved to be wrong, who are convinced that compromises of many kinds are possible, each providing an inevitable mixture of good and not so good and that the possible is at best only asymptotic to the ideal.

If we regard mental health as a state in which the individual can cope without excessive strain with the problems with which life challenges him, can adjust to his society and at the same time play a constructive part in controlling or directing change, then it seems clear that all aspects of his nature, affective and intellectual, must be fully provided for by his environment, in the first decades and until he has achieved sufficient autonomy to bring about more or less unaided adjustments in himself and his surroundings. In this cultural sense there are likely to be as many definitions of mental health as there are different ways of life.

If we attempt to move beyond any such operational definition, we leave psychology for ethics, philosophy or revealed truth. An adequate definition of mental health in more specific terms would involve also a statement of the values prized by society.

MENTAL HYGIENE IN TERMS OF HUMAN NEEDS

It would, however, have to be something more than this. While innately remarkably variable and, at least affectively, markedly modifiable, human beings have certain needs and drives which in themselves are neither good nor bad but the complete denial of which renders any satisfactory adjustment to life impossible. The process of education is the means by which society specifies acceptable outlets for these needs and capacities of the individual and at the same time ensures that they will enrich his personal life as well as serve his society.

Functionally therefore it is possible to base certain principles of mental hygiene upon our developing knowledge of human psychological needs, and on an evaluation of the means of satisfying them. Any given culture, any educational method (for example, highly competitive marking) or any cultural custom (for example, the weaning of the infant) can be evaluated in terms of the outlets which it offers for the instinctive tendencies or fundamental drives called into play and in terms of the relationship it sets up between the challenges to the individual and the means it provides of restoring the psychological equilibrium. It can also be evaluated in terms of whether it enlarges the child's cognitive growth, contributes to systematic knowledge of the environment and moves him towards more effective forms of thinking and coping. Finally.

we can ask questions about the kind and quality of socialization which it implies in ethical terms.

Development is not, however, a matter merely of imposed choices. The child is himself an agent from the moment of birth. As well as being challenged he challenges. Early in his life much of his activity seems to be random and only some of it brings him into positive relationship with his physical environment. As he grows his activity becomes more and more purposive, more and more defined and more and more integrated. Every successful or unsuccessful piece of activity teaches him something which he incorporates into a growing notion of himself as distinct from others, into a notion of values and into a series of patterns which he tends to repeat. Thus almost from the outset, he develops a past which colours the immediate present, determining to some extent what he will attend to or even perceive and tending to give a prepotence in any given situation to one of a number of possible modes of response.

What distinguishes a response which is healthy in terms of future stability from one which militates against mental health is whether it in general brings the child into an acceptable and satisfactory relationship with his environment or tends to withdraw him from it. This is a statement which needs some qualification, particularly in terms of the stage of development of the child and the precise circumstances. It is, however, important that the majority of situations in which a child finds himself should be those in which a forward-looking behaviour is possible and in which socially acceptable forms of success can be achieved by an effort within his compass. For young children, in particular, this demands some degree of modification both of the adult environment and of the expectations and attitudes of those responsible for him.

As the child matures he develops attitudes and patterns of behaviour which become steadily harder and harder to change. In part these patterns are the result of his unique experience, in part they are coloured by the cognitive quality or richness of the experience itself, and in part they reflect norms imposed by the culture in which he lives. In every healthy response to each new challenge, however, there is an element of novelty, a new integration. It is essentially in the formation of such new integrations, their shaping and direction, that the two aspects of development—maturation and education conceived in its fullest sense—play their most important part.

EDUCATION AS A REFLECTION OF THE CULTURE

Education is the means of shaping maturation in accordance with the ecological factors, partly from unconscious causes, partly through its history and traditions, progressively makes. A society agrees to sanction certain kinds of behaviour—for example the acquisition of wealth through work or the resolution of differences by negotiation and majority decision—and to outlaw others—for example the acquisition of property by theft or the solution of differences by violence. Some of these choices appear logical and consistent; some arbitrary or irrational: they range from the acceptance of moral and philosophical values to the smallest details of convention and etiquette; they affect every aspect of the individual's growth and life; their sum total is what is usually understood by 'a way of life'; and their impact on the personality, 'national character'.

Thus in any society, every growing child has to learn to conform more or less to a series of cultural norms; and his ideas of 'good' and 'bad' are based in his early years on what he finds to be acceptable or unacceptable to the adults round him. Since his sense of personal security is very nearly bound up with an easy, warm and well-defined relationship to those with whom he lives, it will be seen that he has the strongest of all motives for conformity. In this way his growth is shaped in one direction rather than in another which may be, psychologically speaking at least, equally satisfactory.

It is in this context of dynamic growth and of interaction between the unique individual and his social environment that we must consider the principles of mental hygiene and the use we make of education as a means to promote a healthy society. Since, even in an area as relatively homogeneous as Europe and the Western World, or indeed even within any one nation, there are increasingly wide differences in cultural choices and cultural sanctions between groups and between generations, we cannot hope to establish universally applicable rules or detailed definitions.[11] The most that can be done is, by a study of growing children and of the impact upon them of their total environment, home, school and community, to point out some of the principles that should be applied and some of the practical measures which might be taken by those who see that human happiness and the capacity creatively to grapple with a changing world, are of critical importance not only to individuals but to the future of mankind.

FURTHER READING

Bantock, G. H. *Education in an industrial society*. London, Faber & Faber, 1963.
Buder, L., et al. *Where we are. A hard look at family and society*. New York, Child Study Association of America, 1970.

Caplan, G., ed. *Prevention of mental disorders in children.* London, Tavistock Publications, 1961.

Didier, P., et al. *Le Bouton du mandarin.* Tournai, Casterman, Paris, Centre d'Etudes Pédagogiques. 1966.

Elvin, H. L. *Education and contemporary society.* London, Watts, 1965.

Gould, J., ed. *Prevention of damaging stress in children.* London, Churchill, 1968.

Heymann, K. *Kindsein in heutiger Umwelt* [Being a child in today's environment]. Basel, Karger, 1964.

Hickerson N. *Education for alienation.* Englewood Cliffs, N.J., Prentice-Hall, 1966.

Illich, I. *Deschooling society.* London, Calder & Boyars, 1971.

King, E. J. *Education and social change.* Oxford, Pergamon Press, 1966.

Levsin, L. A. *Pedagogika i sovremennost* [Pedagogy and contemporary times]. Moskva, Prosveščenie, 1964.

Liardi, C. *Scuola al bivio tra due culture* [The school at the crossroads of two cultures]. Rome, Armando Armando, 1966.

Rattner, J. *Erziehe ich mein Kind richtig?* [Do I educate my child rightly?]. Zurich, Stuttgart; Werner Klassen Verlag, 1967.

Reischock, W. *Die Bewältigung der Zukunft* [The mastering of the future]. Berlin, Volk und Wissen Volkseigener Verlag, 1966.

NOTES

1. 'It is harder to crack a prejudice than the atom.' (Einstein)
2. Hust, P. H.; Peters, R. S. *The logic of education.* London, Routledge & Kegan Paul, 1970 [particularly chapter 3].
3. Young, M. F. D. An approach to the study of curricula as socially organized knowledge. In: *Knowledge and control.* London, Collier Macmillan, 1971.
4. Hirst, P. H.; Peters, R. S. Op. cit. See also Chapter 10 of this book.
5. See: Husèn, T. Curriculum research in Sweden. I: a note with a general appraisal of the empirical approach to curriculum construction. *Educational research* (London), vol. VII, no. 3, June 1965 [especially p. 165]. Husèn points out that vocational relevance, though important, is only one among many objectives. However, the vogue for cost-effectiveness studies of education has tended to stress—or uniquely to consider—strictly economic concerns. See also: Blaug, M. *An introduction to the economics of education.* London, Allen Lane, 1970. Teachers are somewhat in the position of La Fontaine's Miller (*Fables,* livre III, no I, 'Le meunier, son fils et l'âne').
6. See Chapter 10, p. 213.
7. See Chapter 10, pp. 218–221.
8. Mannheim, K. *Diagnosis of our time.* London, Kegan Paul, Trench Trubner, 1943.
9. See Chapter 12, p. 322ff.
10. Caplan, G., ed. *Prevention of mental disorders in children.* London, Tavistock Publications, 1961 [especially the contributions of B. Biber 'Mental health principles in the school setting'; E. M. Bower 'Primary prevention in a school setting'; and R. H. Ojemann 'Investigations on the effects of teaching and understanding and appreciation of behaviour dynamics'].
11. A useful definition, complementary to that outlined earlier in this chapter,

is given by F. Hotyat (*Psychologie de l'enfant.* Bruxelles, Labor, 1972 [2nd ed. in the press]). He says that a mentally healthy person is one who can accept himself in positive and optimistic ways, seeking the esteem and collaboration of others; he has the power to re-establish his balance if he meets with failure or frustration either by systems of defence like compensation, rationalization and sublimation or through his relations with supportive groups; he possesses sufficient reserves of energy to know the joy of giving part of his time to the needs of others and to constructive and enriching leisure.

Chapter six

The role of the family
in mental health

NATURE AND NURTURE

The kind of synthesis of the intellectual and emotional life in the individual which we have described will not arrive by chance or by mere unfolding in a more or less favourable milieu.

Moreover the school, even the nursery school, supervenes rather late in the process. To understand how formal education fits into the whole pattern, we must consider how human beings become what they are. In doing this we must look beyond formal educational institutions to that other immensely powerful educator, the family, which in childhood is the earliest and most continuous bridge between self and society; and try to distinguish how it is that the many facets of the environment —home, school and culture—continuously and cumulatively interact with the individual's natural endowment, elements arising from his inner life and forms of acquired response.

It seems likely that most human environments, even those considered to be relatively deprived, unless they are very extreme, provide minimum essentials for some sort of adaptive growth, if we mean by this the ability to learn by experience, to communicate simply, to sustain life by work, to form simple social relations. However, the quality, the degree of organization, the values implicit and explicit in the environment have profound effects upon the kind and degree of development of the adult personalities that emerge from them. It is thus true to say that most of what we would regard as specifically human in a cultural sense is a product of the environment. It is also true to say that some environments provoke a high level of growth in the individual's capacities. whereas others tend to stunt and permit only minimal adaptation. Given sufficiently nurturing environments, what then matters are the qualitative differences in dispositions to perceive and respond to different stimuli and react in particular ways, in the effectiveness with which intelligence will be used to solve problems, and in value systems.

78

The earliest and for this reason in very many respects the most formative environment of the child is his family in the first five or ten years of growth. It is through the family, rather than through the school, that many of our educational aims will be achieved or nullified. In one very important respect it is to an improvement in the educative quality of the family rather than to change in formal educational institutions like the school, that our efforts should be directed—at least so far as concerns the child under ten.

Every child is born with certain potentialities, the strength of which varies from individual to individual. Some of these are highly malleable whilst others seem to be more resistant to environmental shaping. For example, what we call loosely 'temperament' seems to be highly plastic. Children may originally have a strong or weak tendency to aggressiveness; the strength of aggressive tendencies, however, the objects or situations which provoke them, whether they turn outwards to fight, to violence, to the verbal expression of hostility, or are socialized in some other form, or whether they become directed against the self as in some kinds of neurosis, all these are very largely determined by growth in an environment and particularly the environment at home in the first decade of life.

On the other hand, what we understand by intelligence, learning or problem solving ability seems to have a larger component which is both genetic and maturational.[1] The home environment can depress intellectual functioning generally or in particular ways; it can foster an approach to optimal growth; but it does not seem possible by educational means of any kind to exceed what seems to be a limit for each individual, set by the quality of his central nervous system—though we do not yet know what exactly that limit may be. But here again its directionality, structure, the systems of motivation which underlie its use, and its qualitative character all seem to be heavily influenced by nurture. The content and shaping of intelligence in terms of knowledge, skills and much of the willingness and power to perceive problems as problems and the power to solve them will be very heavily influenced by the home first and then by the school in more formal terms.

Every normal baby is equipped with tendencies to laugh, to play, to imitate, to respond to more or less general stimuli like the desire for food, for sleep, for defecation, for self-assertion and submission. As he develops, such general trends grow into dispositions to react in certain ways, and he may acquire others which take on the force of fundamental biological drives.[2] Many of these dispositions, whether based on innate or acquired tendencies are, certainly in the early years as we have said, highly plastic and little specific, subject to considerable environmental modifications, to deflection but rarely to complete suppression. They constitute the sources of energy, the motive force of the personality.

Even in the most primitive circumstances, a child is born into a society, and hence as well as a purely personal maturation there is always an element of socialization in his growth. As he gets older, the social pressures upon him increase and the process of development is that of reconciling his crude drives and acquired dispositions with the needs both of individual and of social living; human societies may be viewed as means to the satisfaction of instinctive propensities within a framework which reconciles the egocentricity of the individual with the needs of his group.

This interplay between the child and his human and material environment continually involves some frustration. In his earliest months the amount of such frustration may be relatively small; he is fed, sheltered and allowed to sleep; he can exercise his limbs, as a rule, free from marked restraint; and he is cherished physically and emotionally by his mother. The tempo of his development is set by maturational factors, but even thus early, elements enter which are in part cultural and common to all or most children in the same tribe or group and in part arise from the personalities and attitudes of his parents and constitute the beginnings of his unique experience.

SECURITY AS THE BASIS FOR ADVENTURE

This bio-social situation has two distinguishable major aspects which reverberate in the child's emotional life and colour his development. Whenever his activity attains a satisfying end, whenever his impulses towards the outside world meet with success, his tendency to repeat the activity[3] and to value it positively is increased. He tends in fact to incorporate the novel into his schemas and thus to move forward in his understanding of the world. Whenever he is frustrated by his environment in the satisfaction of his needs, then he will react with aggression or retreat or both and will have the tendency to regard the frustrating circumstance as 'bad'. He will assimilate the 'bad' situation to something he already knows and in this sense tend to regress rather than go forward in mastery of the novel.

In this kind of context, intelligence would be defined as the instrument of search for equilibrium between the action of the organism on the environment (assimilation) and the opposite (accommodation). These two aspects always appear together. On the one hand to make an adaptation to a new situation implies that the child incorporates it in to his existing schemas (sensori-motor or conceptual according to his stage of development) without difficulty or change; on the other hand, in so far as the situation is different and novel, the pre-existing schemas must be modified and enlarged to accommodate the novelty.[4] The form of play in which the child uses an object to represent something else—for example, a block which symbolizes a motor car—is largely an activity in which the child is consolidating his concept of a motor car. When, however, the situation presents many novelties which do not relate easily to pre-existing schemas then either of two things may happen. The novelties may provoke the child to learn and to extend his pre-existing schemas to take account of the apparently contradictory novelties. In such situations one will see a child experimenting with material or playing out a situation which interests him until he has 'understood', and has developed and incorporated a more generalized concept. On the other hand, if the novelties are too much for him, if they present no predictable structure or are inconsequent, he is forced either to abandon the attempt at understanding or to imitate stupidly and without insight, leaving his pre-existing schemas at the same sort of level as they were before. Assimilation in fact reinforces the status quo; while accommodation carries the child forward in function of his environment and gives him the confidence and the capacity to go on risking the contact with novelty. If the challenge of the environment is too great for accommodation, then we see frustration and a tendency to play at being someone or something else. In strictly emotional terms, successful contacts with his world tend to reinforce his feelings of being safe; unsuccessful and frustrating ones tend to be perceived as threats to his security.

It is probably a general and innate characteristic of human beings that, unless frustration is too severe[5] and too painful or unless it continues over a long period, they tend to seek other acceptable outlets for primordial drives. Indeed, McDougall[6] defined 'persistency with varied effort' as the mark of an innate propensity of an instinctive kind. The very young child is able to do scarcely anything for himself; but even so he is far from passive. However imperfectly, he is an agent and as he develops physically he shows a growing independence. Bühler[7] in her observation of children's smiles, noted that from about nine months onward babies begin to be independent and selective in their response to a smiling face. Valentine[8] put it even earlier than the ninth month. This independence is greatly increased by the child's ability to crawl and later to walk, but even before he can do either some observers notice an introvert-extrovert rhythm[9] in his reaction to his environment.

This thrust towards independence inevitably brings him up against physical impossibilities and an increasing number of prohibitions imposed by his family. Children vary, probably innately, in emotional stability and in their ability to tolerate these and other frustrations. Some few seem, even in favourable circumstances, destined to become maladjusted; others seem able to survive even when their environment is markedly adverse. In general, whatever the level of frustration tolerance of the individual, healthy development will only be assured if acceptable outlets for his drives are offered by his environment and if

D

the affection of his mother and family are there to sustain him. For child and adult alike the most emotional, and therefore formative, situations are those which lead to a successful discharge of energy or those which threaten his physical or psychological security. In a very fundamental sense the whole education of children, and indeed the whole of mental hygiene, turns upon the solutions sought and found to the twin problems of maintaining personal security and of moving forward to resolve the continual challenges presented by the environment. That the willingness to take a risk depends upon feeling safe enough to do so is only apparently a paradox—at least in the psychology of growing children. Freedom from fears and anxieties which are not directly related to the objective situation is itself a mark of mental health; and it is to the achievement of a state of dynamic equilibrium in a social environment that the upbringing and education of children should be directed.[10]

FRUSTRATION AND OUTLET AS INSTRUMENTS OF CULTURAL SHAPING

This, however, is not to say, as some have done, that children should not under any circumstances suffer frustration. Life in society implies frustration; and one of the marks of satisfactory development is a growing ability to tolerate, without retreat or aggression, an immediate check to a desire while an acceptable outlet is found. This implies that upbringing should progressively do two things: help the child to develop systems of impulse control, and provide him with acceptable habits and techniques of expression for the forces of his personality. It is also the mark of a healthy society that, while it inhibits certain forms of expression, it is rich in adequate outlets for the energy of the needs and drives of its participants and, recognizing the range and variety of human endowment that its practices of child upbringing permit for all children and adults an ultimately smooth adjustment to the environment, human and circumstantial.

It is in fact by the manner in which frustrations are imposed, by the outlets provided and by the selection of responses which gain approval, that a culture sets its mark upon the individual, giving him a distinctive 'national' cast of personality.[11] Culturally speaking, this is what the social psychologist means by education. It is a process which begins at birth and continues throughout life. Artificially we may divide it between various agencies—the family, the school, the milieu; we may single out aspects and call them 'socialization' or 'education'; but to the human being it is a process taking place in different physical environments perhaps and in terms of relationships with different groups of people, but none the less continuous and rendered coherent by the continuity of the experiencing self.

LEARNING

In the case of children under the age of three the intellectual aspects of learning may appear to be relatively very small compared, for example, with adult learning. However, as the work of genetic psychologists has shown us, this is only very relatively true, and learning itself and the power to go on learning effectively later have been shown to depend very much on the structure, predictability and conceptual richness of the early environment, as well as upon the stability of a child's relationships with the adults round him. As children progress through their development the nature of their thinking becomes more complex and effective; and they become more and more able to detach reasoning from perceptual and emotional interference. At a comparatively late stage under favourable circumstances the stage of what Piaget calls formal operations and others 'abstract thought' is attained and intelligence becomes as fully effective an instrument as it is likely to be in the analysis of experience and the choice of response. But there are wide variations as to how far this is attained and in the adult, while the intellect may appear to function in an atmosphere of pure reason, it in fact rarely does so. The selection of what to observe, the weight given to the various factors in a situation and the choice of action will all be heavily influenced by prior affective and intellectual experience, by feelings and emotions and by sets or attitudes deep-rooted in the personality and not readily amenable to rational analysis.

In a primary biological sense, learning is a process of adaptation set in train either by a drive such as hunger originating from a change within the organism or by an alteration in the environment which the experiencing person sees as a challenge or a threat; and it is characteristic of human beings that they are more variable in their responses, more capable of learning and more dependent upon it, than animals or insects. By the time a human being in a modern society reaches maturity, however, primary biological learning has been highly sophisticated by the growth in intelligence, by the effects of individual experience and cultural conditioning.[12] Steadily from the moment of birth, the human child acquires a past and integrates his experience in a complex system of attitudes, sets and habitual responses. An adult has learned adaptive habits and attitudes that enables him to respond more or less efficiently to most of the circumstances in which he normally finds himself. He can also adapt himself within certain limits to the new and unfamiliar.

How far he can do this and continue to do so will be a function of his personal security and intellectual equipment—particularly dependent on how far his early education at home and at school has given him the conceptual skills, the knowledge and the appropriate styles of response which enable him to accept novelty and change without panic and to adjust to them.

It will also depend upon how far the new situation makes demands which are beyond his capacity to adapt. One has only to study, for example, the impact of rapid industrialization on agrarian communities, the effects of a new country upon immigrants, or the changes brought in people's lives by the shut-down of an industry to see that, in such circumstances, the emotional tension of the individual rises and for a time at least many of the old habits break down; adults become insecure and on the *qui vive* like animals that scent danger. If the modifications demanded are too great or the emotional tension too high, some, even many, may break down neurotically temporarily or permanently; alternatively, for a time there may be a retreat into earlier forms of behaviour, many of them anti-social, or partaking of the magical thinking of childhood—such as the revival of superstition during war. If genuine adaptation takes place, the individuals develop new habits, and the group of which they form part achieves a new stability.

Such situations of rapid change used to be relatively rare in the lives of adults. Children, however, find themselves daily—in the first year one might almost say hourly—in novel situations for which they have few developed habits. The very process of growth steadily provides further challenges to their powers of adaptation.[13] They learn to sit up, to speak, to walk, to feed themselves, to make social contacts in an ever-widening sphere, to go to school, to travel unaccompanied ever further and further afield. Their developing physical strength and co-ordination, and their growing intellectual power puts more and more things and situations within their grasp and at the same time the environment represented at first by parents and their immediate family and then by the world beyond the home, increasingly shows that there are expectations which they have to fulfil. Many of these demand forms of thought or response acquired slowly and with difficulty; some of them are outside the child's immediate capacity and therefore bring him the negative feeling of failure; some are achieved only after strenuous effort and bring him the warm positive experience of success; from all of them he learns something more about the people, events and things in his surroundings and more about himself, his capacities and his limitations. He learns ways of adjusting to his environment which begin to form habitual response patterns and attitudes towards the novel. These situations of change confronting the young child are a paradigm of change in general as it confronts adults. A healthy environment provides the changing child with support from his parents and later his teachers in coping with the immense adjustments he has to make. Well managed, such support helps the child to develop positive and successful coping styles which will stand him in good stead throughout his life. If he gets no such support, if it is imperfect or indeed if his environment is too protective or too threatening or if it exacts forms of learning which are beyond his stage of maturity, as happens in some school systems and with over-ambitious, rejecting or anxious parents, then he will tend to be crippled in the face of the challenge of change later in his life.[14]

THE VULNERABILITY OF CHILDREN TO EXPERIENCE

Young children too, because of their egocentric thinking, their lack of analysed experience and knowledge and their imperfect grasp of the distinction between reality external to themselves and their own wishes and fantasies, tend to confound their inner imaginary and the outer 'real' or 'phenomenal' worlds. They may believe, for example, that wishes will come true in a way which, to an adult, is magical. An imperfect grasp of the laws of cause and effect in the physical world, a lack of knowledge of the difference between themselves and other living things and between both and inanimate objects, leads them to project on to their surroundings the feelings and even the impressions made by events of their own mental life. Because the demands to adapt which are hourly being made upon them keep children in a state of emotional alertness, and because so much of what they experience is new, they are all the time, with the imperfect experience at their command, attempting to interpret and thus to learn.

The child's world is a continuous one of which he is the centre. Less even than the adult can he analyse it into separate independent compartments. His learning is global (syncretic) and all his keenly felt experience is educative, reverberating through all he is and does. Much of his learning goes on in situations which parents and teachers do not usually regard as educative ones. The little girl playing apparently quietly on the floor, while her mother in a hushed voice discusses with a neighbour the death of the man down the road, will respond, though she may not immediately show it, to the anxiety in her mother's tones and manner. The little boy who has frequent experience of interpersonal hostility, even though it is not directed against himself (for example quarrels between his parents) will endeavour with his immature knowledge to interpret what is happening and incorporate his ideas of it into his own developing attitudes.

Children do not always learn what the adult sets out to teach or what an adult would expect them to learn. What is selected from a situation, its meaning, is likely to be highly subjective and incomplete. To take a superficial example, a child whose mother prematurely tries to teach him not to make a mess as he eats, and who grows angry at his failures, may learn to fear any new thing he is asked to do, because he expects to fail.

Equally, in the cognitive field one may stereotype a child's learning by always presenting, in number work for example, the same configuration. Similarly exposure to violence as an adult way of solving problems —although a child may not understand what injury and death mean— may make a child fearful of strangers or believe that a punch or a shot is better than an argument. Examples could be multiplied from the case histories of many childish maladjustments which have sprung from situations emotionally disturbing to the child, imperfectly understood by him, and in which he has been unable to meet satisfactorily what he dimly perceives as a threat to his own security.

THE IMPORTANCE OF MOTHER IN LEARNING

From birth the child has strong physical and psychological needs which he is powerless to supply without the aid of his parents, particularly his mother, in connexion with whom his first learning takes place. The satisfaction of a need—for example, for food or warmth—enhances a feeling of security; the denial of a need—for example a loss of physical support—is likely to be felt as a threat to mere survival and a cause of anxiety. Quite early in his life the child begins to respond to other than merely biological stimuli; the very regularity of the major events of his day, the comings and goings of those who care for him, the way in which he is handled, spoken to and looked after, assume an importance psychologically as part of the framework within which he begins to feel safe or in which somehow he feels threatened. In a dim, unspecific way he reacts to the satisfactions or dissatisfactions of those intimately related to him, to their confident consistency or anxious preoccupations.

The importance of the mother-child interaction in the development of children is emphasized by a considerable body of work. Food, warmth and protection from danger can readily be assured in their purely physical sense, and not necessarily through the agency of the family. But an accumulating body of research[15] has confirmed what psychologists long suspected, that impersonal satisfaction of a child's material needs is insufficient for his growth. What appears to be essential are close, warm, affectionate and, at least for the first three or four years, stable ties between the mother or mother substitute[16] and the child. Many mothers for a variety of reasons provide this only imperfectly if at all, at least for the first child. In other cases, babies are early abandoned or separated from their natural mothers entirely, or suffer prolonged separation during the day whilst mother is at work. Where the mother-child tie does not exist or is ruptured, and where the child is not speedily allowed to form a new and consistent relationship to some mother substitute, he may suffer an apparently irreversible warping of his emotional development and be unable throughout his subsequent life to form adequate relationships with other human beings. In most cases his intellectual development is prejudiced and in extreme ones he may be markedly slowed in intellectual development and appear to become mentally defective, developing even tics and stereotyped mannerisms.

The symptoms of severe suffering are not solely psychological in their manifestation. The incidence of rhinolaryngitis and of infantile diarrhoea and the death rate from this and other diseases among very young children in orphanages and crèches where material conditions are reasonably good but where they cannot attach themselves to any one member of the staff, has been shown to be higher than among normal children or those in homes organized to provide separate family groupings in family buildings and adequate substitutes for the mother.[17] Even a relatively short period in hospital may, for example in the case of a child of two, cause so severe an emotional disturbance as to effect at least for a considerable time the child's whole attitude to others.[18]

We are thus led to a closer examination of the role of the mother in the child's earliest years. In the first few months mother and child form a close biological unit and baby's security depends upon the mother's attitude and upon her physical handling. If she is loving and consistent the baby will thrive whether breast-fed or bottle-fed, whether to a schedule or on demand and whether cleanliness training is begun a few weeks after birth or left until the middle of his second year or even later. There is no reliable proof that any one method of infant care is more beneficial than another from the point of view of establishing emotional security as one of the bases of mental health,[19] though different methods may bring about differences in personality structure.[20]

For the child's subsequent mental health, the essential is the development and reinforcement of his sense of security, his feeling of always being loved and acceptable. On the whole the studies indicate that gratification is preferable to deprivation, acceptance better than rejection, and permissiveness superior to coercion. But it is necessary to interpose the condition of 'other things being equal' since the development of personality seems to be an interactive process. Children differ substantially in the equipment or characteristics with which they are born but the implications of these differences for subsequent growth in personality vary according to how others react towards them. The emphasis in upbringing at home and at school should therefore be to adjust expectancies and pressures to individual differences. It should also be added that, while a child should only cautiously and sparingly be put into situations which arouse anxiety or make him fear loss of love, it is not primarily upon the methods used that his mental health depends but upon the meaning which the incidents of his daily life have for him; and more than anything else in his early years this will be conditioned by the mother's attitudes as he senses them.

FATHER

The importance of the mother's role in the first years of life has tended to obscure the important contribution of the father.[21] Economically his part is clearly defined in most cultures. Not always so clearly perceived however, is the importance of his relationship to his wife, on which so much of her emotional security and thus indirectly that of her child depend. If he can accept the woman's inevitable preoccupation with the new baby without being jealous, he can do a great deal to help his wife to accept and rejoice in her maternity. On the other hand he may react in terms of his own unresolved childish conflicts and—to the point of jealousy or outright rejection—complicate the mother's response to her child.

After the first year of life, the infant becomes less and less exclusively dependent upon his mother and the part played by the father becomes more direct. In some groups he is a remote figure of authority, even a bogey man; in others he plays with his children but takes little part in their physical care or in the domestic work of the home.[22] In yet others he represents intellectual and social demands and is a source of more or less benevolent discipline. Current trends, especially in cultures of Anglo-Saxon origin, tend more and more to bring father to share in the whole life of the family—even from the moment of birth at which more and more fathers now tend to be present.

Increasingly, too, fathers are divesting themselves or are divested of patriarchal authority and becoming 'highly participant'[23] in the task of bringing up children even in those aspects of physical care and nurturing traditionally a woman's job. Particularly in middle class families they take an increasing share of domestic chores as well. The sex roles from being distinct and differentiated are tending to become more and more confused. Children begin quite early to interpret their own sex role in terms of the parent of like sex and at the same time to experience relationships between the sexes in terms of what they intuitively feel or comprehend of their parents' married life and their own reactions to the parent of opposite sex. Thus at the core of a child's attitudes to others lie his attitudes to his parents and his perceptions of their attitudes towards each other. In this, the masculine element as represented by father is as important psychologically as the feminine one, and becomes increasingly so as the child moves into adolescence.

Here we may draw attention to the fact that economic changes affect the psychological atmosphere of the family directly. For example the absence of domestic help in middle class homes, the need in many families at all levels for the mother to work,[24] and similar factors, have tended to involve the father more and more in the daily domestic tasks and hence have brought many closer to their children. The very isolation in which so many modern families live, their smallness and the intensity of the relationships to which they give rise, magnify the impact of any changes in parental role and underline the importance, for the healthy development of children, of a consistent loving gentleness in the attitudes of mother and father towards them.[25]

ONE-PARENT FAMILIES

Such isolation affects the one-parent family even more profoundly, at least in social groups where there is no tradition of neighbours helping out. In the United Kingdom, the National Child Development Study of approximately 16,000 seven-year-olds (1958 cohort) showed that nearly 3 per cent lived in homes with no male head and in all nearly 8 per cent were not living with both natural parents.[26] The effect of this seems to differ according to the mores of the social group. In the case of middle class and skilled manual groups, children from typical families showed signs at seven of considerable educational disadvantage compared with their contemporaries from the same social groupings; this was not so in general for children from semi- and unskilled working class groups. Similarly illegitimate children seem to develop more favourably when they are adopted (particularly into middle class families) than when they remain with one parent, partly because of the extreme economic difficulties often involved for the single parent—usually the mother—and partly because of the absence of one parental figure. Illegitimate children who stay with their mothers tend to be retarded in general knowledge, oral ability, creativity, perceptual development and in arithmetic and reading (the adopted illegitimates are twelve months ahead in reading). They tend to be more maladjusted.[27]

Again this is not a simple issue. It is complicated because the un-married mother has to fend economically for herself and her child and, unless she has the kind of professional training which allows her to earn well and adjust her hours to the needs of her child, she may have to leave her infant with child minders and often she sinks lower in the economic scale because of the handicap imposed by her responsibility.

THE FAMILY GROUP

We have so far discussed the part played by the parents in some isolation. It should be emphasized, however, that rarely is the child's relationship with any person an uncomplicated *egoisme à deux* and then probably only in the first few weeks of his life. Normally the child enters what is in fact a social *gestalt* of interacting personalities. As he develops,

D*

the important role of mother, and the supplementary one of father, merge into that of the family group.

In the psychological nature of such groups there is a wide range of variation, even within any one of the developed cultures of Europe. The least 'complete' family is the isolated mother and her child—a phenomenon which shows some tendency to increase.[28] More typical is that by-product of industrial development and a rising standard of living—the small-home centred family consisting only of two generations, the parents and one, two or three children living in greater or lesser psychological isolation from other similar families. This pattern has been emphasized by vocational and social mobility and by the type of housing to which it, and economic factors, have given rise—the small flat or apartment or the self-contained house in the city suburbs. Recently through social planning and through economic measures such as child allowances, there have been attempts in some countries to increase the numbers of children born into such families and to decrease the social isolation in which many of them live.

At the other extreme are what might be called patriarchal families, which consist of at least three generations—grandparents, parents and children—and which, from the child's point of view, provide effective relationships not merely with his immediate parents and siblings but with related groups of cousins, aunts and uncles. He grows within a system of complex equalities and hierarchies. Essentially the patriarchal or matriarchal family is based upon property or upon territory, e.g. an ancestral home or a village, and some of the reasons for its tendency to disappear are to be found in the greater mobility of the working population and the changing nature of work. There are, however, certain factors, such as the great ease of modern travel, which may permit a family of a more or less patriarchal type to exist simply on the basis of a common kinship though without property or a shared daily life.

It has been pointed out[29] that, so far as Europe is concerned, the current 'home centred' society has been developing at least since the nineteenth century; but that the ideals of self-contained domesticity put forward by writers like Rousseau and Cobbett were not easy to realize until recently because non-kinship institutions (clubs, churches, schools) existed and flourished. Knowledge became increasingly public instead of consisting in a jealously guarded craft mystery to be transmitted inside the family and concealed from competitors. As we have seen, a number of trends has diminished or completely erased the structure of most non-kinship institutions. The solitary exception is the school, the importance of which has in many ways increased, particularly as the only counter-weight to the inwardness of the family, and the only source for many of the knowledge and qualifications considered economically necessary.

At this point it is worth attending to the very different structures which exist in tribal Africa where children are part of an extended family group, belong to a band of age mates and become at quite an early age involved in the work, ceremonial and general communal living of the village.[30] Such a pattern provides for very many of the affective needs of children but tends to make them, throughout their lives, very dependent upon the community and unfitted for venturing forth as individuals; their mobility and flexibility may be impaired.[31] This obviously has important bearings upon the way formal education is organized and upon the prospects of its success as an instrument of human amelioration and economic advance. So too it exacerbates by violent contrast the problems of detribalization brought about by the rush to the towns in Africa.

What is perhaps most important to our argument is that different family structures (or even extra-familial caring structures like the *Kibbutz* or the multiple mothering situations of some societies) are likely broadly to provide in different ways for the needs of children, and to facilitate or inhibit different aspects—cognitive, motivational and emotional—of development. We become concerned therefore not so much to bring about changes in family structure even if we could and it were desirable, but to see what it is that any family pattern does well or imperfectly, how it supports or deprives. If we think in this way, it becomes possible to suggest how, within very different frameworks and value systems, families can be helped to educate their children and prepare them for the stresses and possibilities of change.[32]

THE FAMILY AS THE FIRST LEARNING ENVIRONMENT

In very many respects—in all if we regard development as primarily a learning process—the most important aspect is the influence of the family upon the child's ability to learn. This is most clearly and unequivocally shown in measurable aspects of general ability and educational attainment. What we call, rather loosely, intelligence is more closely and clearly associated with home circumstances particularly in the pre-school years[33] than it is with any other constellation of environmental variables, even those of a good school.

Moreover for many decades now and on a wide variety of tests and other cognitive measures, it has been demonstrated in the United States, in the United Kingdom, in Scandinavia and in Europe that considerable mean differences exist between different social groups, with the middle classes being *on the average* superior in all respects to the working classes.[34] Similar differences have been shown to exist, most markedly on measures involving language and the capacity to form and handle abstractions, but on other cognitive characteristics as well, between different ethnic groups. These mean differences whether between social or ethnic groups are not very large but they have tended to be stable over a long period of time; and they are not, of course, inconsistent with considerable overlapping between groups. Thus many members of all groups share characteristics in common although there may be a larger proportion of those with higher or lower 'intelligence' in one group as compared with another. This is particularly and obviously true when we consider the school careers of children up to adolescence. Thereafter the effects make themselves felt in different ways but are nonetheless marked. The evidence, too, is strong for a considerable genetic component in the differences in capacity to reason and to learn which we find among individuals.[35] There is on the other hand no absolutely crucial evidence to prove or disprove any genetic, innate differences in average *potential*[36] between social, ethnic or racial groups; and even if there were, from the social and educational point of view we should be more interested in the ways in which the environment provided by the parents, and later by the community and the schools fosters or stunts, shapes or mis-shapes what inborn ability there is.

It becomes important therefore to ask what are the general characteristics of any environment that maximize potential. It seems also likely to be true that environmental characteristics which favour cognitive development may be compatible with very different characteristics of an environment which bring about differing personality and value structures. If we know what the qualities of an intellectually fostering environment are and can act in consequence, there is hope that inferiorities due to a given familial and social environment can be eliminated without necessarily radically changing other valued characteristics. This is the task of education.

But there are limits to how far we can cultivate the one without affecting the other. We have spoken as though learning ability or intelligence were a separable aspect of growth but we should remind ourselves now that although it is convenient for research purposes and for discussion to separate the cognitive from the affective, in the development of children these are inextricably intermingled and in the early stages at least conditioned by maturational factors.

How these aspects are related to one another depends of course upon the age of the human being and upon the circumstances in which learning takes place. For example a child learns to walk only when readiness has been achieved through physiological maturation. The success or failure which attend his early efforts, the attitudes of over-protective fear, or of encouragement and praise shown by the parents, however, affect him emotionally in a way which not only tinges the immediate experience but may colour his attitude to subsequent situations of effort and achievement.

Moreover, what we understand as the development of personality, of attitudes, of the moral nature, is closely related to the growth of a child's knowledge, power to think, to handle concepts and to make use of language in the analysis of experience and the regulation of behaviour. Personality development, too, is concerned with the moral, social and cultural content of that experience with language, particularly as it deals with human interactions of all kinds.

Conversely difficulties and maladjustments in the emotional life will restrict or inhibit learning in many fields. In a phrase, emotion is the vector along which learning takes place; and if intelligence is the cutting edge of the mind, motivations are what give it direction and provide it with force.

DEPRIVATION, DISADVANTAGE AND UNDERPRIVILEGE

One hears a good deal about 'cultural deprivation', 'cultural disadvantage' and 'underprivilege'. These terms are evocative but somewhat inexact. Few families or cultures deprive their children of experience in their early years; and even the worst slum environment provides— through overcrowding, constant noise and the like—a 'rich' sensory experience in the sense that stimuli are certainly not lacking. It is also worth remarking that the real differences in the functioning of children from different ethnic, social or cultural milieux tend to become marked from about eighteen months or two years old onwards[37]—suggesting that the period of dependent infancy is reasonably well provided for by the more or less symbiotic relationship between mother and child.

Thereafter we may distinguish two different aspects of the influence of the environment. It may, as for example in some African environments, not present the child with particular kinds of experience.[38] In a tribal village, largely because the environment does not provide constant experience of straight lines, rectangles, two dimensional representations and the like, children and adults may have great difficulty in understanding picture material which presupposes such experience.[39] If the prevailing categories of thought are magical rather than causal, if the language is impoverished in concepts of time, space, ordination and cardination and the like, then certain notions necessary to conventional schooling will not ordinarily be acquired without subsequent special teaching and may prove extremely difficult to acquire at all. Similarly, of course, the richness of the child's pre-school linguistic experience has an obvious relation to the way in which his thought develops and his readiness for any learning in which verbal symbolisms play a large part. It is in senses such as this that we can perhaps speak of 'deprivation' since, whatever the culture, the growth of fully effective capacities to think implies contact with a very wide range of concepts of a great variety of kinds.

Some cultures or subcultures within a given society provide all the stimulation necessary to a reasonable flowering of intelligence but the actual content or more usually the value systems, the motivations and the dispositions to act or pay attention are very different from those presupposed by the system of education into which children come as early childhood passes. Such children are not culturally deprived: but they do experience a culture clash and may feel themselves rejected by, and consequently reject, the school. This is a factor, though rarely the only factor, in the problem of immigrant groups; it also tends to complicate, as we shall see later, the adjustment of working class children, or children from genuinely rural areas, to schools whose methods and presuppositions are more or less urban and middle class.

ORGANIZATION AND CONSISTENCY

But the main problems are not here. They appear to reside in how far the environment is organized and consistent—particularly the early environ ment of the pre-school years when the basic transition from the sensorimotor stage to the stage of concrete operations in prepared for: and in the nature of the motivations and attitudes which are built up in children in these early years. The child is both a provocative and a responsive organism, in an environment which itself is provocative and responsive. Children vary in their capacity to learn, to form quickly and to manipulate new concepts of increasing generalizability and abstractness. En vironments vary in the quality of what they offer, in the consistency with which similar actions achieve similar responses, and in how rational the variations in environmental response are.

The environment of the pre-school child consists of one or a number of human beings and of a variety of material objects. The human environment, usually and most importantly at first, consists of mother and father who interact verbally and physically with the infant. It is through them that the child gets his first experiences of human responses to his needs and actions. If their handling on the whole is consistent and flexibly adjusted to differences in circumstances, the child will find them reasonably predictable: on the other hand, consequential variations in their conduct towards him and towards each other will lead him increasingly to accommodate to differences and thus to enlarge and nuance his concepts of behaviour. Where, however, their conduct towards him is irrationally inconsistent and impulsive, it becomes much more difficult for him to build up stable concepts: his own learning is likely to be disorganized in proportion to the disorganization in their behaviour.

LANGUAGE

Into this general picture comes the use of language. Bernstein[40] has drawn attention to the very different ways in which language is used in different social groups: and he distinguishes between 'restricted' and 'elaborated' linguistic codes ('public' and 'formal' language) which tend to be differentially used by different social groups. It is suggested that these language styles cohere with different educational styles used by mothers in the upbringing of their children. Mothers using a restricted linguistic code tend to reward and punish their children directly, to offer predetermined solutions to problems and not to make explicit the relations between objects, situations and consequences. Mothers using more elaborated codes tend to explain more, to insist upon looking further ahead than the moment, to reason with their children and to encourage the delay of immediate satisfactions in favour of something better in the future. The one code tends to stress concrete concepts with a lack of specificity and precision in differentiation. The other emphasizes an increasing differentiation of concepts, increasing abstractness and, particularly, gives a greater part to language in interpersonal relations.

These two aspects—the degree of organization and predictability in the human environment and the richness or otherwise of the linguistic systems employed—have an obvious relationship to the ways in which the child builds up concepts and employs them in his thought. The acquisition of a concept depends upon practice and repetition of closely similar experiences; its generalization depends upon non-arbitrary variations in the environment which provoke attention or vigilance; and as language becomes steadily more important as a means of analysis, of symbolic thought, and of communication, so its richness, precision and the degree to which it draws attention to and helps to catalogue differences within a framework of similarity accelerates and fosters learning.

It is important to point out at this stage that although Bernstein found these differences in linguistic code to be associated with differences of social class, with differences in the ways in which mothers encouraged or punished their children and the degree to which they emphasized looking forward to the future, the three aspects are not necessarily indissolubly linked at all points. From the point of view of intellectual growth, consistency with lawful variation is of manifest importance; so too, as the basis of efficient thinking and ordering of experience, is an elaborated linguistic code. The stress upon immediate or long term satisfactions is to some extent independent of the others and concerned with the development of attitudes, values and motivations which are at least partially independent of sheer intellectual power, though some capacity to inhibit immediate response while the most effective analysis or form of response is chosen is of obvious importance.[41]

MATERIAL ENVIRONMENT

The material environment is somewhat simpler to analyse and under-stand. Here the point of principal importance is that it should provide a wide range of material with which the child can play and which by its intrinsic interest and multifarious possibilities can wean him from too much dependence upon symbolic play. This is not to say that symbolic play should be discouraged. The child who is using a block to symbolize a motor car or a doll to represent a baby is, among other things, prac-tising, learning and exploring the concepts of 'car' or 'baby' which he has acquired. But he is doing something more: the fact that he uses a symbol to evoke a mental image is a step in what Piaget calls the 'semeiotic function' which grows from early imitation, through mental images, symbolic play, children's drawing to language, and even more complex and structured symbolic codes such as mathematics and formal logic. Moreover, as will be seen later, symbolic play in a wider sense plays an important part in emotional growth as a means of playing out interesting and threatening situations and digesting them emotionally as well as mastering them intellectually. But a restricted range of play material or play material with very restricted possibilities deprive a child of learning, by manipulation, concepts of cause and effect in the material world, where they are likely to be more consistent than in the human one.

Nor is it only play material which is of importance. The games which children play among themselves and the games which are played between children and adults can vary in the richness and degree of structuring in their content[42] and the quality of the language they evoke. They can call for more or less of the power to inhibit immediate action in favour of a better and more effective response, and differ in the degree of abstractness-concreteness of the thinking and observation of rules which they demand. One might here notice the difference, for ex-ample, between ludo and draughts, or between the latter and chess. It is noticeable too that western cultures provide their children with many objects embodying simple and more complex mechanical relationships whilst in primitive ones children have few or no such toys, and in some no toys, other than symbolic objects, of any sort.

MATERNAL STYLES—A FOSTERING ENVIRONMENT

The human and material quality, degree of organization, richness in variation and consistency are the constituents of what Reuchlin[43] calls the 'heuristic quality' of the environment. He goes on to point out that these aspects are not the only ones. He gives a considerable weight to the educational style of the mother (and of course subsequently of other adults). If she is content to state the correct choice and to reinforce it in an authoritarian way, neglecting to present her child with a variety of possibilities while leading him to make predictions and choices, she favours the process of 'accommodation'. That is to say the child develops a habit of response with a certain rigidity; he is not encouraged to question or to seek new responses for himself and test them in real situations. Learning which is reinforced by complex and flexible interrelationships in varied situations comes much nearer to the way in which children learn the rules of a game, in which, within the rules, various strategies are possible each based upon the prediction of different consequences. Such a non-authoritarian attitude favours a progressive balance between assimilation and accommodation. It also tends consequentially to foster two other aspects of behaviour: a readiness to approach problems freshly and a degree of personal autonomy and independence.

This is borne out in an excellent series of studies by Burton White.[4] Over eight months he observed intensively groups of 3- to 5-year-old children chosen for their high or low degree of competence. He found them to differ markedly in their ability to get and maintain the attention of adults in socially acceptable ways, to use adults as resources, to show pride in their achievements, to express affection and hostility, to compete with their peers, in their linguistic competence, in their ability to anticipate consequences, to maintain their attention, to plan and carry out multiple types of activity and other similar aspects of development. In their general affective and cognitive development, the highly competent 3-year-olds were more like the highly competent 5- to 6-year-olds than they were like the less competent older children—that is to say that by the age of 3 most of the qualities distinguishing a competent 6-year-old are achieved.

The investigator suggests that the divergences become marked some time during the second year of life and are associated with the emergence of locomotion and the development of language. In a study of 33 families with 1- and 2-year-old children, of lower and middle social backgrounds and with differing degrees of competence in the children, they found that non-social 'tasks' predominate for all 1-year-olds (88 : 12 per cent.) and for all 2-year-olds (81 : 19 per cent.). The predominating behaviour is to 'gain information—visual', that is, steady staring at an object or a scene; but during the third year co-operative tasks increase. Around two years, mothers who develop competence in their children seem to make more demands for co-operation; their children speak more to them and ask for more information; they provide an environment full of small manipulable and visually detailed objects and things to climb. They are generally more permissive and explanatory.

It seems obvious that it is not only early home environments that vary, with consequences for the levels of intellectual functioning attained by children and for their attitudes and values. Schools too can provide more or less richly elaborated situations and materials, can have more or less of organization and predictability in the stimuli which they offer, can be more or less authoritarian in the degree to which they provide, and the ways in which they sanction, choices. And beyond the home and the school, enveloping and deeply influencing both, is the culture of which they form part, with its technological, scientific, religious and moral content, its climate of authority, its values and its systems of sanctions and rewards.

Independently to a large extent of their moral and philosophical values, some cultures seem to make a more effective provision for the maximum intellectual growth of children than do others, just as some by their child-rearing and educational practices augment insecurity or diminish it. In preparing future generations to meet and solve the dilemmas posed by the profound changes of our time, and particularly when we consider the advancement of the developing world and the need to eliminate social and cultural disadvantage wherever we find it, it would seem that we must concentrate effort on improving the heuristic quality of the environments into which children are born and grow up. Though different family patterns, incidentally, may and do favour or disfavour the growth of intelligence through the degree of structure, organization and complexity which they provide, there is no necessary correlation between any one type of family or nurturing group and an intellectually stimulating environment. It should be possible in almost any kind of situation to provide both what is necessary to affective growth and to the highest possible development of the power to learn. Nor does this imply any kind of cultural uniformity, indeed rather the reverse. The cultivation of human intelligence and flexibility based on emotional security is consistent with a very wide pluralism in values, in cultures and in personal life-styles.

SECURITY IN PARENTHOOD

A child's basic security however is by no means uniquely or even principally bound up with the cognitive quality of his environment. It is much more concerned with the confidence with which he is handled by adults, particularly by his mother at first, with the regularity and calculability of the human responses and care in his environment, with the degree of security and affection shown him by his parents, the reassurance they give him that he is wanted, valued, cared for and protected as well as encouraged to venture forth.

How far parents can provide this is subtly dependent upon factors in their own personalities, their relationships to each other and to their own past and present environments. Maternal and child health services in most of the European countries have done much to improve the health of children and to give mothers confidence in their physical handling of infants. The steady increase too of various social and welfare services—maternity grants, schemes of home help for nursing mothers, child allowances—has removed many of the immediate sources of anxiety. On the other hand, such services are themselves contributory to the almost universal phenomenon of the breakdown of the old patterns of child-rearing within which parents found the security of ways established and hallowed by tradition. In the past many parents had themselves frequently been members of large families, and the mother, as an adolescent, had had an apprenticeship to motherhood in caring for a younger brother or sister. Where neighbourhood and kinship patterns were strong and stable, life tended to turn outward and the various members of the family had kinship and non-kinship groups in which they were embedded and which provided experience and supportive frameworks.[45] We now have some confusion in parental roles; and physical mobility and smaller families more and more deprive young parents of support and advice from outside and drive husband and wife into a closer, but more isolated, association. A high proportion of modern mothers have their first contact with very young children only when they themselves have a baby. Such an undivided responsibility, if, as is still common, they are totally unprepared by previous training or experience, may be provocative of anxiety and even be severely disturbing. Better educated than their grandparents, they tend to turn, not to neighbours and relatives, but to more impersonal and generalised sources of advice and guidance—books, articles in the popular press, radio and television programmes. Some of these are good, even excellent.[46] Others merely augment parental insecurity by the conflicting advice, frequently sensational and ill-considered, which they purvey. Even medical and welfare workers, misdirected, improperly, or even untrained in mental hygiene principles, may pass on advice without full realization of its effect in increasing the parents' anxious uncertainty. Similarly books and advice are not wanting which, whatever their intentions, do in fact play upon the anxieties of some parents by suggesting ways of achieving precocious intellectual growth.[47]

This process of the professionalization of advice and of supporting services to the family is one which has been going on for a long time but which has greatly accelerated in the past decades. Our admittedly scanty knowledge of the impact of childhood experiences connected particularly with feeding, defecation, sleep and contact with the mother would suggest that any practice advocated, for example on the grounds of physical health, should be carefully examined in the light of its implication for the development of the child's own personality, and through that, of the society in which as an adult he will participate. Similarly propaganda in the name of hygiene or psychology aimed at improving the handling of young child en should be carefully controlled, since it is apt to arouse parents' anxiety and uncertainty rather than to reassure them in their own ability. This seems to be especially true when, instead of dealing with concrete examples of behaviour in terms of everyday human sympathy and values, articles are written in a pseudo-scientific style with an emphasis on the abnormal.

We must also look carefully at the ways in which knowledge of child development is applied since it is upon the cognitive and affective content of what is done that such things as value structures, motivations and the sheer ability to accept or reject change will depend. It has, for example, been suggested that the greater warmth and permissiveness, the stronger bonds of interest and affection which mark many modern families as compared with those where, as in the past, relationships were more rigid and formal, may militate against the development of a strong motivation to achieve.[43] Further the fact that children and parents in developed countries are more closely and continually in contact may deprive children of privacy and time to be alone, and thus to develop a genuine independence.

Bearing all this in mind, however, it now seems reasonable to suggest that it is with the education of parents that education itself must start. It also seems to follow that in situations such as those of the developing countries, children must be prepared for the kinds of radical change which seem likely to come and parents themselves must be helped to change quite profoundly their traditional child-rearing styles. Even in the developed countries—and particularly as we shall see later among the least privileged sections of the population—this seems to be equally necessary. It is admittedly very difficult to do; even more important is the fact that the task is delicate both ethically and psychologically. The choice however is to leave it to chance, possibly to more or less irresponsible manipulators, or quite deliberately with objectives which are openly declared and defined (and therefore susceptible to criticism), to undertake the preparation and education of parents as a part of the public educational system.

PHYSICAL CONDITIONS AND THEIR HAZARDS

Warmhearted and reasonably insightful parents usually manage not to make mistakes of serious consequence, particularly if their general approach is reassuring to the child. Even in very difficult material circumstances many manage to do this. Nonetheless, apart altogether from the hazards of manifestly poor environments—slums, run-down city centres—there are increasingly seen to be in what are otherwise comparatively good and healthy material surroundings, hazards detrimental to children of which parents may not be fully aware and which social services of various kinds take insufficiently into account. Many of these bear directly upon the effectiveness with which parents discharge their role; others may be less obviously depriving or threatening.

The small apartment which is far from sound-proof and in which children cannot adequately play, the long journeys of adults by crowded trains and buses to and from work, the tiredness of the mother who has another job, poor sleeping conditions and curtailed rest, especially of the children, the frequent necessity of living with relatives or in lodgings with unsympathetic people, these and many similar conditions contribute to fatigue, irritability and tension in all members of the family, making each more vulnerable to emotional disturbances of all kinds. In the small flat, childish mess and untidiness may be crimes. The child who wakes at night crying is apt to get a smack for disturbing his parents' and the neighbours' rest, rather than the reassurance he may need. Quite apart from the possibly damaging experience of sleeping in the parents' bedroom, children in the small house or flat, still more those living in seriously overcrowded conditions,[49] are continuously exposed to interparental frictions, to the anxieties and worries of mother and father. They are too closely and too continuously under adult supervision, and their needs too much and too continuously in conflict with those of their parents, for a relaxation of tension to be easily possible.

The health of the family is however directly affected by many administrative measures over which individuals may have little control, and which create even more serious problems for parents. High flats for example make it difficult for mothers to get their children to and from outside play space, if any is provided, or to supervise them when they are there; landings and stairs provide very often an unacceptable hazard for an unsupervised child as well as making difficult such operations as taking a baby or young child for a walk in a pram or bringing home heavy shopping baskets.[50] Only too frequently in the recent past, such satellite towns and housing estates consisting almost entirely of flats in blocks of twenty or more storeys have been built far away from city centres and without providing the shops, schools, recreation centres and the like which permit the growth of neighbourhood.

Some of the disadvantages can be mitigated, though not entirely removed, by the provision of nursery schools, supervised play areas, adventure playgrounds and club accommodation. A good, energetic and trained community development worker can do something to break down the isolation, the sense of helplessness and the accompanying depression of the mothers; and careful attention to siting, road layout, the provision of shopping and recreational facilities for adolescents and adults will help. But the fact remains that high flats are basically unsuitable for family living and what is saved by high density land use may well be lost in human effectiveness and the cost of social and mental breakdown.

It seems clear that those responsible for housing and rehousing should bear in mind not only such factors as an adequate physical lay-out which includes provision for various sizes of family and for groups of different economic levels and different needs but should do it in such a way that it is possible for a real sense of community to develop.

Families should not be isolated (though having privacy); and children should not be removed from their natural surroundings. A satisfactory housing scheme would be based upon small communities reproducing the best conditions of village life with the hygienic, labour-saving and cultural advantages of a town. There is still in Europe an acute housing shortage and the additional problem that the centres of the large towns that grew up in the Industrial Revolution are now in an advanced state of decay. The high price of land near commercial centres tends to drive housing out to the suburbs or results in high and expensive blocks of flats. It is perhaps utopian to suggest that much more might be done to replan balanced communities in such centres, although some industrial countries have recognized the social value of dispersing commerce and industry, of building complete satellite communities. But even in adverse conditions, such as exist in most of the great cities of Europe, much more might be undertaken at very little cost to foster a sense of community in small groups of families and to provide adequate playing space for the children who so sorely need it.[51]

Migration to housing estates and a generally higher geographical mobility breaks up the neighbourhood structures—children lose their playgroups, wives their friends and working-class fathers their mates. This is in great contrast to the structures of the older established working class areas like, for instance, Bethnal Green[52] in London, or traditional mining towns such as are found in Yorkshire.[53] Even those new towns which have been designed with human social needs in mind, and the housing estates which show consideration for such elementary needs as safe play space for young children, focal points where mothers can meet casually and talk, have not entirely and successfully succeeded in building a supportive community; although many of the older ones now that a generation is beginning to grow up in them are having a much less depressing effect upon their occupants. We have, however, to remember that the growth of the psychological and social structures of a community takes time even under favourable conditions, and that geographical mobility is increasingly a characteristic of western urban populations.

EXTERNAL ANXIETIES

In such a situation, more or less typical of any of the European urban centres, the great external anxieties of our time have their most devastating effect. Economic worries, the threat of unemployment, high living costs, the menace of war, conflicting politics which play upon fears as well as upon aspirations, advertisements for various specifics with their emphasis upon disease, all these and many others bear upon parents and through them affect the healthy mental growth of their children. It is not often realized how closely the total psychological atmosphere in which a child lives affects his whole attitude to himself and to others both at the moment and in his future; nor how even the concealed anxieties of parents are sensed by their children whose whole stability is dependent in the early stages upon the reassurance that nothing terrible can happen if father and mother are there. The sense of helplessness and inability to change their circumstances or even the despair which has often been remarked upon as a characteristic of adults and children in disadvantaged groups is perhaps the most important single obstacle to any attempt to break the cycle of maladjustment, deprivation and underfunctioning which underlies so much general social malaise and inequality.

Modern conditions demand of parents more than has ever been demanded before or than most are able to give without considerable help and reassurance. The mentally healthy upbringing of children in a restricted living space by parents rendered uncertain themselves by great and small anxieties and difficulties is rarely achieved by the simple light of nature or by the coldly scientific application of rules deduced from psychoanalysis or even from child development studies. It demands an optimistic view of oneself and of social possibilities and requires a deeply emotional insight into the nature and needs of children, a readiness to compromise on adult requirements and a spontaneous sympathy which cannot be built by lectures, occasional advice and a flood of more or less well informed pamphlets.

The adverse circumstances of modern life affect children in their early formative years largely in proportion to the parents' own uncertainties and anxieties, expressed or unexpressed. If mother and father, through a calm and accepting temperament, through a religious faith or a working philosophy can reassure their children and meet their emotional needs in all but the most impossible circumstances, then experience has shown that even, for example, the loss of a parent, quite severe surrounding social disturbance and all but the great extremes of poverty can be passed through without very marked or irreparable emotional damage to children. Conversely, even where no objective cause for anxiety exists, parents often fail to appreciate how their words will arouse their children's fears. In many middle class families, for example, parents mention in front of their children their day-to-day financial difficulties, but forget to mention what they know and their children do not—the financial assets which would in fact provide against the starvation the child may imagine to be near. The imperfect knowledge and experience of the young make them vulnerable to anxieties in a way few adults understand.

DEPRIVATION IN THE MIDST OF PLENTY

The social, cultural and economic changes discussed and described earlier have however had a cumulative and general effect on the circumstances in which children now grow up. In very many respects the physical environment is healthier than it was sixty or more years ago; general standards of physical care, hygiene and nutrition are higher. In absolute material terms even the poorest 10 or 15 per cent of families[54] in a modern developed country is better off than was the norm a century ago and are affluent compared with the majority of the inhabitants of developing countries. Children and adolescents are healthier, heavier and taller than they were even in the thirties.

On the other hand, the psychological environment has changed in many ways, not all of them beneficial. Quite apart from the change in the nature of the family itself, with the tendency to inwardness and isolation, there has been a profound change in the communities which surround it. Many of these, even if they are stable as in the older suburbs and satellites of large cities, are not communities in any true sense at all. Most of the workers depart in the morning to labour out of sight in factories and offices, leaving the suburb to women, children and a few tradesmen. Vocational and social roles are not apparent in dress, speech or function: thus children do not grow with an articulated view of inter-relationships.[55]

Their living space too provides for fewer of their needs, particularly the needs for unsupervised play, adventure, exploration and risk taking. In a rural setting or even in a long established urban slum, there tend to be space and materials outside the home, the possibility for children to meet in spontaneous groups, often very mixed in age, to play games, to manipulate materials—even if these are only mud and the gutter water—to explore, even if the object of exploration is only a tumble down house and though the physical dangers may be great. Prior to the advent of intensive scientific agriculture, the fields and woods of the countryside were peopled by working adults who could and did frequently intervene in children's lives—to protect, comfort, threaten or punish; and things were little different in established neighbourhoods.

The salubrious suburb or even housing estate tends not to provide such things naturally and modern traffic makes streets dangerous for young children. This is not to say that a golden age has passed; many of the circumstances in which children grew up in the past were unsanitary and unhygienic both mentally and physically, as they are now in areas of condemned housing in large towns. It is to draw attention to the fact that changes and improvements in the environment may, unless special steps are taken,[56] deprive children and young people of essential stimuli to healthy mental growth.

FAMILY AND COMMUNITY

It is doubtful whether, even in the most primitive tribal organization, the social adaptation of the child and his preparation for the life of an adult rested entirely with the family, even with patriarchal and extended family groups. For many such children, the importance of the immediate family—mother and father—largely ceases at weaning from which time the child tends more and more to spend his time with age mates and to have all or most of the adults of the village in some sort as parents. In the ordinary sense the education of the primitive child is short, informal and acquired in the course of the normal amusements of childhood and in mingling in the work of the community. At the threshold of puberty, he is often admitted at the hands of his elders to adult status by some kind of initiation ceremony which contains an element of formal instruction. Developed societies commence the initiation of the young early and tend to prolong it well beyond puberty; in most, compulsory education begins when the child is between 5 and 7 years old and continues until the middle 'teens or later. As affluence grows a larger proportion of the age group continues in full or substantial part-time education into the third decade. Education is beginning to extend up to and beyond the age of full legal responsibility and independence.

The extent and direction of this conscious cultural shaping of children, certainly after the age of two, varies markedly from one human group to another; and even, within a nation broadly homogeneous in its pattern, from one social milieu to another. So too, does the balance between the role of the child's immediate family and that of the community in general. However, in the earliest years, it is in general through the interpretations of the mother and the immediate family that the surrounding culture, whether it be tribal or urban-industrial, moulds the child.

TELEVISION—A NEW FACTOR IN EARLY GROWTH?

More and more, however, children are exposed to radio and television which intrude into the home. The effects of these probably differ according to how the family makes use of them and to how programmes are themselves organized as stimuli for the young child.

Most developed countries have on radio and television special programmes for children and broadcasting organizations like the B.B.C. in the United Kingdom, for example, exercise considerable restraint upon the kinds and content of programmes shown prior to 9 p.m. because children may be in the audience. Some programmes, like 'Sesame Street' in the U.S.A. are deliberately aimed to help children, otherwise deprived, to gain some of the experiences thought to be essential for mental growth.

Two observations may be made. It many homes, radio and television are left on, and we may suppose that children interested in their own affairs rapidly treat the noise and images as an almost unnoticed background. On the other hand, radio and television programmes, particularly the latter, may provide for some children almost the only experience they have of a fully consequential and organized set of stimuli. This, of course, says nothing about the quality of the content of programmes which children may see nor of the effects upon their attitudes of scenes of violence[57] occurring in recreational, current affairs and news programmes. We have little hard evidence of the effects of this either when it is a parent directed exposure of pre school children to television (and radio) or when it is casual looking and listening to material going on in the background.[53] But it seems reasonable to accept that television in the home provides reinforcing or alternative models of response to the environment at quite an early age—certainly long before literature and school do so. It provides them in highly realistic and powerful forms and for many children without the mediating influence of a known and trusted adult. We do have to recognize that there may be here in the case of children from different backgrounds, a factor making for increased intergroup differences in development. This influence is now added to that of increasing direct contact between the growing child and the world outside his home. From about two years of age with increasing physical independence the process of psychological weaning accelerates and brings him into more direct contact with widening sections of the community's life. As this process grows and develops, social and intercultural differences begin to make themselves most felt, through implicit and rarely more than vaguely expressed expectations, through customs and tradition, and through conscious community organization backed by legislative sanctions.

It is however in the main with the family that we must begin. Psychologically speaking, it is a buffer, a filter and a bridge to the outside world to which for at least five vital years all else is secondary. It should protect its children from too harsh a contact with realities throughout their growing period; it should interpret to them the culture in which they live; and it should act as a base from which they can launch out into the more impersonal world outside the protection of their home. As societies grow more complex and their heritage of skills, techniques and knowledge is enriched, it becomes increasingly difficult for the family—even the patriarchal family group—to discharge completely these responsibilities in the upbringing of its children. Just as economic development alters the nature of the family's food-getting activities and even displaces much of its responsibility, so more and more aspects of the process of shaping children's personalities, their ethical and intellectual standards, are passed into the hands of adults outside the family. Even so, in terms of direct and profound influence, the family seems if anything to grow stronger rather than weaker as compared with the school for example, particularly in the urban centres of Europe where the inward turning isolated family is becoming the norm.

NOTES

1. For example, the stages of growth distinguished by Piaget occur in a culturally invariant sequence but their age incidence varies between individuals in the same culture and between cultures. Some of this may be due to an inevitable sequence inherent in the way experience is built up—percept must precede concept for example—in any culture, in the structure of knowledge and its relationships, and in the process of interaction itself which (by assimilation and accommodation) prepares the next stage and in this sense provokes development. However, no amount of suitable experience or training can, it seems, accelerate the process beyond a certain point or alter the general sequence. Moreover if the concepts—for example, the abstract notions and relationships involved in mathematics—are absent from the cultural experience, they will not arise in the normal individual.

2. Allport, G. W. *Personality: a psychological interpretation.* London, Constable, 1937 [chapter VII].

3. What that early and now neglected psychologist J. M. Baldwin (*Mental development of the child and the race.* 1896) called the 'circular reaction'.

4. Piaget, J. *La psychologie de l'intelligence.* Paris, Armand Colin, 1949 [especially p. 13–14].

5. As for example with children who are repeatedly deprived of a firm link with a mother figure or who later through many family moves constantly lose their friends (World Health Organization. *Deprivation of maternal care: a reassessment of its effects.* Geneva, 1970. / Bowlby, J. *Attachment and loss.* London, Hogarth Press, 1969. [2 v.]).

6. McDougall, W. *An introduction to social psychology.* London, Methuen, 1908. / Idem. *The energies of men.* London, Methuen, 1932.

7. Bühler, C. *Kindheit und Jugend.* Göttingen, Verlag für Psychologie, 1967.

8. Valentine, C. W. *The psychology of early childhood.* London, Methuen, 1943. See also: Ambrose, J. A. The development of the smiling response in early infancy. In: Foss, B. M., ed. *Determinants of infant behaviour.* London, Methuen, 1961.

9. Gesell, A. L.; Ilg, F. L. *Infant and child in the culture of today.* New York; London, Harper, 1943.

10. On this whole field see: El Koussy, A. H. *Usus al-sinhah al-nafsiyah* [Fundamentals of mental hygiene]. 4th ed. Cairo, Librarie de la Renaissance, 1952.

11. The positive and negative contingencies of the Skinnerian psychology (Skinner, B. F. *Beyond freedom and dignity.* London, Jonathan Cape, 1972). Skinner however goes much further and by extrapolation from animal studies suggests that behaviour is entirely determined by environmental reinforcements and leaves no room for states of mind or internal feelings. R. Lynn (*Personality and national character,* Oxford, Pergamon, 1971), analysing broad differences in levels of anxiety as manifested by neurosis, suicide, accidents, alcoholism and stress diseases, suggests that the principal determinants of high-low anxiety are race and climate.

12. Particularly the acquisition of language which leads to an increasing qualitative difference between human and animal learning, rendering hazardous extrapolations from learning experiments with animals to the learning of children and adults.

13. It is the early stages of this process which Piaget (*La psychologie de l'intelligence.* Op. cit.) calls 'sensory-motor intelligence' developing from, for example, the earliest co-ordinations between vision and the ability to grasp an object.

14. For a very full and detailed analysis of the immense amount of research on the effects of early environment on young children, see: Lézine, I. Influence du milieu sur le jeune enfant. In: *Milieu et developpement.* Paris, Presses universitaires de France, 1972 [Symposium de l'Association de psychologie scientifique de langue française]. See also Idem. *Psychopédagogie du premier âge.* Paris, Presses universitaires de France, 1969.

15. See, for example: World Health Organization. Op. cit. [particularly the contributions by D. G. Prugh and R. A. Harlow, by R. G. Andry and the specially valuable discussion by Mary Ainsworth that concludes the monograph]. A more up-to-date analysis, together with extensive abstracts of the research literature, is provided in: Dinnage, R.; Pringle, M. L. K. *Residential child care.* London, Longmans, 1967 [Chapters II, III and IV of this work are specially valuable]. See also: Pringle, M. L. K., *et al. Adoption.* London, Longmans, 1966. / Bowlby, J. *Attachment and loss.* Vol. I: *Attachment.* London, Hogarth Press, 1969.

16. In some societies, e.g., the Samoans, the tie may be highly diffused even at the stage of breast-feeding. In others, as in the Israeli *kibbutzim* (see: Spiro, M. E. *Children of the kibbutz.* Cambridge, Mass., Harvard University Press, 1958) or in the extended families of Africa, the biological mother is only one of a number of substitutes. Within some considerable limits, it seems reasonable to suggest that differing styles of 'mothering' may result in differences of character structure and that discontinuity of style—such as early indulgence followed by rigorous discipline, or the discontinuity of handling brought about by separation in the early years—will also affect

the child's security and learning in subtle ways (Margaret Mead in WHO monograph cited above. See also: Soddy, K., ed. *Cross cultural studies in mental health*. London, Tavistock Publications, 1961). Bruno Bettelheim (*Children of the dream*. London, Paladin, 1971) argues powerfully that the early upbringing of the *kibbutz* child produces a group-oriented personality with an inner life very different from that of the more individualistic and introverted mode fostered by the traditional Jewish family.

17. Lefort, R. Etude des troubles somatiques des enfants séparés, vivant en institutions. Paris, Centre International de l'Enfance [unpublished, duplicated material]. / Spitz, R. A. The role of ecological factors in emotional development. *Child development* (Chicago), vol. 20, November 1949.

18. Cf. film: '*A two-year-old goes to hospital*'. J. Roberts, Tavistock Clinic, London.

19. Orlanski, H. Infant care and personality. *Psychological bulletin* (Washington, D.C.), vol. 46, 1949, p. 1–48. / Sewell, W. H.; Mussen, P. H. The effects of feeding, weaning, scheduling procedures on childhood adjustment and the formation of oral symptons. *Child development* (Chicago), vol. 23, 1952, p. 185–191. / World Health Organization. *Deprivation of maternal care*. Op. cit.

20. Lorenz raises the question as to whether the kind of individualistic character structure required by civilizations of the Western style presupposes the exclusive and intense mother- (or nurse-) child relationship in early years (see: Tanner, J. M.; Inhelder, B., eds. *Discussions on child development*. London Tavistock Publications, 1956).

21. Surprisingly little attention has been given to the role of the father. One of the best discussions is that of R. G. Andry in the WHO monograph cited previously [especially p. 37–43]. See also: Bruce, N. Delinquent and non-delinquent reactions to parental deprivations. *British journal of criminology* (London), vol. 10, 1970. / Wilkins, L. *Delinquent generations*. London, HMSO, 1960. The latter work discusses the effects of war-time absences of fathers.

22. Boutonier, J. Child development patterns—France. In: 'Child rearing practices and social, intellectual and emotional growth of young children'. Evidence submitted to the Regional Conference on Education and the Mental Health of Children in Europe (1952) by the World Federation for Mental Health (later published as: *Mental health and infant development*. London, Routledge & Kegan Paul, 1955).

23. The phrase is that of J. and E. Newson whose enquiries revealed that 79 per cent. of fathers in their Nottingham sample were moderately or highly participant in the upbringing of the family. They conclude that this is a change which has occurred principally since the 1930s (*Infant care in an urban community*. London, Allen & Unwin, 1963). A study in the United Kingdom (Oakley, A. *Sex, gender and society*. London, Temple Smith, 1972 / Are husbands good housewives? *New society* (London), 17 February 1972) suggests that middle class husbands participate more fully than working class husbands in the care of children under five (and in housework) ,but that substantial proportions from both groups do not. Social attitudes seem to differ: 78 per cent. of respondents who were asked how fathers and mothers left on their own with children should cope, responded that a man should go out to work. Women who had children under school age were expected by 75 per cent. to stay at home with their children and maintain themselves by social benefit payments (see: MacKay, A.; Wilding, P.; George, V. Stereotypes of male and female roles and their influence on

people's attitudes to one-parent families. *Sociological review* (Keele), vol. 20, pt. 1, 1972).

24. While throughout this century about one-third of the working force in the United Kingdom has consisted of women, the proportion of married women at work has shown a sharp increase in the past decades (Hunt, A. *A survey of women's employment*. London, HMSO, 1968). However, particularly if mother does not begin work until after the children have begun school, the fact that she works seems to have little effect on the progress and adjustment of her child at school (Davie, R.; Butler, N. R.; Goldstein, H. *From birth to seven*. London, Longmans, 1972).

25. F. Musgrove (*The family, education and society*. London, Routledge & Kegan Paul, 1966) points to the way in which modern conditions (mobility, property ownership on a large scale, the motor car as a 'detachable parlour', the decline of the neighbourhood) have tended to turn the family in upon itself at all levels of society.

26. Davie, R.; Butler, N. R.; Goldstein, H. Op. cit.

27. Crellin, E.; Pringle, M. L. K.; West, P. *Born illegitimate*. Slough, Bucks., National Foundation for Educational Research, 1972.

28. Recent figures in the United Kingdom show a sharp rise in pregnancies among unmarried adolescent girls—see Vol. II, Chapter 6.

29. See: Musgrove, F. Op. cit.

30. See, for example: Read, M. *Children of their fathers*. London, Methuen, 1959.

31. See: Margaret Mead's contribution to WHO monograph cited earlier.

32. There is an inverse correlation between family size and ability and attainment. About 30 per cent of children in the National Child Development Study referred to earlier (Davie, R.; Butler, N. R.; Goldstein, H. Op. cit.) were in families with four or more children, most of them in the working class groups; children from these large families showed a particular disadvantage in verbal skills and were less well adjusted in school. They were also lighter and shorter. These differences have complex causes—diminished resources, less parental attention and probably considerable differences in family attitudes—but this indicates the need for the school to shape its intervention in full knowledge of the differences involved.

33. Bloom, S. S. *Stability and change in human characteristics*. New York, Wiley, 1964 [especially chapter 3 and p. 214–216].

34. See, for example: Vernon, P. E. *Intelligence and cultural environment*. London, Methuen, 1969.

35. Vernon (Op. cit., p. 214–215) concludes: 'There is strong evidence that differences in intelligence . . . between individuals within one culture are largely—certainly not wholly—genetically determined. But when environmental differences are more extreme, as between ethnic groups, their effects predominate. This does not mean that there are no innate racial differences in abilities, but they are probably small and we have no means of proving them. Differences between subgroups such as social classes are partly genetic, not wholly environmental.' See also: Reuchlin, M. Les facteurs socio-économiques du développement cognitif. In: *Milieu et développement*. Paris, Presses universitaires de France, 1972.

36. Some psychologists have argued powerfully that genuine differences do exist in the 'gene pool' of different races and that these produce ineluctable quantitative and qualitative differences. On this whole question see: Jensen, A. R. How much can we boost I.Q. and scholastic achievement? In:

Environment, heredity and intelligence. Cambridge, Mass., 1969 (Harvard educational review reprint series, no. 2); and the critiques of Jensen's thesis in the same volume and subsequent numbers of the *Harvard educational review.* It is also suggested that social mobility and the tendency to assortative mating might in part account for the stability of the mean differences found between social groups in any one community.

37. A striking example of this, and one very complex in its causation, is that generally speaking African children are more advanced in their psychomotor development than are their European counterparts up to the age of two. Thereafter they tend to fall behind, dramatically if the weaning period is abrupt and interferes with nutrition but less so if a European style is adopted by the parents (Geber, M. Développement psychomoteur de l'enfant africain, *Courrier du Centre international de l'enfance* (Paris), vol. 6, 1965. / Geber, M.; Dean, R. F. A. Psychomotor development in African children: the effects of social class. *Bulletin of the World Health Organization* (Geneva), vol. 18, no. 3, 1958).

38. The absence of toys in the environment of many African tribal children has often been noted. Mothers do not play with their children; on the other hand, the very young child goes everywhere on its mother's back and has thus a wider world than that of a European child who spends a good deal of time in a cradle (Geber, M. Op. cit.).

39. A. Zempléni (Milieu african et dévelopment. In: *Milieu et développement.* Op. cit., p. 158–166), analysed a large number of studies, from many cultures, on the development of perception. See also: Cole, M. *et al. The cultural context of learning.* London, Methuen, 1972. This work studies the difficulties of Kpelle children (in Liberia) in acquiring Western style mathematics.

40. Bernstein, B. *Class codes and control.* Vol. I: *Theoretical studies towards a sociology of language.* London, Routledge & Kegan Paul, 1971 [especially chapters 1 and 2].

41. For an excellent discussion of the interrelations of language with the growth of thought, or moral and personal concepts see: Lewis, M. M. *Language, thought and personality.* London, Harrap, 1963.

42. See: Opie, P.; Opie, I. *Children's games in street and playground.* Oxford, Clarendon Press, 1969. / Idem. *Oxford dictionary of nursery rhymes.* Oxford, Clarendon Press, 1951. Similar collections exist for other groups and languages, for example: Baucomont, J., *et al. Les comptines de langue française.* Paris, Editions Seghers, 1961 [with an excellent bibliography].

43. Reuchlin, M. In: *Milieu et développement.* Op. cit.

44. White, B. L. An analysis of excellent early educational practices: preliminary report. *Interchange (Canada)* (Toronto), vol. 3, no. 2, 1971.

45. See: Young, M.; Willmott, P. *Family and kinship in East London.* London, Routledge & Kegan Paul, 1957. See also: Chombart de Lauwe, P. *La vie quotidienne des familles ouvrières.* Paris, Centre national de la recherche scientifique, 1956.

46. See, for example, the goodhearted, reassuring work by B. Spock (*Baby and child care.* London, Bodley Head, 1969), a mixture of the old household adviser on mild ailments and the modern popularizer of methods of child rearing; the series of talks given on the Belgian television by Professor Paul Osterrieth; or the activities (lectures, discussion groups, pamphlets) of the Ecole des parents, Paris. See also: Osterrieth, P. *L'enfant et la famille.* Paris, Scarabée 1957. For a work of a more austere kind see: Lézine;

I. *Psychopédagogie du premier âge*. Paris, Presses universitaires de France, 1969.

47. E. J. Le Shan (*Conspiracy against childhood*. New York, Atheneum, 1968) discusses the whole topic of pressures exerted on children at home and at school. Though its intention was otherwise, a book like *Teach your baby to read* by G. Doman (London, Cape, 1965) has undoubtedly augmented the anxieties of some parents.

48. F. Musgrove (Op. cit., p. 87–89) suggests that: 'Neither humanity nor commonsense seems to pay the highest dividends in the educational system and social order which we have devised.'

49. In 1965, some 15 per cent of the children in the United Kingdom sample of seven-year-olds were living at the ratio of 1.5 persons per habitable room or worse (Davie, R.; Butler, N. R.; Goldstein, H. Op. cit.).

50. Maizels, J. *Two to five in high flats*. London, The Housing Centre, 1961.

51. A good example has been given by the Community Centre Movement in the Scandinavian countries and in the United Kingdom, and by the provision of 'adventure playgrounds' for children in congested areas (Bengtsson, A. *Adventure playgrounds*. London, Crosby Lockwood, 1972). Similarly, the Pre-School Playgroup Movement has done, by voluntary effort, a great deal to decrease the isolation of many mothers and to provide some means of training them in better methods of child care (see Chapter 8).

52. Young, M.; Willmott, P. Op. cit.

53. Dennis, N.; Henriques, F.; Slaughter, C. *Coal is our life*. London, Eyre & Spottiswood, 1956.

54. Poverty is to some extent relative. There is reason to believe that rising general standards of affluence and rising expectations of what is or should be a vital minimum have increased the numbers of urban families who are perceived to live in such dire poverty that the children's personal and intellectual growth is severely menaced (Abel-Smith, B.; Townsend, P. *The poor and the poorest*. London, Bell, 1965). However the worst conditions in affluent countries pale into insignificance when compared, for example, with Brazil (Caldiera, C. *Menores no meio rural*. Rio de Janeiro, INEP, Ministerio de Educaçao e Cultura, 1960).

55. For a thorough study of a typical suburban town in Canada see: Seely, J. R.; Sim, R. A.; Loosley, E. W. *Crestwood heights*. New York, Wiley, 1963.

56. Such as play streets, closed to traffic, 'adventure playgrounds', play centres, pre-school playgroups (see: Bengtsson, A. Op. cit.).

57. Roughly two incidents per hour on British television even before 9 p.m. (Emmet, B. *Violence on television*. London, BBC, 1972).

58. See: Emmet, B. Television and real life violence. *E.B.U. review* (Brussels), September, 1970. / Idem Television and violence—two years and a million dollars later. *E.B.U. review* (Brussels), November, 1972. In the latter he discusses the U.S. Surgeon-General's report on 'Television and growing up', which finds a 'tentative indication of a causal relation between viewing violence on television and aggressive behaviour; an indication that any such causal relation operates only on some children (who are predisposed to be aggressive); and an indication that it operates only in some environmental contexts'. He refers also to a finding by Tannenbaum that there is a general emotional arousal, caused by a variety of filmed stimuli which, whatever the provoking content (humorous, erotic or violent), can according to the individual give rise to pro-social or anti-social reactions.

FURTHER READING

Association de psychologie scientifique. *Milieu et développement*. Paris, Presses universitaires de France, 1972.

Bloom, B. S. *Stability and change in human characteristics*. New York, Wiley, 1964.

Buckle, D., et al. *Aspects of family mental health in Europe*. Geneva, World Health Organization, 1965.

Chombart de Lauwe, P. *La vie quotidienne des familles ouvrières*. Paris, Centre national de la recherche scientifique, 1956.

Davie, R.; Butler, N.; Goldstein, H. *From birth to seven*. London, Longmans, 1972.

Flavell, J. H. *The developmental psychology of Jean Piaget*. New Jersey, Van Nostrand, 1963.

Laing, R. D. *The politics of the family and other essays*. London, Tavistock Publications, 1971.

Newson, J.; Newson, E. *Infant care in an urban community*. London, Allen & Unwin, 1963.

————; ————. *Four years old in an urban community*. London, Allen & Unwin, 1968.

Peaker, G. F. *The Plowden follow-up*. Slough, Bucks., National Foundation for Educational Research, 1971.

Schmidt, M. J. *A família por dentro* [Inside the family]. Rio de Janiero, AGIR, 1965.

Tanner, J. M.; Inhelder, B., eds. *Discussions on child development*. London, Tavistock Publications, 1956.

Winch, R. F. *The modern family*. New York, Holt Reinhart & Winston, 1971.

Wiseman, S. *Education and environment*. Manchester, Manchester University Press, 1964.

Chapter seven

Home, school and community services

We may distinguish in modern Europe some important and possibly conflicting tendencies which are of growing importance. There is first the prolongation of the child's economic and psychological dependence well into the 'teens. This has the effect of intensifying the influence of the family in certain ways whilst exposing adolescents in fact to formal socializing agencies (e.g., schools and youth clubs) which may offer alternative and contradictory models. Secondly, partly because social reformers have perceived isolation as a threat to the stability of families and partly because of an awareness of the immense importance to the child's development of the experience he has at home, there is a vigorous attempt to provide services to help the family in its complex task.[1] Thirdly, we find that some communities seeing the inability of some families to discharge unaided their task of the pre-school care and education of their children tend to intervene in more or less directive ways and to remove children from home and thus in fact to undermine the influence of the parents.

Any measure which seems to break the affective link between a child and his parents, particularly in the case of the very young, or which removes from the family the final responsibility for its children warrants careful examination since it may contain serious dangers, both to the mental health of children and to the moral and political health of communities. On the other hand, it is clear that the efforts at personal and social promotion through the school, may be frustrated by the very home-centredness of the modern family or place children in highly conflictual situations.

A child's family, even an objectively 'bad' one, is important to him throughout the whole of his development—under modern conditions throughout the period from birth until at least the early twenties. Because of the evident importance of the first five or so years of life, there has been a tendency to concentrate attention and support on the parents of the very young child and to think of aid as being primarily material and medical. This has led to a neglect of psychological help generally and to the assumption that agencies outside the home (school and leisure groups) can look after middle and late childhood and adolescence, provided the foundations are laid aright in the early years.

Certainly young children are more vulnerable physically and mentally and certainly in the developing world now, as in Europe a century or less ago, the presenting problems look to be mainly concerned with health and nutrition in the ante- and perinatal period and in infancy. Evidence from the developing countries shows that the effects of severe malnutrition in the first three years are not likely to be entirely remediable either in their physical or their intellectual consequence[2]—although malnutrition later in childhood appears to respond more completely to adequate feeding. Even in these extreme circumstances however the psychological effects of deprivation are in many ways as important as are the direct physical ones and physical care and supervision are insufficient as a positive contribution to the general raising of standards of life.

The broad bases of personality are laid in childhood when, through inexperience and immaturity, the child is liable to intensely emotional experiences with which he is unable to grapple alone; his early learning sets the style of how well and effectively he will learn later. But life steadily thrusts the growing human being forward into novel situations and, in the 'teens particularly, when physiological factors combine with environmental stimuli to provoke another profoundly emotional and therefore formative period, he needs the continuing support and understanding of his family. For the development of a mentally healthy personality and for all that is normally meant by character, the second decade of life is—though very differently—at least as important as the first and offers what may be the last opportunity of setting right any misdevelopments which have taken place earlier. In the so-called developed as in the developing world, modern families are facing situations for which even the best of traditional folk wisdom is not sufficiently adequate. Nothing short of a profound reconsideration and reconstruction of the helping agencies seems likely to suffice.

It becomes therefore important to consider first the relationship between the family and any existing or future outside service. We need to be very clear about the nature of educative support to be given at different periods of the child's growth and how the various professional agencies should combine their efforts rather than, as all too often at present, existing in isolation or in conflict.[3]

Our growing knowledge too suggests that efforts to improve the mental health of communities should be confined neither to the first few years of a child's life nor to the remedying of maladjustments or illnesses when they have arisen. An essentially preventive and constructive mental health service will begin with the family before the child is born into it and will aid—principally through the family but later also through the school—the child and the adolescent throughout the formative years.

The crucial professional problem which such a notion presents is inherent in the historical role of the services themselves and in the attitudes and training of their workers. Most have grown up in response to evident needs—breakdown, poverty, manifest inadequacy, alcoholism, delinquency, major illnesses and handicaps. They are equipped to deal with crises. The temptation is to intervene in directive and authoritarian ways, to take over in some sort the responsibilities of the inadequate parent or family, to treat the child as a case in isolation from the broad social and environmental causes of his difficulties, to use the available social services as a substitute for the family. This kind of help, material and moral, is often easier to give (and sometimes more personally satisfying to medical and social workers trained in the old ways) than it is patiently to attempt through working with parents to help them to learn the skills and attitudes whereby they can help themselves, eventually independently.

There are certainly situations from which children have to be removed temporarily or permanently just as there are physical crises in which massive medical intervention is necessary. But there are many more situations which will only be improved by patient educative support over a long time until the child or the adolescent can find what he needs outside the family.

One of the greatest difficulties in realizing this supportive kind of service of skilled (but auxiliary) help to inadequate families is the lack of staff trained in the rather different human skills (and the humility) necessary and with the time to carry out this form of long-term education. Hard-pressed and understaffed services are almost obliged to concentrate upon crises rather than take long-term preventive action; and their workers are trained more to exercise their curative skills or to operate the administrative machine to bring material help than they are to intervene unobtrusively preventively or constructively to mitigate or fundamentally change the social or individual circumstances which are leading to a crisis or breakdown. Moreover, many services which could combine such a role with their current one, do not see it as their responsibility to do so. This is particularly true of medical and educational services: the first concentrating on environmental sanitation and the treatment and prevention of physical disease by physical methods; the second upon the strictly instructional and cognitive aspects of in-school education.

A big step forward would be taken if legislative, administrative, economic, medical, educational and social action were to be initiated and evaluated in terms of whether it tended to strengthen and support the family in its task of ensuring the healthy personal, emotional, physical and intellectual growth of its children and whether it brought all the potentially educative outside agencies into active cooperation with parents through the whole of the child's period of psychological growth.

THE COMPLEMENTARY NATURE OF THE SCHOOL AND THE HOME

In attempting to achieve this, the role of the school is essential. After the first years of childhood, it is the most important single organization which works with the child and could work with his family. Its influence can be exerted not only on the fathers and mothers, but directly and indirectly in the preparation of the next generation of parents. It occupies a vantage point from which the many other services, medical, social and psychological, could be brought into an educative relationship with the family and its pupils even before they enter school. It occupies a strategic position from which maladjustments can be detected and through which the vicious cycle of deprived or disturbed parents producing deprived or disturbed children who themselves later found inadequate families can begin to be broken.

So far, this broad social role has been neglected and even cooperation between homes and schools and between schools and the community generally has not (for a variety of reasons) developed as fully as it might even in Europe; yet all three are necessarily complementary agencies in the education of children, and parents and teachers have different but complementary tasks. Mothers and fathers, for example, have a far closer and deeper tie with their children than the teacher or any outside worker can have; they know them more intimately and possess a fuller knowledge of the whole pattern of previous growth. The teacher on the other hand should have been trained to know the psychology of children in general; he should be able to draw comparisons from one child to another, to estimate what is normal and what deviates from the average; his attitude to any particular child should be more detached and objective than that of a parent, and he should be able to allay unnecessary anxiety and put the individual child in the perspective of his wide experience.

The child-in-school is in many ways a different person from the child-at-home; his attitude and behaviour towards his parents are markedly different from those towards his teacher. The two environments however interact and what happens in the one will influence behaviour in the other. Many parents, for example, are ignorant of the way in which too heavy a demand on the help of a girl or boy with family chores may prevent satisfactory progress in school; many teachers are unaware that the tasks they set for homework may rouse antagonism in the parents or provoke mother or father to undertake the job of a supervisor of studies. Sometimes newer teaching methods or educational aims are not understood by parents; a subtle or overt opposition to the school begins at home and quickly puts the pupil in a conflict of loyalties. The teacher may treat as lazy a child who goes so late to bed that he has no energy left for work, or fail to understand the irritability, aggressiveness or stubborn non-cooperation of another whose energies are absorbed in anxious fantasies provoked by a mother's illness or the unexplained birth of a baby.

It is even more difficult for both sides when, as is more frequently the case than is generally realized, there is a culture clash between school and home; or when the child lacks the experiences, concepts and attitudes which, tacitly, the school assumes as the basis of its work. In such situations the competence and insight of the school staff are of immense importance. They have first to make an expert appraisal of the situation as it exists and then ask themselves some fundamental questions about how far they should attempt to adapt to a very different set of presuppositions and objectives or how far they should attempt to modify the mores and values of the home. This situation is at its most acute, both practically and ethically, in many developing countries where, unless the child is educated away from many of the ways and customs of his family, progress towards industrialization and modernization (if that is what is wanted) will be slow. On the other hand, the emotional health of the child and of his family may well be acutely shaken by the conflict set up by education itself. Such situations, whether in developed or in developing countries, imply a fairly profound change in the kind of roles traditionally discharged by teachers and schools, in the stance which the school takes towards the community which it serves and in the training of teachers in the psychological, sociological and philosophic aspects of their task.

For other services, who have to work with families and with schools, the change may have to be even more profound—particularly in the stance which they take *vis à vis* the school and the ways in which their particular professional expertise is put at the service of parents and children through the schools. Many administrative and professional barriers are called into question by such a concept and so is the present hierarchy of professional relationships.

UNDERSTANDING BETWEEN SCHOOL AND HOME

With whatever aims in view, the basis of this aspect of education is mutual knowledge and understanding between home and school. The initiative, so far as parents are concerned and perhaps with other professions, will by virtue of his training and his position of responsibility towards a number of children, normally fall to the teacher. Invitations to parents to visit the school and see what goes on, talks and discussions on educational method, upon changes in conception and technique which have taken place since the parents went to school, and upon innovations' which are about to be made, demonstrations and suggestions as to how, without playing the amateur teacher, parents can help their own children to learn and how they can complement the lessons which are given, these and activities like them will do something to bring parents into an understanding participation in the teacher's work. A well conceived scheme of health education which as well as such matters as physical hygiene, nutrition, physical health and disease, deals also with interpersonal problems, human relationships, sex, marriage and the like could and should call upon the specialized knowledge available in other social and medical services, thus bringing them into contact generally with pupils and parents and helping to break down their separation and isolation.

It is more difficult for the teacher, especially in the urban school, to get to know the homes of his pupils and something at least of the personalities and attitudes of parents. Where custom is not antagonistic to it, and where time permits, a visit to the homes of his pupils will tell the alert and observant teacher a great deal that he could not otherwise know. In the case of children who experience difficulties in their educational or personal development, such a direct contact with the home is indispensable and will often go far to explain the cause of the difficulties. Much of the necessary understanding however can be obtained by other means; by personal conversations with the parents; through the reports of school psychologists, welfare officers, attendance officers, social workers and the like; and through the teacher himself making a careful study of the community in which he lives and works, so that he may come to understand the preoccupations of the families of the children he teaches, and the kinds of experience which his pupils are having outside the classroom.

In the course of a child's school career there are, too, a number of occasions when consultation between parents and teacher should be close and where, in the majority of instances, the initiative to bring it about will have to be taken by the teacher. We may list as examples the child's first entry to school or change from one school to another; the times at which he has to be guided in his choice between alternative courses of study; and, as schooling draws towards a close, when the adolescent's future career is discussed. In such circumstances and others like them, it is the task of the teacher to act as adviser (in at least some cases with the help of other services) to parent and child, to present as objectively as possible the facts which bear upon, for example, the choice of a vocation, and to help the family to come to a decision.[5]

PARENT-TEACHER ASSOCIATIONS

It is at least partly from an awareness of these facts that the last 25 years have seen a considerable growth both in general public interest in the social tasks of the school and in the development of parent-teacher activity as means of promoting the general growth of children.

In some countries[6] associations of parents or parent-teacher societies are established by law; in others,[7] legislation or official policy encourages co-operation and even goes so far as to suggest appropriate forms for it; in yet others, responsibility for action is left entirely to the initiative of teachers or parents themselves. Hardly anywhere in Europe do the schools now function in complete isolation from the families of their pupils, though contacts may range from the most rare and casual consultation to highly organized and effective collaboration.[8] One increasing phenomenon seems to be deplorable—the development of parents' associations which act almost as hostile trades unions or as pressure groups against the particular school and its staff or against the providing authority. Not surprisingly where these exist there is also a corresponding tendency for pupils to band themselves together in a group hostile to the staff of their school.[9] Whatever experience of adult ways of social and industrial action such associations may give, the separatism and latent hostility which they imply and sometimes openly advocate seem not to be conducive to the kind of climate of willing trust and co-operation that one would wish to see.

Attitudes in the teaching profession as a whole are not unanimously favourable. There are many educationists who regard the social problems of their pupils and families and even the manifestly medical ones as no concern of theirs, or at best as being tangential. They prefer that any specialized services should operate well outside the ambit of the school. Not a few teachers—and especially, but not solely, those from countries where religious conflict maintains a dual system of education with the fears, rivalries and jealousies that this sometimes means—fear that organizations of parents, especially if they are federated on a national level, will act as political pressure groups. Others see a tendency for parent associations to infringe the professional liberty of the teacher, and are anxious lest there be a direct interference in school organization, curricula, and methods by those who are not fully aware of the complex problems involved. Yet others, perhaps from bitter experience, complain that parents' meetings induce ill-informed and hostile expressions of opinion about the school and about individual teachers. Some few think that close contact between parents and teachers may make children insecure and selfconscious.[10]

There is no doubt that such fears and doubts have some justification. Moreover in the ranks of the teaching profession itself, as in others, there are members whose dictatorial manner or clumsiness in personal relationships are likely to provoke rather than allay stresses and tensions between the school and the home. There are individual parents who are too fearful, too indifferent and, sometimes, too hostile to co-operate in the education of their children.[11] There may well be local or even national situations in which co-operation on an organized basis is undesirable; though it is difficult to imagine circumstances in which informal and personal contacts between members of a school staff and the parents of particular pupils do not have value.

In spite of the difficulties encountered and the fears expressed, most teachers and teachers' organizations recognize that for the good of individual children and for the progress of education as a whole, the home and the school should be brought close together and that they should jointly exercise their complementary functions. As to how it should be done opinions and practice vary. Probably in the majority of European schools, it is at least partially achieved by casual meetings between a parent and the headmaster or headmistress or the teacher of the child's class. In many schools, the head is available to parents by appointment at certain times or invites them for interview whenever particular problems arise. In addition, parents may be invited to school occasions—prize days, exhibitions of work, sports days, concerts and the like—during which personal contact with the school staff is possible.

Many heads and teachers feel that such individual and informal contacts are all that is justified or necessary. For rural schools where the teacher is known to and knows the local community, they are probably sufficient. In towns or where the school draws its pupils from a wide area, such more or less casual contacts are rarely enough to give the teacher real insight into the home circumstances of the pupils, to help the parent to understand the aims and methods of the school or for teachers and parents together to exercise a decisive influence upon the improvement of the total education of children. Hence, usually on the initiative of the head, or of individual teachers, meetings of all parents or of the parents of pupils in a particular class[12] are called on specific occasions, such as first entry to school and when a choice of future studies is to be made, or regularly at intervals of a month or more. The principal object of such group meetings is informational: and, while there is interchange between teachers and parents, they most usually take the form of lectures by the head, his staff or outside experts.

From such regular meetings to the development of a formal parent-teacher association is a relatively small step; and in a great many

European countries associations exist on a regional basis or in connexion with particular schools. The advantage of a formal association is that it makes initiatives by the parents themselves easier and, suitably constituted with a carefully defined field of activities, provides an organization which can give direct and material support to the school. Parent-teacher associations undertake money-raising activities to provide for such things as school expeditions and equipment which would not normally be supplied by the education authorities; they organize social activities, study groups, parent-teacher meetings of informal kinds and arrange for visiting lectures on special topics. More important however is the framework they give for parent education, for the creating of an informed public opinion on educational matters and for bringing parents and teachers, through working together and educating each other, to realize the significance of the social task of the school in its community.

There is a limit to what parents and teachers can achieve alone and a link should be established between the parent-teacher association, or the school, and the more specialized services and resources of the community. This should be a functional co-operation which ensures that research in child development, knowledge of social and medical welfare work, developments in educational technique and the like are harnessed to the practical and constructive task of improving the all-round education and upbringing of children. Ideally, members of the supporting services would themselves be active members of any association. The emphasis should be on normality, upon the everyday problems and upon ways of improving patterns of family and school education rather than upon maladjustments, subnormalities and psycho-therapeutic treatment. Hence the psychologists, social workers, specialized educators, school medical officers and others who may be called on to help, must train themselves in the difficult art of speaking directly and in non-threatening and non-authoritarian ways to parents and teachers in terms of daily life and experience rather than of the clinic or laboratory. Much can be done by the publication of pamphlets, by lectures and demonstrations, by newspaper articles, and by radio programmes if these are very carefully controlled and framed. Many parent-teacher associations seek and obtain help from university departments of education and psychology, from teacher training institutions, from school psychological and medical services, and from the vocational guidance bureaux, in arranging courses of talks which can then be followed up by discussions.

SCHOOL FOR PARENTS AND TEACHERS

An interesting initiative, which began in France in 1928 and which has spread widely throughout continental Europe, is the *École des parents et des éducateurs.* This has in the past decades given rise to an international federation of all kinds of organizations fostering parent teacher contacts and furthering the study of home-school problems. The forms taken within differing national traditions vary quite considerably but the general aims and activities are similar. National or local associations provide a full programme of lectures by educators, medical specialists and psychologists, on various aspects of the physical, mental, and, especially, the psychological development of children.[13] The lectures, supplemented by pamphlets[14] and illustrated folders[15] each bearing upon a concrete problem of development are published and made available to parents and teachers. As an essential corollary to this general dissemination of information, such organizations develop the small discussion group of parents under the guidance of a specialist and an individual service of psychological consultation open to parents and teachers.

SOME TECHNIQUES[16]

Properly developed and under the guidance of teachers who have been more adequately trained than is usual at present for this particular task, the parent-teacher association aided by other services, can perform a most valuable part in the mutual education of parents and of teachers; indeed the teaching staff are likely to draw as much profit from it as the parents themselves. Yet it will largely fail to fulfil the tasks earlier described if it concentrates its activities upon the provision of information acquired at a purely intellectual level. The transition from knowledge to spontaneous practice, from intellectual concepts to intuitive wisdom in handling the growth problems of children and still more in shaping their whole education towards the needs and conditions of the future, is difficult to make. Parents and teachers alike behave towards children more in terms of their own past experience, in terms of barely conscious fears, anxieties and wishes, than in terms of objective psychological insight. General information on child rearing and child development disseminated by lectures and pamphlets may, however carefully framed, do more harm than good if it merely raises doubts and uncertainties, if it undermines an already precarious security in family upbringing, without providing both parents and teachers with the capacity to respond spontaneously as well as correctly to the children in their charge.

The education and orientation of parents and teachers begins long before adulthood and depends more upon directed and analysed experience than upon factual information intellectually acquired. The little girl caring for a younger child is learning some of the responsibilities and joys of parenthood; and girls' secondary schools, as well as teaching the elements of cookery, housecraft and domestic economy, could arrange for their adolescent pupils to have some care of young children, even of babies, in the nearby nursery school or crèche. Nor should contact with young children be confined to girls; boys too can learn much about family life and their future rôle as fathers by taking part in similar activities.

In some research (financed by the Van Leer Foundation) on the problems of underprivileged children, at Mons in Belgium, assistants and students in pedagogy, as well as some adolescent girls have taken part in work with families, thus both giving and gaining advantage. The expectant or young mothers, in the maternity hospital or through the ante- and post-natal clinic[17] can be trained (and not merely instructed) in meeting the psychological needs of their children. In this, demonstration, free and frank discussion, carefully arranged experiences under skilled psychological guidance are worth more than lectures or than the rapid didactic consultation with a busy paediatrician not always well informed on psychological matters. One might mention here the highly successful experiment carried out with negro mothers by Constance Kamii.[18] Each week a trained worker visited the mothers to discuss the education of their children as a means of raising the levels of maternal psychological care even in very unfavourable circumstances. Similarly, in the West Riding of Yorkshire (England) trained social workers have regarded it as part of their task to teach mothers how to help their children to play.[19] The nursery school, with its relaxed atmosphere and its staff trained to put children's needs first can, by welcoming the participation of mothers and fathers, rouse questions in their minds and affect the handling not merely of one child at the school, but others in the family. Indeed it is hardly too much to say that parent education through participation should be as important for the nursery and primary school as is the care for young children.

The parent-teacher association provides the logical framework for a continuation of this process. We are still relatively ignorant of the techniques necessary to ensure that men and women from different social and educational levels will assimilate psychological knowledge and will modify their own attitudes, prejudices and behaviour to children. But it is becoming clear that one means to this end is the discussion group, which systematically explores, from both the home and school standpoints, concrete examples of child behaviour. Such groups should be small—from 8 to 12 persons as a maximum—informal and, as soon as possible, conducted in an atmosphere of complete frankness.[20] This atmosphere will develop only gradually as the participants work together and gain knowledge and security in their relations with each other. Much depends upon the skill with which such a group is initiated and conducted. The ideal is to have someone fully trained in psychology who can at the beginning suggest topics, act as a reference point and as leader, and who can delicately bring the group to understand something of the complex ways in which, consciously and unconsciously, people interact with each other. The fact that such skilled personnel are not available need not however prevent the development of such groups within parent-teacher associations. One member—usually, but not invariably, the teacher—might accept the task of choosing one or two topics for discussion, and of gathering the necessary information both on child development and, of almost equal importance, upon the psychology of small groups. Effective points of departure may be found too through carefully chosen films and filmstrips, especially those of the open-ended variety which lead dramatically up to a practical situation in parent-child, parent-teacher or teacher-child relationships, but break off before a solution is offered.[21] These have the advantage that they can be presented to a large audience which can then subdivide into small groups to continue an intimate discussion; and it is not beyond the resources of a school staff or parent-teacher association to produce such filmstrips themselves or to dramatize incidents of their everyday experience in the form of a radio play recorded on the tape- or wire-recording apparatus possessed by many schools.

Activities of this kind need very careful planning and handling; certainly, unless the leader is highly trained in the techniques of group dynamics, there should be no attempt at deep psychological interpretation or at formal therapeutic work. The most important aspect is that of providing a relaxed atmosphere in which—because the group is an accepting and understanding one—many different attitudes and the variety of human experience can be expressed without fear or excessive anxiety. For this, whether the leader is a trained psychologist, a teacher or a parent, it is important even in the initial stages that the leadership should not be too directive. The leader should be warmly accepting and reassuring, ready to serve the group with information and at times with advice; but the earliest opportunity should be seized of letting the group collectively develop and guide its own discussions, seeking outside itself, if necessary, for information and help.

Some parent-teacher associations have gone beyond this into what is rather pretentiously called psycho-drama or socio-drama. The essence of this technique is that incidents of adult-relationships or adult-child relationships are more or less spontaneously dramatized by parents and teachers themselves without an audience, and as a means of having, at first hand as it were, the emotional experience involved. Carefully handled and with a group which has passed beyond its initial self-consciousness, this can be a most formative and valuable technique. It can even be applied to the many problems of relations between adolescents and their families and teachers, with the direct participation of the adolescents themselves. A further development is for one group, having evolved and discussed a spontaneous drama of its own creation, to construct alternative endings to it and then to present the whole to an audience of parents for discussion.

The success of such techniques depends upon the readiness of participants to accept them, and this is in part a function of individual resistances and self-protective attitudes and in part of the cultural patterns of the particular national or social group. The more an activity penetrates in its effects to the emotional life, the more 'dangerous' is it likely to appear to the adult and the greater the resistance to be expected. In such matters the rule is to hasten slowly; tactfully to encourage the development of frank discussion, of socio-drama and the like rather than to impose them.

Meanwhile there are many other ways in which parents can be drawn into a participation which is something more than passively listening to a lecture. Every form of activity which tends to diminish the isolation of the individual family or parent or which brings teacher and parent together on a creative task contributes directly to mentally healthy living for the adult and thus, at least indirectly to that of the child. The principal need of many adults is for the outlet of doing something constructive, of joining in musical, craft or artistic activities with others, of learning how to learn, and discovering that excitement and satisfaction in a finished and complete product of which their daily lives rob them. The social and cultural activities of a good parent-teacher association therefore are as valuable as the directly educational ones, and may, indeed, by the relief and relaxation they bring, be the essential preliminary to more overtly educational work.[22]

THE FUTURE AND THE NEED

Two things must be stressed. What has been outlined above represents good practices found sporadically in various school systems. They are so little universal in any system, that they must be regarded as exceptional and as affecting only small minorities of children and parents. Even the initiatives described in Chapter 9 concerned with compensatory education for the underprivileged in Belgium, Holland, United Kingdom and the U.S.A., affect only selected groups and are more of the nature of pilot projects than integral and essential aspects of education systems.

Yet, in the light of the kinds of dilemmas education is facing and in terms of the need to ensure that every child has a reasonable chance of balanced social and emotional development as well as maximal educational growth, one is forced to ask the question as to whether what is achieved by the best schemes is sufficient. The recent history of compulsory education in Europe and in North America suggests that, while the early school years are more attractive to children than perhaps they used to be, more and more pupils, from early adolescence onwards, become unadjusted to school and reject what it has to offer. There are not wanting those who attribute this entirely to the schools and who advocate various forms of 'deschooling'[23] as if the withdrawal of all systematic study and any framework of expectations and discipline were the answer to a generation made insecure and to some extent anarchic by the lack of structure in home and community.[24] Others, no doubt with good intentions, perceiving that some schools are not ideal and that some structures are highly authoritarian, promulgate contestatory advice which is likely to set the inexperienced against any form of authority.[25]

There is little doubt that, in many of their aspects, the school systems of the world are in urgent need of change; and it is easy to point to ways in which they fail to meet the needs of a rapidly changing society. Almost every aspect of curriculum, method and organization needs some attention and reform; it is, too, increasingly illogical to think of education as something that necessarily takes place behind closed doors for ten years of childhood and adolescence, during which young-sters are cut off from the daily life of adults. It seems probable that authoritarian directive and paternalistic systems no longer meet con-temporary demands for a high degree of personal autonomy in the adult world.

However the problems and the difficulties, though they are felt most acutely by the schools, are by no means solely or even principally the fault of the schools. They arise from much deeper conflicts—for example from the changes in our notion of society.[26] Some wish to preserve, with suitable provision for merit and hard work to meet its just reward, the élitist concept in which the school and university, as trustees of a hier-archy of values in knowledge, operate as selectors and recruiting agents, classifying pupils and students according to their success in meeting certain criteria. Others wish to break up such a tradition entirely in the name of egalitarianism and open educational institutions to all forms of knowledge and experience, deliberately eschewing any aim of classifying either individuals or forms of knowledge in hierarchies of value or excellence. Under the first system reform would be concerned with the admission to the knowledge hierarchy of bodies of knowledge of con-temporary relevance and with an attempt to make the sorting process more humane, more sensitive, and by compensating for social disadvan-tage, more just. The second concept, in its extreme form, tends to do away with the school as a formal institution with an agreed curriculum. Those who advocate this, wish, in place of formal full-time school, to provide a structure whereby, at any point throughout life, any individual may be helped to learn whatever he wishes or finds it necessary to learn —without at any stage, any element of compulsion of fixed demands. In such a system the 'teachers' would, it is suggested, be men and women engaged in some other profession rather than professional pedagogues.

CRITERIA FOR CHANGE

In considering either of these extremes or any intermediate position, from our point of view, it is important to be clear about certain principles. As we have suggested earlier, satisfactory intellectual, social and emotional growth can only take place in an environment which is organized and predictable in its feedback to the child and adolescent; a disorganized and highly inconsistent environment will depress intellectual functioning and produce a personality in disarray. There are too some forms of thinking which are more adaptive and productive than others —for example, though both are necessary, abstract-symbolic reasoning is absolutely more valuable socially and personally than simple concrete perceptual manipulation—though their embodiment in say any particular form of scientific thought or aesthetic production may not be. Similarly, although their cognitive content may differ in any one case, there seem to be forms of public knowledge, ways of thinking about and analysing experience, with which all men should in some degree be equipped, and without any one of which individual autonomy is at least partially prejudiced.

A TRULY COMMUNITY SCHOOL

Whatever organizational or ideological reform is advocated, its likely effectiveness must be judged in relation at least to these criteria. Beyond them the choice strictly lies in terms of sets of social values and the forms and degree of indoctrination which they imply.

We may return now to make some rather more fundamental proposals about the relationship of the school to the homes of its pupils and to the community in general, remembering that, as was remarked earlier, the school is the only social organization which is potentially in touch with all children and their families for at least ten years and on the basis of normality. It thus occupies a key position in the community which could be exploited and developed. It is, first of all, itself an artificial community of adults and children existing in varying relations to each other. Being artificial, it is fairly readily manipulable and can take many forms, involving pupils and teachers in a variety of roles *vis à vis* each other. Its roles and aims can be made more or less explicit and relatively simply. Thus it can provide what for some children may be their only experience of a comprehensible community bound together by reciprocal duties, aims, roles and privileges. It can, through its age hierarchy, provide a progressive experience of increasing responsibility and autonomy and demonstrate how this is necessarily related to increasing knowledge and experience; it can show how participation implies involvement, a personal contribution, a willingness to sacrifice for the general good and, particularly, the inevitable necessity for effort to make one's contribution worth having. In this way it can provide an orderly apprenticeship to genuine democracy.

By itself, however, though valuable this is not enough. A principal problem for education is the large number of children who are disadvantaged, not so much by sheer material deprivation as by a home environment lacking in order and consistency as well as being linguistically and culturally impoverished. Although something can be done for such children by suitable programmes at the nursery and infant school stage, this is rarely enough nor are there special facilities in any country for all the children who need them. The crucial problem is that of helping parents, long before their children enter a school of any sort, to do a more consistent and effective educational job. A truly community school would be staffed and equipped to do this: to make contact, in conjunction with the health and social services, with the parents of children from their first year, interacting with them, supporting and training them, providing the means whereby mothers could meet together in the presence of some friendly outsider. So too valuable lessons could be learned and real help given by adolescent boys and girls learning about child care and the psychological development of children, about social work and general health protection, as a practical part of their studies in home economics, biology, human relations or elementary psychology.

This process can also be carried out in reverse as part of a general policy of integrating the school with the surrounding community. There are few parents who have not something to give and few indeed who will refuse to help when it is clear to them that what they do is valued and valuable. Many schools encourage parents to undertake jobs like building swimming pools or raising money for equipment. Some, increasingly many, invite outside adults to come and speak about their work. Valuable though this is, it is liable to be partial and insufficient. A much broader and more everyday participation between school and parents is what is needed. Much for example of what a teacher does could be as well, if not better, discharged by a kindly parent with an hour or two to spare. Hearing learners read, playing complex games which help children plan ahead and grasp rules, taking part in small discussion groups with adolescents, teaching aspects of special skills, helping to plan and conduct school visits, helping with preparation of materials, taking an out-of-school interest in children with particular problems, helping to run out-of-school clubs and leisure pursuits—these are only a few of the ways in which parents can be directly involved and by their involvement not only immensely contribute to the quality of the education given but themselves learn more about the education of their children and in an understanding and sympathetic way contribute to the development of the school's ethos.

COMMUNITY FOCUS

The aim, however, can and should go beyond this and stretch into a fully joint involvement by which the school becomes a community focus, making apparent to children, adolescents and parents an interlinked structure of human solidarity. Much of the social work, the provision of voluntary aid to the elderly, community social functions, adult education and leisure activities, youth work and the like could readily be brought together in conjunction with the school in such a way as to give it a truly human (and not bureaucratic) meaning; and in many communities such a focus would be the only neighbourhood group in existence. If it is genuinely co-operative, it can do much to reduce the isolation and alienation which are so marked a feature of our times.[27]

Manifestly such a conception implies changes in professional roles, in professional attitudes and correspondingly in professional training. What we are concerned with is breaking down the isolation of the school from the community—an isolation which exists in the minds of parents and of teachers—and from other community services which tend not to regard themselves as concerned with education, particularly the medical and social services.[28] It implies bringing into a clear working relationship services like the youth service, adult education, community development, health and child care, which at present in most countries tend to work in more or less of professional isolation.[29] This isolation is enhanced by the lack of common elements in training, by interprofessional rivalries and by separate services depending for their finance and administration on different (and often jealously separatist) departments of government.

TEACHER ROLES

For the school itself and the educational professions, it may mean a profound change. In most countries, the professional education of the teacher is relatively uniform and is directed to the task of instruction according to a fixed programme. Such specializations as there are, are concerned with traditional disciplines or newer subjects like physical education. From this and in somewhat belated response to urgent needs, one or two specialities—educational guidance, vocational guidance, remedial education, school psychology, for example—have developed. Nowhere has it been envisaged that even to discharge its conventional task in contemporary society, the school team should be made up on an interdisciplinary basis with staff trained in such areas as co-operation with parents, sensitive social work, the unobtrusive therapy which many young children and adolescents need, and in devising specific changes in curriculum and method to meet acute local social problems. Still less are staff—whether in the education service or in health and social welfare—trained in the skills and attitudes necessary to ensure the informal education of parents and the development of a co-operative, family and community-centred school of the kind suggested. The heads, of even large schools, are rarely trained in any way for their specific job; if they are to orchestrate a wide and interdisciplinary effort, they will have to be carefully selected for their human and intellectual qualities and educated in a very wide range of skills and knowledge, much of it outside the conventional preoccupations of education.

Though the kind and quality of staff are vital to the scheme, other things are needed. Many schools are somewhat dreary places with few amenities; practically none have been designed and built with other aims in mind than the 9 a.m. to 4 p.m. education of children. What is needed is either a centralized campus-type design (housing schools, adult and adolescent educational, vocational and leisure activities as well as social and medical services) or groupings of purpose-designed buildings disseminated through the community which they serve and linked by a common though professionally differentiated staff and administration.

COMPREHENSIVE SERVICES

The value of parent-teacher activity centred upon a community school has been dwelt on because potentially it can span the largest part of the developmental period of children and because it can typify the principle of co-operative effort to help the family to help itself, without robbing it of responsibilities and initiative. The same crucial principle of self-help and of the maintenance of parental responsibility should inform the educational activities of other agencies which aim to bring specialist help to parents or to the school. In an ideal system, as has been suggested, services of medical and social welfare, of educational, vocational and psychological guidance and of the supervision of young workers in industry, all increasingly seen to be necessary, would form an integral part of an embracing scheme along with other services which span the working life and retirement. Unfortunately, while many countries possess such services in wide variety, they are at present only too frequently unco-ordinated, partial in their action, and absorbed primarily in the individual case where something has gone wrong. Moreover the nature of the conceptions by which they have grown frequently leads such services to prefer to exercise responsibility exclusively themselves when in fact they could more profitably act as consultants and auxiliaries to parents or to teachers. They thus undermine with technical expertise a confidence which, by a more disseminated, co-operative and constructive educational function, they could be building up. If this is allowed to continue, and particularly if the services work in mutually exclusive compartments as they tend to do at present, the end results may well be worse than that of a policy of *laissez-faire*. Essentially, unless actual specialist treatment is involved, as in the case of a greatly disturbed or sick child, the specialized individual or service must remain the consultant or adviser to the parents and to the teacher. The aim must be to make it possible for the mother or father, for the schoolmaster or schoolmistress, to use effectively in their work the knowledge gained by the specialist of another kind;[30] and the primary aim of any service should be constructive and preventive, and only secondarily remedial.

Here we need to stress that the authorities should study ways of co-ordinating the various services. Through the joint training of staff, especially in educational work with parents and in interdisciplinary understanding and co-operation, efforts should be directed to ensuring that there is a comprehensive system working for the benefit of all children. In the educational field much could be done officially to stimulate and guide the establishment of parent-teacher associations or committees, to ensure that the training of teachers includes practical study both of the home and family life of children and of the methods of working with parents.[31] Parent and teacher representatives might be invited to take part in the determination of educational policies; and continuous research of a practical kind into the most important educational needs of the community and the results of current educational methods, should be promoted and financed.

High among the priorities should come the whole problem of how, in co-operation, school and home may lay the foundations for successful marriage and parenthood. Parents may make many mistakes in their handling without lasting damage to their children, if they remain affectionate, supporting and consistent. This, however, is just what many parents, without being 'problems', are not fully able to do; and the qualities necessary are those least easy to acquire late and in an intellectual manner. They are the mark of a fundamentally mature personality which has met and adjusted to the strains of its own development. Effective parent education is a lengthy and continuous process beginning long before adulthood, aimed at preparation for marriage and parenthood, helping the new father and mother to understand and to apply throughout the youth of their families and with a genuine spontaneity the intellectual knowledge which the science of child development is putting at our disposal.

What is, if anything, even more important is the preparation for parenthood of those children who come from disturbed or deprived families or whose home circumstances have become through illegitimacy, death or desertion, sufficiently abnormal as to suggest that they are not only maladjusted themselves but are likely as adults to found problem families. The most melancholy aspect of social and educational work is what may be called the cycle of deprivation—deprived parents producing deprived children who in their turn become parents who cannot give their children what they need. In such circumstances, whilst economic aid can improve physical circumstances and a policy of priority help to schools in deprived areas can belatedly do much to help the children, the cycle is unlikely to be effectively broken unless humane and skilful psychological support is given to the families throughout the growth of their children.

The last decades have seen an increasing amount of money, public and private, spent in Europe upon attempts to cure mental ill-health with greater and lesser success. There are child guidance clinics, psychiatric clinics, family service units, social welfare services and a host of similar organizations engaged in attempts to remedy ills which arise mainly from faulty relationships and tensions within the family. Normally little is done until a breakdown occurs. Then the cost to the community of one severely maladjusted person may well be very high indeed, not merely in terms of money and skilled time, but in terms of an expanding circle of self-perpetuating maladjustment and unhappiness. In all forms of social work and particularly where the healthy emotional and intellectual development of children is concerned, a ton of prevention costs less in the long run than an ounce of cure; and its dividends spread over the whole community. Preventive and constructive mental health work requires co-ordinated thinking by all those concerned with the family whether as administrators, architects, teachers, psychologists, medical practitioners, social planners or legislators. The healthy growth of a community cannot be secured by a few specific measures, nor by appointing a handful of experts. It requires, as well as the experts and facilities for the treatment of neurotic or maladjusted individuals, the realization in practice that every social measure has an implication for the life of the family and through the family for the development of the next generation of parents. Few countries indeed have attempted to organize and staff their psychological, social and educational services to do this on the scale which we know now to be necessary.

NOTES

1.   World Union of organizations for the Safeguard of Youth. *Psycho-social resources for families with a view to the adjustment of children and youth in rapidly changing societies.* Paris, 1969 [Opening Address by R. Lafon].

2.   Masse, N. Malnutrition infantile et retard du développement mental. *Science, progrès, découverte* (Paris), no. 3414, October 1969, p. 363–368 [plus supplement mimeographed 4 p. 1972—bibliography]. / Monkeberg, F. Desnutrición y comportamiento mental. *Revista de educación* (Santiago de Chile), núm. 30, septiembre 1970. / Eichenwald, H. F.; Fry, P. C. Nutrition and learning. *Science* (Washington, D.C.), vol. 163, February 1969, p. 644–648.

3.   Andry, R. G. Family participation and the use of psycho-social resources. In: World Union of Organizations for the Safeguard of Youth. Op. cit., p. 152.

4.   See: Chapter 10, p. 233.

5.   All that is said here has profound implications for the training and professional role of the teacher, and for the development of ancillary and consultative services among which the most important is the School Psychological Service. (See. Wall, W. D., ed. *Psychological services for schools*. Hamburg, Unesco Institute for Education, 1955; and volume II, Chapter 8, of the present work. See also: Pedley, F. A. *Education and social work*. Oxford, Pergamon Press, 1967.)

6.   For example: France, Holland and Norway.

7.   For example: Sweden, Switzerland (Zurich) United Kingdom. In Belgium, parents' committees in Poland see: Nalepiński, W. *Dziaalnść komitetów* Their federations are represented in a consultative body set up by the Ministry of Education. Moreover, the authorities encourage the formation, in each school, of management committees made up of representatives of the administration, the teaching staff, parents and students. In the United Kingdom, about 17 per cent of 7-year-old children in the National Child Development Study (1958) were in primary schools having formal parent-teacher associations; between 50 and 70 per cent., however, were in schools which held meetings for parents on educational matters (Davie, R. *The child, the school and the home*. London, British Association, 1970).

8.   See: Councils and their schools, II. *Planning* (Chicago), vol. XV, no. 288, 27 September 1948. For a description of a system which, as well as the usual activities in connexion with the school, also conducts child welfare clinics, an adult education centre, and a service of marriage and family guidance see: Sajón, R., *et al.* Organización y contenido de las escuelas para padres en América. Seminario regional interamericano sobre educación de los padres, 1°, San José, Costa Rica, Montevideo, Instituto Interamericano del Niño, 1970. For a description of the organization and activities of parents' committees in Poland see: Nalepiński, W. *Dziaalność komitetów rodzicielskich,* Warszawa, Panstwowe Zaklady Wydawnictw Szkolnych, 1967. See also: Forst, W. *Das Schulkind von sechs bis zehn.* Berlin, Volk and Wissen Volkseigener Verlag, 1966. / Ghiviriga̧, L.; Dulfu, M. *Sistemul activitătti scolii cu familia.* Bucureşti, Editura didactícă şi pedagogícă, 1963. / Svadkovskij, J. F. Family and school. *International review of education* (Hamburg), vol. XVI, pt. 3, 1970, p. 341–349. / Stern, H. H. *Parent education: an international survey.* Hull, University of Hull; Hamburg, Unesco Institute for Education, 1960 (Studies in education). The last-mentioned work gives a thorough general study of parent-teacher co-operation in Europe.

9.   There are those, both teachers and other adults, who encourage a militant hostility to schools in the name of liberty. Even the Schools Action Union (London), while some of what it claims in its journal, *Vanguard,* seems reasonable enough, has at times a deliberately provocative tone.

10. For an examination of the opinions of a group of teachers on parent-teacher co-operation see: Wall, W. D. The opinions of teachers on parent-teacher co-operation. *British journal of educational psychology* (London), vol. XVII, pt. II, June 1947. For example, whereas one teacher (on a BBC programme in 1969) said: 'I don't think that any system of education which in fact has to enlist the co-operation and sympathy of parents can possibly exist without the parents being in the classroom working alongside the teachers and children'; another, a few weeks later, described the movement for closer home-school links as 'a potential Frankenstein's monster, which could end with teachers losing control of their schools'. See also: United Kingdom. Central Advisory Council for Education. *Children and their primary schools.* London, HMSO, 1967 (Plowden Report).

11. Though, when skilful approaches are made, these are few. M. Young and P. McGeeney (*Learning begins at home.* London, Routledge & Kegan Paul, 1968) provide a detailed action study of an attempt by a junior school in a poor area to work with the parents of its children, and to overcome inarticulateness and hostility.

12. As in the *classes nouvelles* in France. In Geneva a course in modern mathematics is given for the parents of children in the *Cycle d'orientation* (first three years of secondary education) so that parents can understand both how education is changing and something of the demands made upon their children. It seems probable that co-operation on specific problems at particularly important points of a child's career—school entry, the introduction of new methods or curricula, changes in organization and the like —will both attract more parents and be more effective than more diffuse and generalized attempts at co-operation.

13. For example the 'Conférences de l'Ecole des parents' in Paris have included lectures under the four main headings 'L'adolescence', 'Psychologie du mariage', 'Quelques influences premières sur la formation du caractère' and 'L'enfant à l'école'.

14. For example: *L'esprit d'indépendance*; *L'enfant aîné*; *Les parents nerveux*; *La colère*; *Si vous vous séparez de votre enfant*.

15. For example: *Tournants dangereux*; *Paquet-de-nerfs*; *Un petit frère*; *Toto mouillait son lit*; or, from Geneva, *L'entrée a l'école est une étape importante*.

16. The following materials contain representative suggestions of a practical kind useful for parent-teacher activities and discussion: Drouineau, R. *Vade mecum à l'usage des organisations de cercles de famille.* Paris, Union nationale des APEL, 1944. / D'Evelyn, K. E. *Individual parent-teacher conferences.* New York, Teachers College, 1945. / McHose, E. *Family life education in school and community.* New York, Teachers' College, 1952. / National Congress of Parents and Teachers. *Study-discussion group techniques for parent education leaders.* Chicago, 1951. / Pumphrey, G. H. *Juniors: a book for junior school parent-teacher groups.* Edinburgh, Livingstone, 1950. / Taylor, K. W. *Parent co-operative nursery schools,* New York, Teachers' College, 1954 [especially Chapters XI and XII]. / Rogers, J. *Adults learning.* Harmondsworth, Penguin Books, 1971. / De Buena de Baibiene, M. J.; Garabaro, M. N. *Las cooperadoras escolares.* Buenos Aires, Ed. Victor Lerú, 1969. / Pepper, J. *The diary of two groups.* London, Council for Children's Welfare, 1972 [an excellent account of work with mothers of pre-school children but capable of extension up the age range]. / Ecole des parents et des educateurs. *Le guide des parents.* Paris, Larousse, 1955.

17. Partial and promising initiatives of this kind have been undertaken by the

Mutterschule, Winterthur (Switzerland), the Hôpital St Antoine, Paris, and Queen Elizabeth Hospital, Birmingham (England).

18. Kamii, Constance. Socio-economic class differences in the pre-school socialization practices of Negro mothers. 1965. Ph.D. diss., University of Michigan.

19. The 'Red House Project' of the West Riding County Council Local Education Authority, described in: Halsey, A. H. *Educational priority*. Vol. I. London, HMSO, 1972.

20. See: Bierer, J., ed. *Therapeutic social clubs*. London, Lewis, 1948. / Wall, W. D. Ecole et famille en Angleterre. *Ecole des parents* (Paris), no. 10, octobre 1953 (part two). / Anzieux, D.; Dinkmeyer, D. C.; Munro, J. J. *Group counselling: theory and practice*. New York, Peacock, 1971. / Cartwright, D.; Zander, A., eds. *Group dynamics*. 3rd ed. New York, Harper, 1972. See also note 16.

21. In the pre-school enrichment programmes, supported by the Van Leer Foundation at Liège, Mons and elsewhere in Belgium, experiments have been conducted by J. B. Pourtois in making colour slides of educational situations in a family. These he projects with a spoken commentary bringing out different parental attitudes for discussion.

22. Participation in decision making tends to result in positive changes in both the effective and instrumental behaviour of participants. Some studies show that parental involvement in the school enhances children's development and academic achievement. See: Lopate, C., *et al. Some effects of parent and community participation in public education*. New York, Columbia University Press, 1969.

23. The most controversial of these is of course I. Illich (*Deschooling society*. London, Clader & Boyars, 1971), but he was more constructively and thoughtfully preceded by P. Goodman (*Compulsory miseducation*. London, Penguin, 1971) and by the much more constructive work of Jules Henry (*Essays on education*. London, Penguin, 1971) first published in 1960. One of the best short replies to the de-schooler and to sentimentalizers of all kinds has been given by J. Barzun (Sense and nonsense. *The Times educational supplement* (London), 7 January 1972). A well documented discussion particularly of Silbermann's ideas (*Crisis in the classroom*. London, Random House, 1970) has been provided by I. Lister (American mistakes are being repeated here. *The Times educational supplement* (London), July 1971). A quite different movement beginning in some countries, notably in England, is that for 'free schools'. There is no one type of these nor is it easy to describe them in a phrase. In some cases they are rather like other 'progressive' schools, in others they aim to provide for troubled pupils. Some are recognized (and aided) by the local authorities, some are feepaying and some are charities. See news reports and articles by: Hill, B. *The Times educational supplement* (London), 28 July 1971. For an account of experience in American free school see: Dennison, C. *The lives of children*. London, Penguin, 1972.

24. A point very cogently made by J. Henry (Op. cit.).

25. See, for example: *The little red school book*, or 'The bust book', an anonymous article in *Children's rights* (London), June 1972.

26. Fisher, R.; Smith, W. R. *Schools in an age of crisis*. New York, Van Nostrand Reinholt, 1972.

27. Experiments are being conducted along these lines in the United Kingdom, for example, at Sutton-in-Ashfield, Nottinghamshire, at Netherley, Liverpool and, a rather older one, at Countesthorpe in Leicestershire.

28. In the United Kingdom experiments have been made with Family Advice Centres. See: Leissener, A. *Family advice services.* London, Longmans, 1967. / Leissner, A.; Herdman, A. M.; Davies, E. V. *Advice, guidance and assistance.* London, Longmans, 1972. The latter is a study of seven such centres set up in high-need areas by Local Authority Children's Social Departments. Their aim was and is preventive; and they seem to be highly successful in bringing about a good deal of self-help in deprived communities. Their weakness—and it is in the writer's view a grave one—is that they exist apart from that other powerful social agency, the school.

29. A sensitive and practical discussion of this from a psychiatric point of view is given by A. C. R. Skynner (The 'Minimum Sufficient Network'. *Social work today* (London), vol. 2, no. 4, 29 July 1972).

30. This raises the problem of confidentiality of information and of inter-professional confidence. Much progress is hindered by a defensive use of 'professional ethics'.

31. Some schools have social workers officially attached to them (for example, in Sweden and the United Kingdom), in others teacher-social workers are employed (for example, in the United Kingdom).

FURTHER READING

Bengtsson, A. *Adventure playgrounds.* London, Crosby Lockwood, 1972.

Dinnage, R.; Pringle, M. L. K. *Residential child care.* London, Longmans, 1967.

Fédération internationale des écoles de parents et d'éducateurs. Première Conférence, internationale, Bruxelles, 1965. *Transformation et difficultés actuelles des relations et de l'éducation familiales dans les différents pays.* Bruxelles, Ministère de l'education, 1965.

Goodman, P. *Compulsory miseducation.* London, Penguin, 1971.

Hardegger, J. A., ed. *Handbuch der Eeternbiudung* [Handbook of parent education]. Vols. I and II. Zürich, Benziger Verlag, 1966.

Henry, J. *Essays on education.* London, Penguin, 1971.

Illich, I. *Deschooling society.* London, Calder & Boyard, 1971.

————. *The celebration of awareness.* London, Calder & Boyards, 1971.

Klein, J. *Samples from English cultures.* Vols. I and II. London, Routledge & Kegan Paul, 1971.

Leisenner, A.; Hurdman, A.; Davies, E. *Family advice services.* London, Longmans, 1972.

Lopate, C., et al. *Some effects of parent and community participation in public education.* New York, Columbia University Press, 1969.

Myrdal, A.; Klein, V. *Women's two roles.* London, Routledge & Kegan Paul, 1971.

Osterrieth, P. *L'enfant et la famille.* Paris, Scarabée, 1957.

————. *Faire des adultes.* Bruxelles, Dessart, 1964.

Pedley, F. H., ed. *Educational and social work.* Oxford, Pergamon Press, 1967.

Shipman, M. D. *Education and modernisation.* London, Faber & Faber, 1971.

Stern, H. H. *Parent education: an international survey.* Hull, University of Hull; Hamburg, Unesco Institute for Education, 1960 (Studies in education).

Svadkovskij, I. F. Family and school. *International review of education* (Hamburg), vol. XVI, no. 3, 1970.

United Kingdom Central Advisory Council for Education. *Children and their primary schools.* London, HMSO, 1967.

Wall, W. D. *Psychological services for schools.* Hamburg, Unesco Institute for Education, 1956.

World Union of Organizations for the Safeguard of Youth. *Psycho-social resources for families with a view to the adjustment of children and youth in rapidly changing societies.* Paris, 1969.

Chapter eight

The education of the
pre-school child

A. THE NEEDS AND GROWTH TASKS OF THE CHILD UNDER SIX

Before considering the institutional provision made in Europe for children
under compulsory school age, it is useful to set out the ways in which
either the family or the pre-school educator can meet the needs of young
children. Certain aspects of this have been touched upon in general terms
in Chapter VI, more specifically as concerns the child under three.
Greater stress is laid in what follows upon the social and emotional
aspects of growth but we cannot neglect the important interactions
which these have with cognitive and linguistic growth both in stimulating
or inhibiting them and in their turn being affected by the growing power
of the child to understand what goes on around him and to communicate
with others. Few children nowadays enjoy the ideal circumstances of
growth in a large family, living in a spacious home with a garden and
presided over by an intelligent mother who has time and energy to spare
for the education of her children. In very many countries most are denied
even the supplementary opportunities of the nursery class or playgroup (a
description of the pre-school playgroup movement is given on pp. 166-7.
Parents however can, even where difficulties of space and time are great,
do much to ensure a balanced emotional and intellectual growth for
their children if they are helped to develop an insight into their needs,
and ingenuity in meeting them. Therefore in discussing the whole problem of pre-school education, the tasks of home and school, of mother
and nursery school teacher, have deliberately been juxtaposed, since
frequently the mother may have to fulfil as best she can both functions.
Moreover, even where the nursery school cares psychologically and
educationally for children entrusted to it, its full task is not discharged
unless it also accepts an active part in helping the parents to develop
their educative capacity.

SOCIALIZATION

From birth to the beginning of compulsory schooling at the age of five or six, the growing child has a great range of developmental tasks, emotional, intellectual and physical to accomplish if he is later fully to realize his own potentialities. Many, for example, crawling and walking, he achieves mainly by processes of physiological maturation; others, for example, learning to talk, take place under social stimulus as a result of maturation. Every aspect of his early growth, every developmental accomplishment is coloured by the attitudes of those around him. He may be assisted in his growth in a great variety of ways with correspondingly different effects upon his attitudes to himself and to others and upon the shaping of his subsequent life.

Thus there is an element of the social even in apparently maturational accomplishments. As human communities grow at once larger and less isolated, it becomes more essential that self-realization should take place within a framework which emphasizes the need to contribute to the life and development of society as a whole. Hence, the task which, from the viewpoint of society, is of the utmost importance is that of the beginnings of the socialization of the child's crude egotistic and aggressive impulses. From at least the age of two onwards he is normally able to speak and is therefore open to a much more intensive influence by adults and particularly by his mother; it is at her hands that his emotional education begins and he gets his fundamental education in moral behaviour, in co-operation with others, in how to share things and persons with younger and older brothers and sisters and with his parents.

Social and moral attitudes do not grow spontaneously from social interaction but are the results of education, especially of social experience in groups of children playing in the presence of a mother or nursery teacher who comments upon what takes place and acts, not merely to regulate conduct, but to interpret the moral norms of society. The child has to learn to respect the rights of others and to conform to exigencies which are often contrary to his egoistic desires. He should come steadily more and more and in increasingly complex ways to experience and discriminate between situations in which he must abandon or modify a desire of his own in order to conform to the life of a group and others where he must defend his own rights. He must too learn the crucially important lesson that interpersonal physical aggression is unacceptable as a means of resolving conflict although properly socialized aggressiveness is valuable.

The family provides the child with his first social group within which such give and take can take place and, if the family is a relatively complete one, a natural society providing many other experiences of hierarchic and of equalitarian relationships. As the child's experience expands, he comes into contact with other family groups, and with neighbouring children of nearly his own age; later still, wider and different communities are presented to him; the nursery or infant class, the primary school.

These latter, and particularly the primary school, are communities different from that of the family, less personal and intense in their relationships and with a greater emphasis on the relations between equals. The young child, however, cannot conceptualize a large group, even one as apparently little complex as a village or a suburb; but he can experience and come to understand direct relationships among a small band of friends or a class of some 10 or 15 others[1] of his own age and thence be introduced steadily to larger and larger units. It is in the context of such progressive experience, based first on the socialization he has learnt from his parents and brothers and sisters, that he will learn to orient himself more and more fully to others, lay the basis of a widening concept of himself in relation to society and develop moral attitudes and techniques which bring him into satisfying harmony with children and adults outside the tightly drawn family circle. Even a good home well equipped to satisfy many of the personal needs of a child, can only in exceptional circumstances and by much forethought and self-denial on the part of mother fully provide him with such a graded social experience; and the very intensity of the bonds which unite him to his family, even those which go beyond the immediate parents, has an element of exclusiveness which may contribute to raise interpersonal barriers rather than to lower them. If as an adolescent and adult, the child is to develop a capacity to form relationships graded from the intense love of another, through liking to what might be called 'affectionate indifference', it is important for him to experience a considerable range of such relationships even in early childhood. The danger inherent in the home centred family is that it cuts a child off from this experience until he liberates himself, if he ever does so, in the 'teens.

At the age of entry to nursery school (in most countries between 3 and 4 years) the child is still naturally egocentric and obeys almost completely his own impulses. In so far as his attitudes are social they are adult centred. Piaget's early work,[2] though to some extent reflecting the Montessori type of activity pursued by his subjects, has been confirmed by subsequent research.[3] Up to the age of 3 or thereabouts, the child—unless he himself is markedly mature and his early education has provided exceptional opportunities—is scarcely able to take part in co-operative play; solitary and parallel activities dominate all others. Around 3 years of age, however the social integration of the child normally begins to make marked progress, and during the following two or three years he comes to participate more and more frequently in associative and co-operative play, which has been found to reach a first peak, between the age of 5 and 7 years.[4]

Social behaviour, and the moral basis on which it rests, is, as has been pointed out, largely learned. In ideal circumstances and particularly where the child is a member of some sort of extended family in a community which provides opportunities for contacts with children outside the immediate group of brothers and sisters, such learning comes about more or less spontaneously, under the guidance of the mother and father. Where these opportunities are lacking, the nursery school and pre-school playgroup must play an important part in its development.[5] The mere contact of a child with age-mates affords numerous occasions for social learning. Hetzer, on the basis of qualitative studies of the social needs of different children, suggests that they be placed in different play groups according to which aspect of their social behaviour should be fostered. The nursery school teacher or parent may be even more positive. She can not only provide the opportunities but can actively assist the child in his development from egocentricity towards associative and co-operative activities, governed by freely accepted and understood common rules. Her comments and reactions to the social behaviour shown by children, the ways in which she encourages co-operation and self-sacrifice or settles disputes, her praise and blame, even the questions she poses, will train and regulate the behaviour of her charges.

In addition to the concrete and guided social experience which children gain by contact with each other under her guidance, she can help them to become familiar with all kinds of men and things which are foreign and strange. It has long formed part of good nursery—and primary—school practice to take children outside the confines of home or the school from time to time, interesting them in the activities of others, and to invite adults from outside. If there are foreigners in the locality, the teacher can try to bring them into friendly relationship with her children. In many modern communities recently there have been high rates of immigration. In the United Kingdom, West Indian, Pakistani and Indian families are common; in other parts of Europe, Algerians, migrant Italians and Spanish. Many areas of large cities are culturally and often ethnically mixed; and this provides an excellent opportunity for laying the foundations of mutual understanding, tolerance and respect.[6] Even where these conditions do not exist, quite young children by means of pictures and stories, may come to know how, for example, Eskimoes and Africans live and, by singing in their original languages, songs from other countries, come to see that different people use different words to say the same things. It is too much to say that international understanding in the full sense can be trained in the nursery school; but by making the strange familiar, the teacher can help to diminish the aggressive or fearful reactions which foreigners provoke and actively link the socialization of young children with the development of attitudes favourable to other peoples.[7] One should however insist that the fundamental contribution of the home and of the nursery school to international understanding consists, at this early stage, of building up the attitude of good will towards others. This is done not so much by learning about other peoples, as by learning good relationships to playmates.

SECURITY AND INDEPENDENCE

The child's social development however is not only the product of experience with others. The way must be paved for it by the progressive satisfaction of other needs. From the moment of birth, normal psychological progress implies an increasing differentiation of the self from its human and physical surroundings, a steadily fuller distinction between the world of external reality and the realm of fantasy, and a growing physical and emotional independence. None of these processes is completely accomplished before the end of adolescence, but they will be accomplished only partially, if at all, if the child's early growth does not favour them.

The gentle, loving, consistent and reasonable mother lays the foundations of her child's security, the very basis on which his independence is built. Throughout the first two or three years of his life, it is she in general who meets his needs and at the same time takes a large part in adapting him to reality, giving and withholding satisfactions. It is within the secure framework of her affection for him that he is able to assert his independence; it is she whom he imitates and of whom he feels an inseparable part; and it is against her that from time to time he shows opposition. If the child's relationship with his mother is free of anxiety and if his acceptance of the values of his family is healthy, his independence and opposition will be important factors in the growth of his personality and of his ability later to learn and form values of his own. Valentine[8] and others have shown how essential to subsequent character formation is the period of negativism which occurs normally around the age of 2 or 3. This oppositional tendency is likely to become extreme if the parents are over-indulgent or inconsistent; if they are over-rigid and dominating they may provoke rebellion or, by suppression, turn their children into cowards or nonentities. In a stable family most children find enough security and independence for their needs, enough to identify with, and to oppose, for their healthy emotional and intellectual growth. Many parents however need guidance in how to deal with such things as temper tantrums, disobedience, contradiction, refusal of food, and the like, which occur as normal manifestations of opposition and developmental stresses. They need to come to see, too, that much childish disobedience, for example, is simple forgetfulness or due to the child's inability to delay a response; that some selfishness or rudeness or bad manners is merely a phase of development, a sign of normal immaturity. This does not of course mean that they should merely accept or excuse such behaviour; but that they should learn to respond rather in terms of the child's developmental needs than of their own convenience or irritation.

WIDENING RELATIONSHIPS

The parent-child relationship is highly emotional; and everything in the child's life is coloured by it. It is important that as soon as possible his experience of relationships should be widened and the exclusive dependence on mother should be lessened. The little group of friends in someone else's garden or the more regular experience of the pre-school play group or the nursery school containing children who are not brothers and sisters and depending on an adult who is not mother is thus an important step nearer to a wider reality for the child who enters it. He is obliged to compare the new environment with what he meets at home. The only child or the spoilt child find themselves no longer the centre; they have to share the adult's attention with other children; they may receive what, for many only children at all events, is the first experience of 'disillusionment' in that, in the behaviour of other children, they find indifference or aggression and, in the fact that mother leaves them, what may be the first shock of psychological weaning from her exclusive care. For the mother too this may be a difficult experience. Many of the problems of adaptation of young children are due to the mother's inability to release them.[9]

The child's experience of groups outside the home should be more than a series of negatives, however necessary these may be in his adaptation to reality. The nursery class or pre-school playgroup offers the children a field of relationships different from those experienced at home, other kinds of interpersonal tensions and another experience in resolving them so as to bring themselves harmoniously into adjustment with others. Positively, the nursery class can continue and enlarge the mother's task of offering acceptable and happy compensations for the relinquishment of infantile expectations and desires. It fosters the natural drive to independence and gives the children in the person of the adult who is not mother but whom the children recognize as 'safe', someone whom they can 'love' and 'hate' less intensely than their parents. Thus it enriches and makes more real their system of personal relationships. By providing them with a greater variety of concrete experiences with material and with persons than is possible in the average home, the nursery school further leads children forward from the lawless world of their own fantasy into the realm where they realize that others, children and adults, have the same feelings and needs as they; they learn to empathize as the basis of insight into self and others; and they come slowly to see not only that the objective world is governed by laws of cause and effect independent of their own wishes and fears, but that others too have to learn to control their feelings and act in consistent ways.

INTELLECTUAL GROWTH

In young children, emotional, physical and social development go hand in hand with intellectual growth. The child who is insecure will not progress normally in his social development and may thus be held back intellectually. Conversely, as is evidenced by studies of children from institutions and lower economic groups,[10] retardation in intellectual acquirements, if not actual dulling of innate capacity, can be a consequence of a lack of stimulating experience and, through an imposed poverty of concepts and of words, in its turn inhibit social contacts.

The contributions of the home and the nursery school to the child's intellectual and emotional development should arise naturally out of the quality of the environment they provide rather than from any direct teaching such as may be given in primary or secondary schools. Nevertheless the mother or teacher should be aware how experience contributes to the child's intellectual growth and how, by what she offers and her own interventions, she may stimulate and guide, as well as follow and assist, the natural course of growth.[11]

Early cognitive growth, particularly in the prelanguage stage, is of course largely perceptual and sensori-motor but quite early—even before the child speaks for himself—the language of the parents is affecting development both through its cognitive categories and its emotional meanings. From the second year onward, language development and concept formation are closely interrelated and lie at the basis of intellectual development. The child takes terms and expressions from adult language, as he develops at least rudimentary concepts; on the other hand, adult language exercises, through its implicit content of viewpoints and categories, a strong influence on the child's concept formation.

Studies of genetic psychology stress that thought is interiorized and systematized action. The young child frequently must act out in play what the adult can think internally and the objective adult image of the world evolves out of the child's physical and sensory activity where attitude, movement, excitation and his seeking for experience and satisfactions are steadily brought into a closer and closer relationship to each other to form the basis of an expanding and steadily more and more verbalized series of concepts or ideas.[12] Activity and experience (and their emotional accompaniments) are therefore the very food of intellectual growth, and the task of the home and of the school is to provide both in variety.

Reflections of this kind led Maria Montessori[13] to design play material engaging the child in concrete activities to be executed in an isolated manner. However, this type of activity, commonly called functional play (Piaget, 'Jeu d'exercise';[14] Bühler, 'Funktionsübung'[15]) has been shown to make up only a part of the child's spontaneous play. Rôle play (called also 'symbolic' or 'imitative' play) is even more characteristic of pre-school children.[16] It consists in imitating typical real life situations, where father, mother, animals and naturally the children themselves play the main parts. Doll play is a most popular form of rôle play in many countries. Scenes and events taking place away from the house may be imitated also: playing 'train' or 'zoo' are good examples; and stories told by parents or teachers furnish further subjects for children's spontaneous dramatizations.

Properly guided, such activities markedly promote the intellectual development of children. In, for example, playing at 'washing-day' or 'postman', in joining in household tasks with mother, they acquire new concepts in the field of hygiene, money, transportation and the like. Such concept formation is matched by the learning of new words and expressions and an increase in vocabulary takes place. In order that the children may carry on such activities, home or school should be equipped not only with clay, painting materials and simple picture-books, but also with toys for housekeeping, dolls, locomotor toys, large floor blocks, old clothes and scraps of cloth for dressing up and other simple equipment for dramatic play.

Such activities are not of course purely cognitive; they provide release for the emotions, means of digesting conflicts and ways of playing in company, children are led to talk to each other and to communicate in other ways which help their understanding of self and others as well as of the physical world. In a study carried out by Van Alstyne,[17] certain materials appeared to have considerably more 'conversation value' than others. Doll play, blocks, etc., ranked high for the percentage of time that their use was accompanied by conversation. McCarthy[18] indeed makes the suggestion that attempts should be made to stimulate the linguistic development of children who are not naturally very talkative by interesting them in play materials which appear to be conducive to conversation; and, in an interesting series of experiments, Smilansky[19] shows how socio-dramatic play may considerably improve the linguistic functioning of disadvantaged children.

THE PART OF THE ADULT

What should be the function of the teacher or parent in these activities? Certainly to help organize and prepare the material needed for play and other forms of activity. But besides that, should it be her tendency to let children carry out their play of all kinds independently, or should she actively participate in it, even introducing ideas of her own, not spontaneously found by the children? Although for quite irrational reasons, some current educational thought fosters minimum adult participation, much experimental evidence tends to show that contact with grown-ups powerfully promotes the linguistic and intellectual development of the child.

McCarthy[20] found that children who associate chiefly with adults show marked linguistic acceleration. So do only children. At the opposite extreme, several researches show severe retardation in vocabulary development among children in institutions.[21] Furthermore, linguistic retardation is frequently found in young twins, who play mostly together and who may, in fact, develop a kind of jargon private to themselves and unintelligible to others.[22] The fact that their lag is generally reduced as they enter school points to a lack of stimulation in their early language development.[23]

From these findings, it seems reasonable to conclude that the adult should introduce into the children's activities ideas and forms of conduct that lead them beyond the patterns of behaviour that evolve out of their natural growth. As far as under-privileged children are concerned, the need of such active and conscious educational influence, usually by the teacher, is all too obvious.[24] Among children of more favoured social groups, the number of cases where a similar need exists is rapidly increasing. It is of course by no means implied that forms of activity be suggested that are totally unadapted to the child's developmental level or that they be introduced under heavy adult pressure. The teacher should simply do what good parents have always done: look forward to the next desirable stage of growth and guide the child in his search for more developed forms of action and thought. At the same time extremes should be avoided. There are games and activities in which the child has need of adult participation, stimulus and even direction; there are others, equally necessary, where adult interference disturbs the assimilative or other processes going on. The only child frequently suffers from a precocious development in some directions—particularly in language and, apparently, in judgement—through being too closely associated with adults and may later, having lacked the possibility to grow at his own pace and to consolidate his acquirements, regress to infantilisms he has not been allowed to outgrow. Generally, also, over-great association with adults means that the child has been deprived of the social experiences which he gains with his peers.

WORK ATTITUDE

Within the development of creative activities, the Viennese school of child psychology has been able to show certain trends of apparently wide generality and value in our culture. They pertain to what might be called the 'development of purposiveness' or of the 'work attitude'. Purposive behaviour can be defined as being governed, from the outset by a determinate objective, which the individual strives to attain in spite of obstacles and distractions. Normal progress in the development of such purposiveness is of high importance to the young child in our culture, for it is a determining factor in readiness to enter primary school and to accept more directive forms of teaching.

In her studies of the development of creative activities such as building with blocks, drawing, modelling with clay and using the 'Matador' construction material, Hetzer found what she took to be apparently genetic sequences which seemed to correspond to a law of development.[25] An initial stage was characterized by mere functional activity, the child being unconscious of the fact that his product might represent something. Later on, he would discover the resemblance of his product with some person or object after having completed it as a mere functional exercise ('it's a tower', 'it's a man'). During a third stage, he gave his product a meaning while he was working at it, still after some trait accidentally engendered. Only during a final stage was the child found to mention his intention of representing this or that before he set to work and to make definite efforts to attain his objective.[26]

This stage of purposiveness (*Werkherstellung*) was reached in all fields of creative activity studied by Hetzer by the age of 5 or 6 years, activity with constructional material being the last to become purposeful. From that time onward, children were observed to set themselves certain tasks and to struggle towards their solution. When they have reached this stage they are capable of the first simple forms of 'work' as opposed to play, and of the fulfilment of tasks set by the teacher. In respect, therefore, to the development of a work attitude, Hetzer considers them ready to enter primary school.[27]

Two conclusions concerning pre-school education whether at home or in the nursery school might be derived from these and similar studies of child development. Since the stage at which purposiveness is attained seems to be specific for each form of activity and to depend to some extent on the mastery of its particular problems, informed training in the use of crayons, pencils, colours and clay will probably foster the child's readiness for their more purposeful use in primary school. The good home or nursery school will also, as well as developing the child's vocabulary, provide him with pre-reading material and activities—pictures, books, words written on cards and associated with objects and the like—familiarity with which paves the way for more formal learning of reading skills later. In the third place, the adult should help to orient the child's development in the direction of purposeful work. Mother and teacher should gently encourage him from about the age of 4 to finish the piece of work that he has begun and help him to become conscious of his aim in the early stages. In the period immediately prior to entry to the primary school, children might frequently be asked to state their objective before they set to work on any task and they should from time to time be given certain jobs well within their reach, and become steadily more accustomed to working with a number of others on a given task, the completion of which is a collective responsibility. Care for pets and plants, involvement in domestic duties and the undertaking of regular responsibilities within the school or family have proved well suited to help children to develop some sense for the fulfilment of a task and of the beginnings, at any rate, of an idea that there are duties to be discharged in a spirit of service to others, independently of whether one wishes or not to do them.

PLAY AS A DEVELOPMENTAL MEDIUM

So far stress has been laid upon certain aspects and uses of play which have a direct and, to most teachers and parents, obvious value for the physical, intellectual and social development of young children. The part played by the teacher and parent in such play is more or less directive, providing situations and guiding the child's growth. Play, however, to the child is something deeper than this. Studies by psychologists of many schools have repeatedly shown, what the records of work with difficult or disturbed children confirm, that play as well as being an intellectual exercise, is a language of the emotional life and one of the principal means by which children bring fantasies into steadily closer relationships with causal reality and the objective world. If young children are observed closely in their play it will be seen that all aspects occur from time to time alone or in combination; but that, more even than spoken language, it is for the child a means of analysis and control of his own experience, feeling and thought.

A young child is easily made anxious; his latent fears of loss of love, loss of security, and his inner anxieties about his own strong and ambivalent feelings may quickly become overt and appear as either hostility or withdrawal or both. His wishes and desires come into conflict with environmental demands; his imaginative life holds fears and threats and anxieties which are the more terrifying for being secret and unexpressed. At such times play is for him a means of expressing concretely the chimeras of his mind. He is not primarily constructing or exercising; he is exteriorizing his emotions and literally using the only means at his disposal to think. Sometimes he plays out in detail situations which have moved him deeply or he seems to be trying to solve through dolls and teddy bears, problems in his relationships to others. His play may be both intellectual in the sense that he is learning and cathartic in the sense that he is purging his own emotions, unconsciously using a concrete means to the solution of his difficulties and to an understanding of himself and of his relationships to others.

During the recurrent periods of emotional conflict and corresponding behaviour disturbance which are a normal accompaniment of development, children have a special need for acceptance through an understanding relationship with adults. In a good home and in a good nursery school they are fundamentally acceptable to their parents and to their teacher when they are good and when bad, when well and when sick. They can rely on not being rejected. This is the cornerstone of the ability later to accept oneself and consequently others which is one of the main essentials of mental health. Play therefore is not merely to be tolerated but to be encouraged and welcomed. The good mother and the good teacher use the child's play to understand and help him almost intuitively in much the same way as the psychologist does. When, however, the child does not feel that he is loved, when he feels himself rejected or when the adults round him cannot accept the intensity and the reality to the child himself of the experience projected in play and where they react with distaste or aggression to the fears, desires and preoccupations of childhood, he may steadily play less and less until he is unable to accept help in the solution of his difficulties or even to play at all. When this occurs it is not only his affective development which is likely to be stunted but his cognitive growth as well.

Free play is the child's own expression of himself, whether it be the trivial filling of time or the language of his deepest wishes. Approval and understanding of his product—a picture, a construction from junk material, a climbing feat or a relationship with another child—means to him approval and acceptance of him as a person. According to the type of play, this acceptance may mean to him acceptance of him in all his 'goodness', in all his ambition to grow up and be able to do and to understand more and more things, or it may mean acceptance of him in all his 'badness' in the past. For example, a child beating up a teddy bear may dimly be indicating the evil thoughts towards his new baby brother which he either cannot or dare not directly express. The wise mother or teacher (though they may not fully understand this), by their acceptance of the play incident, by the remarks which they make and by the reassurance they give even while they say 'Poor Teddy—I shouldn't do that . . . it's not very nice', help the child to come nearer to real understanding of what is 'good' and what is 'bad'. Play of this type is often a child's way of testing his wishes and desires against adult norms and reactions and a means of learning through imagination what in reality he cannot and should not experience. The attitude and remarks of the adult therefore have great importance for him, in interpreting moral and social values and in commenting upon the adequacy of his learning and conceptual understanding.

The play of children after the earliest years is less and less frequently purely solitary. More and more they tend to play side by side or together; and to them, playing together often means among other things the sharing of a fantasy life. Through play they tell one another these fantasy truths; through being shared these intimate truths become realities, and fall into their true perspective, and the children become real people to one another. They use one another in their seeking to understand the external things around and in their efforts to understand their own experiences.

This assimilative and cathartic function of play is, from the point of view of constructive and preventive work for the healthy, emotional development of children, of great importance. It demands an environment rich in possibilities, in space, in objects and materials (not necessarily nor even desirably, elaborate toys) and, since imposed play is a task, at times at least an atmosphere of freedom in which the adult intervenes, if at all, only with interpretive or regulative comment. There are some adults, parents and teachers, who find it difficult to allow children to play freely: perhaps because they have not come to terms with the child in themselves and fear the fantasies which may be released; perhaps because they have an intense distaste for 'dirt'; or because they consider play a waste of time and are anxious for their children to work hard and get on. It is necessary therefore to urge that children—and not only children of nursery school age—need time and space to play freely. Even though space is at a premium in many homes and in not a few schools, at least a corner and ample time must be allowed.[28]

FAIRY TALES

Allied to the child's need to play out his problems and fantasies is his interest in fairy stories. Many elements of the folk and fairy tales including the cruel and sadistic elements, match the child's own inner worlds, and he can easily identify himself and his circumstances with the story as it is told—the good king and queen with the 'good' aspects of his father and mother; the cruel things done by the 'bad' people who are often giants or wild animals with the 'bad' side of his parents and with his own unregenerate wishes, and the way in which evil is overcome by the cleverness or cunning of the weak and harmless, with his own desire to be 'good' and powerful.[29]

One can readily observe in the responses of children to fairy tales, in their play and in their relations with their parents, a need to experiment with all kinds of different feelings not only of love and happiness but of fear, of terror, of anger and aggressiveness. It is only by experience that the little boy or girl can learn to control these emotions and recognize how far they are caused by things which will never really happen. In this way the fairy tale can be regarded at once as cathartic, and, skilfully used, as a means of aiding the child's adaptation to reality, helping him to distinguish fantasy from truth.

Nevertheless, fairy tales vividly told by adults at home or in the nursery school, sometimes arouse acute anxieties and phobias in certain children; and the danger is particularly acute if the adult telling the story uses it to express her own sadistic fantasies. Many of the folk tales contain elements which, however told, are gruesome, terrifying or sadistic. Some educators therefore would have them either heavily censored or completely banished from the home and nursery school.[30] We do not know, however, how each individual child reacts to various symbols and stimuli and it would be difficult to select an agreed list, though it is clearly necessary to exclude the obviously horrifying. When stories are told, in an atmosphere of security, by a beloved mother or by a teacher who is not herself carried away by the vividness and strength of her own fantasies, and when children are allowed to act out their feelings during and after the telling, fairy tales can be a valuable bridge between the somewhat primitive morality of the child's inner world and the more regulated morality expected of him both by his parents and in his kindergarten.[31] They may even be a useful counterpoise to the very rationalistic and 'hygienic' regime of some modern families and pre-schools. Good current practice, while it does not banish the fairy tale, includes in the stories read or told to children, tales about animals and about children which illustrate positive and optimistic attitudes towards others and towards life. Even in the pre-school stage, children can benefit from true or realistic stories of daily life[32] which serve as a basis for discussion between teacher or parent and the child, and from which the lessons drawn can be directly applied to life. They serve as the basis for a widening emotional and moral education, and of course help to foster the child's growth away from animistic and magical kinds of thinking characteristic of the pre-school period towards more rationally causal thinking. While even adults have need at times for make-believe, to invent stories and the like fantasy activity, the child, as he grows, becomes interested in causality and should pass from pre-causal explanations ('the river runs because it wants to go to the sea') to more objective ones. The educational problem is that of favouring causal scientific thinking without destroying fantasy and imagination,[33] and of showing that 'truth' may have many forms.

DEATH, BIRTH, SEX

In the pre-school period, for most children and for their parents and teachers, certain special difficulties may arise, on the handling of which much of the child's subsequent attitudes and healthy development depend. Sooner or later the child has experience of the death of someone in his environment; sooner or later questions occur to his mind about the mysteries of birth. To both these phenomena, adult attitudes are in general poverty-stricken, full of fears, ignorance and magical feelings and often heavily charged with guilt and anxiety. At first, at all events, the young child is spontaneous in his approach and free of such anxiety or guilt; he can often talk about birth and death much more freely than his parents and teachers, and indeed often shocks adults by his casualness.

Over the death, even of a much beloved person, children's grief is likely to be different from ours and they can express it with more sincerity. When asked incautiously whether he was sad about his granny's death, a four-year-old answered 'Yes—*very*—before dinner!'. So many things and people come over and pass beyond the child's limited horizon that he cannot suddenly be aware of the irrevocable nature of death.[34] The adult should try not to be shocked by this and to accept and respect the child's own way of coping and expressing his feeling.

So too with problems of birth and sex, it seems always better to answer the child's questions as they arise and to avoid imposing a mystery where the child sees none. Many experienced workers feel that adults should merely answer the child's questions without proffering more information than the child actually demands. Grown-ups often, however, by the very way in which they answer the child's first question, make it difficult for him to ask others; and it may seem therefore safer to give rather more information (for example about the father's role in procreation) than the child appears to be demanding because we can be sure that he will put aside, until he is ready to accept them, those parts of what we tell him which are not relevant to his needs.

A purely physiological explanation of sex divorced from the context of the parents' loving consideration, support and concern for each other and for their children, is quite insufficient and may even cause more anxiety than it allays. When for example the first child, before or after the birth of a sibling, asks about where it comes from, it is important to tell him not only the biological facts so far as he can grasp them, but

F*

that he too was carried for nine months by his mother and born of the parents' love: he may otherwise feel excluded.

In the home or the nursery school where children are encouraged to keep pet animals and still more in the country where the phenomena of sex, birth and death among domestic and wild birds and beasts are a daily commonplace, many questions are answered for children before they frame them and in a context unaccompanied by the intense and overwhelming emotion provoked by experiences in their own families. But children learn also from each other and gain ideas in such matters which are often fantastic or even terrifying—and this is more likely to be so amongst those who are deprived of the natural opportunities for observation.

Sex education is not solely a matter of providing natural opportunities to learn and of giving the right information at the right time. It is a part of the whole development of a child as a human being and later as husband or wife and as a parent. The relationships between father and mother, their attitudes towards others, their willingness to give their child the information he asks for, not only on sex but on other things, all shape his attitudes towards others. So too the mixing of boys and girls at work and at play helps each sex to understand that the other is different in certain characteristics but possesses a common humanity. Even information which comes late, after a child has achieved a garbled idea of sex and of the relationships between parents, has value as a corrective and as a means of attenuating shocks caused by premature or erroneous enlightenment. Children's first training in these matters and first questions come at home; and it is from mother and father that early education—good or bad—in intimate relationships between the sexes will come, whether they accept the task or shrink from it. Ideally the school should intervene only in a secondary role, supporting and enlarging the action in this as in other things begun by the family. In the current situation of ignorance and unhealthy attitudes among parents and in the community at large, however, the school may have to do more than this and attempt to help parents to answer their children's questions and even provide collectively or, preferably, individually the information that mother or father do not feel able to give.

Some teachers hold the view that they do not have the right to do this and that it is solely a matter for the parents. Two points should however be made. Many parents shrink from this duty and effectively leave it to chance companions—others feel themselves inadequately informed. It does seem important that children should get such potentially mystifying and disturbing information from someone they can trust and in a context which allows sane and balanced attitudes to develop. In this, home and school should work together by common agreement and teachers should be specifically trained to aid parents and children in this vital area of growth.

More disturbing to many adults than questions children ask about sex are the self-examination and sex play of pre-school children. Parents and sometimes teachers are apt to react with shock or angry moralizing. To the child, his behaviour may be exploratory, an expression of curiosity, or a source of comfort in loneliness or anxiety. The adult attitude most conducive to the child's sound mental development is not that of anxious suppression which can build up pervasive complexes of guilt, but that which accepts such phenomena as natural and gently diverts the child's attention to other preoccupations. The nursery class with its free atmosphere and casual opportunities permits this to happen naturally on the same level as many other forms of training.

In all the situations which arise in the development of children's ideas of sex, birth and death, the essential is to respect the child's personality, to create and maintain his confidence in his fundamental acceptability whatever he may do or ask, and to give answers to his questions which are truthful. Much harm may be done by the parent or teacher who gives an apparently immediately satisfying but ultimately untruthful reply to a child, or who adopts a hypocritical attitude to his behaviour. An even worse situation can arise where home and nursery school are not in accord in the replies which they give to children's questions or in their reactions to children's behaviour. The school cannot act alone or in contradiction to what is done at home without the risk of provoking in the child seriously conflicting attitudes; nor can it provide all the experiences which are necessary to sex education in its widest sense. On this as on other matters a full understanding and co-operation between the home and the school is essential.

EARLY RELIGIOUS EDUCATION

Much the same order of problems may arise in the early religious education of children and, as with other important aspects of the child's life, there should be as little conflict as possible of ultimate values and practices between home and school. There is nothing in current psychological findings about the requisites for healthy mental growth that is contrary to basic Christian teaching and indeed the three great virtues of faith, hope and love can be regarded as fundamental to healthy personality development.[35] And since the moral values of western Europe are still essentially Judaeo-Christian, the humanist education desired by parents, who are not religious believers, will have much in common, at this early stage, with the simple and non-abstract education in behaviour that would be favoured by believers.[56]

Great care must be taken, however, even while inducing a sense of right and wrong, not to make children feel unduly guilty (for example about sexual curiosity). Again certain of the Christian mysteries and symbols (especially that of the death of Christ, and many of the lives of the saints) should be introduced to the child in such a way that confidence and love, rather than perplexity and fear, take possession of his mind. A wrong emphasis can be deeply disturbing.[37] The crucial thing is the attitude of the adult. If, however fervent his own faith, the adult really respects the personality of the child, his immaturity, his imaginative suggestibility, his easily aroused anxiety and his need to be loved and forgiven, young children can get interest, reassurance and moral enlightenment from many of the stories of the Old and New Testaments. But moral education is more likely to proceed from imitation and from the acceptance of the values of their home and school than from precepts, and the question of the relative validity of spiritual and scientific or experimental truth is not likely to arise or be comprehended in the minds of pre-school children—or indeed much before adolescence.

DISCIPLINE[38]

Parents and teachers of pre-school children are daily faced with developmental changes and difficulties occurring in their young charges. The child's need to grow up, perhaps the most fundamental impulse in the whole of his being, is the one need that the adult cannot directly satisfy by reasoning, by argument, by physical care or by all the techniques and means at his disposal. Parents, teachers and adults generally can best help by being unobtrusive and tactful in their educational efforts and by frequently standing aside to let the child experiment alone in the exciting and dangerous business of living, intervening to help him interpret his experience in terms of social norms and attitudes and to save him when physical danger is clearly imminent.

Children do, however, need the support of adult authority, of a discipline imposed first as the framework of an orderly home life which compels by its law-abiding and regular fulfilment of physical needs; they need some few categoric and reasonable imperatives to set the boundaries to their own dangerous thoughts, impulses and desires; and they react with anxiety if such authority and order is withdrawn or is fluctuating and inconsistent. But authority, however consistent and rational, which is neutral or hostile provokes aggression and anxiety; many adults have a highly developed intellectual understanding of children, but, failing to feel respect and deep affection for them, they do more ultimate harm to their development than is done by a loving ignorance which is equally swift to punish and to give affection.

Nowhere is this more clearly shown than in the handling of many childish difficulties. The child's first 'lie', his occasional nightmares, his periods of regressive behaviour, the feeding difficulties that arise from time to time, outbursts of aggression and rebellion, his interest in the phenomena of his own body, his first 'theft', his jealousy of a sibling—all or any of these normal manifestations may become through unwise handling the centre of a disturbance which deflects temporarily or permanently his forward movement to maturity. Many parents and teachers, made unduly anxious by the popularizers of child psychology and particularly by the more extreme exponents of psychoanalysis, see in every temporary deviation from 'normality' the signs of neurosis; and they show horror, shock or anxiety which merely intensifies the child's own problems. We know altogether too little in a scientific way of the distribution of 'abnormalities' among children of any age and less still of the outcome in subsequent development of most of the commonly observed behaviour patterns of childhood, to be as certain as some are, that whenever a child shows deviations and difficulties in growth, psychotherapy is necessary. What, however, we do know is that human material is extraordinarily resilient and adaptable and that, given a stable and consistent home discipline, a rich variety of opportunity to play and a warm accepting atmosphere, all but a few children overcome by themselves the developmental stresses inherent in their drive to grow up. A primary requisite in parents and in teachers is confidence in children's capacity to work through their own difficulties. Teachers particularly must be at once sufficiently detached in their attitude to tolerate a wide range of difference among children in their growth patterns and yet have the ability to love children of many different kinds as human beings. This is particularly important in communities and schools which have migrant or immigrant families. Not only may children from these families have rather more than the normal stresses to undergo but familial and cultural patterns are likely to be different and arouse intergroup tensions. In such situations the attitudes of parents and teachers may be critical, both for the self-image of the immigrant children and for the general atmosphere of relations, whether of races or events or ways of life.

GROWTH AND ADJUSTMENT

For school and parents alike, it is important to grasp, and allow for, the dynamism of normal psychological growth. A child faced with a new demand—the birth, let us say, of a baby brother—may go forward to a new adjustment; or he may regress to an earlier form of behaviour. What in fact happens will greatly depend upon how the matter is handled and interpreted by adults. If in the case of the birth of a sibling, a child is prepared well beforehand to take an interest in the preparations for a new baby, to be ready to adopt the role of elder brother or sister, and to see that this is a step in growing up, he or she may well willingly accept also greater responsibility for certain aspects of his own life. Even so, the effort to adjust may be very great and for a time lead to a breakdown in other habits—he may wet the bed or betray his anxiety at a supposed loss of love in some other more or less unconscious bid for attention. Such phases, carefully and sympathetically handled are usually transitory and if mother, for example, sets aside a time specially for the first child, may be positively educative, increasing the child's subsequent ability to make satisfactory adjustments. Whenever a human being is faced with a demand that is difficult to meet or a renunciation that is difficult to make, there is a choice either to move forward and adapt to it or to regress to a mode of behaviour that was successful in the past. If the demand is greater than he can meet alone, then regression is almost certain unless he is helped; and all children and all adults at times seek refuge in their own past. A healthy environment does not avoid stress or difficult demands; it tries to see that these are adjusted to the child's ability to meet them in positive ways, provides support and ensures the maximum of forward movement, towards adaptation. The wise parent and teacher watch how a child copes with new situations, rarely asking of him more than he—in terms not of the hypothetical average child, but of his own peculiar history and endowment—can give. They are ready to support, praise and make easier his attempts to adapt; and they make him feel that they understand and tolerate his temporary regressions, helping him to learn how he may acceptably surmount them.

FIRST ENTRY TO SCHOOL[39]

The child's first entry to a group outside his family and especially to school whether it be a nursery school or the first-year primary class, may well be a critical challenge to his need to grow up. His experiences and reactions at the time may set the pattern of response to any subsequent change of environment. To him it often means the first lengthy separation from his mother and a consequent threat to his love for and dependence upon her. She too may view it with anxiety and may regard the teacher as a potential rival for the affections of her child. If, in such a situation the child is suddenly introduced into a nursery or infant school and left there or abandoned to the care of an unfamiliar neighbour, despite tears and cries, he may react with an apparent submission which cloaks a real rejection of his mother for deceiving him or he may succeed in literally making himself sick so that he has to be restored to his mother—often to her only half-concealed triumph. If the matter is left there, the child's subsequent ability to adapt to new situations, to wean himself psychologically from dependence on his mother, may be seriously impaired.

Such an example has been sketched to illustrate that the child can never be considered alone. He is always a child with a past which has left its impress upon him and he is always a child who has grown in relation to others with whom we have to reckon at every stage of his development. Children's growth imposes tasks and adaptations on their elders as well as upon the children themselves and this is nowhere more clearly seen than during such a period as entry to school. His acceptance of the new situation of leaving mother for three or four hours or longer each day will be conditioned by his reactions to previous attitudes of his mother and her handling of psychologically similar situations earlier in his life—by what happened when he was weaned from breast or bottle, by the way in which previous brief periods of absence from mother have been managed, by his experiences with other adults, the woman next door, visitors to his home and his visits to other children's homes. Around the age of 3 the normally developing child should have sufficient confidence in his mother's ultimate return to tolerate being left with someone else for several hours, and this tolerance is one of the criteria of readiness for entry to nursery school. Even so, the new faces, the new environment and the new adults may be too much if they are presented all at once. The child who has remained at home up to the age of 5 or 6 may experience similar problems in an even more complicated form on entering primary school. Hence the teacher should make every effort to get in touch with the home before the child comes to school, either, where the cultural pattern allows it, by a personal visit or by inviting mother and child to come and see round the school, perhaps to listen to a story, to join in a play group or to see some other aspects of the children's occupations. Some school systems produce simple, illustrated pamphlets[10] explaining to parents what the school tries to do and such pamphlets can be used by a skilful parent as a way of presenting the school to the child in advance and helping him to prepare himself for it. Another way is for the headmistress to call a special meeting of the parents of new children and talk to them informally about the school day, about what the teachers aim to do for the children and about the child's psychological preparation to take this major step forward from the shelter of his home into a wider and more impersonal world.

PARENT-TEACHER CONTACTS[41]

Not infrequently a child's entry to school brings about the first contact between parents and teachers. For many mothers, especially those from the poorer districts of large towns, the nursery or infant school teacher may well be the only trained worker with whom they have an informal contact and who has a sufficient knowledge of the needs and development of normal children to help them with the daily upbringing not only of the child at school but of younger siblings. The ability of the teacher to take advantage of the keen interest of the mother in her young child depends however on the teacher's humane competence in the psychological and physical care of children, on her knowledge of household management as it has practically to be applied in the homes from which the children come,[42] and upon her ability to build a friendly and co-operative relationship with the mothers. Her work with parents must be based on respect for them as parents, on an understanding acceptance of the values of their culture and a clear perception of the fact that the school and the teacher have as much to learn from mother and father about the individual child as they have to teach about children in general. The approach should from the outset be that of working together from different points of view, rather than a didactic offering of advice. Even young mothers in difficult circumstances who have most need of help do not readily accept it from a teacher, sometimes un-married, who, they think, cannot have their intimate experience of what it is like to have a child and what it is possible to do with limited space, time and money. This is even more difficult if teacher and parent come from different social or cultural groups. One of the most effective tech-niques is the small group of parents meeting with the teacher, herself well-trained in child psychology, to discuss freely their joint problems. In such a group the teacher plays her part along with the others on an equal footing and makes the distinctive contribution of one who is sufficiently detached and knowledgeable to lower the tension of the anxious and to put at the disposal of the group the best current thinking on child psychology and care. Where parents co-operate with the teach-ing staff on other matters and truly participate in the material and moral support of the school, such activity often arises spontaneously and can be guided into channels valuable to the parents and to their children.[43]

Clearly the possibilities and value of such co-operation as well as the most appropriate methods are a function both of the capacities and training of the teachers and the folk ways of the communities concerned. Their success depends in some degree upon how the teacher's role is viewed by society and what status is assigned to it. In part too parents' own attitudes towards school and teacher built up in their own child-hood come into play. What is immediately possible in say a Scandinavian country may not be equally practicable in French-speaking countries and vice versa. The essential objectives however remain the same. The unity of the child's world must at all costs be preserved. Not merely should home and school not be in open conflict: they should present the child with coherent and complementary experiences; and each in its several way should contribute to his growth and socialization. This implies that many methods which are objectively desirable from the viewpoint of child development may in fact have to be, temporarily at all events, modified if they do not accord with the local attitudes and traditions. For example, children from homes where the discipline is very strict and rigid, may not be able to tolerate a very permissive school atmosphere; similarly, the school may have, for the time, to accept that parents are not willing to let their children get as dirty as the teacher would wish to allow them to be. Most difficult of all for the teacher to handle sensitively is the clash which may arise between the uses of language in the home, the style of control and rearing and those which adjustment to the kinds of public knowledge, health practices and discipline necessitate even in a nursery or infant school. This is not to say that in everything the school should follow the standards set by the homes or vice-versa; it implies that the staff should make a direct contribution to the mental health of their community by winning the co-operation of the parents. This can be done by patiently explaining what they are trying to do and why they are trying to do it, and by inviting parents to contribute to and share in the living experience of adapting education to the real needs of children.

This conception of the social and mental health task of the nursery or infant school is one which many gladly, if unconsciously, accept. It throws on the teacher, however, and especially on the headmistress, responsibilities for which she is rarely adequately trained. Some of its implications for the selection, prior experience and the content of training of teachers have already been discussed and set forth elsewhere.[44] Here we need only reiterate that in industrial Europe, the school which begins the education of young children may make so fundamental a contribution to the mental health of the future citizens for whom it cares and be so effective an instrument in the smooth assimilation of techno-logical and social change, both by children and by parents, that no pains should be spared to attract the right type of teacher and no watertight administrative or professional compartments should prevent its drawing on all the available psychological, medical and social services that exist to help in the task.

B. PRE-SCHOOL PROVISION IN EUROPE

It seems clear from the preceding analysis, that even a good modern family may have difficulty in catering fully for all the social and psycho-logical needs of its children, at least from the age of three onwards to the time of entry to formal school. More and more the isolation and sometimes incompleteness of the family, its restricted living space and the urban or suburban environment in which it lives make it highly desirable to supplement home experience and care by some form of education which will give the space, the materials, the intellectual stimulation and the group of other children that the child needs. For those whose home environment is impoverished or disorganized to such an extent that their chances of reasonable intellectual and emotional development are gravely prejudiced, for those whose mothers have to be absent a great part of the day and indeed for any child whose home circumstances are sufficiently abnormal so that he does not get the chance to interact with caring adults and to play and explore freely, some sort of provision is an absolute essential—particularly if we wish the notion of equality of opportunity to have any real meaning.

The truth of this has always been apparent to many reformers like Macmillan and Montessori and in some countries, like France, pre-school institutions maintained by the State have a long history. During the last half century, with halts or even recessions in times of economic stress, there has been an over-all increase in most countries in the pro-portion of the age group catered for in pre-school institutions, partly in response to manifest social need and partly because parents themselves have come to see that guided experience outside the home is enriching for any child.

Yet the picture of organized pre-school provision in Europe is confused and the explicit and implicit aims of many institutions provid-ing day care for young children are conflicting. Nor is it clear which office of State—health, education. or social welfare—should take the lead and the main responsibility, with the differences which are implied in terms of the professional training and objectives of the staff concerned. Although it is true to say that so far as young children are concerned, health, social and educational services are tending to draw together and to see that the needs of young children and their families go well beyond the traditional limits of responsibility of any one of them, we still too often find that the emphasis of a given institution or service depends more upon its appartenance than upon what is really necessary to its clientèle; and that regulations frequently continue to exist which forbid or at least inhibit the kind of inter-professional collaboration which is necessary.

In many countries, the nursery school or kindergarten has grown out of the crèche or *garderie* and still retains, or is even dedicated by its function of social first-aid, children whose mothers are at work or who cannot look after them adequately in the pre-school years. In others, usually those economically more fortunate, the nursery school or kinder-garten is not mainly a social but an educational institution providing for children between the ages of 3 or 4 and the beginning of compulsory schooling, which may be as late as 7 years. In practice many pre-school institutions combine an educative function with that of physical and social protection, some as in France, having two separate staffs, one to conduct the relatively short daily period of pre-school education and the other to ensure the supervision and physical care of children from early in the morning until the end of the mothers' working day.

Though the distinction may perhaps be artificial in practice, it is necessary to point out that there is an essential difference in conception between the nursery, *garderie* or crèche and the nursery school, kindergarten or infant school proper. The first type of institution is custodial and concentrates primarily upon the physical care of very young children, often of babies under the age of 2; its intention may be only incidentally, if at all, educative and its staff rarely trained for an educational task. This is changing; an increasing awareness of the educational importance of the early years has led to a considerable enrichment of the environment of some *garderies* or crèches. There are, however, still too many which are conducted on the principle that very young children —especially if they talk little—can be left simply to amuse themselves under impersonal supervision with not much in the way of toys and practically no interaction with adults.

The second, the nursery school or kindergarten, originated in primarily educational aims and its intention is to provide an environment and a specially trained staff devoted to the psychological and educational needs of children in the immediately pre-compulsory school period, enriching and adding to, but not acting as a substitute for, the educational and the physical care properly given by the mother at home. As such it should occupy only a few hours daily of the waking time of the 3- to 6-year-old child. Indeed the best modern practice takes half-day attendance (2-$2\frac{1}{2}$ hours) as the norm. The extent to which the pre-school is forced to take over tasks not properly in its field will be a function of social and economic necessities which, ideally, should be handled at source by other means. Even the need for, the extent and the kind of the more purely educative activities of the pre-school is conditioned by the capacity—not solely economic—of the parents, and especially the mother, fully and understandingly to educate their children in the years before they enter primary school.

Basically therefore the crèche or *garderie* and the nursery school are different institutions with different purposes: they differ in the age group for which they propose to cater, their staffs tend to be differently trained and they are maintained by different arms of government. However, in many countries they overlap or exist side by side and, because of their differences, provide very different climates for their young charges.

A research by Pringle and Tanner[45] illustrates how differently such different arrangements effect the growth of young children. These workers studied two groups of children initially closely matched for age, sex, intelligence and social background. The one group attended nursery school for part of the day only and the other went to a residential day care nursery. There were of course substantial overlaps in the achievements of the two groups, but it was clear that the children attending the nursery school made markedly superior progress in linguistic development—in the use they made of verbal expression, in social intercourse, in vocabulary and in sentence structure.

Another study, this time of crèches for very young children in France, reported by Lézine[46] provides somewhat contradictory evidence. She draws a distinction between the time and effects of separation from the mother and the greater or lesser educational adequacy of the environment provided. She claims that any difficulties of adaptation are more likely to be shown at home than in the crèche and that adaptation to the crèche is better and easier for children before the sixth month and after the eighteenth. In the case of children between these ages, she suggests that entry should be restricted to those who are already highly adaptable. From her own work and from a sampling of populations of crèches in the Paris region conducted by Brunet and the psychologists of the Infant and Child Welfare Service she concludes that crèches conducted on sound psychological principles not only do little harm but may in fact have a direct prophylactic effect on the mental health of children.

Sjølund[47] analysed some 480 studies made between 1930 and 1968 in twelve or more countries of the effects of day-care institutions on children. He concluded that the effects—certainly the presence or absence of negative ones—are to a very large extent dependent upon the age of entry and upon the quality and type of the institution the child attends.

Although this evidence is to some extent conflicting, it draws attention to two very important things. The first of these has been touched upon in discussing the work of Burton White[48] who, in common with other workers, emphasizes the importance of the mother's style of child rearing in the period from around the sixth to the eighteenth month— the time when the child is moving more freely in his environment when speech is developing and when the child begins a somewhat negativistic phase. Separation at this point is very difficult for the child, as Lézine points out; and it certainly seems hazardous to disrupt the important learning processes which are going on. Hence, and this is the second point, if disruption is for some reason inevitable then any institution catering for such very young children cannot concentrate exclusively upon its health and custodial roles: it must be positively and sensitively educative.

In contradistinction to the later years of pre-school growth, it does seem better not to separate children under three from their mothers if this can be avoided and any measure which does this should be very carefully weighed from the point of view of the child's cognitive and personal development.[49] The effects may be deep and lasting and if they are not to be negative they require very special educational circumstances. In the *Kibbutzim* of Israel, for example, children, often soon after their birth, are confided to trained staff for a very substantial part of the day, if not for the whole of the day and night. But the contact with the parents at critical times—especially in the evening— is maintained and there is a strong general feeling of community. Such a system is said to result in personalities whose inner life is less elaborated but who are highly socially responsive.[50] Apparently too it does much to level out cognitive differences which otherwise might arise from cultural difference between homes. This would lead us to suppose that, if they are really well and sensitively run, even all-day crèches may be positive—as Brunet and Lézine suggest—particularly when children come from hopelessly deprived or disorganized environments.

But in a sense all that is being said is that the best should be made of a bad job. It certainly would seem important by social and industrial organization to preserve the possibility for women to choose freely between making home life and the care of children a career, having a full-time career outside the home or, during critical periods in the growth of their children, combining both in various flexible ways. We are far from having reached such a stage and many mothers of young children have no real choice: they have for economic reasons to be back at work soon after an infant's birth. The present arrangements in many countries which grant short periods of maternity leave—rarely more than six months and generally much less— should be extended so that it is possible without undue financial penalty for a mother to remain with her child for its first two years at least. If this is not the case, then the pre-school institution—and particularly the *garderie* or crèche— should be sited near enough to her work, and her working hours be so arranged, that she can be present with her child at such important times as meals and the beginning and end of sleep periods—thus effectively reducing the length of any separation to not more than an hour or two.

Unfortunately we are far from even this kind of arrangement. Many children and often those who are severely disadvantaged in other ways are separated from their mothers and placed with untrained child-minders or dumped in crèches which are at their best little more than hygienic baby parks. Nor for the most part do the services and the trained staff exist who, by interacting with the mothers and if necessary with the child-minders, could mitigate the deadening influence to which these children are exposed. Even in the most difficult circumstances a skilled worker,[51] frequently visiting the home, reinforcing and extending the mother's competence, helping her practically to meet the child's needs and generally bolstering the mother's sense that she can succeed, seems likely to be more effective and economically less expensive (particularly in the prevention of costly underfunctioning and maladjustment) than the elaborate provision of full-time day care for children under three.

It is also a form of social action different from that intended by the nursery school which caters for children from the age of three onwards. For many children in Europe, particularly those from crowded homes in large cities, but also for those from middle-class flats whose home circumstances may be physically excellent, the three or four hours daily experience at this age with a group of contemporaries in an atmosphere of calm and space is a necessary adjunct to ensure their healthy development. In few countries, however, is the provision adequate, partly because the need is not recognized and partly because this type of education is expensive in space, in staff and in equipment. It is difficult to obtain reliable estimates of the proportions of children between the ages of say 3 and 5 or 6 who attend such schools. In the last two decades, however, there has been an increasing recognition of the value of the nursery school as a constructive, educational institution as distinct from the function of social first aid. The most recent figures from Belgium, for example, suggest that 87 per cent of 3- to 4-year-olds, 95 per cent of 4- to 5-year olds and nearly 100 per cent of 5- to 6-year olds are provided for.[52] In England[53] all children aged 5 and onwards are compulsorily at school but the proportions provided for below that age are well below those for Belgium. The most usual average for developed countries is somewhere around 30 per cent—higher in heavily populated urban areas and lower in the more sparsely inhabited rural regions. Global figures conceal the fact that, in countries where full provision is not made, the available nursery school places in publicly-provided schools are usually allotted to those whose family circumstances make some form of day care imperative, or the schools themselves are sited in the poorer districts. On the other hand in many countries, privately organized and financed nursery schools and kindergartens receive the children of parents in good economic circumstances. For children whose circumstances are between these extremes and whose needs, though different, may be equally great, little or no public provision exists in many countries.[54]

PRE-SCHOOL PLAYGROUPS

Mention, however, should be made of a potentially very significant development principally in England but spreading elsewhere. Recognizing the value of even brief periods of experience with other children, groups of parents have banded themselves into the Pre-School Playgroups Association (P.P.A.). This movement is a co-operative of parents who, in village halls or even in private homes, organize playgroups of children under the supervision of a parent or paid helper. They club together to buy appropriate toys and equipment. Increasingly these groups have developed relationships with official nursery and infant schools and with the psychological services; education and health authorities have sometimes encouraged them by providing small subsidies and, what is more important, by appointing paid and expert advisers to help the volunteer mothers to train themselves for their delicate and important task.[55]

This movement, under whose auspices more than 7,000 playgroups (catering for about 200,000 children) are running in the United Kingdom, is important in two respects, quite apart from the direct provision which it makes on one or two half-days a week for the needs of young children. It brings mothers together outside their homes for various activities connected with the playgroups, thus reducing their isolation in a natural way. Even more important is it that the mothers come to realize their need for knowledge and skills in the bringing up of children and the provision for this in very informal and practical ways reduces their anxieties and increases the security with which they handle their own children.[56]

The important distinguishing feature of P.P.A. policy concerns the role of the expert in relation to the mothers. Such experts do not take over the educational task; their aim is to put their skills and knowledge at the service of the mothers in non-threatening ways: to help them to help themselves. The improvement of mothering is regarded as being of as much importance as the direct provision for children.[57]

CONCLUSION

The evidence concerning the vital importance to subsequent growth of the pre-school period is growing. What is more, studies of all kinds, and notably those cited in this chapter, are increasingly leading us to see an important distinction between two main periods—the second year of life and the period from age 3 to school entry—when the needs of the child are different and which bear differently upon subsequent growth. The second half of the first year and the second year itself is a period when the child emerges from the cocoon of undemanding care and comes into contact and conflict with his human and material environment; and at the same time he has a greater and less predictable interaction with his mother. On the way in which she handles these contacts—verbally, affectively and physically—the general growth of his competence will depend. And, as we have seen, it is also a period when, if a child is separated from his mother, he is particularly vulnerable to disturbance.

From 3 years of age onward, most children are not only better able to accept short periods of separation but have need of wider and more differentiated social contacts, particularly with other children, than mothers can normally provide. Though still, of course, highly vulnerable, their means of communication of their needs and feelings are more adequate, their understanding more developed and they have learned ways of coping with many of their anxieties and problems.

Two things seem clearly to emerge and have a bearing upon social policy. Day care, and particularly full-time day care for children under 2 is a makeshift at the best; at the worst a menace to mental health. If it is necessary, then the adults put in charge of such young children must be very carefully trained and supervised; but in many more cases of social difficulty than we realize at present, a domiciliary service aimed to help mothers to cope and to understand, to recognize the importance to their child's future of the coping styles he acquires in the family seems likely to be a more effective measure than does separation. On the other hand for many more children aged 3 or older and probably for the majority of 4-year-olds, some kind of educative group, nursery school or pre-school play-group, outside the home and away from mother seems highly desirable.

Properly organised, pre-school services of various kinds offer another opportunity—that of the early detection of children, who through physical, social or emotional handicap are deviating in their development, soon enough one would hope for remedial action to have the maximum likelihood of success with the minimum of means. Few maternal and child-health services and few educational ones are as yet equipped to do this adequately and all but the grosser handicaps tend not to be detected until the time of compulsory school—if then.

More positive but more delicate is the action which becomes possible to help families and their children break out of the cycle of deprivation and inadequacy which one finds in many European social and ethnic groups so far as to take advantage of education and raise their whole level of functioning. Educational and social equality and the hope of general human progress have their roots in this very early time of life when, paradoxically, only too often the family is alone and without the means or the knowledge to do what every parent aspires to do for his children.

A word of caution is perhaps also in order. Our knowledge of child development is certainly enough to tell us somewhat better ways of handling these early years and why things go wrong. We are much less certain of how we can intervene positively to make them go better in terms of future adjustment than they do in the best circumstances now. Any rearing style that we use seems very likely not only to have immediate effects but to reverberate all along subsequent growth. What therefore we need are more, and more detailed, action studies of this early formative period of growth coupled with long-term follow through studies of the outcome in adolescence and adult life of different ways of upbringing. These we are only likely to get within the framework of good and well organized interdisciplinary services for the family.

Finally it should be reiterated that, however we organize such services and with whatever social or educational aim in view, the central, primary and most influential worker in them is the mother.

It is to raising the level and improving the quality of the care she gives to her infant that the efforts of social, medical, psychological and educational services should be dedicated.

NOTES

1. The class of 40 or even 60 children in a nursery school makes nonsense of pre-school education as a means of social training for the 3- or 4-year-old. In European schools, the average teacher-child ratio seems to vary between 1 teacher to 59 children and 1 to 18. In many countries, though one fully trained nursery school teacher may have 30 or more children under her charge, she is assisted by nursery helps or by parents who voluntarily undertake some of the tasks of supervision—an excellent way of conducting the informal education of mothers (see Chapter 7, pp. 121–125.

2. Piaget, J. *Le langage et la pensée chez l'enfant.* Neuchâtel, Delachaux & Niestlé, 1924. / Idem. *Le jugement et la raisonnement chez l'enfant.* Neuchâtel, Delachaux & Niestlé, 1924. / Idem. *Le jugement moral chez l'enfant.* Paris, Alcan, 1932.

3. Stern, C.; Stern, W. *Die Kindersprache.* 4. Aufl. Leipzig, J. A. Barth, 1928. / Isaacs, S. *Social development in young children.* London, Routledge, 1933. / Idem. *Intellectual growth in young children.* 1930. / Hoffman, L. W.; Hoffman, M. L., eds. *Review of child development research.* New York, Russell Sage Foundation, 1966 (see paper by S. Ervan-Tripp, 'Language development', especially p. 81 ff). / Lunzer, E. *Recent studies in Britain based on the work of Jean Piaget.* Slough, Bucks., National Foundation for Educational Research, 1960. / Lewis, M. N. *Language, thought and personality.* London, Harrap, 1963 [especially pt. I, 4, and pt. II, 11]. / Russell, D. H. *Children's thinking.* London, Ginn, 1956. / Wallace, J. G. *Concept growth and the education of the child.* Slough, Bucks., National Foundation for Educational Research, 1965 [especially chapter 8]. / Gille, A.; Muylaert, J. *L'étude du langage de l'enfant en âge préscolaire.* Louvain, Vander, 1970.

4. See, for example: Reymond-Rivier, B. *Le développement social de l'enfant.* Bruxelles, Dessart, 1965. / Garrison, K. C.; Kingston, A. J.; Bernard, H. W. *The psychology of childhood.* London, Staples Press, 1968.

5. A study of 500 nursery school teachers in the United Kingdom finds that they regard the broad aims of nursery education as being essentially social, helping children to make stable relationships, encouraging responsibility, self-confidence and self-control and consideration for others. They also appear to reject a more directive cognitive approach. (Taylor, P.; Ashton, P. *A study of nursery education.* London, Evans, Methuen, 1972.)

6. In the United Kingdom there is a small number of multi-racial playgrounds supported by the Save the Children Fund.

7. In France very considerable efforts have been made along these lines in the official *écoles maternelles* using films, models, etc. For illuminating empirical studies of the development of children's ideas of their own and other countries, see: Piaget, J.; Weil, A. Le développement chez l'enfant de l'idée de patrie et des relations avec l'étranger. *Revenue internationale des sciences sociales* (Paris), vol. 3, no. 3, p. 605–621, 1951. / Stevenson, H. W.; Stewart, E. L. A developmental study of racial awareness in young children. *Child development* (Chicago), no. 29, 1958. / Weinshem, E. A. Development of the concept of flag and the sense of national identity. *Child development* (Chicago), no. 28, 1957. / Veness, T.; Norburn, V. *Ethnic awareness in young children* [in the press].

8. Valentine, C. W. *Psychology of early childhood.* London, Methuen, 1942. / Idem. *The difficult child and the problem of discipline.* 5th ed. London, Methuen, 1950.

9. In a recent longitudinal study (Davie, R.; Butler, N.; Goldstein, H. *From birth to seven.* Longmans, London, 1972), it is reported that 6 per cent of children of 5 had not settled in their infants schools even after 3 months. About 9 per cent of those who had not been to a nursery school were reported as not having settled down after 3 months.

10. This is a field to which a great deal of research has been devoted, particularly since 1945. The paper by Reuchlin cited on p. 108 Note 14 gives an excellent survey of the whole topic of socio-economic differences. An important volume of research reports and attempts to suggest applications of our knowledge to current problems is: Pringle, M. L. K. *Deprivation and education.* London, Longmans, 1971. On long term effects of early deprivation see: Skeels, H. M., et al. *A study of environmental stimulation: an orphanage pre-school project.* Iowa City, 1938 (University of Iowa Studies in Child Welfare, no. 4). / Skodak, M.; Skeels, H. M. A follow-up study of children in adoptive homes. *Journal of genetic psychology* (Provincetown, Mass.), vol. 66, 1945, p. 21–58. / Idem. A final follow-up of 100 adoptive children. *Journal of genetic psychology* (Provincetown, Mass.), vol. 75, 1959, p. 85–125. / Skeels, H. M. Adult status of children with contrasting early life experiences—a follow-up study. *Monograph of the Society for Research in Child Development* (Chicago), no. 105, 1966. It is important to remember that deprivation of experiences or of language can occur in any social class; and that some of what seems to the naive observer to be deprivation is in fact the result of cultural difference rather than deprivation (see: Chapter 6, p. 93ff. and Chapter 9, pp. 180–181).

11. See the useful 'how to do it' book: Dickinson, S., ed. *Mother's help.* London, Collins, 1972.

12. Bühler, C. *Kindheit und Jugend.* 3. Aufl. Leipzig, Hirzel, 1931. / Bühler, K. *Die geistige Entwicklung des Kindes.* 5. Aufl. Jena, 1922. / Hansen, W. *Die Entwicklung des kindlichen Weltbildes.* München, Kösel u. Puslet, 1938 and 1949. p. 72–99, 235–63. / Hetzer, H.; Reindorf, B. Sprachentwicklung und soziales Milieu. *Zeitschrift für angewandte Psychologie und Charakterkunde* (Leipzig), 1928. / Kroh, O. Über die intellektuelle Entwicklung der reifenden Jugend. *Zeitschrift für pädagogische Psychologie und Jugendkunde* (Berlin), Bd. 29, 1928, p. 10–34. / Piaget, J. *La psychologie de l'intelligence.* Paris, A. Colin, 1947. Wallon, H. *Les origines de la pensée chez l'enfant.* Paris, Presses universitaires de France, 1945. 2 v. / Brunet, O. Genèse de l'intelli-

gence chez des enfants de trois milieux différents. *Enfance* (Paris), vol. 1, 1956. See also: the perspicuous theoretical essay by: Bernstein, B. *Class codes and control.* Vol. I: *Theoretical studies towards a sociology of language.* London, Routledge & Kegan Paul, 1971 [Chapter 10: A critique of the concept of compensatory education].

13. Montessori, M. *Autoeducazione nelle scuole elementari.* 3a ed. Rome, E. Loescher, 1916. / Idem. *The absorbent mind,* Wheaton, Ill., Theosophical Press, 1949.

14. Piaget, J. *La formation du symbole chez l'enfant.* Neuchâtel, Delachaux & Niestlé, 1945. / Château, J. *Le réel et l'imaginaire dans le jeu de l'enfant.* Paris, Vrim, 1946.

15. Bühler, C. Op. cit.

16. The playing of different roles or the imitation of different persons immediately in the environment has been reported by most observers of young children. Piaget (op. cit.) has subjected it to a most thorough analysis.

17. Van Alstyne, D. *The environment of three-year-old children: factors related to intelligence and vocabulary tests.* New York, Teachers College, 1929 (Contributions to education, no. 366).

18. McCarthy, D. Language development in children. In: Carmichael, L., ed. *Manual of child psychology.* London, Chapman and Hall, 1946. p. 563.

19. Smilansky, Sara M. *The effects of socio-dramatic play on disadvantaged pre-school children.* New York, Wiley & Sons, 1968.

20. McCarthy, D. *The language development of the pre-school child.* Minneapolis, University of Minnesota Press, 1930.

21. See: Notes 2 and 3 (especially Piaget, Ervan-Tripp and Lewis); and also note 14.

22. Lézine, I. *Enfance* (Paris), vol. 1, janvier-février 1951.

23. Davis, E. A. *Development of linguistic skill in twins, singletons with siblings, and only children from age five to ten years.* Minneapolis, University of Minnesota Press, 1937 (Institute of Child Welfare monograph series, no. 14).

24. Smilansky, S. M. Op. cit.

25. Hetzer, H. Die symbolische Darstellung in der frühen Kindheit. *Wiener Arbeiten zur pädagogischen Psychologie,* No. 3, 1926. / Idem. *Kind und Schaffen: Experimente über konstruktive Betätigung.* Jena, 1931 (Quellen und Studien zur Jugendkunde). (The 'Matador' material consists of perforated boards and discs that can be joined by means of small sticks that fit the holes.) These stages correspond in general to those described by G. H. Luquet (*Le dessin enfantin.* Nouvelle ed. pas G. Depouiles, Neuchâtel, Delachaux & Niestlé, 1967) in his study of children's drawings.

26. It is to be asked, however, whether such purposiveness or work attitude is a cultural artefact, an imposed ideal of our culture and not a genetically determined or purely maturational process. In certain African groups for example it does not appear to develop. If this is indeed the case, then the function of parent and teacher in fostering it may be all important.

27. Hetzer, H. Op. cit.

28. On the general topic of play see: Château, J. *L'enfant et le jeu.* Paris, Scarabée, 1967. / Hartley, R. E.; Frank, L. K.; Goldenson, R. M. *Understanding children's play.* New York, Columbia University Press, 1952. / Cass, J. E. *The significance of children's play.* London, Batsford, 1971.

29. Gerstil, Q. *Die Brüder Grimm als Erzieher.* München, Ehrenwirth Verlag, 1964.

30. As *was* the case for example in the U.S.S.R., see: Nečaeva, V. G. *Trudevoe vospitanie v detskom sadu.* Moskva, Prosveščenie, 1964.
81. The writer's own children delighted in the experience of being able to choose alternative endings (happy and sad) to stories such as Hansel and Gretel, modifying their subsequent play acordingly.
32. This should mean daily life as the child knows it. There is a tendency—because teachers may come from a particular social group—to present *all* children with stories about more or less middle class families which are just as strange to them as a tale from a Persian garden. The important thing is variety and contrast in the realistic stories chosen.
33. Laurendeau, M.; Pinard, A. *La pensée causale chez l'enfant.* Paris, Presses universitaires de France, 1962. / Piaget, J. *La représentation du monde chez l'enfant.* Paris, Presses universitaires de France, 1936, 1947. / Idem. *La causalité physique chez l'enfant.* Paris, Félix Alcan, 1927.
34. A quite different difficulty arises when the child—usually the young adolescent—realizes the irrevocability of death in relation to himself.
35. Difficulties do however arise with any religious teaching which teaches that sex activity is sinful, which relegates women to a secondary place, or worse still thinks of them as the 'devil's instrument'. One has to remember that, historically, many religions have such ideas enshrined in their early mythology and in their dogmatic theology. Hence some of the stories—in the Bible for instance—implicitly or explicitly promulgate very different value systems, attitudes or forms of behaviour from those now current. In such cases, the educator's task is rather similar to that with any other story—that of commenting on the bearing of the tale on human relations and of pointing out that as times change so do attitudes and moral positions.
36. That such a common humanism exists and is a sound basis for education is the position of the State school system in France and other countries. Religious groups of various persuasions would go much further. See: Miehle, A. Die kindliche Religiosität. *Akademie gemeinnütziger Wissenschaften zu Erfurt, Abteilung für Erziehungswissenschaft und Jugendkunde.* Erfurt, Stenger, 1928° Pfliegler, M. *Der rechte Augenblick.* Wien, Herder, 1942. / Idem. *Der Religionsunterricht.* Bd. II. Innsbruck, Tyrolia Verlag, 1935. A solidly based psychological examination of religious education is given by: Goldman, R. *Readiness for religion.* London, Routledge & Kegan Paul, 1964.
37. Evidence given by the Catholic Child Bureau to the 1952 Regional Conference.
38. See also: Chapter 10, p. 206 ff.
39. See also: Chapter 11, p. 251 ff.
40. For example the schools of Geneva have such a simply reproduced document.
41. See also: Chapter 7.
42. In a recent study in the United Kingdom it was found that 20 per cent of children in Social Class V (unskilled manual) had no bathroom at home, 24 per cent of children lived in a family which had no exclusive use of an indoor lavatory, 12 per cent of English children and 39 per cent of Scottish children were living in overcrowded conditions—an over-all 15 per cent of children in the United Kingdom. It was also found that young children (7 and under) were more likely to be living in overcrowded conditions than older ones. This must mean, apart altogether from the direct effects such conditions have upon the mother's capacity to organize an effective and re-

laxed environment for her children, that such children are made aware, by advertisements, television, their own school books and the like that they are deprived and different from others. This research showed that children from overcrowded homes are retarded, compared with others, by 9 months in reading at age 7, i.e. after 2 years of schooling. A similar effect is seen in social adjustment. One must remember that these conditions of lack of amenity and overcrowding whilst serious enough would be even more marked in countries not at the stage of relative wealth of the United Kingdom. (Wedge, P.; Perzing, J. Housing conditions and their relationships to educational performance and social adjustment in 7-year-old children. Paper to the British Association, Section N. Sociology, 1970. / Davie, R.; Butler, N.; Goldstein, H. Op. cit.).

43. Such a technique has been developed with success at the United Nations Nursery School, Paris. In the United States, Parent Cooperative Nursery Schools have a history dating back to the 1930s (Taylor, K. W. *Parent Cooperative Nursery Schools.* New York, Teachers College, 1954). Mrs. S. Herbinière-Lebert (Les écoles coopératives: une expérience canadienne. *Ecole des parents* (Paris), janvier 1961) gives an interesting example: in a small Canadian town, the nursery school mistress intended to retire, as much as anything because of overwork, and the parents decided to take turns as nursery assistants; the children, made confident by seeing their mothers taking part in the work, made a more rapid adjustment to the school, and the mothers, seeing the skilled teacher at work, agreed that they had gained more than they gave. The example spread to other schools and towns. Experiments in the United Kingdom in the educational priority areas (mainly urban centres of poor housing and economic stress) have included a close involvement of parents with teachers and social workers in informal ways.

44. *Mental hygiene in the nursery school.* Paris, Unesco, 1953 (Problems in education, IX). Report of a joint WHO/Unesco expert meeting. The training of teachers is also fully dealt with in Volume II, Chapter 8, of the present work.

45. Pringle, M. L. K.; Tanner, M. The effects of early deprivation on speech development. *Language and speech* (London), vol. I, pt. 4, 1958.

46. Lézine, I. L'influence du milieu sur le jeune enfant. In: *Milieu et développement.* Paris, Presses universitaires de France, 1972.

47. Sjølund, A. Effect of day care institutions on children's development. Copenhagen, Danish National Institute of Social Research, 1971 [mimeographed].

48. See Chapter 6, p. 97.

49. See, for example: Janis, M. G. *A two-year-old goes to nursery school.* London, Tavistock Publications, 1964. This is a detailed case study of the separation anxiety, the defensive and aggressive reactions, etc., of the child and suggestions are made as to how a child may be prepared to accept such a situation if it is unavoidable.

50. See: note 16 (p. 108) and note 32 (p. 110).

51. Plowden, B. The way to a breakthrough in nursery education. *Education* (London), vol. 140, no. 2, July 1972.

52. Belgium. Ministère de l'education nationale. *Annuaire statistique de l'enseignement: année scolaire 1965–66.* Bruxelles, 1967. The figures for the Netherlands are: 4 per cent 4-year-olds and 96 per cent 5-year-olds (Nether-

lands. Ministry of Education and Science. *The educational system of the Netherlands.* The Hague, 1970.)
53. Blackstone, T. *A fair start.* London, Allen Lane, 1971. Shows wide variations in provision over the country (0–24 per cent of the age group). Recently the United Kingdom Government has withdrawn a circular which forbade the increase in nursery school places and has decreed a modest expansion in the next decade.
54. For example, B. Trouillet (*Vorschulerziehung in den U.S.A.* Frankfurt a/M., Beltz, 1970) points out that of the 30 per cent of 3- to 5-year-olds estimated in 1966 to be in pre-school education in the U.S.A. 37 per cent come from 'white collar' homes against 27 per cent from working class homes; 41 per cent come from families with annual incomes below $5,000, 38 per cent from those with more than $7,500 and 29 per cent from those in between. Under the age of 4, coloured children predominate; at the age of 5, white children represent 64 per cent and coloured 35 per cent. In developing countries where the need is very great, the provision may, for economic reasons and because of the hostility of parents, be very inadequate. It is, for example, estimated that only 10 per cent of children in Arab countries aged from 3–4 to 6–7 are provided for (United Nations Children's Fund. Problems of children and youth in national planning and development, Paris, 1970 [mimeographed]). See also: Unesco. Pre-school education in developing countries. Paris, December 1970 [mimeographed].
55. Pre-School Playgroups Association. *Local authorities and playgroups.* London, 1969. More recently (1972) the Ministry of Health (U.K.) has provided a substantial subsidy to enable the national organization to appoint fully trained regional advisers and coordinators, and the Ministry of Education has both given a grant and encouraged Local Education Authorities to increase their assistance to playgroups in their area.
56. The Pre-School Playgroups Association in the United Kingdom produces an extremely lively monthly journal, a series of pamphlets of a very practical kind and assists new groups in their early years. It has conducted small surveys of needs and stimulated much other work.
57. See: Crowe, B. *The playgroup movement.* London, Pre-School Playgroups Association, 1970. / Wall, W. D. *Which way next?* London, Pre-School Playgroups Association, 1970. A similar but more isolated development, which has a mainly experimental and research purpose, is the work currently being carried out at the Child Development Centre, Mount Vernon, U.S.A. (Nancy Wimbush). Mothers and children attend the Centre for one hour a day together.

FURTHER READING

Baturina, E. G., ed. *Detskij sad na sele* [The kindergarten in rural areas]. Moskva, Prosveščenie, 1967.
Bergeron, M. *Psychologie du premier âge.* Paris, Presses universitaires de France, 1966.
Blackstone, T. *Pre-school education in Europe.* Strasbourg, Council of Europe, 1970.
Bruner, J. S., et al. *Studies in cognitive growth.* New York, John Wiley, 1966.

Brunet, O.; Lézine, I. *Le développement psychologique de la première enfance.* Paris, Presses universitaires de France, 1965.

Cass, J. E. *The significance of children's play.* London, Batsford, 1971.

Château, J. *Le réel et l'imaginaire dans le jeu de l'enfant.* Paris, Vrim, 1946.

———. *L'enfants et le jeu.* Paris, Scarabée, 1967.

Comitato italiano per il gioco infantile. *Il gioco e il lavoro nella vita del fanciullo* [Play and work in the life of the children]. Rome, 1967.

David, M. *L'enfant de deux à six ans.* Toulouse, Privat, 1960.

Descoeudres, A. *Le développement de l'enfant de deux à sept ans.* Paris, Neuchâtel, 1923.

Douglas, J. W. B.; Ross, J. M. *Children under five.* London, Allen & Unwin, 1958.

Elken, W. *The pre-school years.* Harmondsworth, Penguin, 1967.

Faure, M. *Le jardin d'enfants.* Paris, Presses universitaires de France, 1971.

Herbinière Lebert, S.; Charrier, C. *La pédagogie vécue à l'école des petits.* Paris. Nathan, 1966.

Herzka, H. S. *Jouets pour l'enfant normal et l'enfant déficient.* Bâle, Stuttgart; Schwabe, 1966.

Hotyat, F. *Psychologie de l'enfant.* Bruxelles, Labor, 1966.

Hundertmark, G.; Ulshoefer, H., eds. *Kleinkind-Erziehung* [Early childhood education]. Vols. I-III. Müchen, Kösel Verlag, 1972.

Illingworth, R. S. *The development of the infant and young child: normal and abnormal.* Edinburgh, Livingstone, 1970.

International Bureau of Education. *The organization of pre-primary education.* Geneva, 1961.

Ivanova, N. J.; Lebeleva, E. A. *Samye malen'kie v detskom sadu* [The youngest in the kindergarten]. Moskva, Prosveščenie, 1967.

Karibunzira, M. *Aptitudes des enfants d'âge préscolaire.* Louvain, Publications universitaires, 1966.

Laurendau, M.; Pinard, A. *La pensée causale.* Montréal, Institut de recherches psychologiques; Paris, Presses universitaires de France, 1962.

Lawton, D. *Social class, language and education.* London, Routledge & Kegan Paul, 1968.

Lewis, M. M. *Language, thought and personality in infancy and childhood.* London, Harrap, 1963.

Lézine, I. *Psychopédagogie du premier âge.* Paris, Presses universitaires de France, 1969.

May, D. E. *Children in the nursery school.* London, University of London Press, 1963.

McLellan, J. *The question of play.* Oxford, Pergamon Press, 1970.

Moor, P. *Die Bedeutung des Spieles in der Erziehung* [The significance of play in the child]. Bern, Stuttgart; Verlag Hans Huber, 1962.

Piaget, J. *La représentation du monde chez l'enfant.* Paris, Presses universitaires de France, 1926. 2nd ed., 1947.

———. *La causalité physique chez l'enfant.* Paris, Librairie Félix Alcon, 1927.

———; Inhelder, B. *La psychologie de l'enfant.* Paris, Presses universitaires de France, 1966.

Pourneur, L. *A l'école maternelle.* Paris, Liège; Dessain, 1967.

Roth, H., ed. *Begabung und Lernen* [Talent and learning]. Stuttgart, Klett, 1970.

Sčelovanov, N. M. *Razvitie i vospitanie rebenka ot roždenija do treh let* [Development and education of the child from birth to 3 years of age]. Moskva, Prosveščenie, 1965.

Thomas, A., et al. *Behavioral individuality in early childhood.* London, University of London Press, 1964.

Unesco. *Pre-school education: statistical survey.* Paris, 1963.

Valitutti, S. *Stato e scuola materna* [State and nursery schools]. Roma, Armando, 1962.

Wallon, H. *Les origines du caractère de l'enfant.* Paris, Presses universitaires de France, 1970.

Winnicott, D. W. *Playing and reality.* London, Tavistock Publications, 1971.

World Health Organization. *Care of children in day centres.* Geneva, 1964 (Public Health Papers, No. 24).

———. *The care of well children in day-care centres and institutions.* Geneva, 1963.

Zaporožec, A. V.; El'konin, D. E., eds. *Psihologija detej doškol' nogo vozrasta* [Psychology of the pre-school child]. Moskva, Prosveščenie, 1964.

———; Usova, A. P., eds. *Psihologija ipedagogika igry doškol'nika* [Psychology and pedagogy of pre-school children's play]. Moskva, Prosveščenie, 1966.

Chapter nine

Pre-school education, equality of opportunity and adaptability

ENVIRONMENTAL DIFFERENCES

The conception of the nursery school as developed by Rachel McMillan, Audemars and Lafendel and even Maria Montessori and others has tended until recently to dominate thinking about pre-school education. It has tended to be Rousseau-esque and to adopt a philosophy of 'follow the child'. In general its ethos has been that of a kind of extension of a good home, a complement and auxiliary. Its climate, with some inter-cultural differences, has tended towards the permissive in which, it is assumed, children in contact with good and stimulating materials will 'unfold' and by and large educate themselves and each other under the supervision of a caring but largely non-directive adult.[1] In many such schools there are of course periods of directed activity as well as quiet times when children learn to listen. Many nursery school teachers too as the age of entry to formal school approaches give their young charges experience of more formal work with pencils and crayons and sometimes even of sitting at desks.

More recently many workers have pointed out that children of pre-school age are very active intellectually and that perhaps there are sensitive periods in learning during which they might pick up effortlessly some of those skills which are more laborious to acquire later. A particular case, for example, has been made for associating, even from the eleventh month when the child is beginning to utter his first words, the written or printed form of the word with the sound.[2] More generally reference is made to the poverty in language of children from particular social groups and specific language enrichment programmes have been devised.[3] Most generally of all it is suggested that even children from

177

relatively good homes could benefit from a more systematic and deliberate attempt to accelerate their cognitive growth.[4]

It must be stated from the outset that we have very little evidence one way or the other as to the long-term effects of attempts at accelerating, for example, a child's progress from the sensori-motor stage to that of concrete operations or of helping him to attain concepts of conservation and reversibility by a deliberate training intervention. In some cases such accelerations do appear to occur,[5] though they are rarely very striking. In other fields, for example in the learning of reading,[6] we customarily find that non-accelerated children tend to catch up later. The reason for the rather small success of acceleration programmes of all kinds may well be that most interventions have tended to concentrate upon one aspect of cognitive development and have rarely been very massive in comparison with the weight of a normal child's total experience with his environment. Two of the most important aspects of growth are indeed the great range and variety of situations in which a particular concept tends to present itself to a child thus ensuring an increasing generalization; and the need, very marked in young children, of periods of consolidation, repetition and practice. It seems also likely from our general knowledge of the dynamics of child development, that any marked acceleration in one domain, such as cognition, may bring about a misadjustment in another, for example the affective, which is not correspondingly accelerated. Very high intelligence is rather more frequently associated with maladjustment and frustration in early childhood than is superior or average ability.[7]

In any case the attempt by formal teaching to accelerate cognitive growth always carries with it the danger that—as the child struggles and not infrequently fails in a situation where the adult is clearly seen to wish him to succeed—he will become anxious and even rejecting. If failure means or seems to mean the loss of love and yet the child cannot succeed he will quickly build up all kinds of adverse attitudes. Young children can only be successfully taught in a relaxed permissive atmosphere and even then any failure to live up to what the child believes to be the expectation of his parents is very hard for him to bear.

Nevertheless there are clear, marked and, up to the present, obstinately stable differences in the level of operational intelligence and sheer power to learn between the children of relatively privileged middle class and of relatively less privileged working class groups. This difference holds within every developed country in spite of all efforts to even up formal educational opportunity. A similar and even more marked difference appears between children from the developed countries and children from underdeveloped ones. And these differences within and between countries persist into adulthood.

As has been pointed out earlier there is strong reason to suppose that whatever else such differences may be found to reflect, there are strongly differential environmental influences at work and that it is to these that we must address ourselves if we seriously wish to come within reach of the ideal of equality of opportunity in education and in life itself.

A second line of evidence suggests that the early years, passed outside the walls of the school and beyond the present reach of organized education, are critical for all subsequent cognitive growth. In a major analysis of a number of longitudinal studies of child development, Bloom[8] arrives at the conclusion that, within a relatively unified and advanced culture such as the American, the differential effect of an enriched over an impoverished environment is *on the average* represented by difference of some twenty points of I.Q. in adolescence. More than half of this difference, he suggests, arises between birth and the age of 4 or 5 and about 80 per cent by the age of 8. In his longitudinal studies of a national sample of British children, Douglas[9] was able to show that children from middle class educated homes improved their position relative to others in 'intelligence' as well as in school attainment throughout their primary schooling, whilst children from unskilled manual groups declined. A similar and even more striking finding is reported from a study of 16,000 children born in March 1958.[10] Even by age 7, those children in the lowest socio-economic group were 1.3 inches shorter, 6 times as many of them had speech difficulties, and 15 times as many were non-readers, as compared with children in the highest socio-economic group; they were also less able in arithmetic and had more difficulties in adjustment to school. Such discrepancies installed by age 7 are likely to influence in a cumulative way subsequent growth and progress. It must be remembered that these are figures based upon averages, over fairly heterogeneous groups and populations. Individual cases and severely disadvantaged groups—like those in very impoverished slum environments, in the *favellas* of Rio de Janiero or the *bidonvilles* of Africa—must be even more strikingly and disastrously affected.

Much other research insists also on the point that what schools at present achieve is not only related to the initial effects of the home in the pre-school period but also is continuously affected by the home environment throughout the entire decade or more of education. In a recent follow-up of children in English primary schools and on to adolescence, the conclusion is reached that the influence of the attitudes of the home (even more than the socio-economic level of the home itself) on educational progress heavily outweigh that of the school.[11]

It will be noted here that we are in a somewhat different domain from that of the attempt to accelerate cognitive growth in children who are by and large growing in favourable circumstances. We are, and must be, concerned with an attempt to intervene positively in an environment which not only may not provide the necessary cognitive stimuli for the adequate development of learning ability but which may in fact actually be having a negative effect through its disorganization. In this sense, the early years may be most important in a preventive and constructive sense simply because it is easier to get development right from the start than it is to remedy misdevelopments later on. Moreover, since the sequences of concept development appear to be invariant and prior acquisition determines readiness for the next stage, early deviations or failures inevitably prejudice later learning in a cumulative way. This, incidentally, will be true whether we are considering operational intelligence or attitudinal or emotional learning.

Before we go further into the implications of this, it is important to draw some distinctions. It is possible to have an environment which in itself is favourable to the growth of those aspects of intellectual functioning suitable to the culture in which a child will live. Assuming that such an environment favours all aspects of adult intelligence including, for example, the ability to solve problems involving abstract reasoning or the practical skills required for living, one cannot call it 'culturally deprived'. But it is possible that the systems of motivation which it sets up, the ways in which it shapes perception and attention, the blind spots which it creates are such as not to prepare a child for the kind of formal education which a possibly alien education system provides.[12] The problem then is to decide whether to change the education system and its expectations; whether to attempt to adapt the child to it; or whether to modify both so far as is possible. In varying ways, this has been and remains a part of the problem of the ex-colonial territories in which only the ablest children succeeded reasonably completely in adapting to the demands of schools, the expectations and aims of which were and still are largely European. It is also a problem in developed countries where marked differences in life style exist between widely separated social groups and where children may become increasingly alienated from a school which appears to reject the culture from which they come. However, by far the most important factors in cognitive growth relate to the consistency, degree of organization, conceptual richness and complexity of different environments. These differences are too, not infrequently, accompanied by different styles of child rearing—and particularly the degree of authoritarianism and the stress laid upon immediate or more remote satisfactions and sanctions—which may themselves affect the growth of abstract thought and the ability to conceive and choose alternative hypotheses or to be creative in other ways. The role played by language in the early years, its conceptual richness, lexical and syntactical subtlety, also seems to be of outstanding importance at least in the development of the child's verbal reasoning powers on which so much of education depends and which are of importance in adult life. Other categories of thought also prepare the later structures of intellect. If the culture tends predominantly to magical explanations of events and phenomena, if little experience of mechanical relationships is provided, or if little attention is paid to such notions as grouping and differentiation, then it will be more difficult—if not impossible—later to develop the kinds of thinking which underlie the study of science or mathematics. In senses such as these we can talk strictly and accurately of cultural deprivation. Only too often such deprivations are associated with groups which are underprivileged in other ways and we have to deal not only with cultural difference but with a real cultural inferiority in terms of the demands of modern world.

Finally, and again somewhat artificially, we can distinguish a third situation, this time not confined to a particular social or cultural group. In order that learning may take place and intelligence develop satisfactorily, it is of the utmost importance that the feed back from the environment in response to the child's actions should in general be consistent and, where it is not apparently so, that the inconsistencies should be logically related to a higher and more general order of concepts to which the child can accede by experience and maturation. In one very real sense this consistency and consistent variability of the environment, human and material, is the basis of a child's security; anything which disorganizes it—usually of course adult inconsistencies in emotional or disciplinary responses—inhibits learning, induces insecurity and may lead to maladjusted responses. The child tends to assimilate to earlier successful responses instead of accommodating and moving forward in his learning. Circumstances of this kind are in any extreme form, quite literally, stultifying: if they continue too long, it may be impossible to undo them entirely or even more than marginally. If disorganization is extreme, the whole personality and behaviour is likely to be disorganized.[13]

What has been said so far concerns the relative effectiveness of different kinds and qualities of environments for promoting the child's capacity to learn. Within fairly broad limits, this can be considered to hold good within different value systems both as regard forms of personality and as regards the stress put on different kinds of thought. But, however culturally neutral one might wish to be, one cannot escape some essential value judgements derived from our concepts of culture itself and of cultural change. For example, processes of rapid change seem to demand a flexibility of thought, the ability to conceive and accept new solutions to new problems. Without defining this further[14] we may call it 'creativity'. Such creativity at its most effective depends upon a considerable power to conceive and handle abstractions, to call up a wide variety of hypotheses, and the willingness to pay attention to and profit from a wide range of information. It implies the ability to think ahead and to inhibit immediate response in favour of choice between carefully thought out alternatives. Thus, in considering an educative environment, even at the pre-school stage, one must ask how far it favours the growth of flexible as compared with rigid thinking, of abstract symbolic thought and the ability to look ahead.

If we are fully consequential in the lessons we draw from the kind of research just quoted and from the analysis of the needs of the kinds of society into which we appear to be moving, the pre-school period is of cardinal importance, and should be planned very carefully and seriously indeed as a principal and perhaps even the most important stage of education on which all else depends. Even if our main concern is the somewhat narrower but primarily extremely important one of ensuring that the opportunities offered by free, universal and compulsory education are not lost to substantial proportions of the least favoured children, we shall still find the first eight or so years of life of critical importance.

'COMPENSATORY EDUCATION'

It is largely with this second set of considerations in mind that considerable programmes of what is called 'compensatory education' have been developed, first beginning some ten years ago in the United States and subsequently in many countries of Europe. These programmes, quite logically, have been directed at groups of urban children living in the run-down centres of large cities where poor housing, disease, social disaggregation and general poverty abound. In the United States such areas tend also to contain very high proportions of black children, Puerto Ricans, Mexicans and recent immigrants from poorer parts of Europe. In Europe where until recently at least there was markedly less racial mixture and fewer immigrants the target populations have tended to be the social groups lowest in the economic scale.

Such programmes, with greater or lesser degree of success, have endeavoured to bring to deprived groups of children what are sometimes called 'enrichment programmes' of varying types. Some have assumed that the observed deficiencies are more superficial than fundamental and have tried to give a wider range of experiences; others, basing themselves in the main on familiarity with the sorts of objects—pencils, books, crayons—and the sorts of activities—following directions and the like—met with in school, have sought to give a preliminary experience of these and to impart in fact the more obvious aspects of school readiness. More and more, recent programmes have accepted that deprivation tends to mean that the child's early environment is disorganized, that his experience with objects may be narrow and that his linguistic experience may be less complex and rich than that of more fortunate children as well as being of a somewhat different kind.[15] Hence the attempt has been to provide a structured systematic set of experiences with a strong linguistic content, but also with experience of grouping and differentiating objects, seriation and ordination and such like which form the basis of concepts particularly but not uniquely related to mathematical and causal thought.

Deutsch[16] points out that, whatever the theoretical criticisms that might be made of it and however one might wish to differ in detail, the Montessori system provides a model of an enrichment programme. To it, however, he would wish to add a language training programme 'where the child is allowed multiple opportunities for expressive language demonstrations as well as for receiving language stimuli under optimal conditions and being encouraged to make appropriate responses'. He defends the stress he lays on cognitive development by pointing out the importance to a positive self-image, of success in learning. One might add that since both adjustment and un- or maladjustment are aspects of learning, more effective learning of any kind is likely to lead the child forward rather than to leave him where he is.

Bereiter and his collaborators go somewhat further.[17] They selected specific and significant educational objectives, set up systematic training programmes focused upon what they call the basic information processes that are necessary for thinking. Thus they developed programmes of basic language training concentrating upon the formal, structural content of language rather than upon vocabulary as such and upon programmes concerned with reading and arithmetic. The same information processes are, they state, involved in all three but their application is different. These programmes were run in three twenty-minute sessions spread through a two-hour period on five days a week. The children chosen were fifteen 4-year-old ghetto children from the most severely underprivileged groups. It is claimed that after three months these children gained approximately 20 points in three highly significant language areas and in two others from being at least a year retarded for their age became nearly normal.

There are many kinds of compensatory education programmes which have been or are being tried in many corners of the world[18] including some of the developing countries where conditions are very different from and in many respects more serious even than in the most depressed groups of the western world.[19] The results so far are equivocal[20] for a great variety of reasons.[21] In general they do not appear to have produced the results which even the moderately optimistic expected of them. For example, while immediate gains of as much as 20 points of I.Q. have been reported, they do not seem to be maintained.

Various reasons have been advanced for this relative failure. The most fundamental is that of Jensen put forward in the *Harvard educational review* in 1969. He attacks, with a formidable array of arguments, the notion that social class differences are accounted for, to any but a rather limited degree, by environmental differences. He argues, in fact, that environment is little more than a 'threshold variable'—extreme environmental deprivation can keep the child from realizing what potential he may have from his genetic inheritance; but enrichment cannot push the child above this potential. He seems also to imply two other things: that the processes of assortative mating and social mobility would largely account for the inter-class differences in ability which we so constantly find; and that relatively few environments are really depriving to the extent that they do not give the minimum necessary for development. He suggests too that the structure of intelligence differs from one race to another and that therefore differences in educational treatment and method are warranted.

For reasons which are discussed elsewhere, the Jensen hypothesis, while it is an important corrective to the excessive optimism of the extreme environmentalists, cannot be taken as the last word or even as a too pessimistic limitation on what might be achieved through a careful and well-based educational programme. The very fact that the average level of operational intelligence in the populations of western Europe has increased in the past century with the spread of education and a general rise in the complexity and richness of life seem to contradict any hypothesis which rests mainly upon deterministic genetic grounds.

A contrasting explanation is that which refers to the means of evaluation which have been used—mainly conventional tests of intelligence and educational attainment. These may well be insufficiently sensitive or too loaded with particular skills to detect change. Furthermore we have as yet little evidence derived from long-term follow-up of children in enrichment programmes. From other evidence we know that some effects of early experience at least are latent and reappear only in the 'teens.[22]

Even more likely explanations of the relatively disappointing results are to be found in the structure of many programmes. In most of them the interventions are short—from twenty minutes up to an hour a day— little enough to counteract the effects of a disorganized or impoverished environment which englobes the whole of a child's waking life.[23] Few programmes have been conceived to support the child over a period of years—from pre-school to the secondary stage. It is thus at least likely that whatever effect they may produce is quickly lost when the child moves from one stage to the next.

Furthermore, in part because of the relative inadequacy of the time actually devoted to such programmes, there has been a tendency to isolate, according to the theoretical background of the experimenter, a few aspects of general development and these mainly in the cognitive field. In all too many cases, the concentration has been upon fairly specific skills which have been trained in some isolation.

Perhaps the most pertinent criticism is that few of the early programmes were logically and practically derived from a coherent and embracing theory. This has been taken account of in two related programmes both based on Piagetian theory: the Ypsilanti Early Education Programme[24] which began in 1967 and that carried out since 1969 by the Laboratoire de Pédagogie Experimental of the University of Liège.[25] Neither of these has reached the critical stage of full evaluation but, as well as being rigorously based upon an embracing theory of cognitive growth, each is at pains to train as fully as possible the teachers of the children concerned and to involve their mothers as well. There is thus the chance that the impact on the children will be greater than programmes which are grafted on to an otherwise untouched environment. What is perhaps of crucial importance is that they attempt to fulfil Reuchlin's definitions of an environment with high heuristic value: they p ovide rich and variable possibilities of manipulation and experimentation; and they allow for repetitions which permit a sufficient variety of situations of similar structure, in an environment which is organized, structured and predictable and one which favours the transition from configurations to transformations.[26]

What does seem to be clear from all our experience and knowledge to date is that while relatively specific and brief intervention programmes may be of value in nursery and later school periods for children whose deprivation is not very profound, they are unlikely to be sufficient to remedy the effects of a really poor or disorganized environment. Still less will they serve in countries, such as Africa, where the education of the rural child in his tribe and family is very different from that of the West. Truly to help children from the worst slum environments and those whose home culture is inimical to the development of objective reasoning at any level beyond the stage of concrete operations, a massive change in the environment seems necessary—and that from the earliest possible point in the child's life. And this effort must be continued well into the period of formal school education if its effects are not to be undone by the preponderant influences of the home environment.

We can again restate the necessary conditions. The environment which we create must be heuristic in the sense proposed by Reuchlin. It must provide richly and in variety the appropriate sensori-motor and conceptual experiences and be consistently responsive to the child's inquisitive attack. It must provide the emotional stimulus and support without which learning tends to dry up or turn awry. There must be an

G*

educator who is sufficiently perceptive to accelerate the child's acquisitions at the point when he is hovering in the uncertain state between the absence of a notion and its mastery. None of this will, however, be effective unless the time devoted to it makes it prevalent over the general environment in which the child lives: little short of the whole waking time in the early years seems likely to be fully successful, although the substantial time a child spends in his first compulsory school could be more profitably used by most school systems.[27]

A substantial impact on the learning of pre-school children may seem to be impossible in most circumstances and perhaps in many it is. However, one must return to the experience of the *kibbutzim* and of the all-day crêche. These provide total environments for at least twelve hours of the very young child's day. Furthermore, it does seem that if they are reasonably organized they provide a positive education. There seems some reason to suppose that were the experiences which they provide quite deliberately structured in the ways suggested earlier they might prove very effective indeed.

There remains the very serious problem of the child's need for a firm consistent link with a mother or more or less permanent mother substitute to which attention was paid in Chapter VII. The situation of the *garderie* or the *kibbutz* crêche resembles more clearly the kind of 'multiple mothering' found in some African tribes with its impact upon personality and social relations. It is also difficult to ensure that the staff of such institutions is sufficiently permanent not to cause the rupture of maternal relations which lies at the base of some later pathologies: and this is a serious risk to take.

In some cases the home circumstances are so disadvantageous and the need for the mother to work so preponderant that there is no alternative to the crêche. Thus while one would not recommend all-day pre-school institutions as a general practice, it seems reasonable to suggest that where they have to exist they should be used more fully and systematically than they are as a means of raising the functioning of disadvantaged children.

CONCLUSION

There is no blanket solution, no panacea. A serious commitment to equality of opportunity and more particularly to the raising of human functioning in the developing countries must mean a massive effort to improve early environments. If the line of argument set out earlier, especially in Chapter VI, is correct, we are also obliged both to ensure that interventions do not provoke maladjustments by depriving children of their basic security, and to see that whatever we do increases flexibility and creativity of response. Early experience has profound effects upon character and attitudes.

Thus the problem, in developed and developing countries alike, is the devising of a great variety of programmes for the pre-school and early school years which are carefully designed to ensure both cognitive and affective growth in line with the peculiar differences and difficulties of the country concerned, and which honour the social and personal values of its culture.

NOTES

1. This view is still held as an article of faith by many experienced nursery school teachers in the United Kingdom—they remain 'encapsulated within the shell of holy writ. . . . This is all the more remarkable when one considers that a typical day's programme for nursery school children from deprived areas contains no more than 30 or 40 minutes of structured language teaching, with the rest of day devoted to traditional free activity and play.' (Wiseman, S. Environmental handicap and the teacher. In: Wall, W. D.; Varma, V. eds. *Advances in educational psychology—I*. London, University of London Press, 1972.) See also: Quigley, H. A report on interviews with eleven E.P.A. nursery teachers and assistants using the Peabody Language Development Kit. Slough, Bucks., National Foundation for Educational Research, 1970 [mimeographed]. / Taylor, P.; Ashton, P. *A study of nursery education*. London, Evans; Methuen, 1972.
2. Doman, G. *How to teach your baby to read*. New York, Random House, 1964.
3. For example, *The Peabody Language Development Kits* (an English version is published by the National Foundation for Educational Research, Slough, Bucks.).
4. This is a somewhat different provision of experience and a pedagogic method flexibly based upon a knowledge of how young children learn, such as is advocated by M. Brearley and others (*Fundamentals in the first school*. Oxford, Blackwell, 1969 [especially chapters 1 and 9]).
5. At the Institut des sciences de l'éducation (Geneva) a number of studies have indicated that training can accelerate the acquisition of notions if it intervenes, as Vigotsky suggested, just before they are acquired spontaneously. See for example: Inhelder, Bärbel; Bovet, M.; Sinclair, H. Développement et apprentissage. *Revue suisse de psychologie pure et appliqué* (Berne), vol. XXVI, no. 1, 1961. / Denis-Prinzhorn, M., et al. Des épreuves opératoires au service de la pédagogie expérimentale. *Les sciences de l'éducation* (Paris), no. 3–4, juillet-décembre 1969 [special issue].
6. Morris, J. M. *Standards and progress in reading*. Slough, Bucks., National Foundation for Educational Research, 1966. / Warburton, F. W.; Southgate, V. *i.t.a.: An independent evaluation*. London, Murray; Edinburgh, Chambers, 1969.
7. Pringle, M. L. K. *Able misfits*. London, Longmans, 1970. / Hollingworth,

L. S. *Children above 180 I.Q., Stanford-Binet: origin and development.* New York, World Book Co., 1942.

8. Bloom, B. S. *Stability and change in human characteristics.* New York, Wiley, 1964. It should be pointed out that Bloom's notion of 'half development' has been criticized by A. D. B. and A. M. Clarke, who suggest that the worse the background, the better the ultimate progress—often including substantial I.Q. increases between 15 and 30. For example, of a group of 25, showing a mean increase of 9.7 points of I.Q. over $2\frac{1}{4}$ years (with a correlation of 0.897) one made a 25 point increase, three an increase of 16 points, three of 15 points, one of 13 and two of 12, that is 40 per cent of the group made gains of 12 points or more (Clarke, A. D. B.; Clarke, A. M. Cognitive changes in the feebleminded. *British journal of educational psychology* (London), vol. 45, pt. III, 1954./ Idem. Cognitive and social changes in the feebleminded—three further studies. Ibid., vol. 49, pt. III, 1958. / Idem. Consistency and variability in the growth of human characteristics. In: Wall, W. D.; Varma, V., eds. Op. cit.).

9. Douglas, J. W. B. *The home and the school.* London, McGibbon & Kee, 1964.

10. Davie, R.; Butler, N.; Goldstein, H. *From birth to seven.* London, Longmans, 1972.

11. United Kingdom. Central Advisory Council for Education. *Children and their primary schools.* Vol. II. London, HMSO, 1967 [appendix 4]. / Peaker, G. F. *The Plowden children four years later.* Slough, Bucks., National Foundation for Educational Research, 1971. / Chiland, C. *L'enfant de six ans et son avenir.* Paris, Presses universitaires de France, 1971. These results and those of Douglas have been challenged by H. Goldstein (The home and the school: a re-examination of the Plowden Report's evidence. London, National Children's Bureau, 1972 [mimeographed]. He points out that much depends upon the definition of 'importance' which is given.

12. Bernstein, B. A critique of the concept of compensatory education. In: *Class, codes and control.* Vol. I. London, Routledge & Kegan Paul, 1971.

13. It seems probable that overcrowded living accommodation and lack of amenities in the home operate to depress cognitive functioning and development not so much directly as indirectly through making it extremely difficult for the mother to give consistent attention to her child.

14. But see Chapter XII.

15. Bernstein, B. *Social class, language and socialization* Op. cit. [especially p. 181–187]. / Idem. A socio-linguistic approach to socialization. Ibid. especially p. 152–ff].

16. Deutsch, M. Facilitating development in the pre-school child. In: Hechinger, F. M., ed. *Pre-school education today.* New York, Doubleday, 1966 [chapter 4, p. 87].

17. Bereiter, C., et al. An academically oriented pre-school for culturally deprived children. Ibid. [chapter 6].

18. For an elaborated proposal see: Luckert, H. R. Begabungsforschung und basale Bildungsforderung. *Schule und Psychologie* (München), 14 Jg., No. 1, 1967. For a very thorough bibliography see: *Compensatory early childhood education.* The Hague, Bernard van Leer Foundation, 1971.

19. For example, the *Balwadis* (crêches and *garderies*) recently set up in India to give children the conditions of development which the family cannot provide.

20. An enthusiastic and rather journalistic account is given by M. Pines of many

such programmes and of the rationale behind them (*Revolution in learning.* London, Allen Lane, 1969); Hechinger, however, gives a more balanced viewpoint (Hechinger, F. M., ed. Op. cit.). The United States Commission on Civil Rights (1967) concluded its examination of the effect of the Headstart programme by saying: 'The . . . analysis does not suggest that compensatory education is incapable of remedying the effects of poverty on the academic achievement of individual children. There is little question that school programmes involving expenditure for cultural enrichment, better teaching and other needed educational services can be helpful to disadvantaged children. The fact remains, however, that none of the programmes appear to have raised significantly the achievement of participating pupils as a group within the period evaluated by the Commision (p. 138).' (Cited by: Jensen, A. R. How much can we boost I.Q. and scholastic achievement. *Harvard educational review* (Cambridge, Mass.), vol. 39, no. 1, winter 1969, p. 1–123). Jensen's article, which went much further than a critique of compensatory education, raised a world-wide controversy (see the papers in subsequent issues of the *Harvard educational review,* and the issues of *Educational research* (London), vol. 14, nos. 1 & 2, November 1971 and February 1972, which were devoted to the topic. See also: Jensen, A. R. *Genetics and education.* London, Methuen, 1972).

21. Kamii, C. K. Evaluation of evaluation. *Educational leadership* (Washington, D.C.), May 1971.
22. The so-called 'sleeper effect' (Kagan, J.; Moss, H. A. *Birth to maturity.* New York, Wiley, 1962). See also the Clarke and Clarke references cited on p. 188, note 8.
23. A relatively successful intervention programme in the infant school (age 5–7) however has been reported (Gagahan, D. M.; Gagahan, G. A. *Talk reform.* London, Routledge & Kegan Paul, 1970). It is important to note that these two psychologists working from the socio-linguistic theories of Bernstein, assisted infant teachers to develop their own material. Thus although the intervention was limited to twenty minutes daily, the teacher's whole attitude and strategy changed in line with it.
24. Kamii, C. K. Evaluating pupil learning in pre-school education. In: Bloom, B. S., et al. *Formative and summative evaluation of student learning.* New York, McGraw Hill, 1968. / Ibid. Piaget's theory and specific instruction: a response to Bereiter and Kohlberg. *Interchange (Canada)* (Toronto), vol. 1, 1970. / Kamii, C. K.; Radin, N. L. A framework for a pre-school curriculum based on Piaget's theory. In: Athey, I. J.; Rubadeau, D. O., eds. *Educational implications of Piaget's theory: a book of readings.* Waltham, Mass., Blaisdell, 1969.
25. Directed by A. M. Thirion under Professor G. de Landsheere.
26. Denis-Prinzhorn, M. Discussion du rapport d'Irène Lézine. In: *Milieu et développement.* Paris, Presses universitaires de France, 1972 [Symposium de l'Association de psychologie scientifique de langue Française, Lille, 1970].
27. Brearley gives a very detailed account of how this could be embodied in a programme. Brearley, M., ed. *Fundamentals in the first school.* Oxford Blackwell, 1969).

190 *Constructive Education*

FURTHER READING

Bernard van Leer Foundation. *Compensatory early childhood education. A selective working bibliography.* The Hague, 1971.

Bloom, B. S.; Davis, A.; Hess, R. *Compensatory education for cultural deprivation.* New York, Holt, Reinhart & Winston, 1965.

Durkin, D. *Children who read early.* New York, Teachers' College, 1966.

Education for socially disadvantaged children. *Review of educational research* (Washington, DC.). vol. XXXV, no. 5, December 1965.

Gahagan, D. M.; Gahagan, G. A. *Talk reform. Exploration in language for infant school children.* London, Routledge & Kegan Paul, 1970.

Gray, S. W., et al. *Before first grade.* New York, Teachers' College, 1966.

Hardy, W. G. *Communication and the disadvantaged child.* London, Livingstone (Longmans), 1970.

Hawkridge, D. G., et al. *Foundations for success in educating disadvantaged children.* Palo Alto, Calif., American Institute for Research in Behavioural Sciences, 1968.

Hellmuth, J. ed. *Disadvantaged child.* New York, Brunner, Mazel, 1967–70. (3 v.).

Karnes, M. B., et al. *Investigations of classroom and at-home interventions: research and development program in pre-school disadvantaged children.* Vol. I. Urbana, Ill., University of Illinois, Institute of Research for Exceptional Children, 1969.

Passow, H. A. *Deprivation and disadvantage: nature and manifestations.* Hamburg, Unesco Institute for Education, 1970.

Pringle, M. L. K. *Deprivation and education.* London, Longmans, 1971.

Robinson, R. P.; Rackstraw, S. J. *A question of answers.* London, Routledge & Kegan Paul, 1971.

Wein, N. The education of disadvantaged children—an international comparison. *Educational research* (London), vol. 13, 1970, p. 12–19.

Witty, P. A., ed. *The educationally retarded and disadvantaged.* Chicago, University of Chicago Press, 1967.

Chapter ten

The primary school: aims, methods and mental health

THE ELEMENTARY SCHOOL

In most European countries, the primary school has developed out of the pre-adolescent years of the old elementary school and it is of some importance to remember its origins. The elementary school catered for the whole age range of compulsory education and from its outset was the school of the people. Parallel to the upper end of it, there existed a selective (and often in practice socially selective) system of academic education with very different aims and curricula for those who were destined for one or other of the liberal professions or middle class white collar types of job. Increasingly since the 1939-45 war—although the movement began well before in some countries—there has been a tendency to regard all education after the age of 11 or 12[1] as secondary and to differentiate the kind of provision made, so that in theory at least, all children in their 'teens can have an education adapted to their aptitudes and to their social and vocational aspirations. This has had its impact on the function of the primary schools.

BASIC SKILLS

At present in Europe there is general agreement on many of the aims and much of the content of the primary curriculum. The distinction often drawn between instruction and education is frequently false and misleading but at the primary school level at least we may distinguish certain aspects of the programme which have a large element of formal skill and are therefore properly (in part, though not entirely) matters for instruction. As an instrument of receiving information from others, as the foundation of his subsequent intellectual development and as a means of entry into the garnered culture of his people, a child needs to learn how to decipher written and printed words. He must learn to read as an essential preliminary to that reading to learn which will become a principal means of autonomous development. To communicate in a semi-permanent form he needs to be able to write and to put words together in a coherent grammatical order. For a number of adult purposes (but not nearly so many as is presupposed by most arithmetic courses)[2] a minimum of arithmetic skills is required.

However, if primary education is limited to instruction in a largely instrumental set of skills—the 'three Rs'—useful in primitive forms of clerical work but not contributing greatly to personal and cultural development, then indeed it deprives a child of entering into his society in any but menial ways. The biggest change of the past fifty years or more in Europe has been the recognition that universal education must mean something more than this. It implies at least the attempt to raise the quality of a pupil's thinking, to open access to aesthetic experience, and to enlarge his ability to communicate orally as well as in a variety of other media, rather than merely to give him some useful tricks and a small equipment of knowledge.

Schools conforming to the old pattern of elementary schooling covering the whole of the free and at least partially compulsory[3] period continue to exist in developing countries and many of them with curricula that go little beyond basic skills and some vocational preparation; but in Europe and North America the primary stage ends at or shortly after the first decade of life and occupies four to six years of childhood. It is intended to provide the basis for a much wider education in the "teens' and is no longer directed at the provision of a merely basic literacy for the masses.

The bulk of such schools are provided in developed countries by the State either directly or in association with religious groups, though a privileged private sector may continue to exist alongside them, drawing its children from a restricted social class and often offering a curriculum somewhat different from that of the State schools. In some developing countries, this private sector is very large, often religious and even missionary in its inspiration, very often with a curriculum aimed to prepare an élite to enter a secondary system based upon the norms of a former colonial power. Such schools tend to enjoy high prestige partly because of their privileged social composition and consequently higher academic results, and partly because the indigenous schools are still struggling to develop an education suited to a much wider range of ability and background. There may be, and often are—even in developed countries—very considerable differences between private and State schools in the quality of their staffing, the buildings and equipment and the size of classes. As State education improves and becomes more enlightened, however, it tends, as in the United Kingdom, to be superior in many ways to the private sector—particularly that part of it which is conducted for profit.

The existence of parallel systems of education, particularly when these are based upon economic and social distinctions, is obviously divisive. They tend to perpetuate concepts of élitism which we now know to have little basis in genetic psychology—although some continue to believe that they do. They militate against the realization of the ideal of equal access to education irrespective of race, religion, sex or social class. On the other hand, one would not wish to suggest that all schools should be the same, conforming rigidly to a common ethos. How varied schools are in practice will be governed by a great variety of forces in the culture itself, in the family background from which children come, in the ways in which systems and teachers adapt themselves to the differences in the pupils confronting them and to some extent by how the State itself regards the function of education. Centralized systems like the French and other derivatives of Napoleonic ideas tend to be prescriptive and uniform. Decentralized systems like the British, in theory at least, leave schools and teachers free to choose the curriculum and methods, insisting only on some minimal constraints. Marxist systems, like many confessional schools, have a dominating ideological component which is intended not only to form the basis of curriculum and social and moral training but to prescribe a specific pedagogy.[4]

MANIFEST AND LATENT CURRICULUM

By whatever principles it is guided, however, the school and its demands form a principal part of the influences which shape the pupils; and its explicit or implicit aims have to be accepted as important conditioning factors. Personality development cannot be regarded as an autonomous psychic process; nor can we assume that emotional and moral growth can safely be left to the home while the school gets on with the job of building up basic skills or of intellectual preparation for secondary studies. Even if a school or school system attempts to be neutral and not to intervene either in the moral or the personal growth of its pupils, it cannot do so. In addition to the manifest curriculum of subjects and content, there is the latent curriculum of values implicit in what is put into or left out of the programme, in the methods by which children are taught, in the systems of motivation, incentive and discipline which are used, in the relationships which exist between teacher and pupil, between child and child and among the members of staff. The school is a powerful socializing agent which teaches the child much about himself and about the ways in which other individuals and groups interact with him and with each other. The latent curriculum is likely to be more influential than the manifest one just because it is so pervasive and consistent and because it strikes directly at the emotional life.[5]

We should remind ourselves too that a school is unique as an artificial community set between the often small and intensely emotional family group and the much more complex community of adults in the world outside, and that it is potentially in contact with all children and through them with their families over at least a decade. It is readily manipulable in the sense that the adults within it can, within fairly wide limits, change their behaviour, stress different aspects of the school's intellectual or personal demands and thus foster or inhibit different aspects of personality growth. In situations where the school has an almost complete monopoly of the child's waking time—as in a boarding school or even more markedly in a *kibbutz*—its effects upon behaviour, value structures and personality can be very profound indeed as they can be when school and home are broadly agreed on common aims.

Where, however, there is covert or worse still open conflict between the values and culture of the home and those of the school, in childhood at least, it is the influence of the home that seems to dominate. This may be particularly unfortunate in the case of children who come from difficult or deprived backgrounds or whose home culture is in conflict with that proffered by the school. Longitudinal studies suggest that children, whose parents understand and support the schools' efforts, tend to advance, not only in their attainments but in their sheer ability to learn as the years of childhood go on; whereas those whose family background is culturally different and often less richly stimulating and whose parents are indifferent or even antagonistic, tend to fall, comparatively, further and further behind their more fortunate coevals.[6] Thus differences between children which are already apparent at school entry markedly widen in the five or so primary school years. In this sense, equal access to equal educational opportunities increases rather than diminishes that part of inter-individual differences which is attributable to social background.

It is argued that some societies deliberately and consciously use education as a selective system designed to winnow out the hewers of wood and drawers of water from an intellectual and social élite and that, progressively as school goes on, children are socialized into different roles and expectations which will later govern their station in society. This is particularly the case where elementary education is based on minimum literacy and where a parallel but different system of private schools exist. Certainly the schools in the recent past of most European countries reflected and tended to support the social *status quo*, as many do now; and practices, like selective failure, streaming by ability and even insistence upon particular aspects of curricular content may, not always intentionally, have the same effect. It should also be noted, however, that universal free and compulsory elementary education coupled with an increasing access to academic secondary education on grounds of merit has been a very potent influence in increasing social mobility, particularly from the skilled working class into the middle classes.

Whatever we may think of this on ideological or social grounds—and various positions could be justified—there are two problems which must be clearly distinguished and which have important bearings upon the healthy mental growth of individuals and of their societies. The first of these concerns how best we can provide, in education, for the individual so that, whatever his home circumstances, he can reach the highest mental and personal development of which he is capable. The second concerns the nature of knowledge and whether there is or is not a hierarchy of value in forms of knowledge and kinds of thought. If we can find satisfactory and practicable answers to these questions, the socio-political questions raised by the right to education are more clearly distinguishable and the answers to them can be found in clearly enunciated value terms.

DISADVANTAGE AND REJECTION

We have seen in earlier chapters that the heuristic quality of the early environment seems to have important effects both upon the development of sheer power to learn and upon systems of motivation. There is little doubt that, because of the nature of their early experiences, many children are either deprived or have their thinking disorganized or both. Such children start at a disadvantage in any school, no matter what its aims. If we sincerely believe that equality of opportunity in education is a universal human right, it follows that efforts should be bent in the case of such children to an attempt to remedy their deficiencies and defects. Such an attempt, as far as the schools are concerned must mean positive discrimination[7] and the provision of a programme considerably different from that provided for the more fortunate.

Some of the difficulty confronting these children arises from a clash both of values and experience between their home and the school.[8] There is little doubt that a school which ignores or worse still rejects the experiences which its pupils associate with the warmth and love of home, or with their feeling of identification with a group, tribal or national, or even with their little gang of playmates, may put its pupils in a situation of conflict. Rejection of what a child knows and feels may be seen as a rejection of himself: it certainly gives him difficulty in smoothly constructing a sense of identity. If the conflict between home and school is sharp and intense, the pupil may reject school entirely, bending all his efforts to defeating the attempts of the teacher to help him to learn what the school sets out to teach.[9]

Even at a relatively low level of uniform skills and a standard package of knowledge, it is clear that children from very different home circumstances need substantial modification in the content and style of their education if many of them from the outset are not to experience failure on a massive scale and a sense that what they know and are is completely alien to the school. Indeed at least half of the pupils in many systems still fail to complete the first year at school in a way satisfactory to their teachers and, in countries where primary education is not compulsory, quit education for good.[10]

For these children, and they are many, the school must provide a bridge between the culture of home and the broader cultural aims of education. To do this it must, manifestly, so structure the environment in which learning takes place that it is marked by the consequential regularity which we have seen to be important in pre-school learning; it must provide great variety and increasing complexity in the embodiment of all kinds of concepts and it must present a system of incentives, motives and satisfactions which is consistent. This is, of course, important for all children, but it is crucial for the deprived and disadvantaged.

As well as providing structure, it obviously is necessary to accept, at least initially, the forms of language, the experiences and values which so far have defined what image of themselves children may have developed, as well as to begin from the level of conceptual growth which they have attained. The problem is thus both remedial in the sense that the school may have to bring consistency, organization and richness of verbal as well as of concrete experience, and educative in the sense that among the skills and knowledge which pupils have already acquired some must be fostered and redirected and others gently eliminated without the child feeling that he and his culture are being rejected.[11]

This is true, of course, not only for the initial stage of entry to school but throughout education. The educator is and must always be aware that his is only one of the major influences—home, the peer group, the community at large and particularly the mass media—which are educating the child. He has the advantage that his influence is institutionalized; and that he can structure it systematically if he wishes and knows how.

FIXED CURRICULA AND PRESCRIBED METHOD

The task is made difficult in practice by two things. In very many countries, the curriculum, its detailed content, pedagogical method and even the very textbooks to be used are uniform, prescribed by a central authority, which forbids any deviation even within the timing of the programme. The second difficulty arises from the teacher himself, or rather from his training. The adaptation of curriculum and method, even to broad social differences, requires considerable skill, insight and knowledge not only in the conventional areas of instruction, but in the analysis of the conceptual structure of what he has to teach, in detailed understanding of the background of his pupils, and in what might be called diagnostic teaching—teaching which for each child builds up a picture of the 'lets' and 'hindrances' to learning peculiar to him. Few systems of teacher training even begin to provide the theoretical background which this requires; fewer still arrange the systematic inservice training workshops which would help teachers to develop the practical insights and techniques necessary. Something however could be done by providing alternative curricula, textbooks and methods for widely differing circumstances. This would go some way to help with what is the practical and continual problem of finding an acceptable compromise between the aims and values of formal education, as they are embodied in curriculum, the needs and difficulties of the individual child and the many and powerful outside educational influences with which the school may be in conflict, particularly in societies in rapid evolution and in those which are not ideologically monolithic.

This in effect is one aspect of a general crux in the education of all children whether deprived or not. Education is a normative and socializing process, but it is also concerned with promoting the optimal development of individuals. These two aims are sometimes in conflict; more frequently in uneasy relation; they are difficult to harmonize—at least without taking up some very clear ideological, philosophic or religious position, which in itself may exclude certain possibly valuable forms of non-conformity. However, if, as was suggested earlier, we are concerned with a pluralistic society finding many sorts of adjustments, styles of life and patterns of value acceptable within broad and tolerant limits, then, though by no means simple, the problem is more manageable. The aims which we propose for education at any level will have certain things in common though the importance accorded to particular aspects or particular contents will differ. We can, too, distinguish practices which are conducive to mental health and personal adjustment from those which, under almost any circumstances, are disadvantageous to the individual and to the progress of his society.

Neither for the education of disadvantaged children, nor for primary or elementary education as a whole, is it possible to lay down a precise series of strategies, routines of educational method or curricula content which will serve, even for one particular school. What we can do is to attempt to identify certain broad aims and kinds of practice which are more likely than others to foster the effective use of all kinds of ability, avoid the development of rigidities of thought and personality and of neurotic forms of behaviour, and tend towards a dynamic capacity to adjust to changing circumstances.[12]

COGNITIVE AIMS

In terms of the ability to think, the first decade of life is the period during which the child's enlarging experience leads him to increase and refine a series of concrete concepts about the world, the people in it and relations of cause and effect which govern them. He learns to stand somewhat back from purely sensory impressions imposing on them concepts of constancy and reversibility, and becoming able to carry out concrete operations. He can, for example, in the well known experiments of Piaget, understand that the same volume (of water, or clay) may take perceptually different forms without actually increasing or diminishing. He understands causality in the concrete world and can predict the consequences flowing from clearly perceived causes—for example, directions of movement from an assemblage of interacting levers and cogs. He has moved somewhat from a purely egocentric concept of himself and can project himself in thought and feeling into the circumstances of others in a limited way. He can grasp the rules of simple games and even appreciate that these are relative, to be varied by agreement among the players. He can reason adequately from one concrete situation to another within his experience and even begin 'as if' types of reasoning from hypothetical premises into their, still concrete, logical consequences. He can order, group and classify the objects of his experience. More or less well, he can do all this in imagination using principally speech or other subsidiary forms of symbolism to do so.

How far any given child has moved by the age of 10 or 11 along this path of cognitive growth will depend upon his initial endowment, upon the richness and orderliness of his early environment and upon the quality and variety of his experiences in and out of school. A major cognitive aim of primary education is to foster this development, to help the child refine and increase his conceptual framework, to extend his ability to reason and predict consequences, to assist him to rid himself of sensory dependence and of the magical and animistic notions of early childhood.

In a very broad—but still useful—sense primary education is an important continuing stage in the transition from fantasy to reality, from complete ego-centricity of thought to a more objective view, from notions of the omnipotence of the wish to a realistic notion of the self as an agent in a lawful world. Anything which interferes with this process is likely to tend towards maladjustment or to leave the child stuck at some earlier inadequate level. It is likely too to impede his development beyond the level of manipulation of concrete concepts, to the higher and even more effective kind of thinking which depends upon abstract conceptualization and formal operations of very varied and flexible kinds.

HINDRANCES TO CONCEPTUAL GROWTH

Almost any area of human experience can furnish the raw material of persons, objects and relationships, through interaction with which children may achieve concrete conceptual growth; though, towards the end of the period at any rate, some environments may be depriving in the sense that they are, for example, relatively poor in provoking notions of physical causality or in mechanical types of relations. Much more common inhibiting or disorganizing factors are linguistic poverty which does not present the child with a useful and flexible instrument of thought and conceptual manipulation; and adults whose own thinking is immature, dominated by magical notions of causality and who respond to the 'why' questions of childhood in misleading, inconsequential or even constrictingly negative ways. So too anything which challenges a child to adapt and move to a more general concept or more evolved scheme of causality but which at the same time inhibits him from doing so, is likely to throw him back on some form of rigid assimilation. Familiar examples of this in education are the teaching of routine tricks and methods for the solving of arithmetic problems before the concepts are understood—especially if the child is punished in some way for failure. Only too frequently this results in acquired habits too rigid to be modified when even a small change is made in the situation; and effectively blocks later understanding.

Knowledge of how intelligence, the ability to learn and the capacity to solve problems, develop prescribes, for the primary school, a richly varied programme of experiences which present to the learner a range of concepts embodied in a wide variety of forms, and of increasing degrees of complexity, in themselves and in their interrelations. It also implies a high degree of consistency and organization. It does not however denote any particular content; nor, except in certain limited if important respects, a pedagogic method.

FORMS OR MODES OF KNOWLEDGE

For these we must look elsewhere. There seems to be some consensus that there are forms of knowing and thinking which are relatively distinguishable from each other and initiation into all of which is of value to any participant in a modern society. There are many ways of formulating these for discussion differing in detail. However, one may accept as a set of working categories the formulation of the British philosophers, Hirst and Peters.[13] They distinguish a number of areas each of which 'necessarily involves the use of concepts of a particular kind and a distinctive type of test for its objective claims'.

The first of these is that of formal logic and mathematics involving concepts that pick out relationships of a general abstract kind, where deducibility within an axiom system is the test of truth. In contrast are the physical sciences which are based upon empirical data and concerned with an understanding and knowledge of the sensible world. Different again is our awareness and understanding of our own and other people's minds, a mastery of concepts like 'knowing', 'believing', 'wanting' which are essential to interpersonal experience. Moral judgement and awareness involve a further distinguishable set of notions like 'duty', 'ought' and 'wrong'. The fifth mode which these writers put forward rather more tentatively is aesthetic experience which uses forms of symbolic expression not confined to the linguistic and which has different criteria of truth from any of the others. They also suggest that religious experience may be distinct from other categories and that philosophical understanding seems to involve at least second order concepts and forms of objective tests which are irreducible to those of any first order kind.

Hirst and Peters go on to say that although some at least of these modes of experience and knowledge are radically independent, there is an equally important pattern of interrelationships between them. For example, they point out that while for the solution of many scientific problems mathematical knowledge is necessary it may not be sufficient; similarly either scientific knowledge or mathematics or both may be necessary to moral understanding.

In terms of our rather broad definition of mental health, these categories and their interrelationships are important in rather different ways. Moral judgement and awareness and understanding of our own and other people's minds are closely concerned in all aspects of interpersonal relations, of being at home and in harmony with oneself and others. They are the foundation of what is customarily thought of as adjustment; and many maladjustments—emotional and personality disturbance, delinquency and the like—are clearly related to failures in either or both of these areas. However, logico-mathematical, and empirical scientific thought are in a larger sense equally important, not only for entry into our scientific culture but as the basis of any effective participation in the major social and political decisions which confront us. The aesthetic mode too is not merely a source of enjoyment and 'play', but bound up with the education and refinement of the emotions; it is a means of expression and communication and, very importantly at all stages of life, a therapeutic, harmonizing activity between the inner world of fantasy and feeling and the more constricting influences of the physical and human environment.

Clearly, in view of what has been said about the nature of intellectual development at the primary stage, none of these modes of knowledge and experience can be explored in more than a preparatory and, for most children, very concrete way. Equally clearly, however, if any one is neglected, we are likely to deny full development in some at least of the others if not in all. Essentially the curriculum (both manifest and latent) of the primary school should aim to introduce a wide range of concepts in most of these areas and attempt to draw attention to some at least of the interrelationships between them.

It should lay the bases of those forms of knowing and thinking which bring the child into relationship with the objective world and his community without which his ability to solve problems, his power of dynamic and continuing adjustment and his ability to enter fully into the culture of his society will be seriously prejudiced.

SUBJECT DIVISIONS

We may ask how this relates to the conventional subject divisions—mother tongue, arithmetic-mathematics, craft work, geography, history, general science and the like. Subject divisions in a very rough sort of way do tend to correspond to different modes; but they do not necessarily do so. Still less does a very compartmented syllabus exhibit the interrelations between modes. One may add, conversely, that integrated curriculum units, project methods, centres of interest and the like do not necessarily do so either. Whatever the content or method used, experience of the distinct modes of knowledge and experience and of their necessary interrelationships will come only if the curriculum is planned with the clear aim in mind to foster and develop them.[14]

This leads us back to a consideration of the content of curricula and the pedagogic methods of primary schools. There seems to be no good reason why any one particular subject or any conventional category of knowledge should be the universal pabulum for all primary school children. What we are concerned to do is to develop the power to think in a great variety of ways and in doing this it is likely we shall succeed best if we use the child's own environment, the experiences which greet him daily in his home, his community and his school, his interests and curiosity, to help him build up, through knowledge which he perceives as apposite and useful, the foundations of an orderly and effective analysis of his world.[15] Such an approach too diminishes the disadvantage of those children whose home culture is different from that propounded by most curricula and textbooks. Where, as will be frequently the case, experience which we know to be relevant, immediately or ultimately, is lacking or difficult to come by outside the classroom, it is the task of the school to attempt to provide it. So too there are probably bodies of knowledge, which, although not universally relevant, could and should be possessed by most children and which can only be acquired in the formal setting of a school. An example here might be basic scientific information, some knowledge of the history of his own people, a foreign language and at least an introduction into literature in its varied forms. It is only much later—in adolescence—that the systematic study of bodies of organized knowledge, principally for their own sake, may become necessary, at least for many children.

It is in such a context that learning through activity and experience has most relevance since it becomes obvious that a child will best learn to think numerically on the basis of considerable number activity and real experience of quantities and quantitative relationships. He cannot learn the arts of communication without having experience or thought to communicate, and as he develops the primordial skills of gestural, visual and oral communication so he can be brought to acquire and appreciate reading, writing and visual art as more permanent if less direct media. Similarly the child's curiosity about the external world, his search for causation and crude attempts to predict effect are the basis on which the school can build the willingness to suspend belief, to test hypotheses empirically and formulate laws founded on observed relationships.

At this early stage other knowledge, in the sense of an ordered and coherent body of facts[16] called botany, biology, history, geography, grammar or the like, has little relevance in and for itself. Certainly education, even when conceived primarily as an instruction in techniques, cannot be without content. But the importance of facts in the primary school years lies much more in their instrinsic interest for the child, the stimulus which they give to particular modes of thinking, the raw material their interrelationships provide for the child's developing ability to conceptualize, to think, and to express, than to their place in a systematic adult construct. Nor should it be forgotten that facts can be 'inert' and remain so unless they are actual in their significance for the child. Hence one at least of the teacher's tasks is to provide experience and draw children's attention to it and to help them to order and discipline that experience through thinking and expression. The motive power of learning is the emotional life, and interest is one of the ways in which the emotions point outwards to an analysis of the objective world. Active learning takes place when the whole emotional energy is concentrated on an interest and when intelligence is exercised in its service.

PEDAGOGIC METHOD

Such an orderly and effective analysis of his world is, of course, important in itself as a means of preparing a child (and ultimately the adolescent and the adult he becomes) to enter fully into and participate in his culture and its development. But it is more than this. Genuine personal autonomy implies the ability to make judgements and choices. In any of the modes of knowledge and thought about which we have been speaking, this implies an understanding of the concepts proper to the mode and of the criteria by which its facts can be tested.

It is this aspect which is most deeply concerned with pedagogic *method*. It is possible to construct excellent curricula and textbooks which provide the child with interesting and relevant content in all or any of the areas described above. Indeed it is necessary to do so since— although some progressive educators tend to overlook this—any form of thinking, if it is to be effective, implies relevant knowledge; and it is the task of education to give this and to provide the means to acquire it when it is lacking.

But there is something more. Very young children cannot think about any content in an appropriate way. Yet it is necessary for them to start off with some content ('stealing is wrong', 'flowers bloom in the spring') which they accept initially as beliefs. The problem is to do this in a way which does not fixate them, preventing them from passing on to develop the appropriate form of thought, its distinctive concepts and tests of truth. Indoctrination (which is still the mark of much teaching in primary schools)[17] tends to pass on a fixed and rigid body of knowledge; there is a tendency to lead the child to believe that the only test of truth is whether a statement or a solution is or is not acceptable to authority. Quite apart from the 'verbalism', which marks much of the traditional elementary school ideology, in which the teacher's tick, or the correct reproduction of a formula, is a more important criterion of rightness than the attempt to understand the concept and relationships involved (for example, in mathematical reasoning or in an empirical test of a simple hypothesis 'light things float—heavy things sink'), there is a more subtle dependence upon authority which even good teachers may unconsciously foster. Although the child questions, he is not fully autonomous if he perceives in his teacher's approval or disapproval an arbitrary element unrelated to the rational experiences, questions, judgements and choices which he is encouraged to make. It is thus important that the teacher should give approval rather to the quality of thinking and effort which lead to an answer than exclusively to the answer itself. The teacher's most important task is to help the child develop ways of analysis, criteria of judgement, and learn to apply them, rather than merely to see that the answer is right.

In the physical world, and even more so, in mathematical-logical types of knowledge and reasoning, the principles and knowledge involved are more or less easily made manifest. There is an internally consistent 'rightness' about $6 + 4 = 10$ which is independent of judgements; so too cork can be shown to float on water and lead to sink. Step by step one can demonstrate or find out by experience the conditions under which cork will remain on the bottom and lead be maintained on the surface. This is much less easy with, for example, the historical or aesthetic modes; and the temptation is for the teacher to impose, by example, or worse still *ex cathedra,* interpretations and judgements of value and for children to accept or reject these without the bases of them being made explicit and without their 'rightness' being exposed to any other test than a vague feeling of rightness or a belief in another's judgement, brought about by liking and respect.

INDOCTRINATION OR INITIATION?

Of course, a large part of a teacher's job is to teach, to show relationships, to correct errors in thinking, to provide knowledge, to arrange significant experiences, to question, to provoke and to answer questions. Children do not just 'unfold' by some mysterious maturational process, even in a materially ideal environment, nor do they learn by unadulterated 'activity and experience', 'learning any old thing by doing any old thing'. Education, certainly in our terms, means shaping in ways considered valuable, more valuable than others. The distinction which is being made here is between 'indoctrination' and 'initiation'.[18] If the child is encouraged, in fact and in example, to question and verify the knowledge with which he is confronted by the teacher or by his own discoveries and to do this by methods and criteria appropriate to the mode or modes of thought and experience involved, he is learning to become autonomous—he is being initiated into an independent participation in his culture. If, on the other hand, the teacher does not question his own assumptions and ignores the child's 'why?' and 'how do you know?' questions when they inconveniently call his beliefs into doubt, then however lively his methods, however liberal his attitudes and his curriculum, he is indoctrinating his pupils and keeping them dependent upon some form of authority—whether this be external or ultimately internalized.

MORAL EDUCATION

This is nowhere more clearly seen than in moral education which is a particularly difficult area. It is relatively much easier to maintain rationality in empirical fields than it is say in the aesthetic; it is most difficult of all, particularly for those with a strong partisan commitment, to do so in moral education as against what Church or Party may dictate. It is obvious that anything which can be called 'education' (rather than indoctrination) in religion or in morality must rest upon principles or criteria which are antecedent to any particular religious or moral code.[19] The delicate and difficult task is that of giving the child some rules and habits of moral behaviour, of consideration for others and the like, backed initially by adult authority. This he needs simply because at first his thought is not of the kind that can comprehend. But as he grows he should be given reasons why he should act in particular ways and why others act toward him as they do, be led to question and to rationalize the principles which underly his and others' choices of how to behave, to judge and to choose.

There are those who would go further and insist that there is no basis for ethics and morality except in religion. However, if such a 'religion', whether spiritual in its content or in fact a political system of a monolithic kind, implies a prior belief of a fundamental kind which is not open to question—'except ye believe how can ye know'—then, in one area at least, genuine autonomy becomes impossible. Such religions lead to different theologies and to differences in moral codes. If they are rejected—as they may well be under the impact of questions which arise at maturity—the system built upon them fails. At their heart lies a dependence upon authority, however gentle this may be; and loss of faith means that the internalized 'superego' collapses, leaving the individual no alternative but to seek another authority.

Similar arguments apply to a non-religious moral indoctrination or training. If the child is taught to accept unquestioningly, on the autocratic even if benevolent authority of adults, a moral code, untested or unexplained, he may later be unable to adapt and modify its categoric imperatives to changing situations, or, in a burst of revolt which he takes as a bid for independence, reject it lock, stock and barrel, gaining neither autonomy nor freedom in the process.

This must be taken neither as an attack on religion nor a rejection of moral education. Religious experience and ethical awareness are valid and distinct modes of experience. There is a strong—one might even say in a multi-racial and multi-religious world, an overwhelming—case for teaching *about* religion, even in the primary school. But this is different from moral and ethical education, initiation into the ways of making moral choices, the recognition and application of moral principles.

HABIT AND SENTIMENT

The moral education of children is not something that can be treated apart from normal growth and education. Many of what seem to be moral decisions in the lives of adults are in fact the almost automatic result of deeply ingrained habitual responses, though of course, if challenged, the intelligent adult can usually produce the principle upon which the habit has been built or inculcated in him. A man does not steal money which he finds on someone else's desk, not, usually because in each instance he makes a fully conscious moral decision to resist the temptation to do so, but because he has been taught not to steal and his response has become habitual. Moral principles intervene mainly when the temptation is strong enough to overcome habit.

It is frequently not realized how specific and unorganized such moral habits may be, largely because the individual has not been led by his education, beyond the initial stage where a belief or a habit has been given and supported by authority, into the stage of questioning and test and thence to a genuinely autonomous understanding of the basis of his beliefs. For example, while most European societies inculcate habits of kindness to dogs, cats and other domestic animals, they may sanction considerable cruelty in the hunting of foxes and rabbits. The same man who is horrified if his dog or horse is wantonly hurt, will lay a spring trap for wild animals. One cannot therefore suppose that his kindness to domestic animals springs from an organized and conscious attitude of kindness to animals in general, but at best from a partial sentiment of kindness to specific animals or from habits of response which have not been organized into a sentiment of any complexity. Much the same will be found if we consider honesty. Adults who would not steal a penny from another person, will cheat a railway or bus company or the tax authority of their country.

Such unorganized habits of moral response not infrequently are the result of an education (at home and at school) which in childhood insists, with some justification in apparent success, on the unique importance of habit formation, giving only such explanation of principles as the child can grasp in terms more or less concrete and tied to particular situations; but which fails later to lead older children and the adolescents to refer particular instances to more general principles and thus enlarge and make conscious the intellectual content. Some of the disorganization, however, is due to fundamental theological and philisophical differences as to the source of moral principles and as to what man is, where he came from and what is his final end.

Ideally the moral nature should rest in a series of sentiments— deeply ingrained attitudes organized into a series of intellectually comprehended principles—from which, whenever the individual is faced with a moral decision for which habitual responses are inadequate, he should be able to decide on right moral conduct, and carry it through. The formation of such sentiments in any fully developed and comprehensive way does not take place much before adolescence, partly because of the immaturity of intelligence and partly because of insufficient-ly generalized experience. Prior to adolescence, notions of right and wrong tend to be more or less arbitrary reflections of parental attitudes, of the teaching and examples of other adults and of the social sanctions of the contemporary groups in which the child lives. Frequently one finds among children a dual morality—that which more or less reflects the demands of the adult world and that which has evolved in their own age group with notions of schoolboy honour and a united front against teachers and parents.

Often the child is aware that the demands made upon him by his parents and teachers differ from those to which they themselves con-form.[20] For example, thoughtfulness for others, politeness and considera-tion should be based on a general sentiment of respect for human beings as such. Children are often obliged to be polite to their elders; but they may not in their turn be treated with politeness by teachers or parents. From such a situation they are likely to derive the notion, usually im-plicit, that you have to be polite to the strong and that you may be rude to the weak. Similarly children are expected to be truthful and may be punished for lying; if they then find that their parents or teachers do not always tell them the truth, for example in response to questions about sex, they learn that apparently there are times when lies may be told. Examples might be multiplied of the way in which adults are inclined to apply to children demands in the moral field with which they themselves do not conform, and thus to sanction the attitude that there may be a gap between moral professions and practice.

One must of course remember that access to genuine moral choice and moral principle in any full sense implies knowledge, ability to analyse experience sensitively, to predict consequences and, operational-ly, the capacity to restrain impulses. These, in their fullest development, in turn demand the intellectual power to deal with abstractions and a considerable emotional maturity, not likely to be attained by many children in the primary school and possibly inaccessible to some even at or after adolescence. Thus, in considering the moral and emotional education of pre-adolescents, we must be mindful—just as we are in the education of other modes of thought—of what it is reasonable to ex-pect. Piaget[21] distinguishes three broad stages—premoral; conformity to others' expectations and demands; and internalization of moral rules and concepts—which, in different terms echo his other aspects of intellectual growth and with differences of detail, are similar to those suggested by others.[22]

The difficulty manifestly is that the primary school is concerned at first with the child emerging from a pre-moral phase into one of con-formity to others' demands and expectations and later, towards the end of the primary school period, if all goes well, with his development of an autonomous perception of rules and concepts which he consciously understands, adopts and internalizes. For much of his learning and his sense of security up to the age of 11 or so, he thus has what should be a diminishing need of authority, of extrinsic incentives and sanctions. In many fields of the curriculum, for example mathematical or scientific, he can almost from the outset verify empirically or logically the consequences that follow from alternative actions; he can detect errors. The moral field, however, is different. It depends upon the reactions of individuals and groups: that is to say that the consequences of his acts are visited upon him not by nature but by fellow human beings; and the acts are intentional, their efficacy depending upon their social meaning, itself only to be understood in relation to a set of moral rules and concepts. Thus to understand consequences, a child must be able to project himself into others' feelings, to understand something of his own motivations as well as those of others, and have a grasp in intellectual terms, at least at elementary level, of the rules and concepts involved.[23]

AUTHORITY AND AUTHORITARIANISM

The argument and practice of many would-be progressive educators is based upon the notion that discipline will arise from the free play of natural tendencies in the children and the adults who form the community and that this free interplay imposes, because it is free and non-directive, a kind of self-regulation and observance of the rules essential to social living. It is however arguable that there are tendencies to disorder in human beings—explained in Christian theology for example by the doctrine of original sin—and that at least in the early stages of growth children need the help of adults in coming to terms with these and controlling them. Whether this is true or not, most children have some undigested problems and conflicts, some fantasies, wishes and desires which have to be tested against the rational authority of a society and of more mature individuals. Some have developed minor maladjustments in the course of their growth; others are seriously disturbed. All need an initial authority and profit from the understanding and control which arise from a happy experience of conflict between their egocentric impulses and a comprehensible and supportive system of discipline which they can understand and internalize. Some would-be 'progressive' schools, by allowing an unrestricted satisfaction of their pupils' immediate needs, neglect two fundamentals of healthy mental development: the security which comes from knowing there are limits imposed by a benevolent, reasonable and socially oriented discipline; and the ability to accept, without undue frustration or subservience, the restrictions which are a necessary prerequisite of social living. Because they provide no coherent models, they do not help children to develop that ego-strength which is the basis of a harmonious and effective personality.

We may agree that education should permit, even ensure the fullest possible realization of individual capacities; but self-realization, unshaped by social demands, is merely crude egocentricity. Fortunately every school provides a community of some sort and thus imposes regulation; most schools are staffed by teachers who, whatever their faults, are representative of the adult society into which the child will later pass; and who, often be it admitted blindly and unhelpfully, impose some of the rules by which they themselves live. It is, however, suggested that satisfactory mental and emotional development is ensured neither by a freedom closely resembling license nor by a rigid and unhelpful discipline coupled with impossible demands.

The problem for the adult is that of exercising authority in a rational way and of avoiding an enforced submission to authoritarianism; it is further that of progressively withdrawing external sanctions and rewards as the child's own autonomy, knowledge and sheer power to comprehend develop. For this certain conditions are necessary. The first is that there should be good reasons for obliging children to do this or that—reasons which are not grounded in adult laziness or the defence of adult privilege. The second is that the reasons should be given for any expectations which the adult will insist on. And the third and in some ways the most important of all is that the rules and moral principles should be such that the concepts and principles involved and the judgements and discriminations that have to be made should be broadly within the understanding of the children concerned. Any rules which, for good reasons, must be enforced but which are beyond the child's comprehension at the time, will usually be accepted if trust has been built and the child perceives the adult as inherently reasonable wherever it is possible to be so and be understood.[24]

We must expect notions of right and wrong to be crude and unorganized at first and for the growth in integration and generalization to be slow. This implies that circumstances must be manipulated so far as is possible so that the demands made on children to conform and to resist temptation are nicely graded to provoke effort but also to ensure success, and the reward of praise. For example, it is better not to expose young children to the temptation of stealing jam and sweets at an age when they cannot be expected to foresee consequences other than immediate ones. Similarly the teacher who places great store on success as measured by the number of sums right, or who punishes children who fail in a test, is likely in fact to provoke his pupils to cheat if they can. They may, and frequently do, arrive at the conclusion that it is being found out that matters, not the act itself, and that, while it is

H

teacher's job to prevent their copying from each other, if the end is to gain a sufficiency of marks to avoid being punished, then cheating is perfectly legitimate.

Such an emphasis on individual competitive success may have another unexpected outcome. Cheating is in fact a form of co-operation and it is difficult for a primary school child to make the fine distinction, and to recognize the circumstances in which the one is right and the other wrong.

Just as the psychological principles underlying education apply to moral education as much as they do to, for example, the teaching of mathematics, so do the philosophic considerations. It is of little use adopting an educational style in the teaching of the mother tongue or of science which encourages a child to question the basis of knowledge for himself and to develop an increasing autonomy, if another part of his curriculum or the whole climate in which he moves at school is fundamentally authoritarian. This can only produce a cleavage in his thought and personality and lead to an unconscious conflict. It seems much better to accede to belief and moral conviction by the same processes of increasingly autonomous rationality as one accedes, for example, to aesthetic taste and experience or to an acceptance of some of the fundamental hypotheses of a science. In this way it is possible to know why one believes as one does and hence both to accept that others may legitimately come to other conclusions and, if accumulating knowledge and experience warrant it, to change and to develop. It is the basis of genuine tolerance.

VALUES

In the context of moral education, it is salutary for teacher and parent alike sometimes to take stock of the scale of values which, by their sanctions and prohibitions, they impose upon children; and thence to ask themselves, whether in fact they are not unintentionally inducing guilt and anxiety of a maladjusted kind, through the child's conscious or unconscious interpretation of their actions. If, for example, dirty hands or bad table manners meet with the same apparent (and usually unexplained) threat of loss of love or of punishment as theft or lying or unkindness to others, children may well be confused.

Adults, too, sometimes fail to recognize those aspects of behaviour which are parts of the developmental process and which the child himself, at the stage in which he is, cannot avoid. They may not, for example, understand that the fantasy story of the young child is the projection of his fears or his wishes and punish it as a lie. Thus not only do they not help the child adapt to reality but they teach him to associate imagination with guilt. They may react with shocked horror to his natural curiosity about sex or to his experimentation with 'naughty' words, instead of responding to the first as a legitimate inquiry and to the second as a phase through which most children pass with little lasting harm if adults gently discourage it. This does not of course mean that children should not meet with reproof for actions which are naughty or wrong in the adult sense, but that the grown-up should try to understand the child's point of view and, if he is in fact obliged by circumstances to impose a more adult standard, explain why such things are wrong in terms which the child can understand at his stage of growth.

Perhaps the most difficult thing for teacher or parent to understand and for children to learn, is the distinction we have tried to draw between being authoritarian and the legitimate use of authority—and it is a distinction which lies at the basis of mental health in its most important aspect, that of autonomy. Authoritarianism in any field implies the use of power without exposing to question its rational grounds— 'it is so, because I say so'—and the right to question and to differ for good reasons is denied. Authority on the other hand derives from such things as superior knowledge or analysed experience and is concerned with their use in the enlightenment of the learner. Identification with authorities is a very powerful way for children and adolescents to enter into their culture; and there is an obviously strong case for the exercise of authority in the up-bringing of children and in social life generally providing that it is rationally based and open to question and control. The educational (and mental health) problem is that of exercising it in such a way that children do not become permanently dependent: this implies a willingness on the part of adults to transfer to children so far as possible an increasing responsibility for their own decisions, quite deliberate training in rational choice, a willingness to accept questions and to explain the rational bases for any decisions which have to be made. It is often easier, kindly or coercively, to be authoritarian, to be didactic and *ex-cathedra* than it is to help a child to understand. Frequently too outside factors—for example public examinations—enforce a particular kind of learning; and there are situations in which the adult must exercise a protective authority, the reasons for which the child is not sufficiently mature to understand. Basically, however, if the adult has himself come to terms with authority, is rational in his attitudes and prepared to allow increasing independence to the young in his charge, replying particularly to their—sometimes mutinous—questions with clear reasons, he will help them to wean themselves from an initially necessary dependence into an equally necessary subsequent autonomy.

This will not, of course, avoid all conflicts between children and adults; indeed the more reasonable the adult, the more easy it is for the child, somewhat irritatingly, to question or even defy his authority and reject apparently the reasons which are given. The child's own impulses are strong and, on the whole, much stronger than his power rationally or otherwise to inhibit them, even when he knows they are wrong. Punishment is sometimes necessary to check wrong behaviour and to reassure the child that he is not left unsupported against his own anarchic impulses; but punishment alone is negative. It is important that positive ways of behaving should be pointed out and emphasized by praise and acceptance and that the child should be shown how to make restitution if necessary (not to appease the adult but according to rational principles) and how to set himself right in his own eyes.

CONFLICT WITH ADULTS

Conflict with adult authority is indeed an essential part of growth. It is a way, and an important one, of learning about oneself and others; it tests the limits of the permissible and defines the boundaries of the self. From the temper tantrums of the two- to three-year-old to the bids for independence of the adolescent, it is one of the most important and potentially most effective ways of learning. Those children who rarely or never enter into conflict with parents or teachers are likely later to lack firmness of character or to have been cowed into submission and be unable to free themselves from dependence.[25] What is critical is the context within which the conflict takes place. If the adult is in fact the guardian of a rational and explicable set of rules and at the same time uses his authority to uphold these, to explain them and to help the child understand why he should conform, then the conflicts, though not diminished perhaps, will be constructive. If the adult is merely exercising superior power or influence to ensure unquestioning conformity then, while he may achieve temporary peace, he is preparing explosive revolt or submissive dependence later. And this will be true whether authority is sustained by force or by love and the fear of its loss. The distinction which is being made is that between punishment and reward which reinforce understanding and rational behaviour and systems of discipline which ensure submission and conformity by threat or bribe; between authority which is supportive and educational, and authoritarianism which denies independent growth.

Children are easily made to feel guilty and anxious, even in late childhood; they readily accept what to us is an isolated condemnation of some particular action of theirs, as an outright rejection of all that they believe or fear themselves to be. They recognize in themselves and in their contemporaries, impulses to lie, to steal, to be aggressive, to be 'naughty', to be interested in forbidden things, and they are liable to react strongly in fear against such powerful feelings of badness. If adult authority is suddenly withdrawn and they are left responsible for themselves, the system of punishments which they suggest for each other is likely to be savage—a reflection of their own fear and guilt, and need for external deterrents which their growth and upbringing have led them hitherto to identify with the wholly 'good' authority figures of parent or teacher. In various ways by their behaviour they will demand authority; and if they do not get it, they react with marked insecurity. If the adults with whom they have had to do have never let it appear that they too have 'bad' impulses, and that they have learned to accept and deal with such, both in themselves and in children, and know how to support hard choices by clear reasons, then the discrepancy between the child's knowledge of himself as he is and his desire to identify himself with his picture of the perfect adult, is too great to be accepted without severe anxiety. Many of the very maladjusted children and adolescents we see in our clinics are in fact the products of a parental or school discipline which is irrational either because it is harshly authoritarian or because it mistakes inconsequential *laissez-faire* for permissiveness.

CONFLICT OF VALUES

Most children, sometimes at considerable cost, manage to digest anxieties of these kinds, if the inconsequence is not too marked or the discipline too severe and if the discrepancies between one adult and another are not too great or too irrational. To the outward observer they may appear to pass through middle childhood satisfactorily. Where, however, there is considerable difference or open conflict between the parents, between the values and structures of authority emphasized by the home and by the school, or where either is in conflict with the surrounding community—as for example occurs in some minority religious or cultural groups—the strains may become very great and seriously prejudice future development, and that not only in the moral and personal fields but in ordinary cognitive growth. Such situations demand considerable skill and insight either by parents or by teachers, so that the children can, as concretely as possible, come to understand and accept such differences. Unhappily, parents and teachers alike often find it easier to denounce aggressively, patterns of behaviour and schemes of values which are not their own, and, consciously or otherwise, they try to win the child to their own side. If, however, instead, they try to help him to understand that there can be genuine and sincere differences of opinion, they give the first example of tolerance in their own reactions and at the same time reduce very considerably the strain which a conflict of loyalties may well be imposing on him.

EDUCATION OF THE EMOTIONS

Although moral education has been insisted upon here, it is in fact a paradigm of all education and in one very real sense even the teaching of such apparently non-moral subjects as mathematics or science will reinforce or contradict the tendency towards autonomy and responsibility or towards dependence or revolt which we have been discussing. Moral education, as we have insisted, is not to be considered a thing apart from or even markedly different in the principles on which it is based from the rest of the curriculum.

So far, however, we have tended to stress the cognitive aspects of growth and what we might call the rational and intellectual aspects. But however intellectual or rational the processes of choice or problem solving may appear to be, they are not uniquely intellectual, even in such abstract circumstances as mathematics. The moment we consider choices of action in the everyday world, and particularly when such choices call prejudices and desires into play, we see that the disciplining of the emotional life, the understanding and control of impulse, the refinement of feeling are just as importantly basic as are the more cognitive habits, strategies and knowledge. Hence, however we go about education at any level, we are as much concerned with the education of the emotions as we are with that of the intellect. We are concerned with the balance between feelings of security and the challenge or even the threat proposed by novelty: cognitively this concerns the balance between acquired skill or knowledge and some task which provokes a new synthesis; emotionally and socially it concerns the arousal of a certain measure of insecurity by changing circumstances and the wish to move forward into the unfamiliar from the comfort of acquired habit and response. Psychologically speaking these are not so much different as inter-related aspects of the same thing.

But they are more than this. Although the security-insecurity balance is basic to the emotional life, emotion covers a wide spectrum of feeling states which are not just physiological responses felt as disturbing or enhancing; they involve ways of seeing and interpreting experience, they are a response to stimuli which may be either objective situations outside the individual or arise in a more subjective inner way. For example, a feeling of depression may have an unconscious origin or may be directly related to circumstances or, more probably, partake of both; similarly anger may be provoked by a genuine frustration but be augmented by subconscious, or unconscious dispositions aroused by some symbolic aspect of the frustrating situation. Jealousy may be experienced as much because a child is unsure of his own worthiness to be loved as because another is loved more. Thus, in emotion of any kind—fear, jealousy, pride, sorrow, grief, envy, guilt, shame and so on—there are important cognitive elements which Peters calls 'appraisals'.[26] Particularly in the powerful and primordial emotions, these appraisals are likely to be very greatly modified by unconscious and subconscious elements built up from early intense experiences when any power of appraisal was primitive and uniquely self-referential. One of the most important aspects of education, and especially of the education of the emotional life is that of enabling the individual to recognize in himself the ways in which unconscious elements of these kinds may prejudice his objective appraisals of experience and his judgement of situations. In this sense we are concerned with education, not only as a means of developing cognitive analysis and control but in a way which comes very near to what some would call psycho-therapeutic.

Finally we should point to the connection between emotions and motives—the dispositions to act in certain ways as the result of the emotion experienced; by forms of flight in the case of fear, of aggression in the case of anger and so on, though some emotions may not issue in actions either because of restraint or because there is no specific action towards which an emotion—like grief or wonder—can readily tend, though it may issue as tears or excitement.

This relation between emotion and motive is a very far-reaching one both in education and, even more importantly, in life itself. In all kinds of ways it lies at the very root of mental health, of personal and social adjustment and of the ability to meet changing circumstances with a sufficient degree of confident flexibility. We have only to think of the regrettably frequent cases of pupils cognitively perfectly able to achieve intellectual mastery of, say, mathematics but who fail to do so because, unconsciously, they dare not risk the frustration of failure; or of those whose attitudes to others are tortuously determined by infantile jealousies of which they are not consciously aware, and who see another's independence or achievement as a threat and are therefore motivated either to intense competitiveness or to overt denigration; or, to take another example, those who feel guilt as an inevitable accompaniment of what is, objectively appraised, a perfectly innocent pleasure, and who therefore are unable perhaps to develop a just balance between work and leisure.

In terms then of many of the core problems of mental health, some would say of all, the education of the emotions is central; and it is highly complex since it is concerned with the ways in which the human being learns to appraise and understand experience, how these appraisals are integrated into his personality and determine his disposition to attend to and interpret subsequent experience; and how his feelings issue in and determine his actions.

It is obviously and closely connected too with moral education, since many if not all the appraisals concerned in their more refined and elaborated forms, and certainly most of these connected with the most powerful emotions, are conceptually linked with and dependent upon general moral notions—for instance, shame, guilt, remorse—or rely upon moral notions for control when they are motivations to action—as in, for example, envy or lust or anger.

In attempting to educate the emotions we are concerned with at least three things: the development of the ability adequately to appraise the situation which provokes them, including at least some knowledge and control of the ways in which self-reference may falsify appraisal; the ability to choose an appropriate form of response when the emotion seeks discharge in a tendency to act; and with a refinement of the feelings involved, with the development of sensitivity. Moreover, since some emotions have no morally acceptable direct outlet, we are concerned with sublimations, the direction of motivational energy into constructive rather than destructive or anti-social channels. Finally, since initially young children live almost entirely through their emotions and their powers of objective appraisal are largely undeveloped, few escape in their early experience the deformation of their perceptions by infantile fears, hopes, wishes; we should therefore help towards remedying anything which has gone seriously wrong and aid the development of insight into the ways in which our own and others' behaviour may be irrationally motivated. Again we may draw attention to the fact that we are concerned with weaning from dependence, with the difficult transition from fantasy to reality, with the transformation of the unadulterated ego-reference system of the young child to the hetero- or social-reference system of the developed and autonomous adult.

This is not a process that will be completed in the primary school and in its most refined form it is dependent upon the development of abstract thought. But the primary school period represents a most important, indeed essential, stage in the process, just as it does in the acquisition of moral concepts, habits of impulse control and in the development of cognitive capacities, all of which are related to emotional education.

In some respects, the most important thing about a child's school experience is that it provides him with a great variety of social situations in which he builds up an image of himself in relation to others as well as to the demands and norms of his society. His success or failure in his work, his acceptability to his peers and to his teachers directly influence his feelings of security: they may provide a reinforcement of what he has already learned at home, or they may in some ways compensate for or contradict what he has learned to believe about himself. In school he finds others who are neither siblings nor parents in relation to whom he can learn other ways of feeling and behaving than those he has acquired in the more intensely emotional setting of his family. The others in his environment pass judgements upon him and his actions—he is good, he is clever, he is naughty—which in the absence of other knowledge about himself he introjects as elements in his feelings about himself as a unique individual.

SCHOOL CLIMATE

The process thus sketched will take place in any school more or less well according to its circumstances and the ideas which underly it. A positive education of the emotions implies something more. For example, one of the most important criteria of mental health is a developed ability to form mutually satisfying relationships of kinds which are appropriate in the very varied situations of adult life. This means that not only can one love without possessiveness but that one can maintain friendly and co-operative and non-dependent relations in, for example, working situations. Whether or not a school contributes to this or inhibits its full development will depend upon how far it reinforces personal security and a sense of personal value as a basis from which others can be viewed as non-threatening, how far it provides circumstances in which its pupils can work together and fosters (and overtly values) the appropriate attitudes.

Similarly the ability to curb the aggressive expression of anger in violence against others depends in part upon the capacity to appraise the situation provoking the anger, in part upon sentiments of justice and fair play, in part on the degree to which one can project oneself into the feelings of others and upon a trained ability to inhibit powerful impulses. All children have impulses to hurt and to destroy and control does not come easily. Merely dealing with them by suppression, often even by physical violence or restraint—though it may in some circumstances be a necessary first step—does not positively help. For this, it is necessary that the child should be taught to recognize his impulses for what they are, be encouraged to ask himself what others may feel, to begin to understand notions like fairness, and to develop acceptable alternative behaviours. Similarly opportunities for generosity, for helpfulness, for putting others' interests first, for sharing and the like should be provided and the idea of consideration for others which lies behind them, gently, almost casually, insisted upon.

Such appeals to reason and to rationality, even if they are sensitively and simply made often seem immediately ineffective. They probably will be if it is not manifest that the adults concerned have themselves problems of unregenerate emotional impulses similar to those of children and yet manage to live by the rational principles and rules which they propound. One has to remember that education is a long process and

H*

that too much cannot be expected of children, especially if we wish to wean them towards a genuine emotional autonomy and away from dependence upon a set of rules, respect for which is maintained by the authority of an adult. They need reassurance—and overt reassurance— that feelings and emotion, even powerful, aggressive and 'bad' feelings, are not in themselves wicked or even wrong; what may be wrong are anti-social forms of behaviour, actions which are selfish and take insufficient account of the needs of others.

Of course such rationality is to be tempered by the teacher's genuine acceptance of the child as he is in all his imperfections, by encouragement and by a careful distinction between a rejection of undesirable behaviour and a rejection of an individual. In a very real and fundamental sense the child's faith in his teacher's capacity to accept and care for him whatever he does, even though she reproves his faults, is the basis on which the interpersonal aspects of emotional education are built in school.

THE NEED FOR PLAY IN PRIMARY SCHOOLS

Two other aspects should however be stressed. Children of primary school age are still subject to feelings of aggression, anxiety and fears which they cannot directly express; they are aware of questions which they dare not put into words; they need too to learn how others feel. Play and various non-verbal forms of communication and outlet— painting, clay modelling, spontaneous drama, role play and the like— are important to pre-school children; but they remain essential means whereby the primary school child can come to terms with the many things, situations, impulses and fantasies that continue to puzzle, frighten or worry him. Through play, creative or dramatic work, he can sometimes bring out a conflict or an anxiety without feeling too much committed to it and, by seeing how his teacher and other children react, find ways of easing his tensions and coming to an understanding of himself. He can too project himself into other people and find out what it is like to be them. Often the fact that such expression is permitted, even encouraged, will be sufficient to set right tensions and difficulties or at least to reduce them to a level at which a child can cope. But a sensitive and knowledgeable teacher can do more. By her remarks and comments, particularly if she has a developed ability herself to empathize,[27] and by intervening occasionally in games of make believe, she can foster understanding and help children to develop through words as well as actions an insight into themselves and others; and refine as well as direct the emotions involved.

For many children creative and projective opportunities through play and similar activities will be enough; and for all children it is an essential complement to the somewhat arid intellectualism which dominates many school systems even today. However, some children, for reasons which lie outside the school, are deeply maladjusted; they have developed systems of 'appraisal' and motivations which do not allow them to develop reasonable insight into themselves and others, which falsify their relations and which dictate forms of behaviour which cannot easily be tolerated in the ordinary classroom. For them special remedial and therapeutic help is necessary, from someone trained to understand the rather special problems involved. But it must be stressed, that although its initial aims may appear to be different and different aspects may have to be emphasized, such psychotherapy or special educational treatment is different only in degree rather than in kind from what is a good education of the emotional and social life under normal circumstances. In the open expressive atmosphere of a good primary school many minor maladjustments and behaviour disturbances, covered and repressed in a more authoritarian environment, emerge and it is good that this should be so. But such phenomena can appear threatening and difficult to a teacher untrained in recognizing them for what they are— especially if in dramatic or visual creative work she is confronted with the expression of half conscious fantasies by her pupils which reactivate her own childish conflicts or represent an intolerable expression of primitive emotion.[28] The teacher may need reassurance and support from a psychologist if such behaviour is not to provoke a rejecting and suppressive reaction.

Emotion can and should be explored in other ways; and it is here that literature, the dramatic and other arts come very much into their own, not only as valid forms of knowledge and thinking in their own right, but as important ways of learning about oneself and others, about emotions, the springs of behaviour about how others think and feel and the ways, acceptable and unacceptable that people behave towards each other.[29] Adventure stories, fables, tales of family life, even fairy tales all provide situations of direct appeal to children and provoke reflection and comment on behaviour. Drama allows one to feel into a different role and win understanding of others. Poetry, music, expressive movement and dance and the visual arts help children to experience and to express wonder or other emotions, as well as providing sublimations and acceptable ways of expressing dark and difficult impulses. Apart altogether from the aesthetic aspects, which are important in themselves, what we are concerned with is the extension of the experience of emotion, the shaping of perception and the disposition to attend to emotional stimuli, the development of sensibility to the world and to others and of a language in which to formulate and express it. Much art too, particularly literature, embodies moral principles and provides examples of desirable and undesirable behaviour, ways of understanding and adjusting to others from which children extend their experience and learn as much as, if not more than, from direct exhortation and advice, and the inevitably limited situations of real life.

As with play and other forms of spontaneous expression mentioned above, the teachers' role in aesthetic and emotional education is not necessarily and always a passive one. It is they who, in the case of literature and the arts, are mainly responsible for the introduction of the stimulus, the selection of books and music, proposing the themes of dance or movement—although, of course, children too should themselves be encouraged to select and propose experiences for themselves and others. The adults should encourage children to discuss, to judge, to test the validity for themselves of the experiences, to help them find categories of expression; and while not imposing their adult judgement, be nonetheless prepared to explain and interpret and to expose the basis on which they find value in the arts.

ORGANIZATION

We cannot however limit ourselves to specific content or aspects of the curriculum, important as these may be; nor can we be content with narrow improvement of pedagogic methods used by the teacher in front of his class. We are as much concerned with the kind of information conveyed to children by the forms of organization used, by the tissue of relationships—among children, between children and teachers, teachers and parents and among teachers—which impinge almost unconsciously on the child's idea of himself and others, constructing for him his earliest and most influential picture of a functioning community. In this, the ways in which children are grouped for their learning, the implicit and explicit hierarchies not only among staff and children, but also of knowledge and the value set upon persons and forms of behaviour, the code of rules and general system of discipline, and the overt relationships with the surrounding community are of critical importance.[30]

Thus practices such as streaming which are aimed to adjust curricular demands to the differing abilities of children may in fact be perceived by pupils (and by parents) as a rejection of the less able and a valuation of intelligence, or rather particular kinds of school success, over other qualities such as effort.[31] Inter-individual competition, systems of marks to be gained or lost may stress conformity rather than questioning and place a value on mechanical attainment rather than understanding. Similarly, a rigid distinction between forms of knowledge appropriate in the classroom and experiences in the out-of-school lives of children, or between the reproduction of learned answers and more spontaneous and 'creative' uses of thought can easily introduce conflict with so strong an emotional loading for children, that they completely reject what goes on in school; and efforts made by individual teachers within the curriculum proper to lead the pupil along the road to intellectual and personal autonomy may be completely nullified. We may add that this will be true whether the child perceives that the system is enforced by a punitive or by a loving authoritarianism; though revolt or cowering submission are more likely perhaps where the authoritarianism is punitive and dependent submission where it comes from a loved and loving adult. In either case—to the degree that the ends sought or the hierarchies of value established are not seen to be fair and rational by the child and his failure to conform fully is perceived by him as rejection—he may either withdraw from any active participation in his own education or attempt to internalize models which he cannot understand in any full sense, relying on the teacher as a kind of external 'policeman'.

Curriculum objectives, teaching methods, classroom and school 'climates' and systems of rules and discipline are thus parts of a whole. The educational task—and this is particularly important in the primary school where the foundations of a method of learning, of attitudes towards knowledge, of moral behaviour and understanding, the expansion of experience and of a more complex basis of personal security and autonomy are laid—is that of helping the child to shape his motivations and interests, to identify for himself his own aims and goals and to help him to reconcile these with social needs and pressures. The teacher is or should be aware of remoter ends concerned with the nature of knowledge and culture, with the ethical basis of the 'rational unity of mankind',[32] notions of justice, fair play, consideration for others and the like, and with standards to which effort should tend. This conscious and reasoned awareness is the source of his authority. He will draw out from his pupils what they wish to do, help them choose and set their own, increasingly exacting, standards, initiate them into experiences chosen to open different modes of thinking, to provoke questioning of the bases of knowledge and he will intervene to help understanding and knowledge, of the self and of others. He will reinforce the will to achieve or to work, where it is weak, against discouragement or conflicting impulse; he will provide outlets for emotion, conflict and unconscious preoccupations; he will provide for aesthetic and emotional experience and education and only rarely will he compel, in situations where the necessity is overriding, to something which his pupils cannot yet understand.

The value of proposals for the reform of curriculum, method or organization must then be judged by whether they make the tasks of teacher and learner easier. About such innovations as, for instance, modern mathematics, integrated science or integrated humanities, and such organizational devices as family grouping, activity methods, the integrated day or team teaching, we have to ask three questions: do such proposals favour an understanding of some or all of the essential modes of thinking and experience? do they lead the child to choose with increasing insight the aims of his own activity and set himself advancing standards of achievement? and do they create a climate which promotes the intellectual and moral autonomy of the pupil?

B. SOME HARD REALITIES—METHOD AND ORGANIZATION

INDIVIDUAL DIFFERENCES

Any attempt at embodying a more truly educational set of aims in the primary school will be largely frustrated unless teachers are fully aware of the immense range of individual variation between children, even at the age of 6 or 7, and the increasing differences which make themselves felt with advancing age. For example, in sheer intellectual power there may well be a range of four years or more of mental growth between the dullest and brightest of a group of 7-year-olds,[33] a divergence which at 10 may well have widened to some six or seven years. Similar but less measurable differences are apparent in the strength and organization of the emotional drives, in the ability to tolerate frustration, and in levels of aspiration. Some children of 6 are little more mature socially and emotionally than 4-year-olds, and where children are drawn from very dissimilar social backgrounds, their levels of development towards maturity will not only be different in degree but in kind. Physically and physiologically too there will be differences—in size, in susceptibility to fatigue, in neuro-muscular control, in the acuity of the senses and in the psycho-physical developments which underlie such skills as visual and auditory analysis, fine muscular co-ordination, and the like—on which learning to read, to spell and to write in part depend. In verbal development, in range of spoken vocabulary, in sentence structure and in comprehension, social differences and differences of individual experience will show themselves as marked almost as differences in the sheer power of intelligence. Thus the greater the emphasis upon formal skills, upon uniform instruction and upon homogeneous standards of attainment, the more likely is it that inter-individual differences will become increasingly marked—particularly in such instrumental skills as the recognition of words in reading and mechanical calculation.[34]

Even if the teacher is encouraged to regard his task as that of giving a lesson, the learning of which is the responsibility of the children, he cannot afford to ignore this variety in the human material in front of him. If on the other hand he fully accepts its implications, he is faced with developing a highly flexible programme, much study of each child and a grading of his demands to meet the capacities of each.

This does not mean that we must wholly give up class teaching or group activities in favour of individual attention. A sum in simple arithmetic will show that the primary school teacher with a class of 45 children could devote only five or six minutes of individual attention to each one daily, if he worked without interruption. Quite apart from the factor of time too, children need experience in groups working together; just as they enjoy and profit from class lessons. The problem is one of careful organization in function of what is to be achieved and the needs of the pupils.

THE CLASS LESSON

Hence the teacher of children aged 7 to 11 or 12 must scrutinize carefully his curriculum and decide which parts of it are appropriate for direct teaching to the whole class, which are appropriate for group activities and where individual attention is necessary. This can be done by no rule of thumb formula. It has to be based upon an assessment of the pupils he is teaching and an examination and modification of the goals set by his curriculum if he has one imposed upon him by outside authority. If necessary (and it is likely often to be so), he will find it better to discard some as impracticable since in attempting everything he may well achieve nothing except confusion and distaste.

The class lesson should have as its core those relationships, facts or techniques which are essential and which can be grasped by the slowest learner; but it should contain meat even for the brightest. The Shakespearian play which appealed for different reasons to groundlings, men of the world and the literary critic is essentially the perfect example of what a lesson should be: something within the grasp of everyone and much to challenge the capacity of the most able. The object of a lesson is to cover ground relatively quickly and to add to the common stock of the class. As a lesson of this type proceeds the teacher is aware of the shortness of the attention span of even the brightest child and by variety of techniques maintains interest: didactic, expository, questioning, inspirational by turns, the good lesson moves at a tempo determined by the class and differing from class to class. It is essentially a creative and artistic activity in which the media are the children and the subject matter varies in ways, subtle or marked, every minute.

GROUPING[35]

Grouping or the establishment of 'sets' has uses too within the large class. In its simplest form it is a way of dividing the whole body of pupils into sections each more homogeneous than the whole. For example, it is common to have groups for reading or for arithmetic who are moving slower or faster than the average and for whom the instruction and the exercises are appropriately graded. This is a device not to be despised in practice unless it becomes rigid and in fact stratifies the form into the able, average and the dull by the criteria of the basic skills or, as is often the case, by only one of them. Development, in the early stages of primary school at all events, is so uneven that grouping by attainment and ability carried out systematically for each skill to be acquired, should mean (though it rarely does) differently composed groups for each, and a continuous process of interchange between them. The overcrowded classroom or school makes grouping (and of course any work which involves movement by the pupils) much more difficult; some would say impossible. Yet the large class in fact makes grouping the more necessary.[36] Provided children can all be seated in a classroom (even where the desks are of the three or four to a bench type) it is possible for all members of any one arithmetic or reading set to be in geographical proximity. In most circumstances too it is possible to turn the desks in different directions according say to four sets or to four co-operating cross-sectional groups and thus break up the spurious homogeneity and teacher-directedness of the usual classroom layout. In order to adapt instruction to the varying possibilities of his pupils and to ensure that the various groups progress with sufficient to challenge their activity and interest, a careful system of recording is necessary. Here the record card maintained by each child for himself is of inestimable service for keeping track both of the work and practice done by the groups and of individual progress. Properly designed, such a card and the assessments on which it is based also enable the pupil to see for himself how he is achieving his goals.

Grouping of a different kind has other educational uses. For instruction in arithmetic or in reading skills, the group may need to be homogeneous; but for wider educational purposes, the class may be divided into what may be called cross-sectional groups. Each of these might reproduce, as far as possible equally, the spread of ability in the whole class, and they can then work as a series of teams, the members of which assist each other on joint projects. In this way certain important attitudes may be fostered and developed. The abler children come to realize that their better endowment imposes duties towards their fellows; the less able learn that they have a contribution to make. Competition between individuals, which is a usual incentive in the classroom, is destructive for the majority of children who, however hard they work, can rarely beat the few outstandingly able—and who therefore frequently lose heart. Competition between equally matched groups, however, is a different matter, since success depends upon a joint effort and upon the smoothness of the integration of the team.

A third form of grouping, where the accent is perhaps more on social than on strictly cognitive learning, is that of 'friendship grouping', where children choose their own companions. This sometimes has the disadvantage that like chooses like both intellectually and socially and the groups may in fact deprive children of certain kinds of contact and stimulation. This is not to condemn it as one of a number of forms; it is doubtful whether any form of grouping or individual work used exclusively as a basis is without some major disadvantage.[37]

INDIVIDUAL WORK

In the early stages of number work and reading considerable purely individual learning is necessary and this cannot readily be achieved solely by group work. What happens still in many schools is that the whole class repeats a lesson out loud, chants arithmetical tables or number combinations, and reads collectively or round the class. The result is that many children perform mechanically and little or no learning takes place, certainly if the method is frequently practised.[38] If, however, the rhythmic chanting is considerably reduced and replaced by a series of very short assignments—for example, cards containing many of the number combinations up to 100 arranged as subtractions and additions, or a short passage to read followed by questions to test comprehension, or lists of 5 or 10 words to learn to spell—then, working individually or in pairs, children can check and record their own increasing speed and accuracy, logging their results on their own record cards. They can be taught to maintain a graph of their own progress and thus be stimulated to compete against themselves.[39]

If periods of class instruction are kept short and employed only when it can reasonably be expected that all children will follow them; if a careful distinction is made between the teaching of techniques to homogeneous groups and class or group activities which have a value in stimulating social and co-operative learning; and if skilful use is made of individual assignments progressively graded and as far as possible self-checking; then the teacher can be free to devote attention for short periods individually to children who have an immediate difficulty or to those who through absence have missed a critical step. Such help prevents children from falling further and further behind, growing more and more discouraged until, at 10 or 11, they have developed major emotional difficulties as well as marked educational retardation.

Methods of the type suggested above lend themselves to a wide variety of uses within the primary school. They demand of teachers considerable sensitivity to the particular class of children with whom they are working, some ingenuity in the preparation and production of material, and rather more attention to systematic recording than older methods. In the early stages at any rate the uniform textbook possessed by each child in the class is inappropriate. What is needed is a wide variety of exercises of all types printed or duplicated, single examples of a range of books, small sets only of some, and plentiful raw material in the form of paper, cardboard and the like. The school or class library is a tool of inestimable value. In countries where the primary school syllabus and even the textbooks are prescribed by the central or local authorities the initiative of the progressive teacher may be somewhat hampered. Even so, individual and graded group work, self-checking and self-testing devices, the stimulation of self-competition, and intergroup competition and the elimination of direct competition between individuals are not impossible to achieve.

ACTIVE METHODS

It is in the light of these modifications of the chalk and talk teacher-directed classroom that we should return to examine practices like 'learning by activity and experience', systems like those propounded by Cousinet and Freinet[40] and indeed the conflict between proponents of traditional versus 'active' methods.[41]

A number of studies throw some light on this.[42] Gardner[43] studied the results of different practices—roughly progressive or active versus traditional—in infant schools with a follow-up in junior schools.[44] Her conclusions tend to indicate that more child-centred methods result in formal attainments which are little if anything below those of traditional schools; but that in such things as originality and enjoyment in free writing, and width of reading, the willingness to use books for a variety of purposes and the like, pupils from active schools are markedly superior. A much later study is that of Barker Lunn.[45] This major research was based upon a very large sample of ordinary English schools. In some of these children were streamed by ability, and their teachers emphasized formal attainments, a reasonably formal discipline, class teaching and a systematic emphasis on a predetermined curriculum. In the contrasting group, the teachers themselves tended to be rather more 'progressive' in their outlook, the children were in groups heterogeneous for ability and attainment, discipline was freer and the methods used involved more self-directed activity by the pupils. It must be emphasized that within each of the contrasted samples, there was wide variation in the degree of 'traditional' or 'progressive' emphasis and that within any one school not all teachers adhered to the philosophy of the organization involved; nor, it should be said, was it possible to identify and match a group of very good traditional with a group of very good progressive schools or classes.

Nevertheless, the results suggest that formal subject-centred methods with an emphasis on measurable attainment in reading, writing and arithmetic calculation, tend to produce results in these areas only slightly if at all higher than those of the more informal schools.[46] When, however, one investigates the use which is made of reading, the ability to comprehend, the degree of mathematical understanding, the imaginative quality and quantity of writing and a general ability to use divergent as well as convergent thinking,[47] then it is the children educated in a generally more 'progressive' atmosphere who have the advantage. What is more, the evidence suggests that the levels of anxiety produced by the two systems are different; the more child-centred schools had fewer anxious children and a lower level of anxiety, generally, and more children who were considered a pleasure to teach.[48]

IMPORTANCE OF THE TEACHER'S ROLE

There is little doubt that one cannot afford to be dogmatic and ideological on matters of method and organization. Three things seem to be of importance and each can be realized by almost any system along the continuum formal-traditional to progressive. Teachers must be perceived by the child, not as arbitrary judges whose standards and aims are unclear or undefined, impossible to attain and in conflict with everything else in the child's life at home, in the community and in his own intellectual growth. They must be seen predominantly as adults who co-operate with their pupils to further learning and whose authority, reasonably exercised, supports resistance to impulsive weaknesses or sustains the interests of the group against the individual or vice-versa, in terms of manifest principles of fair-play and justice. They should foster the development both of linear or reproductive and of creative thinking in the sense that they enable children to see that both kinds of activity are according to different criteria and in different circumstances involved in learning and in the solution of problems. It is largely the teacher who will arrange to bring together different kinds of experience and different subjects in such a way that the connexions between them can be discovered by the pupils, so that they can learn how to generalize and extend their concepts beyond the subject compartments. So far as it is possible, teachers should encourage children to seek and find their own goals and establish their own standards of performance; and where, as is often the case, they themselves have to set objectives in relation to aims too remote for their young charges to conceive, they must try to win understanding or build so trusting a relationship that the pupils will accept adult guidance. The aim is progressively to wean children from dependence on adults for extrinsic incentives to learn, for discipline and even for help. This means that much of the time the teacher must permit children freely to choose, limiting his or her role to ensuring that the knowledge on which choice depends is really available to the pupils and that they can foresee the consequences. The good teacher then sustains the child in his choice, even if it appears to be a wrong one, intervening to mitigate consequences which the child cannot be expected to bear.

In very many ways this is easier to achieve in an informal, active classroom climate where children are encouraged to be spontaneous. But there are real difficulties. It is not easy to ensure for all children that the sequencing and pacing of their learning is adequate and does not leave serious, even crippling gaps. It is difficult to see that children do get a systematic exposure to and practice in the various modes of knowledge and thought and that the generalization and correlation of diverse experience really does take place. Some at least of this desirable systematization and control of learning is considerably easier in a more formally organized situation—and this is particularly true of that early development of basic instrumental skills like reading, basic calculation, handwriting and spelling.[49] So too, because of the rather authoritarian nature of their home background, some children feel more secure in a highly structured school environment and many very intelligent children may at first desire to be taught in directive ways, rejoicing in competition because they tend to be successful, and seeking the safety of an externally imposed black and white discipline. We must remember too that teachers are people. They vary in their capacity to sustain their tolerance of the 'untidiness' which spontaneous activity appears to engender, to maintain their faith that the lightest of guidance supported by a systematic overall and flexible plan will result in secure learning. Teachers too vary even more in their security in the face of the challenge to their deepest and least conscious fears that the uninhibited activity of young children not infrequently proposes.

VARIETY OF STYLE AND METHOD

One is led therefore to suggest that there is no ideology, no method, no one kind of climate which is practicable and good for all children, all teachers and in all school circumstances; but that methods should be chosen in terms of how far they bring teacher and learner into a wide variety of satisfying relationships in terms of the kinds of cognitive and emotional objectives we have discussed. This implies a considerable variety of style and method; but it implies too that the teacher is clearly aware of broad objectives, systematic in his or her approach and flexible in adjustments to the differing needs and capacities of individual pupils.

Of recent years, there have been a number of methods and forms of organization developed to provide just this combination of formal and informal activity, mixing overtly systematic teaching with more spontaneous interest-centred and self-directed work. Two contrasting but not incompatible systems may be mentioned here which can in fact be used alone or in combination.

THE INTEGRATED DAY[50]

The so-called 'integrated day' is one. It is based on the facts that children naturally work at different speeds and levels, that the boundaries between subjects like reading, arithmetic, writing and the like are highly artificial and that the compartmentalized timetable frequently breaks up an activity long before the child himself is ready to finish it, thus rupturing his interest. Schools which practice the integrated day tend to abandon all but a few essential fixed points in the timetable—meal breaks or activities requiring specialized facilities like physical education—as well as reducing or eliminating entirely the class lesson. A great deal of material of all kinds (paint, paper, water, sand, simple craft materials, mechanical objects to take to pieces or reassemble, modest scientific apparatus, large and small building material) is provided, along with a large and varied collection of books for consultation and reference and very carefully prepared work cards, covering all those kinds of activities which subtend reading and communication skills, mathematical skills and insight, or the systematization of knowledge acquired through experiment with the materials and the use of the books provided. The children are formed or form themselves into groups who sit together in different parts of the classroom and are assigned or sometimes choose projects or activities on which to work together or individually. They are free to move about as they need and wish, encouraged to converse and to help each other.[51]

The teacher's role is quite different from the conventional instructional one. Very much of his or her work is that of preparation, of making sure that the diet offered is sufficiently varied, rich, stimulating and comprehensive, ensuring as well some systematic work on the instrumental skills, in some ways the most difficult aspects of the task. While the children are at work, he or she circulates, encouraging here, helping with a difficulty there and seeing to it that each child over time does get both the range of experience and learning he needs and the individual teaching sometimes necessary to achieve a real mastery. From such a system, the class lesson, or the short period of instruction to part of the class is not excluded. Nor should children be denied the delights, for example, of singing together, or of sitting quietly and listening to a story, or being the audience for a play presented by some of their number.

TEAM TEACHING[52]

It is obvious that, the moment one accepts the challenge of opening experience to children in this way and of breaking down the in-school and the out-of-school barriers, the pupils will find interests demanding knowledge which goes beyond that possessed by their teachers. Books are a help but, in some spheres (for example music, handicrafts and much science), adult skilled aid is necessary. Moreover adult enthusiasms or lack of them are infectious: so children tend to reflect the strengths and weaknesses of their teachers. Hence *team teaching* has been used as a means of bringing children into contact with adults who have complementary interests, specialisms, knowledge and gifts. The team may consist of two, three or more teachers and the equivalent number of classes—something like 100 or so children. It may consist of one highly experienced and gifted team leader who inspires a group of collaborators or it may be a number of co-equal members each with a particular flair in one direction or another. The children concerned are grouped in different ways for different purposes. There may, for example, be two relatively small groups working at reading and mathematics while the third team member undertakes a large group activity such as singing, dramatic work or games. The three or more classrooms may be arranged and equipped for specialized purposes—dramatic work and movement, expressive play, environmental studies, craft work, and a quiet area for reading or other 'pencil and paper' types of activity. Members of the teaching team tend to be available in one or other of these, the children moving between them as the needs of their own work prompt them.

This kind of team teaching, of course, combines very well with the integrated day and permits the individual child or groups of children to put themselves in touch as they feel the need with those members of the team whose knowledge and skills they require at the time. It also allows each member of the team to make himself particularly expert in one or two important areas. For example, one might concentrate upon mastering modern mathematics or the newer forms of integrated science teaching, whilst another is the musician or artist of the group and a third specializes in the teaching of reading both as a basic skill and as a meaning-information getting process linked with a school or class library. If children are encouraged and trained to get on by themselves either singly or in groups, then from time to time two or even the whole team of teachers can concentrate with some of the children on, for example, orchestral, dramatic or movement activities or on expeditions into the surrounding community.[53]

NO MAGIC PANACEA

Again, however, it is important to reiterate that no form of organization is a magic panacea. The two outlined above are ways of managing the teaching environment which permit, but do not by themselves ensure, a better use of all kinds of resources, human and material and, from the children's point of view, a varied, rich set of experiences from which they can profit at their own pace and in their own way. They can readily be used to stress independence in learning and the correlation of knowledge; they may allow the school to open itself to the world, and they can foster cooperation. But they are not easy for the teacher; they demand extensive and careful preparation based on skilled appraisal of the children, a clear and systematic analysis of objectives and real insight into how children learn. Without these they readily degenerate into gimmickry and in fact waste children's time and frustrate their learning.

Such methods do not imply undisciplined running about or even, invariably, overt action, they do not mean merely 'following the child'; they imply that through a consciously guided series of experiences in which the child participates he is led to mental activity of many kinds. The teacher should provide perhaps even most of the raw material of experience though advantage should be taken of the child's out-of-classroom life; and he or she should see to it that whatever is offered is such as to evoke ever more complex and varied types of thinking. But the task does not end here. A teacher has to teach, has to use, to stimulate, and to channel enthusiasm, and to show pupils how from specific relationships, or elements, or techniques, they may increasingly generalize. It is only in this way that a transfer of training of value to the whole mental development of the individual will take place. The teacher, too, has to be the guardian of standards and, while not carping at the imperfections of immaturity and the errors that increasing mastery will eliminate, to help to set goals immediate and more remote toward which the pupils will strive.

A CLEAR AWARENESS OF AIMS

Demands which are clearly understood, goals which are attainable with effort and values which the child can appreciate, are not merely the marks of a curriculum and method which is educationally sound; they are the very framework within which the child can build a feeling of security and confidence in school. Children will learn because they are emotionally stirred by the situation in which they find themselves; because they recognize and are challenged by the element of novelty which they wish to integrate into their existing schemas. Gradually, if they have been trained by undertaking at first small tasks with an easily seen and relatively immediate result and, later, progressively tasks with more and more distant objectives, accepted by them as worth while, they will undertake the apparently unrewarding toil, because they feel confident that the remoter end towards which they work is both attainable and worth attaining. The fault of many of the traditional methods lies in that fear of blame and punishment is the motive which leads to learning. Not infrequently, if the learning takes place, it is joyless and often impermanent; where, in spite of his fear and sometimes because of it, a child fails, his morale may be completely undermined and he may well lose the will to try again. On the other hand, many modern methods fail because, relying solely on arousing the child's immediate interest, they do not lead him progressively to perceive and wish to attain steadily more remote ends through an effort which may not in and for itself be immediately enjoyable.

As we have seen earlier, the degree of consistency, organization and complexity is a most important environmental element in the structuring of ability and, indeed, of the moral and emotional life. Hence a crucial condition for successful education is that the teacher should have a clear (albeit flexible) awareness of the aims of what is being done, both immediate and remote; and without being rigid he or she should organize systematically the education of the children confided to his or her care. It is not without significance that in much work concerned with methods of teaching particular skills, or aspects of the curriculum, like reading,[54] the quality of the teacher, the degree of order and system employed, prove to be more important to success than any specific method used.

EXPLICIT GOALS

It would be inappropriate here to develop in detail the means by which the broad objectives of education as outlined earlier can be defined and broken down in precise behavioural terms. In some respects it is difficult to reconcile the 'modes of thinking and knowing' of the type outlined by Hirst and Peters with such developed taxonomies as those of Bloom and his collaborators.[55] What, however, is important about the work of Bloom is that it provides a model whereby broad aims may be broken down into a hierarchy of levels and objectives, each one of which it becomes possible to define, in terms of an observable form of behaviour. This is most readily done with specific items of knowledge and fairly simple processes of thought and problem solving, but it can also be achieved with higher and more complex intellectual functioning. The crucial point is that any such analysis should be systematically developed from a synthesis in which considerations derived from learning theory and child development play their part alongside careful conceptual and philosophic analysis. Such an analysis helps teachers themselves to become more fully aware of what they are doing and why they are doing it. They can develop detailed and sensitive criteria by which to diagnose the progress and learning difficulties of their charges and help each pupil to make his own goals explicit so that he can see clearly what he is aiming at. A systematic framework provides the means, too, whereby children can measure their own progress—very much as they do, for example, in acquiring physical prowess. The accent is then shifted from teacher-centred praise and blame to the pupil's independent assessment of himself, tempered by the teacher's encouragement and co-operation in the difficult places.

PARENT CO-OPERATION

Suggestions of the kind which have been made throughout this chapter are revolutionary for most contemporary school systems in that they imply a profound change in adult-child relationships, and in the concepts which underlie traditional curricula and methods. The emphasis shifts from incentives, inter-individual competition or adult decided rewards and punishments to motivation and self-determined goals, from imposed discipline to increasing personal autonomy, from subjects with carefully maintained boundaries to the opening up of all kinds of knowledge as the pupil sees need for it in the process of constructing his own mind and his own capacity to learn. They also imply a certain open-endedness in the attitudes of teachers to the answers which children give, a willingness to recognize that, in different ways, divergent and convergent thinking are equally acceptable, the only criterion being that of their effectiveness for the purpose in mind.

So fundamental a modification in the way teachers, parents and children view formal education cannot be introduced at a stroke. Children have to learn how to handle themselves and their impulses in open, permissive and self-directed situations and to cope with the anxiety which many feel if the firm directive discipline of the formal classroom is withdrawn. Parents, too, may be made anxious about the progress of their children and tend to judge this by mechanical attainment in reading, calculation and spelling. They may even demand formal homework and formal instruction of the kind they themselves underwent. They may find it hard to believe that learning which is not difficult and painful but spontaneous and indistinguishable from play can really be effective, or react with anxiety to the kind of problems chosen by their own children which have more than one answer without criteria of rightness or wrongness which are clear to them. A curriculum content which deals with controversial ideas—like race for example—may seem subversive or threatening to their prejudices, just as an open explanatory system of discipline may be seen as a criticism of their own methods of control. It is essential that attempts be made to get them to understand what the school and the teachers are aiming to do and why they adopt the means they are using. So far as possible parents themselves should become involved with their children in the absorbing tasks which opening the school to the outside world provokes; and should, by learning with their children, learn to learn in new ways themselves. For this, they have to be as closely consulted and involved in the education of their own children as possible.

Open days, exhibitions of children's work, concerts and dramatic presentations help with this but by themselves are rarely sufficient. What is needed is a climate in which parents can feel that they are welcome to drop into school, informally and without appointment, and see that they truly have a responsible role to play in education. It is valuable to arrange evening contacts with groups of parents to discuss how children of the age of theirs can be helped to learn at school and at home and to arrange that pupils profit as far as possible from the special knowledge, experience or skill that most parents, even the least qualified, have. In this way the school clearly places value on the culture of the home, instead of ignoring or, worse still, rejecting it. The education of children must be seen to be a joint affair in which teacher and parent have different but complementary responsibilities and tasks[56] and it is very much a part of a school's professional duty to help parents to realize this in concrete ways. The more disadvantaged the social group or environment from which the pupils come, the more important is it to build such mutual understanding and co-operation, since so much of the success or failure of education in school depends upon whether there is complementarity or conflict of aims in the two sides of the child's life. This is not easy in the best of circumstances; few teachers are trained to communicate with adults of a very different background from their own and still less to understand the delicacy of their relationship to the surrounding community, particularly if this is a very disadvantaged or culturally different one. But such bridging must be undertaken if the increasing alienation of many children and their families from education is to be halted.

STAFF RELATIONSHIPS

It is equally important that the school staff should achieve some unity of purpose among themselves. Children of primary-school age are still immature; they are still liable to feelings of insecurity, to unassimilated love and hate, and to aggressive impulses. Anything in their environment which divides their loyalties or presents them with conflictual situations which they cannot understand or resolve will be seen as a threat. Hence it is essential that the aims of the school as expressed through the attitude of all members of staff should be consistent and calculable. This does not mean absolute uniformity; nor does it imply that the head should impose his ideas *ex cathedra*. It means that the whole staff should, through free discussion among themselves, arrive at agreement and work together as a team—even if this involves them in some compromise on particular aims and ideals. Differences there may and will be; but these should be seen by staff and children as reflecting the diversity of life itself, be rooted in tolerance, and be recognized and explained rationally to pupils. It is particularly essential that children should not pass from a class in which they are taught by one method into another where the approach in entirely different. Children can and do adapt themselves to adult inconsistencies; they learn to be one person at home and another at school; they learn to respond to Miss Y in one fashion and to Mr. X in another. This kind of adaptation is necessary at certain stages, since the adult in a modern society moves in a number of mutually inconsistent worlds; for the child under the age of 10 however, marked and unexplained clashes of ideology between adults, abrupt changes in their attitudes and expectations can delay if not inhibit his learning and be destructive of his security, provocative of aggression either turning outward to the environment or inward to himself. This may be particularly marked where the teachers are openly at loggerheads among themselves and emphasize their difference of method or expectation as an expression of their mutual hostility; or where the school manifestly despises or is hostile to the homes from which the children come.

This is something of a crux; and it must be faced. Responsibility for the education of children is peculiarly liable to make those who bear it critical and antagonistic to the many outside influences which appear to undermine their work; and children not infrequently exploit manifest or covert conflicts among their teachers and between the ideas and ideals of their schools and other aspects of their lives at home or presented to them in the mass media. To some extent this challenge is healthy; it is a child's way of testing out and understanding adult differences; and sometimes it is an anxious exploration of how far differences are tolerable, and how far the admired teacher can be accepted as well as the loved but very different parent; sometimes the child sees himself forced to an anguished choice because the two cannot be reconciled.

The understanding of a school staff, their ability to accept, tolerate and work with differences, to value in a discriminating and non-condemnatory way views different from their own, and to accept that a child's family and life out of school are intensely important to him, are crucial to the effectiveness of education and critical to their pupils' healthy, mental adjustment. In doing this, as we have said, it may frequently be necessary to compromise or even, temporarily at least, to abandon some ideals as impracticable. Teachers will certainly have to question their own prejudices and values very closely indeed and ask how far their own particular formulations may be but one set among many equally acceptable ones. They may well have to accept that, while education is dedicated to change, there are many models of adequate and effective human development; and that their task is that of fostering the integrity of a child's growth in terms not of what they may wish ideally for him but of the possibilities and limitations of his whole environment.

SELF-IMAGE

How teachers resolve problems of this kind in practice goes far to determine the climate in which children extend and refine the idea they have of themselves. Quite apart from the task of equipping them cognitively to deal with their world, of helping them to develop their moral and emotional nature, education is very much concerned with this self-image. Lacking any objective criteria for self-evaluation, children are dependent upon what they think others wish them to be or suggest they are; and they incorporate their experiences of success and failure, of acceptance and rejection by parents, teachers and coevals as well as their perception of the interpersonal relations which they see daily, in highly subjective ways, sometimes with considerable disturbance and anxiety masked by the apparent calm of the later years of childhood. Hence markedly divergent attitudes among members of staff or conflict between school and home are likely to be reflected in incompatibilities in the child's own idea of himself and may even provoke crises which emerge in disturbance of behaviour. This early and necessarily incomplete self-image is the foundation too for the much more subtly differentiated personality which should grow out of the changes of adolescence. While it is true that some problems set themselves right under the impact of the restructuring of the emotional life that occurs in the 'teens, it is also and more often true that prejudicial development in childhood prepares greater difficulties in adolescence.

It is important for teachers, and parents, to realize that remarks which to them seem casual and of transitory importance may fall into a matrix of sensitivity in a child and have a bearing upon his emotional life out of all proportion to what is meant. The unsaid things, the minor injustices or the rejection implied by a harsh criticism—especially if they coincide with a crisis at home or in the child's friendships at school—may be deeply and lastingly damaging. And outward appearances can be very deceptive. The mutinous, aggressive child, the silent, withdrawn one, the boy or girl who ostensibly ignores what is being said and draws even harsher treatment from his teacher may in fact be putting up a protective barrier against unbearable feelings. They certainly call for deep empathic sensitivity from any teacher who wishes to get through to them.

Most parents and teachers for example at one time or another complain of children's manners, forgetting how much these are dependent upon the kinds of examples which they themselves set in a number of subtle contexts. All young children are learning how to behave, how to make and maintain contact with others, age equals or older; all have periods of imperfect adjustment and of covert or overt hostility, anxiety or insecurity; many of the things which they are expected to do—wash their hands, hang up their clothes, say 'please', 'thank you', 'sorry'—even at the age of 8 or 9 are far from automatic habits and are not clearly accepted as spontaneous desires and may seem to be forced upon them by naked adult power. What is more the abstract moral bases of behaviour, the real reasons why, are beyond the stage of concrete conceptual manipulation which they have attained; and they will learn more by what they see and experience and from simple practical explanations than they will from abstract appeals to evolved moral concepts. When they themselves are treated by adults with discourtesy or when they see that grown-ups do not perform the tasks which are enjoined upon them, such examples reinforce their own unsocialized impulses. If the adult is one with whom, out of fear or love, their identification is close, then the example of that person's behaviour is the more striking.

EXPECTATIONS

Of particular importance not only educationally but for subsequent development are the expectations which teachers (and to a lesser extent parents) appear to the child to have of his capabilities. A child's confidence in his power to succeed is likely to be critical when he meets a challenge which is at the limit of his possibilities: if he and those around him are optimistic, then he will try and probably manage; if his idea of himself is that a task is too hard for him, then he is defeated before he begins. It is for this reason that experiences of failure (and not merely failure in school learning) may be so critical. This does not mean that a child should never be allowed to try and to fail: failure which is recuperated is in fact a powerful support to confidence and morale. It does mean, however, that success should predominate and that in any failing situation the wise teacher or parent will either intervene with discreet help to enable him to succeed or will reassure the child that he will be able to succeed later when he is more mature.

The influence of adult expectations is more general and pervasive than this. Children tend to conform to the ideas which are held about them by influential adults. Hence any practice which labels a child or appears to him to do so is likely to influence his behaviour and profoundly affect his image of himself. Thus a child labelled as naughty or rebellious or as the clown of the class is likely to live up to his reputation—particularly if this is the only way of getting the attention he seeks and needs. Similarly if a teacher appears to be convinced that Johnny is dull and rather stupid and that there are many things that he cannot be expected ever to understand, it is likely that Johnny will accept this picture of himself and fulfil the prophecy made about him.[57] The world is in fact full of people who are convinced that, however hard they try, certain accomplishments are beyond them—for example, simple mathematics or the capacity to make an adequate visual representation by drawing.

It is with this in mind that one should carefully examine any practice which appears to label children. The assignment of an I.Q. for example if this is interpreted as a prediction of an inevitable future and not as anything more than a measure of immediate functioning; practices like streaming by ability or rigorous selection for different levels of education; expectations based upon racial, cultural or social differences; all these tend to become to some large extent self-fulfilling prophecies, particularly if they are adverse and underestimate real capacity.

On the other hand, in spite of one rather inadequate research to the contrary,[58] there is little to support the view that expectations greatly in excess of immediate possibilities will produce striking improvement in general intellectual functioning. Indeed if children's levels of aspiration are raised unrealistically above their possibilities, the way is prepared for what can be a very damaging disappointment, and a correspondingly excessive swing towards an equally unrealistic set of high expectations.[59]

In very many respects, the problem of building up a realistic but on the whole optimistic self-image in children is the core problem of helping each individual to a satisfactory adjustment and the acceptance of self. Certain aspects of development are much more malleable than others—the emotional and moral life for example are more readily modified profoundly by the environment than is sheer intellectual power, at least once early childhood is passed. Such attributes as social behaviour, readiness to help others, willingness to put forth effort for the common good are more or less independent of the kinds of cognitive ability expected in normal school learning; and any child can learn to excel in social activities. On the other hand academic success of the conventional sort is much more dependent upon endowment and the cumulative effects of environment and the differences between individuals are marked. It is, however, true that some at least of the differences we see are as much the result of the ways in which children conform to the ideas we have of them as they are to intrinsic differences.

REALISM IN ASPIRATIONS

The problem then is that of bringing about an increasingly refined and accurate knowledge of oneself—of one's possibilities and of one's limitations—of developing a system and level of aspiration which invites to effort and anticipates that, although hard to achieve, success will come. If this is to be ensured for all children, very careful thought has to be given by the school and its teachers to the kinds of model of human beings, the kinds of values which it offers and the system of incentives and motivations which are used. The first and most obvious—but nonetheless difficult—attitude is that of valuing children for what they are, of seeking out what is good and fostering it and of not rejecting the child for what he does or fails to do, even though one may condemn the act itself. The second aspect is that of ensuring a balance in favour of success, not only in school work but in many other aspects of growth. This involves clearly and manifestly accepting that there are many forms of excellence of which intellectual achievement is only one and not of exclusive importance. Formal education in schools tends to accentuate sheer cognitive skills and often in a competitive way which gives few winners and many losers. On the other hand self-competition and self-pacing methods accentuate the value of individual effort; forms of group work emphasize and nourish the ability to make a personal contribution for the good of all and one which may be different in kind from that made by others but just as valuable. Acts of kindness and services to other children or by groups of children undertaking a task for the old or less fortunate, willingness to do a menial job for the common good—these and many other things can be fostered and given open value by the school. Children can be brought to see that the prime values are care for others, contribution to the common wealth, the putting of one's gifts and capacities at the general service. Within such a framework, it is possible for each child to build up a positive and realistic image of himself as different from others but with as much claim to esteem and as much confidence in what he can do and contribute as anyone else.

THE WHOLENESS OF GROWTH

The child's mental and emotional development, his moral growth and his image of himself are deeply and lastingly affected by all that happens to him at home, at school, in the playground, or in the streets and fields. His world cannot be fragmented without danger to the unity of his development: a separation between instruction and education, between home experience and school experience, between intellectual education and moral training is artificial and frequently adverse in its effects. The task of the adults who deal with him is complex: they represent authority, they offer objects of identification, they give security and acceptance, they proffer experience and stimulate effort. What they appear to value will exert a potent influence, even if the child rejects it. Hence the explicit goals, the rules and relationships of school, the casual words of praise or blame may be of immense importance, the more powerful very often because they are not consciously examined, rejected or accepted—though they are integrated in the child's growing concept of the sort of person he is. Children are liable to develop exaggerated ideas of the goodness of the adult, especially the teacher, in each of his or her many roles; or they may, as frequently happens in late childhood, seem to turn away somewhat from adults and find refuge in a world of concrete experience, seeming almost to postpone consideration of the grown-up world in favour of a simpler more extraverted and primitive society of contemporaries. If teacher and parent are tolerant, understanding, manage to maintain some degree of harmony and above all are able to convince the children in their charge that they are accepted and loved for what they are, they can help to interpret and give unity to the child's worlds and to the diversity which is characteristic of modern cultures. Thus they help to develop a positive image of the self as an acceptable and successful person and prepare constructively for an enrichment and deepening of the personality in adolescence. The challenge of contemporary life to the educator is that while its lack of unity, its tensions and its threats make a coherent picture of oneself more difficult to attain, and constitute a graver menace to the personal security and mental health of child and adult alike than some at least of the more uniform and explicable societies of the past, its heterogeneity of demands and possibilities offers much greater scope for almost any individual to achieve a healthy personal development, to gain success in some field and fully to realize his endowment.

NOTES

1. Earlier in some countries, later in others—the span is from about 10 to 13.
2. Wilson, G. M.; Stone, M. B.; Dalrymple, C. O. *Teaching the new arithmetic.* New York, McGraw Hill, 1939. Ninety-five per cent of adult figuring is covered by the four fundamental processes (addition, multiplication, subtraction and division), simple fractions, elementary percentages and simple interest.
3. In Europe attendance is compulsory and virtually 100 per cent of the age groups are in attendance. In most developing countries, the situation is very different. By 1964–65, for example, in 37 out of 42 African countries, less than 50 per cent of the 5–14 age group was in attendance, in 27 less than 33 per cent and in 10 less than 16 per cent. The Addis Ababa Conference of African Ministers of Education fixed 1980 as the target for achieving 100 per cent provision but this is not likely to be realized everywhere. See: Institut régional pour les constructions scolaires, Khartoum. Intégration de l'école et de la communauté en Afrique. Khartoum, 1970 [mimeographed].
4. Bronfenbrenner, U. *Two worlds of childhood: U.S.A. and U.S.S.R.* London Allen & Unwin, 1972. / Idem. Another world of children. *New society* (London), 10 February 1972.
5. See, for example: Dreeben, R. *On what is learned at school.* Reading, Mass., Addison Wesley, 1968. / Overly, N. V., ed. *The unstudied curriculum.* Washington, D.C., Association for Supervision and Curriculum Development, National Education Association, 1970.
6. Douglas, J. W. B. *Home and school.* London, McGibbon & Kee, 1964. [2nd ed., London, Panther, 1967.]
7. United Kingdom. Central Advisory Council for Education. *Children and their primary schools.* London, HMSO, 1967 (Plowden Report).
8. Chapter 7, p. 118, and Chapter 11, pp. 254–259.
9. The National Child Development Study researchers report that even at age 7, for some children from lower socio-economic groups, the process of alienation from school has clearly begun (Davie, R.; Butler, N.; Goldstein, H. *From birth to seven.* London, Longmans, 1972.
10. See Chapter 11, section B, 'Failure to learn', p. 266 ff.
11. This is dealt with in greater detail in the next chapter.
12. For a detailed exposition see: Brearley, M., ed. *Fundamentals in the first school.* Oxford, Blackwell, 1969.
13. Hirst, P. H.; Peters, R. S. *The logic of education.* London, Routledge & Kegan Paul, 1970 [especially chapter 4, 'The curriculum']. The remainder of this chapter draws heavily upon the work of Hirst and Peters and upon R. F. Dearden (*The philosophy of primary education.* London, Routledge & Kegan Paul, 1968). There are, of course, other formulations, though few have been as carefully analysed conceptually or made as explicit. For example P. H. Phenix (*Realms of meaning.* New York, McGraw-Hill, 1964) proposes four basic types or realms of meaning—the symbolic (language, mathematics, usages and customs, etc.), the empirical (physics, biology, psychology, etc.) the aesthetic (arts, literature, etc.) and the synoptic (history, religion, philosophy). An existentialist analysis is given by G. F. Kneller (*Existentialism and education.* New York, Wisley, 1964). The writers of *Fundamentals in the first school.* (Op. cit.), by implication at least, accept a classification into: science; art; literature; movement (action feeling thought); mathematics; music; and morality. B. S. Bloom and his collaborators have a very different, more directly behavioural view and provide the means whereby the larger aims may be systematically placed in hierarchies, broken down into behavioural items and objectively evaluated. Though much criticized

by philosophers of many schools, Bloom's taxonomy because of its insistence on clearly stated behavioural criteria has been and continues to be very effective as a means of analysing and testing the effectiveness of many aspects of cognitive educational growth (*Taxonomy of educational objectives. Handbook I: Cognitive domain,* and Handbook II: *Affective domain.* New York, McKay, 1965 and 1967. / *Handbook on formative and summative evaluation of student learning.* New York, McGraw-Hill, 1971). See also: Vargas, J. S. *Writing worthwhile behavioural objectives.* London, Harper Row, 1972. For a Marxist analysis, see: Agostin, G. L'idéal humain de la pédagogie socialiste. *International review of education* (Hamburg), vol. XVI, no. 3, 1970.

14.   B. Bernstein (*Class codes and control.* Vol. I. London, Routledge & Kegan Paul, 1971 [chapter 11, 'On the classification and framing of educational knowledge']) proposes an admirable set of classifications for curricula. He distinguishes type 1 'Collection' where boundaries are sharply drawn between subjects, and type 2 'Integrated' where previously insulated subjects are subordinated to a relational idea. He points out that each of these can be strongly or weakly framed, specialized or non-specialized, teacher based or based on teams of teachers. The ways in which this is done influence such things as the degree of access which pupils are permitted to various forms of knowledge or subjects and the ways and degree to which pupils and teachers find an identity through knowledge. This is much more clearly applicable at the secondary stage (see Volume II of the present work) but nonetheless helps us to understand varieties of primary school curricula, and their implications for the aims suggested above.

15.   This would correspond to Bernstein's 'Integrated' code type: weak classification—weak framing.

16.   A 'Collection' type curriculum in Bernstein's classification.

17.   Bealing, D. The organisation of junior school classrooms. *Educational research* (London), vol. XIV, no. 3, June 1972.

18.   Snook, I. A. *Indoctrination and education.* London, Routledge & Kegan Paul, 1972. For a much wider philosophic context see also: Bantock, G. H. *Freedom and authority in education.* London, Faber, 1965.

19.   May, P. R. *Moral education in school.* London, Methuen, 1971.

20.   In a comment on this passage in particular and on the whole of this section in general, experts consulted by the Catholic Education Council (United Kingdom) write: 'This (i.e. discrepancies in the behaviour of teachers) is always a difficult situation and can only be met, at least as far as the school is concerned, by proper teaching of moral principles. Not all will agree that this can be done, nor will there be agreement about how it should be done, but the following extract will give some indication of the Catholic approach: "From this it follows that the forming of the Christian conscience of a child or youth consists, before all else, in enlightening their minds regarding the will of Christ, His law, and His way, and also in acting on the inner self, in so far as this can be done from without, in order to bring it to the free and constant carrying out of the divine will. This is the highest duty of education".' (Pius XII broadcast message on 'The Christian conscience as an object of education', 23 March 1952: *Catholic documents,* vol. VIII. London, Salesian Press). They also comment concerning the reason behind moral behaviour: 'It is I suppose possible to teach children to behave socially without any reference to God and our duties towards Him, but if a child asks why should one behave socially, it is surely difficult to give him a satisfactory answer merely on the principles of a non-religious deontology. . . .

One can teach children to do what is right for love of God. The principle of morality then is no mere categorical imperative but a strong and vivid love for the person of Christ.'

With some slight difference this probably represents the position of most religious groups. In the text, however, an effort has been made to present as fairly as possible the psychological and technical considerations of which any particular conception of moral training would have to take account. Necessarily this is incomplete since, ultimately, while moral education must take account of psychological principles and of the intellectual and emotional reactions of children and adolescents, the content and inspiration of that education will be drawn from the moral, philosophic and religious belief of the educators, parents and teachers.

21. *The moral judgement of the child.* London, Routledge & Kegan Paul, 1932.
22. R. Goldman discusses, in the light of research, Piagetian and other theories, the child's grasp of the concepts involved in religious and moral education (*Religious thinking from childhood to adolescence.* London, Routledge & Kegan Paul, 1964).
23. Dearden, R. F. Op. cit.
24. For a different and 'non-directive' viewpoint see: Rogers, C. *Freedom to learn.* Columbus, Merrill, 1969; and the devastating review by: Peters, R. S. *Interchange (Canada)* (Toronto), vol. I, no. 4, 1970. See also: Association pour la recherche et l'intervention psychosociologiques. *Pédagogie et psychologie des groupes.* Paris, Editions de l'Epi, 1964.
25. Valentine, C. W. *The abnormalities of normal children.* London, National Children's Home, 1951. / Idem. *The difficult child and the problem of discipline.* London, Methuen, 1950.
26. Peters, R. S. The education of the emotions. In: *Feelings and emotions.* New York, Academic Press, 1970. Peters distinguishes emotions from motives in saying that the first is a state of feeling as a result of an appraisal and the second connects the appraisal with things we do.
27. Most human beings—and especially those concerned with professions like teaching, medicine, social work or psychology—need some explicit training in empathy (Natale, S. *An experiment in empathy.* Slough, Bucks., National Foundation for Educational Research, 1972).
28. The writer recalls the case of John whose complicated love-hate conflict around ideas of death and his father and mother expressed themselves in a long (and for the teacher very trying) series of playful attempts to bury dolls, class comrades and eventually the teacher herself (in boxes fortunately!). Gradually because the teacher did not reject him or his play fantasies, but indicated casually and conversationally that his fears were not justified and emphasized the good sides of love and care for others, John worked through his conflict, digested it and made a good general adjustment. The important aspect in helping John was the general tolerance and affectionate acceptance of him in all his feelings of badness which was provided by his teacher. She would not have considered her attitude as anything other than educational, certainly not 'psycho-therapeutic' in the sense of providing 'interpretation'.
29. Hourd, M. *Relationship in learning.* London, Heinemann, 1972.
30. Oeser, O. A., ed. *Teacher, pupil and task.* 2nd ed. London, Tavistock Publications, 1960. / Mollo, S. *L'école et la société.* Paris, Dunod, 1970.
31. Ferri, E. *Streaming: two years later.* Slough, Bucks., National Foundation for Educational Research, 1971.

32. Popper, K. *The open society and its enemies.* London, Routledge & Kegan Paul, 1962.
33. See Chapter 9, p. 179 and notes 9–11.
34. On these differences, their educational and personal consequences and their long-term effects, see: Chiland, Colette, *L'enfant de six ans et son avenir.* Paris, Presses universitaires de France, 1971.
35. On this whole topic see: Yates, A. *Grouping in education.* Hamburg, Unesco Institute for Education, 1966. / Miller, R. I. *The non-graded school.* New York, Harper & Row, 1967. / Meyer, E. *Gruppenunterricht.* Worms, Ernst Wunderlich, 1964.
36. This form of grouping by ability is not in essence different from streaming a whole year group by ability into a series of allegedly homogeneous classes; but, if it is used sparingly with other forms of grouping, is less likely to have some of the adverse attitudinal effects attributed to streaming when it is applied rigidly to a whole year group.
37. Yates, A. Op. cit.
38. Like the small boy who, asked whether he knew his multiplication tables, replied that he knew the tune but not the words.
39. This method is not advocated except as an occasional supplement to systematize the much better practice that comes through well motivated use.
40. See for example: Cousinet, R. *Une méthode de travail libre par groupes.* Paris, Cerf, 1945. / Idem. *Pédagogie de l'apprentissage.* Paris, Presses universitaires de France, 1959. / Freinet, C. *Les techniques Freinet de l'école moderne.* Paris, Armand Colin, 1964.
41. For a thorough-going psychological and philosophic rationale of child-centred, active education see: Brearley, M., ed. Op. cit.
42. Of the considerable body of research devoted to this problem, much is vitiated by basing contrasts on indifferent examples of the one compared with good examples of the other. Some studies have failed to perceive that the objectives actually attained under the different systems are at most differently accentuated and only sometimes incompatible; and that the ultimate upshot is a matter of judgement between two or more sets of results each more or less desirable.
43. Gardner, D. E. M. *Testing results in the infant school.* 2nd ed. London, Methuen, 1948.
44. Gardner, D. E. M. *Long term results of infant school methods.* London, Methuen, 1950.
45. Barker Lunn, J. C. *Streaming in the primary school.* Slough, Bucks., National Foundation for Educational Research, 1970.
46. From another small study (Gooch, S.; Pringle, M. L. K. *Four years on.* London, Longmans, 1966.) it seems that, by the end of secondary schooling of the more or less traditional type, boys taught traditionally in their junior schools do marginally better in reading than do boys from more progressive schools. Girls on the whole do better if they have come from a more progressive junior school. It also seems that the duller children, of either sex, profit most at the secondary stage from having had a progressive primary schooling. E. Ferri (Op. cit.) also shows that there is some evidence to suggest that children from non-streamed schools are better at creative thinking, though in general there was little to choose between children from streamed and non-streamed in conventional academic attainment. Her case histories, however, show the traumatic effect on children who, having been in a high stream in their primary schools, find themselves in a lower stream in a secondary school.

47. The topic of creativeness is dealt with more fully at the end of Chapter 12 (especially p. 322ff.)

48. V. S. Sherman (Two contrasting educational models. Research Memorandum EPRC 6747-9, Stanford Research Institute, n.d.) suggests that highly structured educational methods favour socialization and open progressive methods favour the development of individuality—and that teachers tend towards one or the other extreme because of their own personalities. The educational problem is in fact the achievement of a just balance between, on the one hand, security, order, conformity, the accumulation of systematic knowledge and emotional control and, on the other, the flexibility, the ability to tolerate and use ambiguity and uncertainty, and the imaginativeness and emotional freedom which are equally necessary for fruitful change and adaptability.

49. B. Cane and J. Smithers (*The roots of reading: a study of twelve infant schools.* Slough. Bucks., National Foundation for Educational Research, 1971) bring together studies of reading attainment in twelve infant schools, many in the most deprived areas of London. It is clear that the level of mastery of reading attained at age 7 is considerably higher in schools where teachers insist from the outset on systematic phonic instruction, not waiting for 'reading readiness' to develop. Such an insistence on a systematic approach is not incompatible with a generally permissive and child-centred climate, with considerable individual attention and work in small groups. The schools—even those in good middle class areas—which practised permissive non-directive and unsystematic methods had much lower levels of attainment. See also. Chapter 11, p. 275 ff., especially p. 280.

50. See: Moran, P. R. The integrated day. *Educational research* (London), vol. 14, no. 1, November 1971. This gives the results of a survey of the very varied practices of some 200 teachers in English infant and junior schools. See also: Walton, J. *The integrated day in theory and practice.* London, Ward Lock, 1971.

51. As Moran (Op. cit.) points out, no one method is covered by the term 'integrated day'. Some teachers allow free choice in the afternoon concentrating on the three Rs in the morning; others direct groups over a lengthy period of time (from one day to a fortnight) allowing a limited choice of topics, etc.

52. This is more commonly practised at the secondary stage but as a method is differently but equally applicable to primary schooling. On the whole technique and methods see: Lovell, K. *Team teaching.* Leeds, University of Leeds Institute of Education, 1967. / Shaplin, J. T.; Olds, H. F., eds. *Team teaching.* New York, Harper & Row, 1964. / Warwick, D. *Team teaching.* London, University of London Press, 1971.

53. For a sympathetic and practical analysis of these and other methods in action with children in English infant schools (5-7+) by an American educator, see: Weber, L. *The English infant school and informal education.* New Jersey, Prentice Hall, 1971.

54. Morris, J. M. *Standards and progress in reading.* Slough, Bucks., National Foundation for Educational Research, 1966 [p. 327-9]. / Cane, B.; Smithers, J. Op. cit.

55. Bloom, B. S., et. al. *Taxonomy of educational objectives.* London, Longmans, 1956 (Vol. I: *Cognitive domain*; Vol. II: *Affective domain*).

56. *Children and their primary schools.* Op. cit. [especially vol. I, pt. 3, chapter IV and vol. II, appendix I] Hubbard, D. V.; Salt, J. *Parents: participation*

and persuasion in primary education. Sheffield, The University Institute of Education, 1972. This is a most valuable and detailed study of the ways in which a sample of 40 schools (8,000 children) co-operate with parents; and has an excellent bibliography.

57. Pidgeon, D. A. *Expectation and pupil performance.* Slough, Bucks., National Foundation for Educational Research, 1970.

58. Rosenthal, R.; Jacobson, L. *Pygmalion in the classroom.* New York, Rinehart & Winston, 1968. But see also: U.S.A. Office of Education. *Do teachers make a difference? A report on recent research on pupil achievement.* Washington, D.C., Government Printing Office, 1970. / Fleming, E. S.; Anthonen, R. G. Teacher expectancy or my fair lady. *American educational research journal* (Washington, D.C.), vol. VIII, no. 2, March 1971, p. 241–252. This research, based on 1,087 second grade pupils in 39 classes, gives no support whatever to a generalized self-fulfilling prophecy.

59. One of the characteristics of failing children is that they tend to have unrealistically high or low estimates of what they can achieve.

FURTHER READING

Aebli, H. *Grundformen des Lehrens* [Basic forms of teaching]. Stuttgart, Ernst Klett, 1964.

Atkinson, J. W.; Feather, N. T., eds. *A theory of achievement motivation.* New York, John Wiley, 1966.

Banks, O. *The sociology of education.* London, Batsford, 1971.

Bantock, G. H. *Freedom and authority in education.* London, Faber & Faber, 1965.

Baścik, S. *Uaktywnienie metod nauczania* [Active teaching methods]. Krahow, Nakladem Uniwersytetu Jagiellonskiego, 1966.

Bataillon, M.; Berge, A.; Walter, F. *Rebâtir l'école.* Paris, Payot, 1967.

Bernstein, B. *Class, codes and control.* Vol. I: Theoretical studies towards a sociology of language. London, Routledge & Kegan Paul, 1971.

Bloch, M-A. *Philosophie de l'éducation nouvelle.* Paris, Presses universitaires de France, 1968.

Bloom, B. S.; Hastings, T. J.; Madaus, G. *Handbook on formative and summative evaluation of student learning.* New York, McGraw Hill, 1971.

Bochinger, E. *Anschaulicher Religionsunterricht* [Illustrative religious education]. Stuttgart, Calwer Verlag, 1964.

Bruner, J. S. *Toward a theory of instruction.* Cambridge, Mass., The Belknap Press of Harvard University Press, 1966.

Burnie, I. H., ed. *Religious education in integrated studies: a symposium.* London, SCM Press, 1972.

Charlier, H.; Collin, R. *L'éducation morale à l'école primaire.* Paris, F. Nathan; Bruxelles, Editions Labor, 1965.

Clegg, A. B., ed. *The changing primary school: a statement by teachers.* London, Chatto & Windus, 1972.

Davie, R.; Butler, N.; Goldstein, H. *From birth to seven.* London, Longmans, 1972.

Dearden, R. F. *The philosophy of primary education.* London, Routledge & Kegan Paul, 1968.

Douglas, J. W. B. *The home and the school.* London, McGibbon & Kee, 1964.

Eggleston, S. J. *The social context of the school.* London, Routledge & Kegan Paul; New York, Humanities Press, 1967.

Ferri, E. *Streaming: two years later.* Slough, Bucks. National Foundation for Educational Research, 1971.

Gagné, R. M. *The conditions of learning.* 2nd edn. London, Holt Rinehart & Winston, 1970.

Goldman, R. *Religious thinking from childhood to adolescence.* London, Routledge & Kegan Paul, 1964.

Gurvitch, G. *The social frameworks of knowledge.* Oxford, Blackwell, 1971.

Hameline, D.; Dardelin, M. J. *La liberté d'apprendre.* Paris, Les Editions Ouvrières, 1967.

Hirst, P. H.; Peters, R. S. *The logic of education.* London, Routledge & Kegan Paul, 1970.

Hourd, M. *Relationship in learning.* London, Heinemann, 1972.

Jackson, B. *Streaming: an education system in miniature.* London, Routledge & Kegan Paul, 1964.

Jadoulle, A. *Devenir quelqu'un.* Paris, Editions Universitaires, 1965.

Johannesson, I. *Effects of praise and blame.* Stockholm, Almqvist & Wiksell, 1967.

Krathwohl, D. R.; Bloom, B. S.; Masia, B. B. *Taxonomy of educational objectives.* Handbook II: *Affective Domain.* New York, David McKay, 1964.

Lovell, K. *Team teaching.* Leeds, Leeds University Institute of Education, 1967 (Paper No. 5).

Meng, H. *Zwang und Freiheit in der Erziehung* [Constraint and freedom in education]. Bern, Stuttgart; Verlag Hans Huber, 1961.

Miller, R. I., ed. *The nongraded school.* New York, Harper & Row, 1967.

Mollo, S. *L'école et la société.* Paris, Dunod, 1970.

Monoszon, E. I., ed. *Formirovanie mirovozzrenija učaščihsja vos-miletnej školy* [Formation of a world outlook in students of the eight-year school]. Moskva, Prosveščenie, 1966.

de Moura, I. C.; da Silva, C. M. L. *Estudo-inquérito em lôrno de um programa experimental de ensino* [A research study of an experimental educational programme]. (Recife, Pernambuco, Instituto de pesquisas pedagógicas, Secretaria de Estado dos negocios de educaçao e cultura, 1961.)

Musgrave, P. W. *The sociology of education.* London, Methuen, 1965.

Muszyński, H. *Podstawy wychowania spoleczno-moralnego* [foundations of moral and social education]. Warszawa, Państwowe Zaklady Wydawnictw Szkolnych, 1967.

Niblett, W. R., ed. *How and why do we learn?* London, Faber & Faber, 1965.

Nuttin, J. *Reward and punishment in human learning.* New York, Academic Press, 1968.

Oeser, O. A., ed. *Teacher, pupil and task: elements of social psychology applied to education.* London, Tavistock Publications, 1960.

Okoń, W., ed. *Szkoly eksperimentalne w świecie 1900–1960* [Experimental schools in the world, 1900–1960]. Warzawa, 'Nasza Księgarnia,' 1964.

Ozerskij, I. Z.; Berdnikova, E. M.; Hmelev, A. N. *Nravstvennce vospitanie vo vneklassnoj rabote po istorii i obščestvovediniju* [Moral education in extra-curricula activities in history and social sciences]. Moskva, Prosveščenie, 1965.

Phenix, P. H. *Realms of meaning.* New York, London, McGraw-Hill, 1964.

Pidgeon, D. A. *Expectation and pupil performance.* Slough, Bucks., National Foundation for Educational Research, 1970.

Robinson, W. P.; Rackstraw, S. J. *A question of answers*. London, Routledge & Kegan Paul, 1972.

Rose, B., ed. *Modern trends in education*. London, Macmillan, 1972.

Selleck, R. J. W. *English primary education and the progressives 1914–1939*. London, Routledge & Kegan Paul, 1972.

Skinner, B. F. *The technology of teaching*. New York, Appleton-Century-Crofts, 1968.

Snook, I. A. *Indoctrination and education*. London, Routledge & Kegan Paul, 1972.

Stenhouse, L., ed. *Discipline in schools: a symposium*. Oxford, New York, Pergamon Press, 1967.

Thouless, R. H. *An introduction to the psychology of religion*. Cambridge, Cambridge University Press, 1972.

Vasquez, A.; Oury, F. *Vers une pédagogie institutionelle*. Paris, François Maspero, 1967.

Wallace, J. G. *Concept growth and the education of the child*. Slough, Bucks., National Foundation for Educational Research, 1965.

Walton, J. *The integrated day in theory and practice*. London, Ward Lock, 1971.

Warwick, D. *Team teaching*. London, University of London Press, 1971.

Weber, L. *The English infant school and informal education*. Englewood Cliffs, New Jersey, Prentice-Hall, 1971.

Wheeler, D. K. *Curriculum process*. London, University of London Press, 1971.

Yates, A., ed. *Grouping in education*. Stockholm, Almqvist & Wiksell; New York London; John Wiley, 1966.

Young, M., ed. *Knowledge and control*. London, Collier-Macmillan, 1971.

Chapter eleven

Some special problems of the primary school

A. THE GENERAL PROBLEM OF INDIVIDUAL DIFFERENCES

THE COMMON SCHOOL

In many parts of the world the primary school, with few exceptions, is the common school which all children attend; in very many it is the only school available to most children, and in countries barely emerging from serious underdevelopment, even two or three years of primary schooling may not be available to more than half the child population. Governments and public opinion have, however, increasingly come to see that education, at least basic elementary education, is not only a human right but essential to cultural and economic development. More recently it has been perceived that without sound education in the pre-adolescent years, there is little hope of extending effective secondary, technical and higher education or indeed of getting the teachers for the system as a whole. Furthermore the paradox is becoming steadily more apparent that the younger the child and the less support he gets from his home and general culture, the more he needs a highly skilled teacher. Just as the teacher's job in an urban slum school in France or Britain is different from and more exacting and more critical for his pupil's development than that of his colleague in a comfortable middle-class area, so the teacher in a primary school in Africa or Latin America is confronted with psychological and cultural problems which demand insight, knowledge and skill well beyond those needed in Europe. But he is generally less well educated, less well trained, enjoys few of the supportive advisory services available to his European or North American counterpart; and he is often obliged to instruct, rather than teach, to a curriculum derived from that of a developed country and unsuitable to the needs of his pupils.

In spite, however, of the extraordinarily wide differences which we

J*

find in the circumstances in which education has to be carried on in the world and the immense practical difficulties which face schools in all but the most favoured circumstances, the principles and aims outlined in the previous chapter remain the same. We are concerned, from the point of view of the mental health of the individual, of his society and of the world society of which they are increasingly a part, with the development of human beings equipped with the knowledge and the skills required to achieve dynamic adjustment in rapidly changing situations, with the personal security and flexibility to withstand and profit from tensions and with the intellectual and emotional autonomy without which genuine freedom is not possible.

In this, the processes of intellectual and social development particularly related to education in the primary schools are of critical importance. Education is a normative and socializing process which confronts children with expectations and demands. Success or failure in meeting these growth tasks, largely culturally imposed, is a vital element in the child's growing notion of identity and image of himself and of his capacities to succeed, and they are critical in determining the ways he adopts to confront and cope with difficulties and challenges. We have too, to remember that for the most part the thinking and powers of analysis of pre-adolescent children are limited to fairly concrete and largely egocentric modes; they have little power to stand back and regard themselves or their circumstances objectively; still less have they much insight into adult motivations; and they are very dependent for their own evaluation of themselves upon the implicit and explicit criteria of success and failure set up by their own age-group and by the adults in the school community. The school, just because it is a structured community with explicit intellectual goals and some considerable affective distance between children and adults, in a very different environment from the family and discrepancies between a child's capability and others' expectations—particularly in intellectual attainment but also in social behaviour and physical powers—tend to be sharply perceived.

The interaction between home and school in this is complex. We may simplify it somewhat by drawing a distinction between the effects on a child's adjustment to school of emotional disturbance or personality defect arising at home and the effect upon a child's learning and personality growth brought about either by a clash between school and home or by a school environment which is itself inimical to sound adjustment. It is rare, of course, to find any clear-cut dichotomy in practice except in fairly severe cases of maladjustment. Nevertheless many childhood difficulties and deviancies, and many cases of failure to learn, derive principally from the one and may be aggravated or mitigated by the other. For our purposes, it is true to say that while the school itself can do little to improve seriously or even mildly disturbing home circumstances it can do a great deal to see that each child is offered experiences which lead on the whole to success and which positively contribute to his intellectual, emotional and social adjustment. For not a few children, even modest intellectual success at school and the feeling of worth created by their teachers enable them to pass through very disturbing home circumstances and emerge, scarred perhaps, but reasonably effective, balanced and happy human beings.

Thus it is insufficient merely to consider the general aims, ethos and pedagogic methods used by primary schools. We must look closely at particular practices, at sensitive stages in growth and at least some of the more obvious demands, because mental health and intellectual progress depend upon the way in which the school adapts itself to the developmental level and the background of its pupils and, while not abandoning its reasonable and essential normative demands, adjusts these to the processes of growth and maturation. This is the most difficult of all educational tasks, the point where the aims and theories outlined in the previous chapter have to be embodied in realistic and practical compromise, mainly by the teacher, but also by those responsible for educational policy, administration and the allocation and use of resources. Upon such compromises depend the mental health of individuals and of communities, and the very effectiveness of education as a means of enhancing human ability.

FIRST ENTRY TO SCHOOL

In working towards this compromise, the child's first experience of primary school may be crucial and determinant of later success. In most European countries, compulsory schooling begins at the age of 6,[1] and for many children who have not previously attended nursery schools or kindergartens, this may be their first contact with a school of any kind, the first time they have found themselves in a group of age mates supervised by one adult only.

At this age children are neither quite like the kindergarten child whose principal means of learning is symbolic and functional play, nor the fully-fledged primary child who is eager to acquire skills and build up a world of causal relationships. Emotionally they have not achieved detachment from fantasy and a purely hedonistic or pleasure-pain attitude nor have they markedly progressed towards a close and real acceptance of the world and people as they are. Their personal and social independence is precarious, and though at times they may show considerable realism in their understanding of others, adults and contemporaries, they will revert frequently to subjective projections of their own fantasies. Their behaviour may show surprising swings from one extreme to the other, particularly in such things as the habits of cleanliness imposed by earlier training. Adjustments are less stable and fixed than most parents and teachers realize; and children of 5 or 6 are only provisionally and transitorily oriented in their world.

This first entry to primary school, to a world which is more specific in its demands and more impersonal than home, is likely—even for children who have already had experience in a good nursery school and who have no unusual difficulties in development—to be provocative temporarily at least of mild anxiety and insecurity. It is by no means unusual, for example, to find a breakdown in what seemed well established habits. Some children show difficulties in sleeping or eating or even a reversion to bed-wetting and temper tantrums; others seem to become particularly vulnerable to minor ailments, coughs and colds, stomach upsets, bouts of sickness. Most show considerable fatigue. Many find the effort of adjustment to school so great that when they return home, they 'let go' in a bewildering bout of bad behaviour, which may provoke repressive action by parents. Almost all betray their immaturity and their anxiety by projecting on to the teacher, much in the same fashion as younger children in the nursery school, their attitudes to their own parents. They 'love' and 'hate' them in a fashion which usually seems exaggerated, and which may arouse the jealousy or hostility of those parents who are themselves more or less immature. For children who have not successfully detached themselves from mother at the normal 6-year-old level, or who for any reason are nervous or insecure, the new circumstances may prove to be so severely disturbing as to be intolerable, a disturbance which is likely to be reflected in their whole ability to respond to the intellectual demands made upon them.

INTELLECTUAL DEVELOPMENTS

The stage of fragile and delicate adjustment which coincides with entry to school is accompanied by a transition in the intellectual life closely dependent upon it. Many research workers have noted that the early primary school years are marked by a change from numerical, spatial and physical concepts that are rigid, inconsistent, seizing only the exterior aspect of things, to concepts and operations which though still concrete are more generalized, mobile and consistent and allow objective apprehension of reality.

The pre-school child apprehends and interprets objects and events very subjectively, in close dependence on his personal interests. For example, young children define objects in terms of the activity which they allow ('a puddle is to step in'). Normally[2] as they approach the age of 7 years however, they tend to define an object in terms of the sphere to which it belongs; and from then onwards, begin to name distinctive features showing thereby that they apprehend things as they are, and can adopt objective criteria.[3] In his studies of child thought, Piaget[4] notes that during the period between 6 and 8 years of age, the logical structure of the fundamental concepts and mental operations pertaining to number, physical quantities, movement and space undergoes a marked change. Concepts and operations that had previously depended on the perceptual configuration and were subject to all the illusions suggested by their superficial aspect (apparent variability of physical quantities, errors in comparing distances and movements, etc.) were found to acquire constancy, coherence and reversibility for most children around the age of about 7 years. While the child was not yet capable of carrying out thought processes based on mere assumptions and hypotheses, he could reason logically if confronted with concrete materials or when remembering them. Authors affiliated with the school of *gestalt* psychology have put the matter in another and complementary form. They note that during middle childhood, a transition from syncretic to more analytic apprehension of data takes place.[5]

INDIVIDUAL DIFFERENCES

These related processes of socio-emotional and of intellectual growth in young children are profoundly and indistinguishably affected by genetic and environmental factors. The intellectual changes referred to above, for example, will proceed more or less rapidly according to the child's level of operational intelligence which sets an upper limit to his immediate learning potentialities and, in a cumulative way, to the speed of his growth. Any age expectation derived from the work of Piaget or others can only be very approximate even for European children. Children in developing countries, though they tend to go through similar stages, seem also after the early years, to progress more slowly on the average than their more fortunate European counterparts.[6]

Quite apart from these general cognitive differences there are considerable differences in temperamental endowment which alone would make for differences in the child's capacity to adapt to the social demands of school. If in addition his previous circumstances have not met his fundamental needs then he will not have travelled far enough along the road towards emotional freedom, without which he cannot achieve an adequate conceptual development. Environment, too, plays a direct part in his intellectual growth, both cognitively and in the emotional context which conditions his willingness to learn. Children for example who, at home, have watched or happily helped mother with the cooking, who have weighed, measured and counted are likely to have had the opportunity to develop rudimentary number concepts and a certain pleasure in using them. Similarly, children from environments relatively unfavourable in other respects, from their early experience in, for example, buying food at the local shop, may have a marked and realistic knowledge of money values denied to the more sheltered. Those who come from families where parents talk intelligently to their children, where stories are told or read, and where their attempts to express themselves verbally have been fostered with an accepting affection, are likely to be advanced in their vocabulary and have a joyful readiness to use and understand words on which much of their subsequent educational progress will depend. Some indeed may be well begun along the road to reading.[7] Examples of these kinds might be multiplied to show, in practical terms, that no two children even from a relatively unified cultural background at the beginning of their primary school career will be at the same stage of development. Indeed, since they have not yet been submitted to the uniform influence of schooling, children of 6 or 7 are perhaps more heterogeneous in their general development, in their cognitive abilities, in their social growth and in their attitudes than at any other stage except very early adolescence.

LANGUAGE AND CULTURAL DIFFERENCE

However, in very many schools in Europe—and one might almost say generally in countries striving to develop an education system—teachers are faced with a problem which goes well beyond that of adapting to the social and individual differences normally present in a group of healthy, well cared for children coming from a reasonably homogeneous social setting.

We have already drawn attention to the ways in which, even within one western country, the cognitive style and affective development of children may differ radically in different cultural and social groups. In bilingual areas or in developing countries these differences may be complicated by differences between the language of the home and that of education, a difference which extends to the content of pictures, books, to clashes of attitudes and assumptions, of rules concerned with acceptable and unacceptable behaviour, standards of personal cleanliness and of environmental hygiene. It may go deeper still if the education offered is largely based upon a rational approach, whilst the surrounding culture is animistic, magical and highly authoritarian. Unless this is handled very carefully indeed it can set up overt conflicts between school and community from which children inevitably suffer; more importantly for the child who succeeds in overtly conforming, it may lead to an enduring confusion of identity and to attitudes which are compartmentalized and inconsistent.

THE CHILDREN OF MIGRANT WORKERS AND IMMIGRANTS

Though we have become aware recently of the problems of children from culturally deprived, culturally different and culturally disorganized backgrounds, such more acute and overt forms of culture clash are still often thought of as peculiar to developing countries striving to modernize themselves through education. This, however, is not by any means entirely true. Prosperous western communities like Sweden, for example, or Switzerland, have attracted labour from Southern Europe where economic levels are lower and cultural standards, beliefs and life styles very different. The United Kingdom has always received immigrants and migrants from Southern Ireland and in the 1950s and 1960s there began a heavy influx of families from the West Indies, from India and from Pakistan. France has for many generations received individual workers and families from North Africa and Asia.

The children of these migrant and immigrant families pose problems for the schools which in some ways are different from and often more difficult to resolve than those of deprived indigenous children. In some respects too, the problems of children of migrants are not the same as those of immigrants. Migrant workers are usually adult, often semi-or un-skilled and come from a more or less neighbouring country to work abroad with the object of returning to their native land when they have made sufficient money to settle. If they are married and have children, their families frequently remain at home and for the children the problem is that of the absence of father with what that may contribute to the child's sense of insecurity and his difficulty of identification. Sometimes, however, children are left with grandparents or relatives. Such separations undoubtedly cause strain, particularly if the children are young; and when the arrangement breaks down—for example, if the father contracts a new liaison, or if the grandparents cease to be able to care for the children who are hurriedly sent to join their absent parents— can be highly provocative of emotional disturbances.

If children accompany their parents to the new country, there are acute problems for them—the clash between the culture and schools to which they have been used and the new, often the problem of a foreign language and, if the parents are truly migrant moving from casual job to casual job, a constant change of home and school, often with lengthy periods of uncertainty and absence from school of any kind.

Most normal children find changes of school and of teacher some-what difficult, provocative of at least a measure of anxiety, though a certain amount of change if the adjustments are satisfactorily made can act as a healthy stimulus. However, adjustment demands an effort to make new relationships and implies the sometimes painful rupture of

old friendships; if a child is not to suffer from this he must be fundamentally secure, particularly in his relationships with his parents. Migrant
workers and their families tend to be economically among the least
favoured, to have considerable difficulties in finding accommodation,
to be regarded with some mistrust by their neighbours and for these and
a variety of other reasons the parents themselves are likely to be more
anxious and feel more threatened than normal. This means that their
children, quite apart from linguistic difficulties, discontinuities between
the methodis programmes and expectations of different schools and such
obvious problems of adjustment, may well meet a disturbing series of
changes without the confidence which comes from a stable home background. Even where circumstances are ideal, as they were for the British
Army stationed abroad, with its specially adapted system of schooling
and arrangements for moving and housing families, the evidence suggests that the level of emotional disturbance among children was much
higher than normal.[8] Many children of migrant families appear dull and
educationally markedly retarded; some, having had to make several
efforts at a short-lived adjustment, give up and refuse to attempt to make
new friendships, withdrawing into themselves; others become aggressive
to a marked degree, wreaking their unhappiness and sense of rejection
on their human and material surroundings wherever they find themselves.

The children of immigrant families have some of the same problems
and difficulties but there are others. The greatest difficulties arise where
the immigrant group is ethnically markedly different from that of the
host country—as it is, for example, with Pakistanis, Indians and West
Indians in the United Kingdom. There are self-evident differences in
colour, in religion, even in dress; styles of life and family discipline may
be in marked contrast. For some groups, the language of the host country
is a foreign one, acquired only very imperfectly and, if at all, with great
difficulty especially by mothers from cultures where education for girls
and women is rare.[9] Even where physical differences are not marked,
and the language is the same, the immigrants may be seen as foreigners
competing for scarce work and accommodation, having a different way
of life and religion, despised if they are in a minority, feared where
they predominate. Often, too, immigrants come from countries with lower
standards of health care, social protection and the like and appear to
have more children and adults with physical defects, making greater
demands upon the health, social and educational services.

Finally, both for economic and for socio-psychological reasons,
immigrants tend to congregate in the poorer quarters of the towns and
to develop more or less closed communities set over against those of the
new country. This raises social and ethical problems concerning integration, multiracialism and the like which issue in difficult practical questions. For example, how far should one prevent particular schools or

classes from becoming all or predominantly filled with immigrant children by artificially bringing native born children in to redress the balance? How far should one attempt acculturalization and integration, and how far should one preserve cultural variety? Questions which raise issues of pedagogic method, curriculum content and the overt values of the school.

These are broad general problems affecting the mental hygiene of communities and at least partially amenable to forms of social and legislative action. They have been the subject of much study particularly in the United States of America where, for historic reasons, the problems are somewhat different from those of Europe and in many cases more grave.[10] They are different, too, for a State like Israel pledged to the admission and cultural assimilation of immigrants from all over the world united only by their Jewish origins. Immigration in Europe is very much a question of relatively small cultural or ethnic minorities[11] not economically very powerful.

The education of the children of immigrants represents in sharpened form some at least of the difficulties and disadvantages which will be found in indigenous populations but there are qualitative differences as well as differences of degree. For example, as we have noted earlier, many children from working class homes suffer from a clash of cultures and expectations between what they have been used to and what the school offers and appears to favour. They find themselves at a dis advantage linguistically and the experiences with which they have grown hitherto are at odds with, or appear to be rejected by, the school. For the children of immigrant parents this clash of expectations may be acute, even if the parents themselves are relatively highly educated. Family discipline may be very much more authoritarian in some respects and very much more lax in others, there may be marked religious and dietary differences and marked conflicts, for example, over expectations of sex roles as between girls and boys. Basically too, particularly for Asiatic and West Indian children, there is a conflict of identity—with their own group or with the host group—which is complicated by differences of colour and the differential valuations put upon it by the surrounding group. As a result, too, of differing family styles, there are differences in such things as the spontaneity of emotional expression or of inhibition, levels of anxiety, the degree and kinds of motivation to conform and the like.[12]

It is important to reiterate that none of these differences is likely to be racial in any genetic sense; all or any can be modified by environmental circumstances; and most will be found in differing degrees in any group of children coming from homes with differing child-rearing methods. The only exception arises from skin colour, not because of the colour, but because it marks an unalterable difference and acts as a signal for various social responses from other groups. In so far therefore as the social responses to skin colour can be modified one might expect that it could be brought to have no more effect upon the personal, emotional and social development of children and adolescents than any other physical characteristic such as height or hair colour. In present circumstances it tends to operate psychologically and socially like some physical handicaps, provoking over-reactions of compensating (and often condescending) acceptance or hostility and rejection; it acts as a focus for stereotyped kinds of reaction and response.

There are, too, differences in average measured ability and in school performance which, at present, characterize immigrant groups and, particularly, those of Asian and African ultimate origin. In England, for example, one finds many more immigrant children (particularly West Indian) assigned to special classes for the educationally subnormal than one would expect from non-immigrant groups of a similar economic background. Correspondingly, there are fewer high achievers than one would expect.[13] The same is true of black pupils in the United States, and it has been argued that since the means of performance ascend from Porto Ricans, through Mexicans to European immigrant groups, this corresponds to a genuine genetic difference, if not inferiority.[14]

One might remark that even if any genetic difference could be shown it is not likely to be so marked as are the overlaps—that is, all groups have high, low and average achievers, the differences being in the frequencies with which they occur in the various ethnic groups. This in itself would strongly suggest an environmental rather than a genetic cause, particularly when one considers the very different life styles and family educational practices associated with them. In education, however, they cannot be ignored any more than individual differences in general: for example qualitative differences in general ability, probably reflecting cultural differences and having a bearing upon educational provision, certainly exist and call for modifications in initial curricula and method. On tests such as the Wechsler which have verbal and non-verbal scales, it is not uncommon to find children of West Indian parents (and indigenous working-class children) scoring relatively much higher on the non-verbal than on the verbal scales and for children of Indian and Pakistani origins, but with a good command of English, the reverse; and some are selectively and generally weak on both, particularly if they come from rural or tribal backgrounds.[15]

The teacher who has immigrant pupils in her class, therefore, is faced with a series of problems which are complicated by social, personal and cultural differences. The most obvious one, that of the language of instruction. is in some ways the most readily understood and solved, by well organized reception centres and classes concentrating upon language teaching and upon helping the new immigrant to understand the host culture and its expectations.[16] The less obvious ones may call for specific remedial work; they certainly demand a considerable effort of sympathy and understanding by the teacher and often by the native born class-mates—particularly if the immigrant child has already had some schooling in his native country.

Most difficult of all are the emotional problems which arise for the immigrant child either because his home culture, his religion, and the behaviour which he has learnt are completely alien and not understood or because of the very fact that he and his parents are strangers, and not privileged strangers, in a strange land. Parental difficulties of adjustment are likely to be reflected in the anxieties of their children; and very often it is the mother who finds it most difficult to adjust to a country where the roles and functions of women are very different. Not infrequently the parents, the mother particularly, cling to the old ways which represent their own identification whilst their children try to adhere to the new; and the clash of cultures aggravates the clash of generations, making apparently trivial pretexts—clothing, hair styles, even the choice of friends—the cause of violent conflict inside the family or between family and school.

Where families are split, the father and the older children coming first to be followed later by mother and younger brothers and sisters, or where the culture from which they come has very different marriage customs and forms of family organization, family breakdowns may arise. Some children, for example, have a succession of 'uncles' or 'mothers'; others find the translation to the new country a traumatic separation from friends and relatives and suffer physically and morally from changing a pleasant, free and open climate for a more dreary, friendless and restricted environment.

SCHOOL READINESS

This immense variety in the circumstances and development of the children, immigrant and indigenous, the primary school receives, the great quantitative and qualitative differences in children's learning abilities, the capacities to adjust and their familial backgrounds, are in sharp contrast to the school's normative expectations. It is in this context that we can consider the narrow but important concept of school readiness, work on which began more than sixty years ago.[17] Danzinger and the Viennese child psychologists[18] established as main criteria of readiness: a certain level of intellectual development; an ability to engage in purposive work; some sense of duty and capacity to respond to set tasks, to concentrate, persevere and resist distraction; and the power to participate in collective activities and to respond to suggestions and tasks given, not to the child personally, but to the class as a whole.

It will be noted that some, if not all, of these qualities are clearly dependent for their emergence upon what a child's pre-school environment has fostered, and upon more or less specific training.

School readiness tests have been devised on these and similar criteria, but in, practice, have rarely been applied except experimentally, though in some countries, the age of entry is delayed for children who are markedly immature in any or all of them.

More recent work is that of Breunig[19] and Bernart.[20] The first of these considered the attainments of children who, because the age of entry was changed from 6.0 to 6.3, entered school somewhat later. He found that a later entry age meant fewer retarded and more advanced children and suggested that diagnostic tests should be used in connection with two entry points in each school year. Bernart's enquiry, conducted in a school in Bielefeld, suggests that a battery of cognitive tests and measures of motor development should be used in conjunction with a trial or diagnostic period of teaching during which the teacher should note the child's behaviour in semi-standardized situations.

In contrast to this are studies of English children who begin compulsory schooling at the age of five. Since practices vary throughout the country and since children's birthdays fall throughout the year, the time spent by children in the infant school varies by as much as two terms or even a year. It has repeatedly been shown that children who have the longest time in the infant school tend to have superior attainments throughout the primary school proper at least to the age of 11.[21]

Hence it is manifestly not a simple question of age or 'readiness'. We have to ask the question 'ready for what'? If the exigencies of the first years are more or less standardized for all children, then readiness means the ability to meet them, whatever they are, and assessments of readiness easily become a form of selection, the more so the less flexibly they are used and the more rigid the demands of the curriculum.

What in reality work on school readiness has done is to draw attention to the fact that the expectations current in the State primary schools of Europe—evolved from a combination of 'experience' and more or less intuitive hopes about what can be achieved—do not generally reflect the known realities of children's development and particularly the very wide variations among individuals and between different social and cultural groups, even within one more or less unified culture.

They are even less appropriate where the schools receive children from families with very different behavioural norms, or from disorganized, deprived immigrant or primitive backgrounds. For such children, emphasis upon a conventional curriculum, a rigid time-table and the like imposes a pressure to adjust, and adjust rapidly, which they are not equipped to meet. Nor is it likely that merely delaying entry for a year or causing them to repeat a grade will help by processes of simple maturation over time.

However, the problem remains. Children do enter school with very different levels of intellectual, emotional and social maturity, with very different attitudinal patterns, motivational systems, backgrounds of knowledge, experience and expectation; there are marked qualitative differences in such things as attention and memory, conceptual growth and power. Quite legitimately education makes certain normative demands. What we must therefore be concerned with is a progressive reconciliation between the child's capacities and the school environment. We have to help him to make himself ready for the successive levels of learning; but we have also to adjust the actual tasks and the methods used to what particular children can be expected to do and learn.

Tests and assessments of children and careful observation of them in at least semi-structured situations, particularly at the initial stage but later on in school also, have a clear diagnostic purpose—that of establishing what the child can do, what immaturities he may have and of developing at least the outline of a programme which will help him to develop the aspects of maturity without which he cannot progress in semi-formal situations, like learning to read,[22] beginning on the more systematic aspects of mathematics, or even feeling at home in a group. Such a diagnostic and remedial approach involves a corresponding adjustment of the methods used and the demands made, certainly in the first two years of schooling and probably for many children for much longer. Where this is done certain kinds of failure tend to be reduced.[23]

THE RECEPTION CLASS

In some countries the attempt is made generally to adapt the first years of schooling to the great heterogeneity of the children by the establishment of a reception class or a special infants school covering the first two or even three years of the primary course. More recently, the proposal has been put forward in England that a first school, covering the years from 5-8 or even 5-9 should be established[24] with only very general goals and allowing great freedom of content and method.

Such infants schools or reception classes should be in the charge of a teacher specially trained and alive to the needs of children in their early schooling. Where these schools or classes work best, both to ensure healthy development and a satisfying adjustment to formal learning, they tend to be child-centred and, by a great variety of activities, to cater for many levels of emotional and intellectual growth, continuing many of the symbolic and active play ways of learning of the nursery school and at the same time giving opportunities for the acquisition of skills in a steadily more systematic manner. In such a class or school it is possible to accustom the children gradually to general disciplinary and organizational necessities of classroom teaching with large numbers —to sitting at least for short periods at desks, to habits of orderliness, to persistence in a task, to waiting one's turn to speak and the like, which often come so hard. It is also possible to develop and continue for children who need it a carefully directed programme of intellectual, verbal and conceptual enrichment.

If such classes are kept small and remain with the same adult for a year or two, then as she progressively comes to know her pupils, the teacher can herself assess their readiness for formal learning without the need for specially constructed tests, though these have an auxillary use-fulness. She can estimate how far a child has formed elementary con-cepts of number and knows that, for example, however grouped, five blocks are always five. She can gauge the child's comprehension of spoken language, the range of his vocabulary and the development of perceptual ability to the point where he can embark on learning to read. So, too, her day-to-day observations will indicate to her the growth of purposiveness, concentration and capacity to respond to set tasks in the members of her class. She can adjust her programme accordingly.[25]

PREPARATION FOR ENTRY TO SCHOOL

Though the teacher is there to ease and assist the child's development from infancy to stable happy childhood, bridging procedures in school, important as they are, are not likely to succeed fully if the child's prior experiences have not been helpful and if there are marked discrepancies between the environment from which he comes and that into which he goes. If he has already attended a nursery school he should have had, particularly in his last year, experiences similar in nature to those of the first primary or infant school year. Provided there is no abrupt change of method between the nursery school or kindergarten class and that of the primary school, the transition is likely to be smooth and adjustment easy. Where, however, the nursery school or the home are free and active and the primary school rigid and repressive, difficulties are almost bound to occur. It is of the utmost importance that the nursery school teachers and those of the reception class in the primary school should meet and agree on an approximation of methods, which though it may mean compromise for both, cannot but be of assistance to the pupils.[26]

Children who do not attend nursery schools or kindergartens, need to be prepared by their parents and to be handled with care and insight by their first teacher. As with younger children entering nursery school, it is ideal if parents and teacher can meet sometime before the child enters school, and the child himself visit the school in company with his mother. If, as is common in small, tightly knit communities, there are older children close at hand who attend the same school, a skilful mother can increase her child's confidence by enlisting their help to reassure him.[27]

This can in most circumstances be extended by a method which has been tried with success in British infant schools. It is called 'family grouping'.[23] Instead of being arranged in classes corresponding more or less to age levels, children are grouped heterogeneously, each group having older and more experienced children as well as some younger newcomers in it. New entrants thus come to a group whose members are already familiar with school and who take them in charge. Quite apart from the additional security which this gives the young entrant and the possibilities it provides for the older ones to stimulate the maturation of the younger, the family group system embodies a principle of mutual aid and assistance, of responsibility for others, very important in general social and moral development.

The teacher, either through speaking to parents individually or by means of a meeting with the mothers and fathers of new children, can help the family to understand what the school is about and prepare them also to tolerate the difficulties of behaviour which may occur, especially towards the end of the school week—the reluctance to go to school or the sudden, almost compulsive secrecy, and independence which their child may show. If contacts with the family begin soon enough and the teacher possesses the tact, skill and knowledge, she may be able to influence the early upbringing of her pupils even before they come to school so that they get the opportunities of social and intellectual development which facilitate later educational growth.

COMPENSATORY EDUCATION

Practices like these may be sufficient where the gap between schools and a relatively homogeneous surrounding culture is not too great and where homes and schools have many even most expectations in common. But the existence of large deprived groups in European cities, of increasing numbers of children of migrants and of immigrant children and their families, leads us to question whether even this is likely to be fully effective; and to look again at the notion of compensatory education in a rather different light from that of a largely school-based cognitive stimulation, language development and enrichment—important and vital though these may be. With immigrant groups, the subcultural groups of children in large towns and for most children in countries endeavouring to raise the functional levels of populations with a tribal background, the problem is not simply that of p oviding experimental enrichment, accelerating conceptual growth, bringing consistency and order into the environment at school or even helping children to adjust to school with minimum strain. Such attempts will be successful only according to how far a genuinely effective bridge is made between the values and culture the school appears to sustain and those of the home, the parents and the surrounding community.

Thus compensatory education (if in the face of the great number of children who need it it can still be called so) should be as much concerned to understand and reconcile its aims with the powerful influences affecting children out of school as it is with narrowly educational or intellectual goals and the adjustment of children to its normative demands. In very many, one might say all, cases the school is likely to fail if it adheres to its traditional more or less isolated role, even though marked by some points of contact with willing parents; children who appear to thrive in it will either be those whose homes already share its preconceptions or those who come to do so at the heavy price of rejecting much of their own background and not fully assimilating the alien norms.

The fact is that whatever is attempted for and with children in school will be seriously prejudiced if not entirely negatived if there is overt or even hidden and passive hostility or incomprehension from the home. Schools which cannot count upon a majority of families agreeing with and intelligently supporting their work have only very limited success in trying to graft some education onto their pupils. Where as is increasingly the case the pupils come from very different and often very deprived backgrounds, schools and teachers cannot ignore their social role; the school has to be positive in its approach to parents, to act as a community centre, a development agency involving parents as well as children in the process of social change.

This does not mean just inviting parents to lectures and school functions; still less does it mean defensively or aggressively explaining how the school's goals must be accepted by parents as better than their own. So often the very parents one most wishes to be in contact with are those who do not respond because they are already convinced of their own inadequacy and believe that they have nothing to give: they renounce their function as partners in the education of their children and even feel themselves threatened by the school and its teachers. In depressed groups this renunciation extends to a feeling of complete helplessness and self-devaluation in all areas of life.

Few cultures, even the most debased and disorganized, even the most primitive, are without values, customs, systems of personal relationships, knowledge, experience and wisdom which are worth preserving. Few parents are without something they can valuably contribute to their child's education and fewer still will reject uncondescending help which they can see as setting a value on them and their support for their own

child. Few aims of education, even the highest, do not lend themselves
to an immense variety of embodiment in human experience of different
kinds. What then is clearly needed is a continuing attempt by the school
to identify and use those elements in its pupils' experience and culture
which can—if we set prejudiced notions of superiority aside—be welcomed, reinforced and directed to the achievement of the broad aims
of education. This must imply the development of a true partnership
with parents, even the most depressed and inadequate, eliciting from
them their aims and aspirations for their children, helping them to feel
truly needed in the work of the school, enhancing their status in the
eyes of their children and patiently trying with them to reconcile the
aims and values of the school with what exists in the surrounding
culture. Where, as is sometimes inevitable—particularly in developing
countries—there is a clash between what the school believes to be right
and what are the customs and preconceptions of the culture, the school
must question its own rightness and recognize that even when it is
justified in its view, nevertheless at least a temporary compromise may
be better than a damaging conflict.

Such an attempt implies resources of skilled workers which few
systems as yet possess and levels of training and insight not common in
the teaching profession, committed as it tends to be to more or less
standard packages of knowledge and skills which children are expected
to pick up. But any genuine attempt at levelling-up social differences by
education, and still more the urgent tasks of education in developing
countries, must mean a massive attempt to develop the educational
skills of those most present and pervasive educators the parents.[29] There
is a growing series of experiments along these lines taking place in the
United States, in England and elsewhere.[30]

It may be suggested that this is Utopian and that many, even most,
children somehow survive the experience of a plunge into more or less
formal schooling, changes of school, class or country with very little
help from their parents or teachers. Human beings are indeed remarkably resilient and at a greater or lesser apparent personal cost, children
do make some sort of adaptation.

However, the proportions of partial or total failure to make satisfactory educational progress, the amount of maladjustment, the huge
and increasing differences in sheer learning as school goes on which are
revealed by the studies undertaken in European systems—and the even
more alarming figures from the developing countries, where as many as
60 per cent of children may drop out in the first year[31]—must give us
pause. We cannot afford to ignore the possibility that even in favourable,
Western circumstances more than one child in four may be seriously
unadjusted in school with consequences for his attitudes to himself,
towards education and towards the society which insists upon it. On

the other hand—and subject to proper handling by parents and by teachers who are profoundly aware of the psychological reverberations of the clash between what the child is and what the school reasonably sets out to do—entry to school, change of school and even change of culture, just because they are stressful and heighten sensitivity, can contribute greatly to the child's conviction that he can succeed, to his knowledge of self and others, his own capacities and limitations and to his ability confidently to enter novel situations later on. For very many children, the early years of infant and primary school represent the only chance they will have to break out of the cycle of deprivation.

In a world where the ability to think and to adapt, where smooth even if effortful adjustment to change is increasingly seen as a major factor in the mental hygiene of adult life, one cannot too greatly emphasize the importance of the primary school. What happens in the first excursion outside the family, the first contact with public demands and group pressures will settle how the child reacts to education generally, and how as an adolescent and adult he will adjust to subsequent periods of transition and change, determining his general style of coping with life and its challenges.

B. FAILURE TO LEARN

RETARDATION AND BACKWARDNESS

The consequences of rigidity in school programmes and of a general failure to recognize and allow for both differences in ability to learn and the effects of social and cultural background on children's adjustment to school are shown in the proportion of children who are labelled, early on in their school careers, as failures. As we have seen, the causes and possible remedies are complex and not easy either to understand in terms of a few generalizations or to set right by a stroke of the administrator's pen. We can, however, profitably ask some more detailed questions about the role of the school itself in causation and prevention.

The pioneer work of Binet and Simon in France and of Burt in England,[32] drew attention to the fact that success in school may have a large genetic component and that children's ability to learn certainly shows marked variation. This is, of course, not to say that all low scores on tests of general ability reflect entirely genetic factors or that all failure to learn is caused uniquely or even principally by a lower than average level of operational intelligence. Many other factors enter; notably, for some children specific physical or physiological defects and for very many more, inhibitions or deviations in the structuring of intelligence stemming from their home background. There is, as we have noted, a strong correlation between socio-economic factors, measured ability and success or failure in school. Moreover, socio-economic factors reflected particularly in such things as parental co-operation with the school, willingness and ability to support the schools' intellectual effort, continue to have a cumulative effect at least until well on into adolescence. It seems highly likely too that the expectations of teachers themselves are influenced by their knowledge of children's home backgrounds[33] and tend in their turn to influence pupils' ideas of themselves and levels of aspiration.[34]

From whatever causes, however, there are some children whose ability to learn is markedly below average and who cannot, whatever is done for them by the school, maintain the same pace of learning as their contemporaries. Repeated testings of population samples indicate that about 2-3 per cent of children are so markedly subnormal that they fail conspicuously to follow the curriculum considered suitable for the normal child. A proportion of these, particularly those in the lowest category of all have serious neurological impairments.[35] Most European school systems recognize this by the provision of special schools or classes for children whose intelligence is markedly subnormal[36] though not as yet in sufficient numbers.

THE DULL

There is, however, a much more numerous group of those who, while not being subnormal, nevertheless as they progress through school fall increasingly behind the others in the development of cognitive skills and usually in many other social and personal aspects of growth. If we take as a borderline an I.Q. of 85—that is, a level of development in sheer all-round capacity to learn (not standard of attainment) which is 85 per cent or less than that of the average child of the same chronological age —then we should expect to find in any unselected age group of children about 12-13 per cent who are, while not markedly subnormal (i.e., not below I.Q. 70), unable to keep up with their better endowed fellows. It is important here to realize that rates of growth in operational ability are roughly proportional to the degree of that ability—that is to say that brighter children mature intellectually faster and duller children slower than the average. Hence the dull child, even if he works up to the limit of his operational capacity, is likely in the course of the five or six years of his primary schooling to fall further and further behind his abler contemporaries.

Few European countries fully recognize in their primary education systems that the dull need a programme more closely adapted to their slower development. Indeed the age-grade system, or any other which implies norms based upon the capacities of the average child,[37] dooms the dull to increasing failure as they go through school. One would expect, for example, the child with an intelligence quotient of 80 to be working at the age of 10 at the level of children two years younger than he is. One would expect such children, in fact, to complete no more than five or six of the nine years of a standard package of compulsory schooling within the normal time, though given a more flexible curriculum and a rather slower pace they might well get a great deal further than they do now.

Of recent years attention has been turned to the problem of grade repetition in the schools of Europe and we now have statistics showing the chronological ages of children actually working in the various age grade levels of primary schools. An early and detailed study[38] revealed that the proportions of children backward by one year or more in Belgian schools in 1951 were as follows: second year (age 7) 22.1 per cent; third year (age 8) 25.9 per cent; fourth year (age 9) 32.3 per cent; fifth year (age 10) 40.2 per cent; sixth year (age 11) 41.3 per cent.[39] Later figures 1965-66, for the French speaking part of Belgium, show no substanial change, ranging from 20 per cent in the first year to 43 per cent in the fifth.[40]

A similar study made by Haramein[41] of nearly 17,000 children of compulsory school age (6-14) in the Canton of Geneva in 1959-60 showed that in the second primary year, the percentage of children backward by one year or more were 17 per cent of boys, and 13 per cent of girls; in the third year 25 per cent boys, 21 per cent girls; in the fourth 34 per cent boys and 27 per cent girls; in the fifth 42 per cent boys and 36 per cent girls; in the sixth 45 per cent boys and 34 per cent girls; in the seventh 47 per cent boys, 31 per cent girls; and in the eighth 52 per cent boys and 41 per cent girls. Moreover the percentages of children advanced by a year drop steadily from 12 per cent boys and 14 per cent girls in the second year to 5 per cent boys and 5 per cent girls in the eighth. From the fifth year onwards less than half the boys are in the grade appropriate to their age. A comparison with similar figures obtained in 1954 suggests that apart from the second year, the number of children retarded by a year or more has increased and this most markedly in the fifth, sixth and seventh years—an over-all increase of 6 per cent.

In France the 1963-64 figures for all children show that in the first year of the primary school (putative age 6.9-7.8), 58 per cent of children are normally placed, 8.6 per cent advanced by a year or more and 33 per cent retarded by a year or more (of which 13 per cent are two or more years behind). By the sixth year of primary school (i.e. the second year of the *cours moyen,* putative age 9.9-10.8), 8 per cent are advanced, 41 per cent normal for age and 51 per cent at least one year retarded (of which 7.5 per cent are two years or more retarded in grade for age).[42] There is some indication that the percentages for retarded children have *risen* slightly since 1950-51 and those for advanced children have fallen. From these figures—which are probably typical of Europe—it is possible to infer that failure as represented by inability to conform to the standards set by the school programme is very much more widespread than would be expected from the known proportions of the dull.

In the developing countries and for a great variety of reasons, the figures for grade repetition and drop-out from school are much higher, so much so as to represent a very serious waste of the scarce resources available for education. Not uncharacteristically there is an annual 20 per cent dropout rate but this may be as high in some countries as 60 per cent or more.[43]

RETARDATION AN ARTEFACT?

The reasons for this are complex. In the first place if, for example, at the end of each school year 70 per cent of children in each age group are promoted to the next grade, then by the end of the sixth year not more than 16 per cent of children will have passed normally from grade to grade without doubling a class. Thus some 'backwardness' may be an artefact of the age-grade promotion system itself, indeed certainly is, particularly when the thresholds of promotion are arbitrarily and unobjectively fixed. Actually it seems from the Belgian figures that the promotion rate is rather more favourable[44] since Hotyat and his colleagues found (1951) that approximately 50 per cent of pupils complete the cycle of six primary years without remaining more than one year in the same class, but significantly they point out that the proportion of failures is highest in the first year.[45] An examination of the Belgian figures for 1938, 1945 and 1951 for two main school districts[46] indicated a deterioration of the situation as a result of the Second World War and a steady recovery afterwards, though it seems that the consequences of the war were still exerting an influence on children born in 1941 and earlier,[47] even in 1954.[48]

Since 1950, there has been some improvement in some countries (but not in all) because attention has been drawn to the problem and the strictly artificial aspects of failure have to some extent been eliminated. However, particularly in developing countries, the rates are still very high, very much higher than one would expect from any knowledge we possess of the distribution of sheer ability to learn, and the reasons in part lie in the background of the pupils as well as in the schools' promotion policies and the attitudes they imply. In a study from Brazil,[49] for example, it is pointed out that very many children of school age have to work to supplement the family income, and that in few of the 180 countries, is the general level of literacy above 30 per cent of adults.

A Hong Kong study[50] stresses the seriously adverse socio-economic factors and the clash between the Western values of the school and the very different ones of the home.

The Haramein study cited earlier is one of the most thorough and it gives for the schools of Geneva a more detailed picture—and in its broad lines probably for similar systems elsewhere. There are the usual strong correlations between socio-economic background and sex and levels of attainment. In addition Haramein notes that the average marks obtained by pupils, normal for their age-grade, diminish as they go up the school, especially in the fourth, fifth and sixth years; moreover, because probably the curriculum after the first two years puts more stress upon comprehension and verbal skills and becomes more abstracted from the daily experience of children, the socio-cultural quality of the home seems to have a greater influence. By the fourth and fifth years new subjects—geography, history, geometry, for example—appear on the time-table and any failure in basic learning tends to become compounded. Haramein suggests that the school is not adapted to children as they in fact are; it has a particular idea of what children should be and in reality rejects a large proportion of those for whom it should be catering.[51]

This in fact is the principal indictment of the traditional school—that its notions of childhood and its models of what a child should be, can do and learn are based, unscientifically, upon the socially more fortunate groups (and on the whole even then of children of somewhat above average ability) and that it has not yet fully accepted the implications of universal education and genuine equality of educational opportunity. It is acting as a rigidly selective mechanism which from the earliest years is rejecting children who cannot conform to its restricted and exacting model.

A more positive view is taken in the U.S.S.R. where the stress is laid upon the school's obligation to adapt itself to the pupils it receives. It is claimed that between 1952 and 1964 repetition of grades has been reduced by 1 million from 2.5 million and that this has been due to an intensive effort on the part of the teachers—refusal to confront the child with demoralising failure, abolition of practices tending to fail the slower pupils instead of helping them, and a firm belief that a normal child should always be able to follow his class level.[52]

Obviously we are confronted by a problem which in its main lines is similar in countries at very different levels of development. In detail, however, it varies not only with broad social and economic circumstances but with factors in the school systems and in individual children or groups of children. Basically, the solution must be sought, as the Russian study suggests and as Haramein proposes, in a much more sensitive adjustment of the school's expectations and methods to its human material, an adjustment most likely to be successful if it takes a constructive and optimistic view of human potential. One thing is certain: the mental health of any human being and particularly that of a child is put at hazard if demands are made upon him which he cannot possibly fulfil and if he senses that his failure means rejection by the system. Failure and drop out rates of the kind which exist today in the majority of primary schools in the world represent an intolerable wastage of economic and human resources as well as the seed bed of delinquency and antisocial behaviour of all kinds.

BRITISH STUDIES

Further light on the matter is thrown by studies of a rather different type which have been made in Great Britain since Burt began his inquiries as psychologist to the London County Council in 1913. For more than forty years now promotion according to standards or grades has ceased to be a feature of English primary education. Children pass from class to class with their age mates, though in many schools there is a system of streaming and of special classes by means of which children of similar age are grouped in classes very roughly homogeneous in ability. In this sense therefore, there is no failure marked by a repetition of grades. However, there is evidence to suggest that children in lower streams are often given the worst teachers and tend to view themselves as failures unless very special efforts are made to maintain their morale.[53]

Investigation has tended to concentrate mainly upon the basic skills of reading, spelling, arithmetic and written composition, and on the relationship between a child's level of attainment and his general ability. Though the correlation between general ability, as measured either by group or individual tests, and attainment in the basic skills is by no means perfect,[54] the correspondence between school performance and intelligence is sufficiently close to enable us to estimate approximately how many children are likely, because they begin with lower than average levels of general ability to learn, necessarily to be backward educationally. Burt[55] suggested that any child whose attainments at the age of 10 are equal or inferior to those of the average child of $8\frac{1}{2}$ should be considered backward and in need of special help. This gives us as a rough borderline an educational quotient of 85. If we assume that developed general ability sets limits on the child's power to learn at least up to the age of 11 or 12, then children whose intelligence quotients are inferior to 85 will in most cases also be backward educationally.[56] We should expect some 10 to 12 per cent of children inevitably to be backward at the chronological age of 10. solely because of a lower than average general ability.

THE UNDER-USE OF ABILITY

Prior to the Second World War, repeated testings of groups of children in primary schools revealed that between 13 and 15 per cent of children in English schools were backward in these terms. This suggests that there was a small proportion[57] of children—between 2 and 4 per cent—whose backwardness may probably be attributed to causes other than that of markedly lower than average ability, that is they were retarded.[58] When, however, the actual conditions of backward groups were closely investigated[59] it was found that nearly half the children were in fact achieving even less than might be expected of their limited ability and that some 15 per cent of them were of normal or even of superior ability.[60] In such groups therefore we may expect retardation to be a phenomenon not confined to any particular intellectual level.

The effects of the Second World War, with its disruption of education and general disturbance of the social and emotional security in which children lived, were clearly reflected in a striking increase in retardation. The British Ministry of Education organized the testing of the reading ability of large and representative samples of children in 1948.[61] Accepting a borderline for backwardness somewhat lower than that adopted by most other authorities,[62] the investigators found that 30.1 per cent of 15-year-old children, and 20.5 per cent of 11-year-old children were backward or worse. These figures indicated a substantial increase in the proportion of retarded children, especially among those whose whole primary schooling took place during the war.

More recent surveys in the United Kingdom[63] show that between 1948 and 1964 the reading standards of children at the end of their primary school careers (age 11) have risen steadily—11-year-olds in 1964 achieved an average level of performance equivalent to that of pupils 17 months older in 1948. Between 1964 and 1970, however, there seems to have been no significant improvement, if anything slightly the reverse. However, if we take a reading age of 9 years or less[64] at 11 as indicating backwardness in 1970, some 15 per cent still fall into this very low category. Of the 15-year-old school leavers in 1948, 6 per cent were judged by pre-war standards to be semi-literate (reading age 9 or less), and just over 3 per cent were so in 1970; many more than this (about 22 per cent) of course were three years or more behind the average level for their age.

A detailed study made in 1964-65 by Rutter, Tizard and Whitmore[65] of the entire 9-11 year groups (3,500 children) in the Isle of Wight (U.K.) distinguished *reading retardation* as a specific disability in reading not explicable in terms of a low level of intelligence. For this purpose they adopted as a criterion a discrepancy between I.Q. and reading level of approximately 28 months—a rather more severe standard than usual—and for reading backwardness a similar discrepancy between chronological age and reading. They found 3.7 per cent of children exhibiting specific reading retardation as compared with 6.6 per cent who were backward. These figures are not directly comparable with those cited earlier since the criteria used are dissimilar; but what is important is that they indicate that in any generally backward group will be found a considerable proportion of children who are under-functioning, that is not realizing educationally even the level indicated by their operational intelligence.

There is reason, too, to suppose that children who get off to a bad start in the basic skill of reading are increasingly handicapped as they progress through a curriculum which in the later primary stages and in the secondary presupposes the ability to get information rapidly from print. Moreover, as Morris[66] found in her study of children in Kent schools, of the 14 per cent who had barely made a start on reading at eight, more than half remained very poor readers throughout their schooling—they did not catch up, even in reading.

The problem of retardation, of the underuse of ability, is not however confined to the backward group. Wall[67] in 1949 and 1950, investigating attainments in arithmetic, reading and spelling in a sample of some 1,500 8-year-old children in 15 junior schools, found that among children of ability superior to the average, more than half were two years retarded in reading comprehension, one-third two years retarded in arithmetic, and three-quarters, two years or more retarded in spelling as compared with their mental ages. Retardation among children of superior intelligence is apt to escape the attention of the teacher since such children, mentally sometimes two or three years ahead of their contemporaries, frequently achieve an average performance which passes muster.

BROAD SOCIAL CAUSES

However educational systems operate and by whatever criteria we judge, we are obviously confronted by a complex problem. Failure which is apparent to the individual has emotional consequences for him, for his image of himself in relation to others, and ultimately it colours his attitude to the school and the society which it appears to represent. As Bloom,[63] citing a good deal of American evidence, suggests repeated success in school appears to increase the likelihood that an individual can withstand stress and anxiety more effectively later on in life; and conversely that repeated failure appears, for many, to be the source of emotional difficulties and mental disorders. If, moreover, we recall that the ability to make the kinds of dynamic adjustment essential in a

K

world of change depends upon the acquisition of knowledge and skills, then a denial of these by a failure to progress through a well conceived curriculum imposes a very severe handicap indeed.

The objective causes of such failures are not far to seek. The evidence from European countries of the disturbances wrought by the Second World War not only to the schools but to the framework of home and community life shows how these were reflected in generally lowered standards. The return to more settled conditions is reflected in the English figures by a steady rise at least up to 1964.

There is, too, some evidence which suggests that rising standards of literacy and general educational aspirations in populations lead to a rise in average operational intelligence:[69] roughly we can say that the more educated the parents, the more likely is it that their children will be able and willing to learn. A principal problem of developing countries is illiteracy, particularly of the mothers; and this is certainly reflected in the greater difficulty of children in many developing countries to adjust to school and its demands.

There are too, the causes, cited earlier,[70] in the general background of the pupils which lead to a depression in the general level of intellectual functioning and which produce a clash between the culture of the school and that of the child's home. Probably also, partly because of this and of the widening gaps between the more successful and less successful groups in the wealthy societies of the West, some of the élan of popular education has been lost and the role of the teacher has been devalued.[71]

CAUSES IN THE SCHOOL

There is no doubt that the tasks of the school have become more difficult, particularly in societies which no longer recognize schools as authoritarian and selective institutions while not having clearly assigned to them a new role (and the resources necessary) to provide for the personal and social development of children of all kinds. Large classes impose mass teaching and a largely authoritarian and directive approach. Centrally determined programmes and lock step curricula tend to demand a uniform progress in which the slower are bound to fall behind, whilst the abler may be kept back. A general lack of human resources, not only of well-trained teachers but of auxiliaries and ancillaries, make it difficult to give each child, particularly those who have some disadvantage in their background, the kind of individual attention or skilled help in small groups which could do something to realise the ideal of ensuring that all children reach adequate levels in the simpler and more complex educational skills. What is perhaps even more important, in the present context, is that the attitudes of school systems and of teachers are excessively deterministic, tending to regard children's abilities as fixed quantities which irrevocably set limits to what can be learned.

While evidence does not support the extreme opposite view—that all children can reach any level of attainment if they are suitably taught —there is reason to believe that, at differing rates of progress, all children can potentially be brought to minimum levels of education somewhat in advance of present standards. It is also true that the influences operating to depress in-school learning probably have also operated (and continue to do so) to depress the general level of operational intelligence or general ability to learn. Hence the fact that educational attainment and general ability roughly coincide and that both may be low for many children should not be accepted as a reason for abandoning an attempt at improvement in both.

The crux lies in fact in the climate of expectation in the schools and in what the teacher teaches the child about himself and his possibilities. We know that repeated failure or low performance has emotional consequences for the pupil; we know too, that the pupil's perception of himself as a success or a failure, certainly early in his school life, is directly associated with his teacher's marks and judgements. Whatever the degree of accuracy and objectivity they may have, they tend to be relative—to compare the pupil with others. Hence any group, however generally high or low in ability, will have its inevitable (but relative) successes or failures with attendant effects on the self-image and emotional responses of the winners and losers.

In this sense then the elimination of comparisons—inter-individual by marks and exams, and intergroup by streaming and setting—might help to eliminate the sense of failure. This does not mean that real differences will be eliminated or that failure should or will not occur. What it could do is to transfer to the child the determination of realistic objectives for himself, and help him to use his own progress as a standard of comparison, with the teacher aiding his pupil to determine reasonable goals and providing the means of self-evaluation. In this context failure can be clearly and manifestly related to such things as degree of effort, realism in setting targets; it can be detected and remedied by the child himself, again with assistance and reassurance from the teacher, and he can learn that failure is neither absolute nor irremediable. In terms of what has been called the latent curriculum[72] the customary use of marks, grading and competition assigns (often inaccurately) to each child—at least as he perceives and incorporates it in his self image—a place in the academic and social pecking order[73] and at worst implies rejection of all who are not among the best; whereas more stress upon self-comparison provides the setting in which pupils can accept themselves as they really are, equally valuable but different and helps them to recognize that they can choose the kind of person they wish to be.

It should, however, be remembered that the elimination of inter-individual competition and the stressing of personally set goals is not to be achieved overnight; and there is always the danger that standards may slip if teachers too readily accept children themselves as pace-setters. What seems to be critical is that the pupil should develop aspirations and standards of performance which lead him to efforts likely to be crowned with success. In this the interaction of teacher and taught is crucial: the teacher always helping the pupil to set his sights a little higher and seeing to it that the essential masteries are in fact steadily acquired. Unthinking and unsystematic 'progressive' methods do children little service.

INDIVIDUAL CASES

Even when broad causes have been allowed for and under the most enlightened system, there will remain a hard core of children, representing the whole range of ability, who are underfunctioning for a combination of reasons which can only be estimated by a careful individual clinical study, and who can be helped only if some special effort is made by a skilful teacher or psychologist. Most investigators are agreed that in any one case the causes are multiple, combining in different ways in different children. It is clear, however, that failure to learn nearly always has emotional connotations. Social, physical, and physiological factors, unless they are very extreme, though they may sometimes slow down a child's progress, are not insuperable obstacles unless they reverberate adversely in his emotional life. Not infrequently retardation is the symptom of a series of attitudes to oneself, habits and maladjustments in the entire social and emotional development of the child which find their roots in experiences in the family or in the early years of school. Furthermore we are beginning to see that retardation, either as a symptom of deeper disturbances or directly by what it may mean in terms of wasted talent and lowered morale, is related to many cases of adolescent and adult breakdown and delinquency. As such it is worthy of the continuing attention of research workers in every country in the world.[74]

REMEDIES

The school, and especially the primary school in the first years of the child's educational career, is in the first line of defence against backwardness and retardation. This defence is most likely to succeed upon the basis of constructive mental health work applied to the education of all children, supplemented by some special remedial work where this proves necessary.[75] By a sensitive knowledge of their pupils, by close co-operation with parents, by the adaptation of method to differing capacities and above all by the quality of the human relationships they build up, teachers can play a key part in such constructive work, even where the earlier circumstances of the child's life have been adverse and even where the social milieu is unfavourable.

Failure to learn, and particularly failure to learn to read because reading is the key to so much in later education, is always to be taken seriously. This does not mean in the early stages putting an increased pressure to learn or even the undertaking of elaborate remedial work. It may mean an attempt to reduce the anxieties of a child who finds he cannot keep up simply because he is not yet developmentally ready. On the other hand, failure to read persisting beyond what is the range of normal expectations—say around the age of 8 in an otherwise apparently normal child—does call for expert attention and probably for some special help, if only to sustain morale while the processes of growth catch up. One thing appears to be quite certain. Making a child merely repeat a year in which he has failed in one aspect of learning, particularly if the assessment of failure is based on arbitrary criteria, does not seem to result in satisfactory progress.[76]

Unhappily in many schools in Europe reading and arithmetic are regarded as the major task of primary education and are taught as formal instrumental skills which the child must acquire in step with his contemporaries. Often a start of an instructional kind is made, directed at a whole class of whom some at least have not achieved the necessary physiological and mental maturity necessary to a fair prospect of continuing success. Since in the eyes of parents, children, and teachers alike, the acquisition of these basic skills ranks as the major task, failure is immediately apparent to the child himself and usually to his parents who read into it misgivings prompted and intensified by their own anxieties. Hence there is the tendency, always a danger to good education, to attempt to start too early, to go too fast and to devote so much time and energy to formal teaching that little is left for other activities, which would both develop the child's expanding curiosity about his world and help him to increase his stability and self-confidence which lie at the root of his power to learn.

CRITICAL PERIODS

Recent research tends to indicate that for each child, whatever the method used and whatever the prior preparation, there is a stage at which he is insufficiently mature to learn certain techniques. Time spent in trying prematurely to teach him is not merely wasteful, but the result-

ing failure builds up in him adverse attitudes and actually delays subsequent learning. Similarly it seems, though this is not so certain, that
there may be critical periods at which learning of particular skills or
processes takes place more readily and surely than later. Such critical
periods are difficult to determine with precision since, whilst ultimately
dependent upon a general maturation which varies greatly from individual to individual, they are much affected by prior experience and
environmental stimulation which are only partly under the control of
the school.

READING READINESS

This is well illustrated by the studies of reading readiness, the upshot of
which is that learning to read depends upon a sufficient level of general
intellectual development, a physical and physiological maturation which
makes possible the fine perceptual discriminations on which the deciphering of print depends, and a growth in personality such that the child
wishes to learn and has sufficient emotional energy to devote himself
to the task. Learning to read moreover in part depends upon the child's
own spoken vocabulary, which in turn largely reflects environmental
stimulus. Other things being equal, the child from the culturally stimulating home is likely to be advanced by as much as two years or even
more in his verbal development at the age of 6 as compared with his
contemporary from a poorer environment; he is thus not faced with the
double task of acquiring the concepts and of learning how to read the
words in which they are embodied.

Much attention has been devoted to physical and physiological
defects—for example cross-laterality, visual and auditory weaknesses—
as causative factors in reading difficulties. Such weaknesses may call for
special attention and, if neglected, operate as severe handicaps. Many
more children are found to have weaknesses in visual and auditory
perception, independent of sensory defects; indeed up to the age of 7,
confusions between the letters b/d, p/q, m/n and the like are rather
the rule than the exception.[77] In themselves, however, neither sensory
defects nor weaknesses in visual and auditory perception will prevent
learning to read if the child is well motivated and taught.

DYSLEXIA

A special word should perhaps, however, be said here about what is
sometimes called dyslexia or 'word-blindness'. Ever since the turn of
the century attempts have been made to define a syndrome of reading
failure which is due neither to lack of intelligence nor to any form of
linguistic or cultural deprivation.[78] Similar, though less intensive, efforts

have been made to identify dysorthographia and 'acalculia'. In the sense that these are definable disease syndromes with features common to a group of sufferers, and calling for a more or less uniform method of treatment, they do not appear to exist. But it remains true that there are children of normal or superior intelligence who, at least initially, have no motivational or emotional blockages or inhibitions, and who nevertheless find it difficult or even impossible to learn to read, write and spell adequately under even reasonably favourable classroom conditions.

In the intensive study made of children between 9 and 11 in the Isle of Wight, referred to earlier,[79] a thorough comparative neurological study was made of the intellectually retarded (below I.Q. 70), the specifically retarded in reading (reading level 28 months below measured ability—means I.Q. 103) and a control group of normal children. It is clear from this study that on most measures used, intellectually retarded children showed an incidence of cerebral dysfunction and other neurological disorders along with abnormalities in speech and motor function much higher than those of the reading retarded or the controls. In the group of children with specific reading retardation, however, there was only a slight (and statistically non-significant) difference from the controls in possible neurological abnormality. But reading difficulties were associated with clumsiness, a lag in language development, difficulties in the perceptual field and in concentration. There was no evidence to support a single syndrome of a genetically determined sort but the study did suggest that developmental, and probably constitutional factors were important, principally as lags in language, motor and perceptual development, and that in some at least there was a family history of such lags coupled with educational difficulties.[80]

It seems probable that the main factor in readiness is that of general personal development. Intelligence and physiological maturation set downward limits below which teaching is likely to be ineffective; but the decisive factors, given adequate intellectual maturation, seems to be orectic and to be a reflection of the child's whole prior developmental experience, and in particular of the stimulus which his environment has given him. If home and nursery school have satisfied his needs, if he is, at his level, stable, confident and enterprising, then he will welcome the challenge of new and difficult tasks.

If, however, his verbal experience has been limited or if he is manifestly unable to tolerate failure or if he exhibits marked developmental lags, the wise teacher will postpone formal teaching in favour of activities aimed at enlarging his experience, remedying verbal or perceptual weaknesses, and building up a sense of security.[81] Such aspects of maturation cannot be mechanically determined or assessed solely by tests;[82] only by careful study and understanding of each individual child with all his idiosyncracies of ability, experience and development, can the teacher in fact adjust the programme to the widely differing capacities which will characterize a group of 40 or more children at the outset of their school career.

At what age then may we expect that the child who is developing normally will begin to learn to read? There used to be a fairly general agreement that a *mental* age of 6-6½ is optimal for the conditions prevailing in most schools. However, much depends upon method and motivation. Gates,[83] for example, pointed out long ago that modifications of reading material and teaching method make an earlier start possible. Taylor, studying Scottish children,[84] indicated that they may profitably start reading as early as 5 if, but only if, words of very simple structure and expressing a very limited range of ideas are used; and, as we have seen,[85] Doman[86] and others have advocated teaching at ages between 2 and 3 both for 'normal' children and for children in deprived circumstances. There seems, however, no reason to suppose that anything is lost by a later start;[87] much harm, however, may be done by a premature beginning which increases the chances of failure among those of an insufficient maturity.

What does seem to be important is that, in nursery schools and particularly in the early years of primary schools, children should be surrounded by books, have a rich and varied contact with the spoken word related to vivid experiences and should be brought to associate spoken words and printed symbols together by constant exposure to them. When actual learning to decipher print begins it is important that the teacher's method, the vocabulary used and the ways of presentation should simplify rather than complicate the task of the child. To this end various simplified media[88] have been developed of which the best known (and the most heavily tested and researched) is the *initial teaching alphabet* (i.t.a.). This medium provides a version of the Roman alphabet augmented to 40 characters so that words are presented in a wholly regular form and the child is not confused by non-phonetic orthographies until he makes the transition (once reading is an established skill) to the less regular orthography. Experimental trials by means of tests of attainment of this alphabet in English speaking countries do seem to show, quite conclusively, that the proportion of poor readers diminishes markedly.[89]

So far as methods of teaching the decoding skills of reading are concerned there is more doctrine than conclusive research. Advocates can be found for global or whole word methods, for alphabetic methods and for more or less systematic phonic approaches. Successes (and failures) are obtained with any method. What seems to be important is that the teacher should be systematic in her approach, knowing what she is doing, why she is doing it, making clear to children the ends to be served and that she should have an encouraging and enthusiastic faith that children can and will learn to read. In these conditions almost any method and materials which do not raise unnecessary obstacles for the learners will prove successful. Furthermore it seems best if reading is seen from the outset by the pupils not to be something apart, a 'subject' on the time-table, but a vital aspect of general work in the development of language, a means to experience and a reflection of it.[90] Reading is certainly a skill and as such requires to be taught but its main value is as an extension of communication and information getting; and no method which obscures or hinders this is likely to be educationally successful in the long run.

ARITHMETIC

Even more than in the teaching of reading, teachers (and the framers of curricula) tend to go too far and too fast in pushing children to learn formal arithmetic. The ability to handle numbers in the abstract form of figures and to comprehend such processes as multiplication and division, depends upon the acquisition of concepts of quantity, size, extension and the like through repeated concrete experiences.[91] It depends, too, upon a *gestalt* of experiential and emotional factors similar to those involved in learning to read.

Where such concepts are inadequately formed or where the concrete experience is lacking, arithmetic very readily appears an incomprehensible puzzle around which children build feelings of inferiority. The results of their efforts are so clearly right or wrong that failure is immediately apparent. Moreover, an imperfect mastery of one basic process may entirely prevent subsequent progress. Hence it is of vital importance educationally that each stage of teaching and each new process should be introduced only when it is clear that the ability to understand and to learn is mature enough to give the best chance of success.[92]

Under the chairmanship of C. Washburne, a committee of seven educationalists carried out a large-scale experiment in the United States of America, designed to determine the optimal placement of practically all processes involved in primary and early secondary school mathematics. Washburne himself, however, points out that results for grades higher than the first depend more on the previous mastery of operations that enter into the new topic than on the mental age reached by the pupil. They are therefore not directly applicable to school systems where different sequences of subject matter are followed and where general levels of scholastic attainment differ from those in the United States. The one or the other condition probably obtains in most European countries. Reference here therefore will be made only to the age of the

K*

learning of the basic addition and subtraction facts, since these affect the age at which formal instruction in arithmetic could be appropriately begun. According to Washburne, these operations can be successfully learned at a *mental age* of 7 or 8 years,[93] a finding in accordance with Piaget's discovery that it is only somewhere around the seventh or eighth year that most children acquire the notion of the invariance of discrete quantities.[94] Before that age, the normal (i.e. not superior) child will believe that 'there are more pennies' or that 'there are less pennies' according to their being spread out or put together on the table, even if he has counted them. It is obvious that under these circumstances understanding of arithmetic operations is impossible and that memorized number combinations remain vocal reflexes.[95] Washburne also showed, and subsequent inquiries have confirmed, that while there is a minimum mental age below which a notion will not be comprehended, however presented, the method of presentation profoundly affects the age at which learning can successfully take place.

Only too frequently failure is induced in children by the teacher not drawing a distinction in his method of presentation between the logical structure of a subject, process or technique and the psychological mode in which it is taught. This distinction is at the root of successful pedagogic method and deserves more attention—particularly in the teaching of mathematics but also in reading—than it usually gets. When we speak of such notions as simple common fractions or the inclination of a slope, we refer only to their logical structure. A fraction can be used concretely by handling sticks and surfaces or it can be expressed by symbols and handled representatively (abstractly). Similarly the inclination of a slope can be conceived as its steepness as experienced when one climbs it; it can be appreciated perceptually when looked at from the side; or it can be expressed as a ratio between the vertical and horizontal distances of two points.[96]

Thus almost any given notion, process or operation found in the primary school curriculum can be dealt with concretely (by actual perception or by real action or experience) or symbolically or abstractly, and in a more or less generalized way. These are psychological dimensions. Moreover the context in which the latter occur will determine the amount of energy which the child will bring to their handling. If a given notion, operation or technique is seen by the child to be of immediate interest and value to him, and if it is dealt with by the teacher in a way which allows a pupil to comprehend it, in relation to the concepts he already has, then it can be acquired both more surely and at an earlier age than if it is unrelated to his interests and presented in a form which is beyond his present experience and grasp. Thus, though logically the 'content' may be the same, psychologically very different processes are involved, and it is not so much that the notion itself is too abstract which causes failure, as the mode of presentation.

MODERN MATHEMATICS

Some of the impetus towards the reform of mathematics teaching in primary and secondary schools has come from considerations such as these, though by no means all. In terms of the amount of use made of it by the average adult, there could be little justification for the teaching of arithmetic as an instrumental skill much beyond the four rules, elementary fractions, percentages and money. But as we have suggested, the modes of thought and of knowledge involved in mathematics have a general educational importance well beyond that of everyday calculation. Moreover, much of what we tend to think of as mathematics belongs as much to empirical science and is a way of looking at and ordering the evidence of our senses.

What is called modern mathematics then has more than one aspect. The first concerns the view of mathematics itself and of what constitutes within it an order of importance and priority. This leads to the introduction into syllabuses of material not traditionally taught in schools but which is thought to be of more value.[97] The second consideration is that pupils should be given a deeper insight into the fundamentals of mathematics itself; this implies explicit attention to the structural features, set theory, elementary logic and so on. The third aspect is that pupils should be provided with more opportunity to learn by discovery, using heuristic and inductive methods to build up more generalized concepts and schemas of relations before particular symbolic systems (e.g., numbers) are used to denote them.

In terms of primary school curricula this tends to lead to much experience both with structured material of various kinds and with ordering and classifying real objects in the environment. When it is well done, modern mathematics in its initial stages merges with work in integrated, everyday science.[98] Pupils learn to group objects in sets, which provides the conceptual basis for set theory and ultimately for matrix algebra. By manipulating blocks[99] and shapes they can come to discover such concepts as that different bases may be denoted by the same (arbitrary) symbols or build up notions of area and of equivalence as the basis of equations. Even the notion of negative number can be acquired in a concrete way either by simple balances or by marking out lines upon the ground. Similarly all kinds of phenomena—differences in height, shoe size, hair or eye colour—can be grouped in graphical form and distinction be perceived between continuous and discrete series. Problems of probability and sampling can be worked out in relation to simple estimations. The teacher's skill lies in understanding and systematically introducing the concepts and notions which underlie mathematical thought by profiting from (and encouraging) the interests of children in the world about them. Almost any interest can be pressed into service by a teacher who sees mathematics as one of the ways of ordering experience and thereby helps children to see its value for their own purposes.

The difficulty of modern mathematics is that it requires of the teacher (and often of the parent) a much deeper and more complete understanding of mathematical thinking (though not of formal mathematics) than is normally acquired in the older curricula; and the ability constantly to return to first principles applying them rigorously afresh rather than regurgitating them in conventional form. Moreover, the conventions of number tend to come later in the learning process and to be seen, by the child, for what they are—conventions rather than absolutes. Formal masteries of the old instrumental kinds come somewhat late and the conceptual understanding which it is the aim of modern methods to develop is sometimes more difficult to demonstrate. However, it does seem clear that, under the care of a teacher well trained in the newer material and methods, children not only progress more securely in understanding but develop positive attitudes to the general subject of mathematics.[100]

THE ANXIETIES OF PARENTS AND TEACHERS

In many, if not most, countries in Europe, teachers and parents alike are reluctant to postpone the beginnings of formal teaching of reading, arithmetic and written composition even by as little as six months. Still less are they likely to accept modern freer methods unless these are well explained and they are reassured as to their rationale and effectiveness. In some countries the tendency is noticeable for parents to enter children in primary schools if possible before the minimum compulsory age; other countries well provided with nursery schools have had to forbid the formal teaching of reading and number in such schools. In many communities parents insist upon homework being set and exercise pressure on the primary school to force children forward in formal attainments as rapidly as possible. Where two systems of education exist side by side in competition for pupils, such pressure is liable to be very marked and difficult for the teachers to resist.

There is little doubt that many of the objections to innovations, to ideas of making education more child-centred and of adapting it more nearly to the conclusions of an increasing body of research in child development, are motivated, in parents and teachers alike, by a genuine if perhaps mistaken anxiety for the child's good.[101] Education and educationists are rightly conservative and well-tried methods should not be lightly abandoned. On the other hand it is as well to consider carefully whether, in order to ensure the best possible future for children, we are not submitting them to such heavy present disadvantages that we defeat our own ends.

C. BEHAVIOUR PROBLEMS

MALADJUSTMENT

Hitherto we have in this chapter tended to concentrate upon the cognitive tasks of the school, dealing only incidentally with the personality and affective growth of children. This is on the assumption that the majority of children are socially and emotionally developing normally and satisfactorily and that the school's task is contributory to that of the home. However, although it is true that most children are considered by their parents and by their teachers to have settled down happily at school within a month of starting,[102] there is a considerable number who show signs of unsettlement or maladjustment in themselves or in their attitudes, both in the early years and later in their primary course.

It is often said that educational failure, particularly difficulty in learning to read, and maladjustment go hand in hand; and there is little doubt that continued failure—particularly when school or home apply misguided and ineffective pressure and punishment—has a seriously disturbing effect upon general personal morale. It seems probable also that in a number of cases maladjustment will inhibit learning or at least some important aspects of it: a refusal to learn to read, for example, may be the only way for a child to express his rejection of an environment which he perceives as itself rejecting and aggressive.

In their study of 7-year-olds—who had been in school for two years and were at the stage where initial mastery of reading is generally expected—Davie, Butler and Goldstein[102] found that nearly four out of ten of their backward readers were maladjusted; of those who, at this age, were virtually non-readers more than half were maladjusted. Hence in a substantial proportion of young backward children, it seems that maladjustment may be a cause or at least an accompaniment of their failure.

But certainly at this age, there are more children considered[103] to be maladjusted and unsettled in school than there are backward and the two groups though they overlap are not coincidental. Over-all, 14 per cent of 7-year-olds were 'maladjusted' and 22 per cent 'unsettled'. Nearly twice as many boys as girls were found in the maladjusted group and the proportions increase from the highest socio-economic group to the lowest and are particularly striking when the non-manual and skilled manual are compared with the lowest social group of all. When, however, maladjustment at home is considered, while it is still true that boys seem to be more difficult (particularly more aggressive and restless) than girls, social class differences, though in the same general direction as is shown in school, are much less marked. Probably, since for home behaviour mothers are the reporters, there are differences between social groups as to what is regarded as acceptable and what as deviant behaviour.

In this enquiry the investigators were able to look at the incidence of particular constellations of behaviour in the 6 per cent of children considered to be most deviant. These are revealing. The over-all pattern shows that in general more boys than girls, and more manual working class children than middle class children, show extremes of behaviour. This is particularly true for behaviour which indicates a 'writing off' of adults or adult standards, which was twice as frequent in working class manual groups as elsewhere. The largest individual difference between groups was for 'inconsequential behaviour—frequent and recurrent mis-behaviour with little or no regard for consequence'. Few middle class girls showed this and between 6 and 7 per cent of middle class boys; for every one middle class girl displaying this feature there were four working class girls, six middle class boys and ten working class boys. Nearly three times as many boys as girls (irrespective of social class) showed anxiety for acceptance by other children, while more girls than boys—particularly working class girls—were anxious for adult accep-tance. Twice as many working class as middle class children were 'unforthcoming' in school but there was no difference between the sexes.

It will be remembered that this was a national sample of 7-year-old children who had been in school since the age of 5. The assessments were not value judgements by teachers but reports of specific items of behaviour readily observable in the classroom and that the over-all incidence of deviant behaviour ('maladjusted' 14 per cent and 'unsettled' 22 per cent) was established statistically in the standardization of the instrument used. Furthermore the 'syndromes' were derived from the most deviant 6 per cent. Other estimates[104] derived in various ways from groups of different age ranges and in different countries suggest that 'seriously maladjusted' children constitute from 4 to 12 per cent of school populations, whilst a further 20 to 30 per cent display symptoms which call for some special attention. The figure from the Isle of Wight study[105] of 9- to 11-year-olds, based upon a detailed clinical examination and a severe criterion is 6.8 per cent of children having clinically significant psychiatric symptoms.

In a very detailed individual follow-through study of 66 children— the entire 6-year-old intake of a school in a district of Paris—Chilland[106] found that 20 children were seriously disturbed: 9 pre-psychotic, 2 with serious neurosis, 3 with marked neurotic depression, and 6 marked school failures. A further 28 had considerable problems of a neurotic or behavioural kind suggesting a poor outcome if no effective help was given. Only 18 were considered psychiatrically normal. At the end of their first school year (age 7), 32 (48 per cent) were judged good at reading, 11 (17 per cent) average and 23 (35 per cent) virtually non-readers—and at this stage a learning failure was not only predictive of future failure but a strong indication of serious psychological difficulty. Moreover, in so far as this small sample can do so, the link between behaviour problems, school failure and social class was confirmed.

We are here in the presence of a very complex and disturbing phenomenon, and one which probably varies markedly in specific detail from country to country and from social group to social group. The British figures display a marked difference, in general, between children from manual working class homes, and particularly from the homes of unskilled manual workers, and the rest. Children from the least favoured social circumstances seem to give the most unease and anxiety to their teachers and to be least adjusted in themselves and in their school environment. As we have seen earlier, they are also the children who for a variety of other reasons are likely to be the least successful in learning. It seems to be likely also that some forms of behaviour, such, for example, as aggressiveness or destructiveness, have very different meanings in different social groups. This is shown by very different incidences in social groups and by the fact that, when mothers are reporting, differences related to socio-economic class are much less in evidence than they are in data derived from the more normative situation of the school.

One thing seems to be clear. The normality or deviance of any form of behaviour has to be judged in terms of its frequency and acceptability in the group to which the individual belongs, in terms of social background and sex particularly. What might be relatively normal behaviour for a working class boy, might be a sign of considerable disturbance if it occurred in a middle class girl.

It seems likely, too, that many problems of behaviour and personality seen by teachers in the school setting are rather part of the clash of expectations and values between school and home which we have noted earlier than signs of a maladjusted personality—at least initially. With these children the problem for the teacher, and for the psychologist, is how far a form of behaviour, which may well be adjusted to the outside environmental circumstances of the child, should be modified, since a successful modification in school may well result in difficulties for the child elsewhere. It seems best in such cases to stretch the limits of tolerance as far as possible and to accept—and help the child to learn to accept—that standards of behaviour within limits are relative and that particular codes are in no absolute sense the right ones. There is no harm in a double standard of conduct if the individual understands why it may be necessary.

Nevertheless there are forms of behaviour which are intolerable and states of feeling or attitudes which either bring the individual into an increasingly maladjusted relationship with others or are self-destructive in various ways. From the teacher's point of view, any behaviour which sets up a barrier between the child and his group, which noticeably impedes his free entry into social contacts with other children and adults or blocks his ability to learn, should be taken as a sign that the child needs help. This does not necessarily imply psychiatric treatment, though this may be necessary; but it does imply a study of all the circumstances and probably some attempt to modify aspects of the environment, home or school, in positive ways. In many such cases, a fostering accepting attitude by the teacher, a genuine attempt to give the child success, even if only modest success, in his school work will at least prevent matters getting worse and may in fact be sufficient until greater maturity enables the child to make more satisfactory adjustments.

It should be remembered too that many forms of behaviour which are signs of maladjustment in older children are perfectly normal at younger ages—for example temper tantrums accompanied by screaming and kicking are normal in the early pre-school years but by no means so with, for example, a 7-year-old. Processes of socialization, of impulse control and the like take time; and not all children progress at the same rate, or indeed as we have seen, in the same general direction. Developmental lags are probably as common in this aspect of growth as in any other. Marked delays and discrepancies should always be brought forward for expert study and attention by the psychologist. But, while limits to what is tolerable must always be set, be explained and be insisted upon, it is the task of the teacher to understand and care for the individual child at grips with a problem in his own growth. A firm and understanding tolerance gives the best chance for developmental difficulties to diminish or disappear with advancing maturity.[107]

D. HIGHLY INTELLIGENT AND GIFTED CHILDREN

The belief still seems to be widespread that children of well above average ability tend to be physically weak, vulnerable to illness and highly liable to maladjustment. This stereotype dies hard, partly because of its link with the romantic notions of genius as being queer, maladjusted and destined for an early death. The facts tend to be the reverse. In his study of children with I.Q.s over 140 (some 2 per cent of the population) Terman[108] found them to be healthier, heavier, taller, less liable to illness, gayer and less susceptible to emotional disturbance than their fellows; a set of characteristics generally confirmed by work in New Zealand[109] and the United Kingdom.[110] In later life they tended to be more successful both personally and professionally.

This is, of course, what one would expect. From the outset the somewhat accelerated achievement of such children is likely to attract favourable attention and lay the basis for a positive self-image. They will tend to learn faster in early childhood and this has a cumulative effect, particularly in widening their interests in all kinds of ways. They read earlier, as a general rule, and they read more—rubbish as well as good books; they may develop a passion for general information, have demanding hobbies, invent games with complicated rules. They tend to have a wide and rich vocabulary and to be superior in such things as 'memory', originality and common sense. In very marked contrast with the dull or even with the average, they seem actively to seek intellectual stimulation and wring from the environment what they need for their cognitive growth. Perhaps, also because of their accelerated ability to understand and to verbalize, they are often much better able to cope with stress and difficult situations, escaping into imagination, imaginative play or absorbing hobbies when life is temporarily too hard for them.

However, the highly intelligent may have special problems created for them by disparities between their needs and abilities and the environments in which as children they find themselves. In their early years, the differences from others are not too great; but as they progress through the primary school their rate of cognitive growth means that they draw away in conceptual development from their average fellows. A very bright child of 9 or 10 may have already reached the stage of formal operations and be able to deal with highly abstract notions. He will certainly be well in advance of his age mates, and many older children, in his command of concrete operational thought.[111] Such a child is disconcerting for his teachers and may seem very queer to his contemporaries. Only too often he finds the games and occupations of his age group unsatisfying and dull; he wants to complicate them beyond what his companions can accept and understand. He runs the risk of being rejected and solitary, the odd man out. He may find his school work far too easy and boring but nevertheless deliberately try for acceptability by conforming to the general level, and thus develop adverse work habits. It is, in fact, characteristic that highly intelligent children, though their formal educational achievements are well above average, do not perform as well as their level of general ability would lead one to expect.[112] On the other hand they may seek to fashion the demands of the school to meet their own capacities, seeming to challenge the teacher and to be showing off to their mates.

In many school systems, those children who show their high ability in school work are somewhat accelerated through the grades—though rarely as many or as much as, for example, is conversely true for the dull.[113] It is, however, fairly characteristic that such acceleration is insufficient to challenge the ablest fully and many of the brightest children are considerably underfunctioning in their school work. This may not be particularly serious if, out of school, they have a variety of stimulating occupations and hobbies.

What is perhaps more important is that accelerated cognitive growth, although generally accompanied by some acceleration in physical, emotional and social growth, does not fully go hand in hand with it; towards the end of the first decade a bright child may have powers of learning and reasoning, a level of intellectual activities and a fund of knowledge well beyond that of the average adult, but still be emotionally and socially a child. Thus the bright accelerated child may find himself working with much older and more mature companions, and his differences from others be accentuated. It seems better to keep the very able with children no more than a year older or at the most two and to meet their cognitive needs by considerable enrichment in and out of school.

SPECIAL GIFTS

Marked special gifts and abilities are in some ways more difficult to deal with even than generally high intelligence, particularly if they do not fit nicely into the aims and facilities of the school, and what may be worse, if they are seen by the teacher as a threat to his pre-eminence. The helpfulness of the mathematically gifted child in pointing out a mistake or suggesting a better way can be very threatening to a teacher unsure of his own skills and knowledge. Some gifts may be denied and frustrated altogether if, for example, neither home nor school provides musical or artistic opportunities. Others, if they are to be really effectively exercised later like dance must be detected early and fostered before it is too late. It is also, in the early years particularly, difficult to distinguish between a special talent and the operation of high general ability on a passionate interest.

Although high intelligence tends to make adaptation easier, very high intelligence may make for quite severe maladjustment.[114] The discrepancies between cognitive growth and other aspects of development are exaggerated as are those between the child and his contemporaries; and this puts considerable stress upon the child. He may, in the simplest cases, find as so many intelligent children do, that his powers to conceive far outrun his powers to execute and react with frustrated rage; or he may become cripplingly self-critical. The frustration may be or become more general: he is so advanced and so 'queer', that others are frightened of him and react with teasing or open aggression and because he can find no success or companionship he withdraws into fantasy; he may reject the exercise of any special talent he has just because it singles him out and perhaps makes others jealous.

Unfortunately there are many able misfits produced by schools and homes inevitably geared to the needs of the average and a bit above and insufficiently sensitive to the needs of the very able and insufficiently resourceful in meeting them.[115]

From the point of view of the mental hygiene of the individual and of the community, maladjustment with high ability or special giftedness is a serious problem. It is from the highly intelligent and gifted that a community recruits its leadership and social output seems to follow an exponential or J curve in function of intelligence. Thus anything which impedes the harmonious growth of gifted individuals very greatly impoverishes their society. Perhaps even more immediately important is the damage which a highly intelligent but maladjusted child or adult can do to himself, to his immediate surroundings, and, later to his society as a whole if he attains, as he is likely to do, a position of leadership.

It is not to advocate a policy of élitism to say that special attention should be given to the needs and education of the very able. In some cases, usually towards the end of the primary school, this may involve an element of segregation.[116] For most, the best solution is to make special arrangements within the ordinary school, to give help where necessary to the family and to provide out-of-school opportunities. For example, since the able child can master rapidly some or all of the basic demands of the programme for his class, he can be given additional and more complex work to do; he can be asked to undertake an individual project for presentation to the class, or to lead and inspire a small group to do so. He can be invited to assist his less able fellows with their learning, supplementing the work of the teacher and, at the same time, becoming aware that great gifts imply great responsibilities to others. In any sizeable community, there is likely to be a number of very able children who can be brought together in their leisure or even —since they cover the normal work rapidly and easily—be released during school time to join a group where they can pursue their more complex interests.[117]

E.   SELECTIVE AND OPEN SYSTEMS

PREDICTIVE AND COMPETITIVE EXAMINATIONS

One of the major external causes of anxiety in parents and teachers and therefore of pressure on schools to maintain a safe uniformity rather than to become more open and child-centred is that in most European countries, after five or six years of primary education, the choice between the various forms of secondary education is determined by some kind of selection process, usually an examination. Some children, as a rule the least able intellectually, continue with studies similar to those of the primary school or a watered-down version of the academic curriculum; others enter various technical or prevocational courses; and a smaller group passes into some form of academic education which may be the only way of entry to a university or to a profession, and is regarded as the gateway to economic and social advancement.

The guidance of children between these different forms of secondary education has always presented a problem. Sometimes the simple but undemocratic expedient of charging relatively high fees for some of the courses is the favoured way. Other systems have a sufficiently generous provision to allow parents and children a free choice between secondary schools. The method of economic selection results in a very considerable waste of talent among those children whose parents cannot or will not pay fees. On the other hand unrestricted entry to a particular form of education having high prestige leads to a number of children entering schools for which they are intellectually unfitted and therefore to a very considerable rate of failure and premature school leaving.[118]

Until quite recently in most European countries children have been allowed to enter selective secondary schools, whether academic or technical. only after passing some kind of examination, set by the school itself. by the responsible local authority or by the State. This tends still to be true of developing countries where secondary education is a comparatively rare privilege. Partly because of the apparent economic or social value of particular forms of education, partly because of the prestige of particular schools. parents and teachers attempt to ensure that a child shall gain entry irrespective of whether the particular form of education provided is the one best suited to his aptitudes and interests.

In countries which retain them such selection examinations tend to be based upon some or all of the primary school syllabus. Most examine solely or mainly the standard of attainment in the mother tongue and in arithmetic. More rarely other subjects are brought into the examination, particularly geography and history. Clearly the form of the examination and its content will affect the primary school curriculum; in so far as it is competitive, it may lead both to cramming and overwork for the children and to a concentration by teachers on the teaching of those subjects chosen by the examiners at the expense of activities equally valuable but not examined. It also tends to an emphasis on linear reproductive types of thought and to the exclusion of the more open ended and creative kinds.[119]

Beside the possibility of a distortion or cramping of the primary school syllabus, there is also the danger that the natural eagerness of parents and teachers to do their best for their children will result in a period of mounting anxiety as the examination approaches. There is evidence that many children—even among the most able and whatever the form taken by the examination—experience emotional stress as the result of which they fail to do themselves justice; others, straining their ability to the utmost and nevertheless failing, develop apathy and a sense of inferiority which pursues them throughout the rest, at least of their school, life; yet others, carefully and expertly coached, pass the examination only to find that they have entered a form of education for which they are not genuinely suitable.

It is easier to criticize current examinations for entry to secondary education than it is to suggest remedies. The effects of such examinations on primary schools and upon children, parents and teachers are closely related to social attitudes in the community, to the amount and types of education offered at the secondary stage, to the effectiveness of the examination itself and to the means used to decide in doubtful cases. Where, as exists almost nowhere in Europe,[120] all forms of secondary education enjoy an equal prestige and are equally accessible to all children irrespective of economic or social factors, the problem is at its simplest—that of devising some series of tests, measures or observations which will enable us to guide each child to that form of education best suited to him. Even here, however, many problems arise. Such guidance depends upon the reliability and validity of the instruments—examinations, tests, interviews, or records—used to predict how children will develop. In most European systems, mainly for administrative reasons, most children make the change from primary to secondary education between the age of 10 and 13; guidance or selection thus operates at the threshold of adolescence which will bring about a profound change in the emotional, social and intellectual life. Predictions are perforce made at a period when many factors combine to make them difficult and not fully reliable.

Prior to the Second World War and in the two decades that followed it, much research was devoted to the refinement of selection and guidance procedures for the allocation of children to different courses of secondary education.[121] This work indicated that standardized tests of verbal reasoning, arithmetic-mathematics and the native language predicted better than any other form of examination, success in academic secondary education as shown in the results of public examinations four of five years later. Less success was obtained in predicting success in technical education but the addition of tests of spatial ability for example helped.[122] It was also found that selection could be much improved and the weight of testing considerably diminished if the assessments made by teachers were incorporated in the procedures.[123]

Such standardized and objective procedures are undoubtedly more just than the usual examinations. However, they are open to a number of different objections. All examinations and tests at whatever stage they are used tend to exert an influence on the curriculum, and the methods of teaching which are used. Although coaching and special preparation has a relatively small and rarely decisive influence on the results of properly divised objective tests, parents and teachers tend not to believe this and it was found that pupils were being extensively coached in 'intelligence' test questions and in the types of arithmetic operations which were used, to the exclusion of more liberally educative experiments in the primary school. Because of its critical importance as a gateway to academic education, this 11 + test, as it was called in England, tended to become the focus of anxiety and pressure by schools and parents. Moreover no procedure of selection, however accurate, is free from error; and some injustice is always done at the borderline of success and failure, particularly when we consider that such non-cognitive aspects as motivation to succeed, home support, temperamental stability and the like may, given the minimum necessary ability, be determinant of subsequent success or failure in a five- or six-year period of secondary education—and that these are only indirectly assessed, if at all, by an examination coming at the threshold of adolescence.

However, the arguments for and against any particular form of examination at the end of the five or more years of primary education, important as they are to the mental health of individuals and to the nature of primary school curricula and methods, are less crucial than the general arguments concerning the merits of selective or comprehensive systems. Here, as is usual in education, we tumble into a mixture of philosophical, economic and psychological considerations which do not lend themselves to neat, absolute and logical conclusions.

In situations where the most valued form of education (usually the liberal academic studies leading on to the professions) is relatively scarce and expensive, some form of selection seems essential. The intention is to make the best use of facilities by allowing access to them only of those with the most chance to succeed. So long therefore as all available places are occupied by pupils who can follow the course with success, the fact that there may be as many or more who do not get in is 'irrelevant'. Provided that entry is not gained uniquely on social grounds but mainly upon sheer ability as shown by performance, the system can be said to be just. There is equality of opportunity, apparently, to compete for places. This was the situation in most European countries in the decades following the Second World War and in some since the interwar years; it is still the situation in most developing countries and in a considerable proportion of southern Europe.

Two things should be noted. The abolition of fees for secondary education, the provision of bursaries and grants and the attempt to make selection upon merit by means of objective tests which reduce (but do not by any means eliminate) the effects of good and bad teaching and favourable and unfavourable social backgrounds, have contributed to an opening of opportunity for children from social groups which prior to 1914 had no hope of access to academic studies. This has been accelerated by a steady increase in provision for academic secondary schooling in most developed countries.

Apart altogether, however, from the adverse backwash effects of a competitive examination upon primary school curricula, selectiveness in a system has itself very complex influences upon pupils. The most obvious ones are shown in the statistics of failure and doubling of classes dealt with earlier in this chapter. Even, however, where failure is not made so manifest, it seems to be clear that the more selective the system, the more it tends to exaggerate the differences in functioning between individuals passing through it; and this not only in attainments but in general ability[124] as shown by performance tests. Moreover, the effect of home circumstances on the growth of ability and on motivation tends to be exaggerated. Broadly it would seem that, to some extent, selection induces a self-fulfilling prophecy. Those who are favoured by it believe themselves more capable, are believed to be so by their teachers and tend to receive better educational treatment; they tend to conform to the expectations held about them and actually to improve. Those on the other hand who are not selected diminish their aspirations; their teachers expect and obtain less; and only too frequently the facilities offered are inferior. They too conform to what they perceive as the expectations and decline relatively.[125]

Selective systems, however humanely they are handled and however justly and accurately selection is made, are evidently inimicable to broader philosophic concepts of equality because they tend to reinforce social and genetic differences. Economically, too, they appear to be wasteful since they ensure that a considerable proportion of children do not realize their full potentiality either as human beings or as producers —though in fact their output may well be roughly adjusted to an economic system requiring much labour and relatively few in the innovative, technical or administrative groups.

The problem of mental health, particularly in the terms in which we have earlier defined it, is somewhat different. Selective systems are inevitably competitive and inter-individual competition directly and deeply affects the image a child builds up of himself, his capacities and his acceptability; for most, this effect must tend on the whole to be negative; and the evidence suggests that while repeated success in school over many years tends to increase resistance to stress and anxiety later in life, repeated failure may be a source of emotional difficulties and maladjustment, particularly if it adds to a pre-existent problem of growth.

It is equally serious that the non-selected may be denied a full initiation into their culture, and consequently leave school unequipped with the forms of thinking and the knowledge necessary to participate in the value decisions with which, as adults, they will be faced. Inability to cope, the belief that understanding and responsible decision are beyond their capacity, seems a major source of the alienation from or rejection of their culture by an increasing number of people.

The problem for the primary school is, in effect, a reflection of the organization and provision of secondary education and ultimately of the relation between this and the value in economic and social terms placed by society upon particular classes of vocation to which education leads. In this sense selective practices in the primary school, and procedures for allocating children to different forms of secondary education are processes of socialization into various vocational roles; educational selection is vocational selection, itself a form of social determination and thus the wheel comes full circle.

This is not the point at which to discuss fully the various developments in secondary education which are taking place. However, because the first five or so years of education lead up to education in adolescence, the expectations of the secondary school and the means used to guide children's and parents' choices of study after the first decade have an important bearing upon the primary school.[126] Currently many countries are moving towards a comprehensive form of secondary education in which all children are educated together in the same institution. Sometimes this takes the form of a middle school catering for an age band between 9-10 and 13-14[127] and followed by more differentiated schools from the mid 'teens; in others the school accepts all children up to 16 with some going on to a more selective gymnasium or various general and vocational courses after that; and there are many variants.

Many countries in Europe, notably France, Belgium, Switzerland and Italy, have recognized the diagnostic nature of the early pubertal years and established formal *cycles d'orientation* which lead on at the age of 13 to different types of more specialized secondary schools or courses. Others like Sweden, with its nine-year compulsory school from 7 to 16, or in the United Kingdom, having established comprehensive schools, attempt progressively throughout the first years of the second decade to differentiate their courses according to the needs and interests of the pupils as they declare themselves. Systems like this avoid the sense of success or failure in a critical examination and the invidious distinctions of prestige between schools[13] of different types. They do, too, allow pupils to keep their options somewhat more open and because they allow all children to move forward from the primary courses without examination their exigencies do not bear so heavily on curricula and method of the first crucial years of education.

However, *cycles d'orientation,* middle or comprehensive schools ana such like devices do not by themselves abolish either the genuine inter-individual differences or those due to the cumulative effects of the environment. They do not automatically ensure equality of opportunity or of esteem, not only in so far as the major determinants of these are outside the school in the attitudes and the opportunities offered by society, but also because educational values and practices have difficulty in freeing themselves from more or less élitist views of the value of particular subjects or courses. In any system it is difficult to prevent parents (and teachers) from trying to press children into moulds which they believe lead to the best chances later. But the more flexible and open system which such forms of organization provide can allow transfers from course to course and can, by grouping and setting devices, meet differences in ability and interest without openly segregating the abler from the less able. They can offer more children more chances of trying for the highest standards and they do provide a kind of safety net which allows earlier failures to be retrieved. They are more 'wasteful' in that more children are exposed to more opportunities and therefore more may fail or give up after a trial; but their output tends to be higher in the over-all realization of human potential. They will, however, only realize fully what their idealist proponents desire for them, if parents, teachers and pupils genuinely accept that success in what one can do is better and more healthy than a failure in a high prestige course: when in fact differences are accepted as valuable in themselves rather than as points in an academic pecking order.

No system gets rid of the fact of individual differences. It is obviously important, as primary education draws to its close, that two things should be achieved. The first of these is that progressively the individual's strengths and weaknesses should be diagnosed, and diagnosed accurately so that a choice of appropriate studies at the secondary level can be made and, equally importantly, so that any difficulties or weaknesses that have revealed themselves can be remedied.

Even more important to the individual's mental health and to the adjustment with which he enters the stresses and difficulties of adolescence, is a realistic and positive image of himself. Guidance at any stage, and particularly in this critical transition period is concerned not so much with selection (and the implication of rejection) as with an increasing knowledge and acceptance of oneself as one truly is as the only rational basis for choice of courses and ultimately of career. Thus, while tests, assessments, traditional types of examination and the like are important means to understanding, the guidance function of the school is that of interpreting the results to the pupil and his parents and helping them estimate the chances of success in different sets of circumstances, as a basis for conscious choice. If a pupil decides, after a full, impartial and objective assessment of his strengths and weaknesses, to undertake a course on which he has a lower probability of success than on some other easier one, there may well be a fair chance that he will succeed simply because he has himself consciously chosen to try and is therefore motivated to succeed. All our knowledge of human function shows that for given levels of ability there is a wide range of difference in achievement which is related to temperamental and motivational factors.

On the other hand, the school has an obligation, on the basis of the surveys of pupils' possibilities and needs, to adjust its methods, curricula and expectations to the human material it has. In this sense then the middle school, the *cycle d'orientation*, or the early years of comprehensive secondary education is a stage of diagnosis and guidance not only for the individual but for the school itself. Chronologically too, because it is set between childhood and adolescence it represents a chance to set right anything which may have gone awry in the basic skills of reading[129] and writing, in basic mathematical notions, in general ability to learn and, one would hope, in the general development of personality.

F.   CONCLUSION

CONSTRUCTIVE MENTAL HEALTH IN THE PRIMARY SCHOOL

Throughout this chapter, attention has been drawn to the important differences which exist between children and to the more obvious ways in which our European primary schools may be imposing upon some or all children needless stresses which individual parents and teachers often feel themselves powerless to alter or even to control. It will be argued that none of the difficulties or problems discussed in the present chapter is new and that, in the past, the pressures have been even greater, maladjustments and learning difficulties just as severe and yet the large majority of children have passed through their primary schooling relatively unscathed. We may admit that this seems to be largely true; backwardness and retardation, for example, are only seen to be problems when in fact we begin to evaluate the results of education in scientific ways.[130] Disquiet about the effects upon children and upon the primary school syllabus of selection at the age of 11 or 12 for various forms of secondary education only came to a head in England with the institution of universal and free secondary education. Increased knowledge of psychological disturbance, rising incidences of delinquency and mental breakdown have made us more sensitive to the origins of malad-justment in childhood. Since the Second World War, however, and increasingly since 1960, almost every country in Europe has shown itself uneasy about some aspects of its education system as is evidenced by the volume of new legislation and of expert reports since 1945.

It is also clear that, as our cultures develop and become more affluent, they demand more of more people in the way of an ability to continue to learn, to judge and to make responsible choices. We have become increasingly uneasy at the numbers of young people and adults who seem, as the result of their schooling, in fact to have turned against and rejected education, a process which may begin towards the end of the primary school—or even earlier in terms of 'writing-off adults'. The change to secondary education offers a chance for a new start to re-trieve lost ground; but it may in fact merely discourage, if it is seen to be a selective, rejecting process, or if the secondary schools are not equipped to remedy some of the failures and deviations left at the end of the primary years.

The school is, after the home, the most important single shaper of the child's personality. As such, its part cannot be merely to avoid needless difficulties for its pupils; it has, or should have, a positive and constructive part to play in the healthy mental and emotional develop-ment of all children. This does not necessarily mean that the school should preach a particular social philosophy or that it should do more than provide the stimulus to and the opportunity for the fullest possible realization of individual potentialities within a social framework; but the needs and potentialities of each child are different, and there cannot be, without loss, a complete standardization of curriculum and of method, a kind of blind mass teaching.[131] For a very considerable pro-portion of children, perhaps as many as 1 in 4, it has to be in a broad sense a positively therapeutic environment.

Yet, in fact, what most schools in Europe are forced to provide is a set of circumstances and expectations which are manifestly not adapted to something like half their pupils. The class of some forty, fifty or even more children in a room crammed with serried rows of desks, makes individual attention difficult if not impossible; it forbids all but the most limited activity on the part of the pupils and makes it almost impossible for a teacher to help, or even tolerate, a seriously maladjusted child or indeed to cater for the most able in any adequate way. Such overcrowding is often at its worst where the need for the most enlightened methods is greatest—in the dingy slum areas of large towns. A second major problem is that of the official syllabus, often laid down by the central authority with scant attention to what the bulk of children can reasonably be expected to learn, and given greater force in the teacher's eyes by the competitive examinations for secondary school entrance. In many countries, recent reforms and directives have tended to make the primary syllabus more permissive; nevertheless our ideas on curriculum have remained substantially unchanged since the nineteenth century and the model is that of the child of rather above average ability from a secure and fostering home. New subjects have been added; little has been dropped. In many countries the syllabus is so crowded that children from the age of 6 onwards have an hour or more's homework to do at night in addition to a school day of at least six hours.

The results of all this are seen in a primary school programme in which the formal elements of reading, writing and arithmetic predominate, where music, creative work, dramatics, and even physical education are regarded as 'frills', secondary to the grim purpose of ensuring by hook or by crook that as many children as possible attain a standard level of literacy and ability to calculate mechanically and are equipped with a body of more or less arbitrarily selected knowledge. The fact that, with traditional methods and traditional curricula, so much time is spent in achieving this purpose and with a success which is not unqualified,[132] is the strongest of all arguments in favour of continued practical research work into the psychology of teaching method and of the basic subjects. Verbal expression, oral and written, reading and calculation are all essential skills and, given time, it is certainly within the power of all but a very few children to acquire them; but they are not the only means of culture nor the sole skills of value to modern man; and they can be bought too early at too high a price. More and more the evolution of our industrialized civilization is thrusting on teachers the duty of consciously analysing the needs of the local and wider community and its children and of adapting curricula to supply the stimulus and experience which may be lacking in the homes or in the streets. The greater the stresses imposed upon children, the greater is their need for expressive activities and particularly for all forms of play by means of which they can come to grips with their problems and solve them. Free dramatic work, drawing and painting, mime, discussion, music—none of these are luxuries in the primary school, except perhaps to children whose home background is rich in possibilities of a similar kind. They are essential to healthy growth. Not only can such activities form the basis of an insight into great cultural media but, for those who need it, they give an outlet by means of which children themselves may work through some at least of their own emotional problems. Education in Europe regarded even as the transmission of a minimum culture is only relatively efficient; regarded as a way by which children are prepared emotionally for the enjoyment of a full and happy adult life it still has far to go.

NOTES

1. In many developing countries at age 7. Recent tendencies in Europe have been to extend the age downwards, even though attendance is voluntary.
2. There will be considerable variation in this. Some children, especially those from deprived backgrounds, will not attain this stage until two or even three years later. One of the great difficulties in primary education in developing countries is that we lack information concerning the conceptual growth of children from rural and tribal backgrounds very different from those of Europe.
3. C. Bühler following Binet, in whose scale for the measurement of intelligence, definitions of objects formed a considerable feature and who distinguished several levels of development in interpretation. *Kindheit und Jugend*. Verlag Göttingen für Psychologie, new edition 1967.
4. Piaget, J.; Szeminska, A. *La genèse du nombre chez l'enfant.* Neuchâtel, Delachaux & Niestlé, 1941. / Piaget, J.; Inhelder, Bärbel. *Le développement des quantités chez l'enfant.* Neuchâtel, Delachaux & Niestlé, 1941. / Piaget, J. *Le développement de la notion du temps chez l'enfant.* Paris, Presses universitaires de France, 1946. / Piaget, J.; Inhelder, Bärbel, *La géométrie spontanée de l'enfant.* Paris, Presses universitaires de France, 1948.
5. Werner, H. *Comparative psychology of mental development.* Chicago, Follett, 1948. / Wallon, H. *Les origines de la pensée chez l'enfant.* Paris, Presses universitaires de France, 1945 (2 v.).
6. Evans, J. L. *Children in Africa.* New York, Teachers College, 1970 [especially chapter VI]: / Ivory Coast. Ministère de l'éducation nationale. *Bibliographie analytique des recherches effectuées sur la psychologie de l'enfant africain anglophone.* / Idem. . . . *de l'enfant africain francophone.* Abidjan, 1970. (2 v.). (Programme d'éducation télévisuelle, vol. IV et V). / Cole, M. et al. *The cultural context of learning and thinking.* London, Methuen, 1972. The last-mentioned work suggests that the marked differences which exist in cognition are attributable more to the situations in which particular cognitive processes are applied than to the existence or absence of any process in one or other group.
7. In reading ability, for example, the difference between the advanced and the retarded may be as much as four years at the age of 7 (Davie, R.; Butler, N.; Goldstein, H. *From birth to seven.* London, Longmans, 1972).
8. Williams, H. L. Progress reports on discontinuity studies (mimeo.) 12 Feb. 1964, 8 April 1964, Royal Army Ed. Corps. United Kingdom. We are aware, too, how greatly the absence of fathers and the disturbance of education during the 1939–45 war affected average educational standards and was reflected in the statistics of delinquency—especially recidivism (see this Chapter, p. 265 & 370 ff). See also: Wilkins, L. T. *Delinquent generations.* London, HMSO, 1961.
9. Of roughly a quarter of a million immigrant children in English schools, 43,000 were unable to follow a normal school curriculum because of language difficulties. Even where the mother tongue is a form of English, it may have important differences (as in the case of West Indian) from the English of England. See: Townsend, H. E. R. *Immigrant pupils in England.* Slough, Bucks., National Foundation for Educational Research 1971. / Townsend, H. E. R.; Brittan, E. M. *Organisation in multi-racial schools.* Slough, Bucks., National Foundation for Educational Research, 1972.

302   *Constructive Education*

10. See, for example: Goldman, R. J.; Taylor, F. M. Coloured immigrant children: a survey of research, studies and literature on their educational problems—in the U.S.A. *Educational research* (London), vol. IX, no. 1, November 1966. Taylor, F. *Race, school and community.* Slough. National Foundation for Educational Research. 1974.

11. For example, in the United Kingdom population of some 55 million, there are not more than 2 million immigrants from Asia and the West Indies. In Israel at present, the proportion of 'oriental' immigrant children in schools to those often of parents from Europe who have been settled a long time in the country has risen to 50 per cent or more.

12. There is some evidence, for example, that among girls in British schools behaviour is worse in West Indian and African immigrant children and in those from Europe and Ireland, and best among immigrant children from Japan, China, India and Pakistan (Herman, D. L. S. Asian girls are the best behaved. *The Times educational supplement* (London, 12 May 1972). Later in this Chapter (p. 286) it will be seen that within indigenous groups in the United Kingdom there are marked cultural differences in forms of behaviour considered to be signs of maladjustment by schools and by parents respectively.

13. Townsend, H. E. R. Op. cit.

14. Jensen, A. R. Op. cit.

15. On the whole problem of testing the abilities of immigrant children, see: Haynes, J. M. *Educational assessment of immigrant pupils.* Slough, Bucks., National Foundation for Educational Research, 1971. / Vernon, P. E. *Intelligence and cultural environment.* London, Methuen, 1969 [especially chapter IV and part V]. See also: references in this Chapter, p. 301, note 6.

16. Townsend, H. E. R. Op. cit.

17. Winch, W. M. *When should a child begin school?* Baltimore, Warwick & York, 1911. See also: the researches of C. W. Valentine and his students published in *Forum of education,* 1925, and following years.

18. Danzinger, L. Der Schulreifetest. *Wiener arbeiten zur pädagogischen Psychologie,* No. 9, 1933. See also: Bühler, C. Op. cit. / Strebel, G. *Das Wesen der Schulreife und ihre Erfassung.* Solothurn, St. Antonius, 1946 [contains full bibliography of French and German literature].

19. Breunig, W. *Schuleintrittsalter und Reifedifferenzierung.* Freiburg, Herder, 1964.

20. Bernart, E. *Der Probeunterricht.* München, Ernst Reinhart Verlag, 1965. See also: Dey, J. D. *Theory and practice governing the time of school entrance.* Edmonton, University of Alberta, 1960 (Monographs in education, no. 4). / Schlevoigt, G.; Roth, F. *Schulreife und Einschulung.* Frankfurt a/M., Moritz Diesterweg, 1964.

21. Pidgeon, D. A.; Dodds, E. M. Length of schooling and its effect on performance in the junior school. *Educational research* (London), vol. III, no. 3, 1961. / Jinks, P. C. An investigation into the effect of date of birth on subsequent school performance. *Educational research* (London), vol. VI, no. 3, 1964.

22. See this Chapter, p. 278 (Reading readiness).

23. For one such experiment conducted by a highly sensitive schoolmistress, see: Valdes, J. S. *Amelia: maestra de primer año—narración de una experiencia.* Mexico, Secretaría de Educación Pública, 1965 (Cuadernos de informaciones tecnico-pedagógicas para los maestros de educación primaria,

vol. II, no. 8). For a thorough examination of ways to smooth the transition from home to school see: Palmer, R. *Starting school.* London, University of London Press, 1971.

24. United Kingdom. Central Advisory Council for Education. *Children and their primary schools.* London, HMSO, 1967 (Plowden Report). These 'first schools' continue to the age of 8 or 9 because it is considered that by then the children should be at home in their basic learning. The middle or second school then takes them to age 12 or 13—the end of childhood and dawn of puberty and adolescence.

25. A good infants school does much more than this. See: Weber, L. *The English infant school and informal education.* New Jersey, Prentice Hall, 1971. / Brearley, M., et al. *Fundamentals in the first school.* Oxford, Blackwell, 1969.

26. Where separate infants schools (5–7+) exist as preparation for junior schools, similar bridging between the two is necessary.

27. See Chapter 8, p. 159ff.

28. For a description of the various practices see: Ridgway; L.; Lawton, I. *Family grouping in the infants school.* London, Ward Lock, 1965.

29. Donnison, D., et al. *A pattern of disadvantage.* Slough, Bucks., National Foundation for Educational Research, 1972.

30. Misline, J. Group therapy in an elementary school. *Social casework* (New York), vol. 52, pt. I, 1971. / Vasquez, A.; Ouvry, F. *Vers une pédagogie institutionnelle.* Paris, François Maspero, 1967.

31. For example in Laos (see p. 304, note 43.

32. Binet, A. Le développement de l'intelligence chez les enfants. *L'année psychologique* (Paris), vol. 14, 1908, p. 1–94. / Burt, C. The relations of educational abilities. *British journal of educational psychology* (London), vol. IX, pt. 1, 1939.

33. Goodacre, E. J. *Teachers and their pupils' home background.* Slough, Bucks., National Foundation for Educational Research, 1968. / Idem. *School and home.* Slough, Bucks., National Foundation for Educational Research, 1970.

34. Pidgeon, D. A. *Expectation and pupil performance.* Slough, Bucks., National Foundation for Educational Research, 1970.

35. Whether the dullness is of genetic or social origin (or both), by the time a child reaches the stage of formal primary schooling it is very difficult to avoid it having a cumulative impact on his rate of subsequent development. It has yet to be proved that retardation of growth in operational ability due to environmental factors in the pre-school period can be more than partially remedied. Hence, while it is important for the teacher to adopt an optimistic stance about any child's potential, it is most unwise to fail to adjust one's expectations to what the child's actual level of operational intelligence permits him to achieve. A recent study which surveyed all children aged 6–9 in the Isle of Wight (a relatively favoured area of the United Kingdom) 2.53 per cent of children were in the group I.Q. 70 or below; about 7 per cent had a discrepancy of 28 months between their chronological age and their reading attainment and 4 per cent between reading attainment and level of ability (Rutter, M.; Tizard, J.; Whitmore, K. *Education, health and behaviour.* London, Longmans, 1970).

36. In terms of standardized, individual intelligence tests with a mean and standard deviation of approximately 100 and 15 points respectively (e.g., the various Binet derivatives), the borderline of subnormality requiring

special provision is usually taken to be an I.Q. of 70. There are of course other factors to be taken into account—for example, social development, kind and level of motivation—which very considerably modify this border-line.

37. It should be pointed out that rarely indeed are these 'norms' more than notional. They represent expectations rather than average performances determined in any scientific way.

38. Hotyat, F. *et al.* The instruction, education and mental health of Belgian children and adolescents. *La Revue pédagogique* (Bruxelles), vol. 27, no. 9, November 1953, and subsequent volumes (a report prepared for the Unesco Regional Conference on Education and Mental Health by the Centre de recherches de l'Institut supérieur de pédagogie du Hainaut). The figures cited are based on information collected by school inspectors from all the schools subsidised by the Primary Education Administration in the Flemish, mixed and French speaking areas. They do not include data for the approximately 7.5 per cent of the school population who are to be found in the preparatory sections of lycées, athenées and intermediate schools, etc.

39. Hotyat states that the final figure (41.3 per cent, sixth year) is smaller that it otherwise would be because of the numbers of retarded children who leave before the sixth year.

40. F. Hotyat in a personal communication. Sand et al. (Sand E. A., Emery-Hauzeur C., Buki H., Chauvin-Faures C., Sand-Ghilain J. and Smets P. *L'Echec scolaide précoce—variables associées—prédiction.* Bruxelles. Université Libre. Laboratoire de Médecine Sociale : Ecole de Santé Publique; Laboratoire de Calcul Scientifique de la Faculté de Médecine 1975) in an intensive study of French-speaking Belgian children in their second primary school year found that 28 per cent had repeated at least one year and of these 15 per cent had repeated twice and 5 per cent three times—the biggest proportion of repetitions was of the first year. Their analysis of associated factors showed that, next to the pupils' general level of ability, the influence of the mother, her methods of discipline and general interest in her child's school progress, seemed to be the most important constellation of predictive factors.

41. Haramein, A. *Perturbations scolaires.* Neuchâtel; Paris, Delachaux & Niestlé, 1965.

42. Cited by : Chilland, C. *L'enfant de six ans et son avenir.* Paris, Presses universitaires de France, 1971 [p. 63].

43. Conference on Children and Youth in National Planning and Development in Asia, Bangkok, 1966. *Selections from the documents of the Conference.* Vol. II : *Problems of children and youth.* New York, United Nations Children's Fund, 1967. See also : Arab Republic of Egypt. Ministry of Education. Centre of Educational Documentation. Redoublement des classes et pertes d'effectifs scolaires dans l'enseignement général en République Arabe Unie. Cairo, 1970 [mimeographed]. / International Conference on Education, XXXII session, Geneva, 1970. The statistical measurement of educational wastage. Paper prepared by the Unesco Office of Statistics. Paris, 1970. [mimeographed]. / Wastage. *Bulletin of the International Bureau of Education* (Geneva), no. 173, 1969 [special issue]. / Wall, W. D.; Schonell, F. J.; Olson, W. *Failure in school.* Hamburg, Unesco Institute for Education, 1962. / School drop-outs and the social background of students. *Unesco courrier* (Paris), June 1972.

44. About 89 per cent on the average. In the Netherlands the figure seems to have been 91–92 per cent in 1952 as compared with 87–89 per cent in 1947 (Netherlands. Central Bureau voor de Statisteek. De Ontwikkeling van het onderwys in Nederland. Utrecht, 1953).

45. About 20–22 per cent for 1965–66 (Netherlands. Central Bureau voor de Statisteek, Op. cit.). A situation shown in the Dutch but not in the Genevan figures.

46. This seems likely to have been a general phenomenon in the belligerent countries—see also under heading 'Broad social causes' in this Chapter— and is supported by the Dutch figures (Netherlands. Central Bureau voor de Statisteek. Op. cit.).

47. In France since 1952 the situation has also sensibly improved at least in the first school year—though it is difficult to distinguish the real improvement from the effects of increased promotions due to the influence of an increased birthrate. This again draws attention to the possibly artificial nature of some 'retardation'.

48. For the French-speaking area of Belgium, the percentages of pupils in the grade appropriate to their chronological age (6th year) were successively the following: 1938, 45; 1946, 41; 1951, 45; 1961, 57; 1966, 58. (Belgium. Ministère de l'education nationale. *Annuaire statistique de l'enseignement.* Bruxelles, 1970.)

49. Caldeira, C. *Menores no meio rural.* Rio de Janiero, Ministerio de Educaçao e Cultura, 1960.

50. Rowe, Elizabeth, *et al. Failure in school.* Hong Kong. University Press, 1966 (Hong Kong Council for Educational Research, Publication no. 3).

51. Haramein, A. Op. cit., p. 171–173. See also: Sand et al. Op. cit. sup. note 40.

52. Demencev, A. D., *et al.*, eds. *Puti preodolenija vtorogodničestva.* Moskva, Prosveščenie, 1966. In a seminal paper (Innocence in education. *School review* (Chicago), vol. 80, no. 3, May 1972) Bloom claims that 'as many as 90 per cent of the students can learn these school subjects up to the same standard that only the top 10 per cent of students have been learning under the same conditions' and that 'much of what we have termed *individual differences in school learning* is the effect of particular school conditions rather than of basic differences in the capabilities of our students'. In support of this he cites, particularly, the work of L. J. Cronbach and R. A. Snow (1969) and R. M. Gagné (1967).

53. Jackson, B. *Streaming: an education system in miniature.* London, Routledge & Kegan Paul, 1964. / Barker-Lunn, J. C. *Streaming in the primary school.* Slough, Bucks., National Foundation for Educational Research, 1970. It is interesting to note that the idea is still widespread among economists, administrators and some sociologists, that slow learners (like young children) require less able and less experienced teachers and can tolerate larger classes than older and more academically intelligent groups. For example, a recent OECD report (*Politiques de croissance économique et d'investissement dans l'enseignement.* Paris, OCDE) states innocently as a self-evident truth: 'Les études de niveau élevé exigent des professeurs mieux qualifiés, des classes moins nombreuses.'

54. Correlation ratios vary between $r = +0.5$ and $r = +0.9$. It is essential to be clear as to exactly what a correlation between a test of intelligence and an educational test really means. Theoretically a test of educable capacity or operational intelligence should adequately sample a child's abilities to learn and to solve problems as they have been developed by his

experience in the relatively unstructured home and out-of-school environment. There will of course be factors in the subject and in the test which will make it an imperfect measure and reduce its validity as a test of the ability concerned. The score on an educational test, however, is more complex. A child's attainment is a function of his general level of operational intelligence, any special intellectual abilities involved in the particular form of learning concerned, and of his opportunities to learn reading or any other school subject, as well as of his motivation to do so, i.e., in some way it measures his response to the more structured environment offered by the school. If a group of children could be found who differed only in innate capacity but who did not differ on the kind and length of teaching they had experienced, we might be able to estimate more closely the relationships between intelligence and the acquisition of educational skills. Our correlations between scores on tests of intelligence and scores on tests of, say, reading or arithmetic, are likely to be reduced considerably by the fact that the samples on which they are based consist of children who have had very different home experiences which modify the expression of their 'intelligence' and, as well, have been exposed to schooling of different degrees of suitability and effectiveness. It seems arguable that, given identical conditions of prior experience and of methods of teaching, the correlation between intelligence and the acquisition of educational skills would be much closer than is usually indicated by empirical studies.

55. Burt, C. *The backward child.* London, University of London Press, 1937. / Idem. *Mental and scholastic tests.* London, King & Co., 1923. Later investigators in England have tended to set the borderline lower (around 80) or to speak in terms of a discrepancy score.

56. A Belgian study of more than 1,200 children (Jadoulle, A. *Le laboratoire pédagogique au travail.* Paris, Editions du Scarabée, 1951) individually tested at entry to primary school found that all those with an initial I.Q. of 85 or less were at least two years retarded in school eight years later.

57. It could be argued that this discrepancy is a statistical artefact, a regression effect, due to the imperfect correlation between tests of intelligence and tests of reading. When tests, say, of 'intelligence' and 'reading' are standardized upon the same population, there is a tendency to find as many children whose attainment level exceeds their intelligence level as the reverse. However, when one examines the deviant groups, one finds a whole constellation of different factors—motivation, presence or absence of marked verbal ability, forms of maladjustment, social background (and particularly parental encouragement) which differentiate 'over-achievers' from 'under-achievers'. Thus the regression of tests of intelligence on tests of attainment is, at least in part, a function of genuine, i.e., not statistically artificial, elements in the normal educational experience of children. This, of course, does not mean that out-of-school factors do not contribute also to depressing or elevating both general ability to learn and the learning of reading and mathematical skills. Broadly, while the results of suitable tests of verbal ability reflect, for example, the interaction of the general environment and innate ability, tests of attainment more nearly reflect the child's response to the more factual and structured environment of the school.

58. English usage in this field of research and practice reserves the term 'retardation' for that condition in which educational achievement is markedly less than that to be predicted from the level of general ability. This is a rough but operationally important distinction which should be borne in

mind in what follows. A child whose educational age is 8 years and whose chronological age is 10 years is backward. If his mental age is 10 years, then he is backward and retarded; if, however, he has a mental age of 8, though he is backward he is *apparently* making the most of a limited ability and is not retarded. Similarly, a child of 10 years old with a mental age of 13 years who is working at the level of an average 11-year-old, though he may appear to the teacher to be advanced by one year is in fact retarded. His attainment level is considerably less than that to be expected from his superior ability. It must be emphasized that, although these are useful operational concepts, neither the terms nor the I.Q.s used should be taken in any deterministic sense. Even if a child is functioning educationally at the level equivalent to his mental age, there is no reason to suppose that this represents an optimum for him. It may still be possible to raise his level of genuine operational intelligence and his formal educational attainments—particularly if social and emotional factors have depressed his function in both areas.

59. Burt, C. *The backward child*. Op. cit. / Adams, R. H. An investigation into backwardness in arithmetic in the junior school. 1940. M.A. thesis, University of London. / Sleight, G. The diagnosis and treatment of the dull and backward child. 1952. Ph.D. thesis, University of London. / Schonell, F. J. *Backwardness in the basic subjects*. Edinburgh, Oliver & Boyd, 1942.
60. Hotyat's investigation in 1951–52 of 107 children in Charleroi who were in classes corresponding to age levels two or more years younger, showed a similar figure: 10 per cent had I.Q.s (T. and M.) between 100 and 90; and 61 per cent between 90 and 70. Adjusting his borderline of I.Q.90 to meet Burt's criterion of I.Q.85, his figure would slightly exceed 15 per cent.
61. United Kingdom. Ministry of Education. *Reading ability*. London, HMSO, 1950 (Pamphlet no. 18).
62. The convention before the Second World War was to accept an educational ratio of 85; the Ministry of Education survey accepted a borderline reading age of 8.8 years for 11-year-old pupils and of 12 years for 15-year-old pupils, i.e., a quotient of 80. This would nearly halve the proportion deemed to be backward.
63. Start, K. B.; Wells, B. K. *The trend of reading standards*. Slough, Bucks., National Foundation for Educational Research, 1972.
64. As compared with a 1938 baseline for attainment.
65. Rutter, M.; Tizard, J.; Whitmore, K. *Education, health and behaviour*. London, Longmans, 1970.
66. Morris, J. M. *Standards and progress in reading*. Slough, Bucks., National Foundation for Educational Research, 1966.
67. Wall, W. D. Problems and methods of dealing with retardation in junior schools. Paper read to the British Association, Birmingham, 1950. See also: Wall, W. D. Le retard scolaire en Grande-Bretagne. *Enfance* (Paris), vol. VII no. 4, 1954.
68. Bloom, B. S. Op. cit.
69. Scottish Council for Research in Education. *The trend of Scottish intelligence*. London, University of London Press, 1949.
70. Chapters 7 and 10.
71. In a private communication, Fernand Hotyat (Belgium) writes: 'Teachers in urban and industrial areas . . . complain that they have no longer the same prestige in the eyes of parents as they used to have. Most parents (at least those from disadvantaged environments) they say are indifferent to

the teachers' remarks or advice and care less about the education of their children.'

72. See p. 193ff.
73. Bloom, B. S. Op. cit. It will be noted that if one wishes individuals to fit into a stable, hierarchial society based on some kind of meritocracy, an efficient grading system is probably the best way of doing it. However, most of our school systems use grading systems which have many arbitrary and inaccurate features, notably the unreliability of the marks and assessments made by teachers on which they are based. A self-evaluation system such as that outlined above tends towards a different concept of society based upon the value of individual contributions. It has equal need for accurate evaluation and assessment but inaccuracies are likely to be less damaging to the individual's knowledge of himself.
74. See: Volume II, Chapter 9, 'Problems of special groups'.
75. For methods and organization see: Burt, C. *The backward child.* Op. cit. / Schonell, F. J. *Backwardness in the basic subjects.* Edinburgh, Oliver & Boyd, 1942. / Wall, W. D.; Schonell, F. J.; Olson, W. C. *Failure in school.* Hamburg, Unesco Institute for Education, 1962. / Younghusband, E., *et al. Living with handicap.* London, National Bureau for Co-operation in Child Care, 1970. / Gulliford, R. *Backwardness and educational failure.* Slough, Bucks., National Foundation for Educational Research, 1969.
76. Pupils who have repeated a grade once tend in about half the cases to repeat again subsequently (Wall, W. D.; Schonell, F. J.; Olson, W. C. Op. cit.).
77. Schonell, F. J. Op. cit.
78. See for example: Orton, S. T. *Reading, writing and speech problems in children.* New York, Norton, 1937. / Hallgren, B. Specific dyslexia. *Acta psychiatrica Scandinavica* (Copenhagen), sup. 65, 1950. / Critchley, M. *Deveplopmental dyslexia.* London, Heinemann, 1962. / Franklin, A. W., ed. *Word blindness or specific developmental dsylexia.* London, Pitman, 1962.
79. This chapter p. 272 and note 65.
80. United Kingdom. Department of Education and Science. *Children with specific reading difficulties.* London, HMSO, 1972. / Vernon, M. D. *Reading and its difficulties.* Cambridge, Cambridge University Press, 1971.
81. The contradiction between what is said here and the results cited from other research on p. 245 (especially note 49) is only apparent. The successful teachers in the schools studied by Cane and Schroeder did not wait for readiness to develop by some mysterious and autonomous process; they fostered systematically those aspects of readiness which help bring success in the formal element of reading in the early stages, and did this within a generally encouraging optimistic atmosphere.
82. Though tests may be useful if carefully and expertly used. See, for example: Inizan, A. *Le temps d'apprendre à lire.* Paris, Bourrelier, Armand Colin, 1963. There has in some quarters, notably in America, been pressure for the earlier teaching of reading and in particular to children well before the age of school entry. Sometimes this has been undertaken with at least apparent success, especially where the children concerned are well above average in ability and where the methods used have been relaxed and child-centred. In more cases, however, the results have been negative, any acceleration has later been lost or the pupils concerned have been somewhat disturbed (*The First R—Harvard report on reading in the elementary school.* New York, Macmillan, 1963. / Delogue, R. De l'opportunité

d'apprendre à lire avant l'âge de 6 ans. 1968. Mémoire de licence, Université libre de Bruxelles.). What seems to be important is a state of interest and development in the child, which is the product of a favourable environment as much as anything, and good conditions for learning, such as appropriate methods, small groups and help of good quality from adults and older children (Downing, J. Reading readiness re-examined. In: *First International Reading Symposium*. London, Cassell, 1966. / Downing, J.; Thackray, D. V. *Reading readiness*. London, Unibooks, 1971.).

83. Gates, A. I. The necessary mental age for beginning reading. *Elementary school journal* (Chicago), vol. 37, 1937, p. 497–508.

84. Taylor, C. D. The effect of training on reading readiness. In: Scottish Council for Research in Education. *Studies in reading*. Vol. II. London, University of London Press, 1950. p. 63–80.

85. See p. 308, notes 81 and 82.

86. Doman, G. *How to teach your baby to read*. New York, Random House, 1964.

87. Gardner, D. E. M. *Testing results in the infant school*. London, Methuen, 1942.

88. Including various uses of colour codes, some of which are very old. Those holding the field in England at present are: Gattegno, C. *Reading with words in colour*. Reading, Educational Explorers, 1969. / Becasdale, E.; Becasdale, W. *Reading by rainbow*. Bolton Moor, Platt Press, 1966. / Jones, J. K. *Colour story reading*. London, Nelson, 1967.

89. Downing, J. *The i.t.a. Symposium*. Slough, Bucks., National Foundation of Educational Research, 1967. / Warburton, F. W.; Southgate, V. *i.t.a.: an independent evaluation*. Edinburgh, Chambers, 1969. By itself formal attainment in the decoding skill is not, of course, sufficient but it is necessary to the development of a love for and a capacity to use reading as a means of personal enrichment.

90. Chall, J. *Learning to read: the great debate*. New York, McGraw-Hill, 1967. / Southgate, V. *Beginning reading*. London, University of London Press, 1972. / Morris, J. M. *Standards and progress in reading*. Slough, Bucks., National Foundation for Educational Research, 1966.

91. Scottish Council for Research in Education. *The early development of number concepts*. London, University of London Press, 1942. / Piaget, J.; Szeminska, A. Op. cit. / Buyse, R. *Etudes et recherches louvanistes sur le calcul élémentaire*. Congrès International de Santander (R. Buyse, University of Louvain).

92. This, it will be observed, is only a special case of the need for security or confidence.

93. Washburne, C. Grade-placement of arithmetic topics. In: *National Society for the Study of Education, 29th Yearbook*. Bloomington, Ill., Public School Publishing Co., 1930 [p. 641–670]. / Washburne, C. The work of the Committee of Seven on Grade-placement in Arithmetic. In: *National Society for the Study of Education. 38th Yearbook*. Part I. Bloomington, Ill., Public School Publishing Co., 1939 [p. 299–324]. Some of Washburne's findings have been questioned on methodological grounds by Curr (Curr, W. Placement of topics in arithmetic. In: Scottish Council for Research in Education. *Studies in arithmetic*. Vol. II. London, University of London Press, 1941 [p. 183–218]). Any student of age placement should familiarize himself with Curr's analysis of the methodological problems involved in this kind of investigation.

94. Piaget, J.; Szeminska, A. Op. cit. [p. 33–48]. / Piaget, J. *La psychologie de l'intelligence.* Paris, Armand Collin, 1947 [p. 167].
95. For a penetrating monograph on the development of arithmetical thinking during the first grade, see also: Oehl, W. Psychologische Untersuchungen über Zahlendenken und Rechnen bei Schulanfängern. *Zeitschrift für angewandte Psychologie* (Leipzig), Bd. 49, 1935, p. 305–351. The concept of 'vocal reflexes' (*réflexes relatifs au maniement des symboles*) was proposed by H. Aebli (*Didactique psychologique* 2ᵉ éd. Neuchâtel, Delachaux & Niestlé,1963).
96. For illustrations of the discordances which can exist between what curricula propose and the stages of development see: Wall, W. D., *et al. Failure in school.* Hamburg, Unesco Institute for Education, 1961 [especially p. 79–81].
97. *New thinking in school mathematics.* Paris, OECD, 1961.
98. Brearley, M., ed. *Fundamentals in the first school.* Oxford, Blackwell, 1969 [especially chapters II and VI].
99. For example the multibase blocks devised by Dienes; a full description is given in: Williams, J. D. *Educational research* (London), vol. III, no. 3, 1961. See also the Nuffield material in mathematics and elementary science.
100. Gilbert, R. *L'enfant et la mathématique moderne.* Paris, Fleurus, 1971. / Jaulin-Mannoni, F. *Entrainement pre-mathématique progressif.* Paris, Editions Sociales Françaises, 1970 (2 v.). / Williams, J. D. *Teaching technique in primary maths.* Slough, Bucks., National Foundation for Educational Research, 1971. / Idem. ed. *Mathematics reform in the primary school.* Hamburg, Unesco Institute for Education 1967. / Idem. The teaching of mathematics I–VI. *Educational research* (London), vol. III, 1960, to vol. V, 1963 [especially 'Teaching arithmetic by concrete analogy I—miming devices'; and 'II—structural systems', vol. III, nos. 2 and 3, 1961; and vol. IV, no. 3, 1962].
101. See for example: Brogan, C. The decline and fall of State education. *Daily Telegraph* (London), 16 December 1952. / Cox, C. B.; Dyson, A. E., eds. *The Black Papers on education.* Rev. ed. London, Davis-Poynter, 1971.
102. Davie, R.; Butler, N.; Goldstein, H. Op. cit. p. 118.
103. On the results of the Bristol Social Adjustment Guide. This requires the respondent to rate a large number of specific pieces of behaviour according to their frequency of occurrence in each particular child. It has a high consistency and reliability and does not call for judgements. Scores are estimated in terms of the frequencies of particular forms of behaviour (which can be favourable or unfavourable) and allow deviant groups to be identified statistically.
104. See: Volume II, Chapter 9, 'Problems of special groups' (table 2).
105. Rutter, M.; Tizard, J.; Whitmore, K. Op. cit.
106. Chilland, Colette. *L'enfant de six ans et son avenir.* Paris, Presses universitaires de France, 1971.
107. A much fuller treatment of maladjustment will be found in Volume II, Chapter 9, 'Problems of special groups'.
108. Terman, L., *et al. Genetic studies of genius.* Vol. I: *Mental and physical traits of a thousand gifted children.* Stanford University Press, 1926.
109. Parkyn, G. W. *Children of high intelligence.* London, Oxford University Press, 1948.
110. Lovell, K.; Shields, J. B. Some aspects of a study of the gifted child. *British journal of educational psychology* (London), vol. XXXVII, no. 2, 1967. See also: Shields, J. B. *The gifted child.* Slough, Bucks., National Foundation for Educational Research, 1968.

111. Shields, J. B. Op. cit. [Chapter IV].

112. See: Parkyn, G. W. Op. cit. / Terman, L. Op. cit.

113. In the Genevan figures given by Haramein (see p. 268) only 5 per cent of boys and 5 per cent of girls are advanced by a year in the eighth year as compared with 52 per cent and 41 per cent of boys and girls respectively retarded by a year or more. Parkyn found his New Zealand children to be accelerated on the average by half a grade, Terman calculated that the average grade placement of his group was only 14 per cent above the norm.

114. One of the earliest studies was that of L. Hollingworth (*Children above 180 I.Q.* New York, World Book Co., 1942).

115. Kellmer Pringle, M. L. *Able misfits*. London, Longmans, 1970.

116. As, for example, in schools for the very musically gifted, ballet schools and schools for those with a high degree of mathematical talent such as are found in the U.S.S.R. There are also schools for very able children who cannot adapt to the normal school or whose homes are insufficiently stimulating or tolerant.

117. In the United Kingdom, this has been done in association with a local technical college which has not only scientific laboratories but advanced art, craft and other facilities. For a much fuller and more detailed discussion of the education of the gifted, see: Wall, W. D. Highly intelligent children. Part II: The education of the gifted. *Educational research* (London), vol. II, no. 3, 1960. / Bereday, G. Z. F.; Lauwerys, J. A., eds. *Year book of education 1962: the gifted child*. London, Evans, 1962 [especially contribution by C. Burt and F. Waddington). / Shields, J. B. Op. cit. [Chapter V].

118. The rates of failure in secondary schools as shown by the repeating of grades or premature leaving are similar to those for primary schools. See: Volume II, Chapter 7, 'Special problems of the secondary school'.

119. See Chapter 12.

120. The attempt is being made in Sweden and to some extent in comprehensive secondary schools elsewhere.

121. In Belgium, Holland, Norway, Sweden and the United Kingdom principally. See, for example: Van Waeyenberghe, A. Une batterie de tests d'instruction pour l'orientation scolaire. *Revue belge de psychologie et pédagogie* (Bruxelles), 1947. / Idem. La valeur prognostique d'un test de connaissance appliqué à l'entrée de l'enseignement moyen. Ibib., 1950. / Schlepens, M. Intelligentiemeting en schooluitslagen. *Persoon en Gemeenschap* (Antwerp), vol. I, no. 2, 1947, p. 6. / Nutsseminarium voor Paedagogiek aan de Universiteit van Amsterdam, 1945–52. / Sandven, J. *Opptakinga til den högre skolen*. Oslo, 1949. / Sundet, O. *Eksamen og skolearbeid*. Oslo, Cappelen, 1945. / Arvidson, S. *Skolreformen*. Lund, Gleerup, 1948. / Hallgren, S. *Grupptestning*. Stockholm, H. Gebers, 1943. / Sweden. Ecklesiastikdepartementet. *Sambandet mellan folkskola och högre skola*. Stockholm, 1944 (Statens offentliga utredningar, 1944: 21). / Husén, T. *Testresultatens prognosvärde*. Stockholm, H. Gebers, 1950. / Wigforss, F. *The entrance examination in view of later school performance*. Stockholm, Norstedts, 1937. / Magdeburg, H. *Versager auf weiterführenden Schulen*. München, Reinhart, 1963. / Schultze, W., *et al. Uber den Voraussagewert der Auslesekriterien für den Schulerfolg im Gymnasium*. Frankfurt, Max-Träger-Stiftung, 1964. The British work is the most extensive and cannot be quoted in detail. The reader is referred to the following which cover the principal researches which have been made and each of which has an extensive bibliography: C. Burt, W. P. Alexander, V. J. Moore, E. J. C. Bradford,

J. J. B. Dempster, E. A. Peel, C. M. Lambert, A. Rodger (Symposium on the selection of pupils for different types of secondary schools. *British journal of educational psychology* (London), 1947–50). / McClelland, W. *Selection for secondary education.* London, University of London Press, 1942. / National Union of Teachers. *Transfer from primary to secondary school.* London, Evans, 1949. / Yates, A. F.; Pidgeon, D. A. *Admission to grammar schools.* London, Newnes, 1957.

122. See: Peel, E. A. Selection for technical education. *Educational review* (Birmingham), June, 1952. / Bradford, E. J. G. Selection for technical education, Parts I and II. *British journal of educational psychology* (London), vol. XVI, pts. 2 and 3, 1946.

123. See: Yates, W.; Pidgeon, D. A. Op. cit.

124. Foshay, A. W. ed. *Educational achievements of thirteen-year-olds in twelve countries.* Hamburg, Unesco Institute for Education, 1962.

125. Pidgeon, D. A. *Expectation and pupil performance.* Slough, Bucks., National Foundation for Educational Research, 1970. / Barker-Lunn, J. *Streaming in the primary school.* Slough, Bucks., National Foundation for Educational Research, 1970.

126. This is unfortunately true for most countries. However, if we believe that education at any stage should cater for the child's development at that stage and that stage only, then it would follow that subsequent stages should build upon what children are and not demand that they should have been brought to a particular standard. Any selective system tends to impose its selection criteria on the precedent phases of education. An open and truly comprehensive system would make it possible to avoid this. This situation is similar to that discussed already in this chapter under the heading 'School readiness'.

127. The ages of entry from the first school to the middle school and of passage from middle to high school, vary considerably; in some places in the United Kingdom the ages are 8 to 12, in other 9 to 13; in Europe it may be 10 or 11 to 13 or 14.

128. Though they do not as a rule avoid prestige distinctions between courses.

129. Surprisingly high proportions of children pass from primary to secondary schooling with basic difficulties in reading; for example, about 1 in 4 children entering secondary schools in England have reading ages two years or more behind their chronological age.

130. During the Second World War and subsequently, repeated testings of recruits to the British Army have revealed that between 1 and 2 per cent of adult men are to all intents and purposes illiterate and a further 20 to 25 per cent so backward in reading that only the simplest forms of printed material are comprehensible to them. The figures for the Belgian Army were very similar—1.31 per cent illiterate (Delys, L. La mesure de l'enseignement primaire. *Revue des sciences pédagogiques* (Bruxelles), 1948). More recent figures (1970) show some improvement: among French-speaking recruits of the 1970 class, 0.9 per cent were judged illiterate and 15.8 per cent had not passed the sixth primary year; the figures for Flemish-speaking recruits were respectively 0.5 per cent and 12.8 per cent (Belgium. *Statistiques du Centre d'études sociales du Ministère de la défense nationale*). The various publications of the examiners of recruits into the Swiss Army do not state figures for illiteracy as such but give, on the other hand, valuable qualitative analyses of the knowledge of such things as history, geography, politics, shown by these recruits (Burki, M. F. *Rapport sur les*

examens civiques des recrues en 1948. / Idem. *Rapport sur les examens pédagogiques des recrues.* Berne, Office Fédéral des imprimés et du matériel, 1949, 1950-.).

131. MacDonald, D. Culture ou masse. *Diogène* (Paris), no. 3, juillet 1953, p. 3–30.

132. Vernon (personal communication) writes: 'There is strong evidence of most loss after leaving [school] in the most drilled subjects: arithmetic and spelling.'

FURTHER READING

Note: The literature on the topics covered in this chapter, especially that on failure, on reading difficulty and on maladjustment, is very extensive. Only a highly selected list is therefore given here to supplement the works cited in footnotes.

Ajuriaguerra, J. de, *et al. L'écriture de l'enfant.* Neuchâtel, Delachaux Niestlé, 1964 (2 v.).

Aurin, K. *Ermittlung und Erschliessung von Begabungen im ländlichen Raum* [Identification and development of talents in rural areas]. Villingen, Schwarzwald, Neckar-Verlag, 1966.

Auvinet, J. *L'école et la réussite scolaire.* Paris, Vrin, 1968.

Bertolini, P.; Cavallini, G. *La scuola elementare e il disadattamento sociale minorile* [The primary school and the social maladjustment of minors]. Milano, Istituto Editoriale Cisalpino, 1965.

Borel-Maisonny, S. *Langage oral et ecrit.* Neuchâtel, Paris; Delachaux & Niestlé, 1966 and 1967 (2 v.).

Cane, B. *The roots of reading: a study of twelve infant schools.* Slough, Bucks., National Foundation for Educational Research, 1971.

Carroll, J. B. 'The analysis of reading instruction: perspectives from psychologists and linguists. Jn: National Society for the Study of Education. *63rd Yearbook,* P4. 1. Chicago, University of Chicago Press, 1964.

Clark, M. M. *Reading difficulties in schools: a community study of specific reading difficulties.* Harmondsworth, Penguin, 1970.

Dehant, A. *Etude expérimentale des méthodes d'apprentissage de la lecture.* Louvain, Librairie universitaire, 1968.

Flavell, J. H. *The developmental psychology of Jean Piaget.* Princeton, N.J., Van Nostrand, 1963.

Gilbert, R. *L'enfant et la mathématique moderne.* Paris, Fleurus, 1971.

Gilly, M. *Bon élève, mauvais élève: recherche sur les différences de rëussite scolaire à conditions égales d'intelligence et de mileu social.* Paris, Libraire Armand Colin, 1969.

Girolami-Boulinier, A. *Prévention de la dyslexie et de la dysorthographie dans le cadre normal des activités scolaires (l'enfant, l'adolescent).* Neuchâtel, Delachaux & Niestlé, 1966.

Jaulin-Mannoni, F. *Entrainement pré-mathématique progressif.* Paris, Editions sociales françaises, 1970.

Jornadas sobre dislexia. *El niño limitado* [The limited child]. Vol. II. Santiago de Chile, 1970.

L

Kern, A. *Die Schulreife in paedagogischer und psychologischer Sicht* [School readiness from the pedogogical and psychological point of view]. Frankfurt, Akademische Verlagsgesellschaft, 1970.

Kirchhoff, H. *Versager in der Grundschule* [Failures in the primary school]. Basel, New York; Karger, 1965.

Klasen, E. *Das Syndrom der Legasthenie* [The syndrome of legasthenia]. Bern, Huber, 1970.

Kupisiewicz, C. *Niepowodzenia dydaktyczne* [Teaching failures]. Warszawa, Panstwowe Wydawictwo Naukowe, 1964.

Limbosch, N.; Luminet-Jasinsky A.; Dierkens-Dopchie, N. *La dyslexie à l'école primaire*. Bruxelles, editions de l'Institut de sociologie, 1969.

Merritt, J., ed. *Reading and the curriculum*. London, Ward Lock, 1971.

Mialaret G. *L'apprentissage de la lecture*. Paris, Presses universitaires de France, 1966.

Moyle, D.; Moyle, L. M. *Modern innovations in the teaching of reading*. London, University of London Press, 1971.

Oden, M. H. The fulfilment of promise: 40-year follow-up of the Terman Gifted Group. *Genetic psychology monographs* (Provincetown, Mass.), vol. 77, 1968, p. 3–93.

Peters, M. L. *Spelling: caught or taught?* London, Routledge & Kegan Paul; New York, Humanities Press, 1967.

Piaget, J., *et al. Rechenunterricht und Zahlbegriff* [Arithmetic instruction and the conception of numbers]. Braunschweig, Westermann, 1964, 1965.

Raph, J. B.; Goldberg, M. L.; Passow, A. H. *Bright underachievers*. New York, Teachers' College Press, 1966.

Schenk-Danzinger, Lotte, *et al. Handbuch der legasthenie im kindesalter* [Handbook of legasthenia in childhood]. Weinheim, J. Beltz, 1968.

Schools Council for the Curriculum and Examinations. *Mathematics in primary schools*. 2nd edition, London, HMSO, 1966.

Seminario Latinoamericano Sobre Dislexia, 2⁰, Montevideo, 1965. Dislexia escolar [Second Latin-American seminar on dyslexia, Montevideo, 1965. Student dyslexia]. Montevideo, Instituto interamericano del niño, 1965.

Tansley, A. E. *Reading and remedial reading*. London, Routledge & Kegan Paul; New York, Humanities Press, 1967.

Zazzo, R. *et al. Des garçons de six à douze ans*. Paris, Presses universitaries de France, 1969.

Chapter twelve

Conclusion

PRE-ADOLESCENT CHILDREN

The first eleven or twelve years of a child's life are critical in determining the broad cognitive and affective style which he will carry into the disturbances of adolescence. What has happened to him since birth will have been largely determinant of his present and future ability to learn, to go on learning, to solve problems and to react with confidence and understanding to the changes in his circumstances and transformations in his environment which he will meet with in the second decade and later.

In his first ten years his acquisitions are immense and far-reaching. He acquires a spoken language which even at its most primitive is yet a highly complex and flexible system of thought, of handling concepts and of communication with others. If his education has been only moderately successful, this command of language will have been greatly enlarged and he will have acquired a mastery of reading as a means of extending his learning and experience. He will, too, have gained some grasp of other forms of symbolism and expression like music and mathematics or visual presentation, which open up independent routes to thought, knowledge, culture and the expression of feeling. He will have learned to distinguish between reality and the wish, to some extent; and, through expanding knowledge and experience, have acquired a considerable understanding of the physical world, though his knowledge of the complexities of human feeling and behaviour will still be limited and relatively simple.

He has, too, acquired ways of interacting with others in social situations, learnt ways of behaving and knowing which should provide him with the means of being at harmony with himself, with children of around his own age and with adults in their varying roles in relation to him. He has a developed, but not necessarily very subtle or objective, image of himself built up from his experience of success and failure, from his rather primitive introspections, from what others—his friends, his teachers, his parents—have said to him about himself and by what he has inferred from their actions towards him.

For most children, the first year or two of the second decade of life is a period of relative tranquility. Physically they tend to be solidly developed and rather less vulnerable than earlier to illnesses; emotionally they are less liable to upset than they were as young children; and socially their role as school children is fairly clear in their own and in others' eyes: they know what is expected of them and have learned to be pretty much at home in their world. This is a period of relative calm before puberty and adolescence brings about a fresh wave of physical and emotional change.

How far all this has come about successfully for any individual child and how far the way in which he has developed leads him towards a general ability to make dynamic adjustments without damaging stress to the changing situations which await him in the mid and later 'teens will depend upon all that has so far happend to him at home and at school. In part it will have been a function of the way in which the ordinary growth tasks—weaning, walking up-right, first entry. to school, response to formal learning, and particularly to the learning of skills like reading which others regard as an important acquisition—have been accomplished. In part, too, it will depend upon how far any child is generally sure of being loved and accepted, particularly, but not solely, by parents and other important adults and by contemporaries.

SOMETHING MORE THAN ADJUSTMENT

But there should be more than this—at least in terms of the kinds of adjustments which will be required of children as they pass into adolescence and if as adults they are to cope with the unforeseeable demands of the end of this and the beginning of the next century. We have to remind ourselves of the changes in thought, feeling and environment which were sketched in the introductory part of this volume and the kinds of decisions which will have to be taken by democratic States all over the world. These are decisions which will imply, in each participant individual, the ability to understand complex public issues, to undertake new forms of learning and training and to react with confidence to far-reaching and probably initially threatening alterations in personal habits and styles of life. Much of the intellectual and emotional equipment which men and women will need for this will have to be the product of their education in adolescence. Unless, however, the first decade of life has prepared them well, they will enter adolescence with disturbances of feeling and of thought, with rigidities and uncertainties in their thinking, lacking in some essential grounding in the simpler or more complex cognitive skills, or with attitudes which prejudice a satisfactory transition from childhood to adolescence.

THE EFFECT OF FAILURE

We see this most clearly with those children who have failed to develop an easy mastery of the skills of reading or, if they can read reasonably well, take no real pleasure in it and find it difficult or impossible to use reading as a way to independent learning.

The recent figures quoted in Chapter XI from a large-scale survey of primary school leavers (11-12-year-olds) in the United Kingdom suggest that, at this age, one leaver in twelve has a reading age less than that of an average seven-year-old and one in four reads less well than the average nine-year-old. The figures of grade repetition from the schools of Europe tell the same tale. Reading, as measured by standardized tests (even when these measure reading comprehension) or grade repetition are, of course, only crude indices of the failure of education to equip substantial proportions of children with a minimal means of entry into a wider culture. Many, even most, poor readers have associated difficulties in the use of oral speech and poor verbal skills which account for accumulating failure through the grades. Partly at least because we are not managing to make an effective bridge between the restricted forms of language and culture of the homes and communities from which very many children come and the 'public' forms of elaborated speech and knowledge which are essential to a citizen in a complex modern State, by the end of their primary schooling many children have decided that what is offered is not for them. They cannot compete with satisfaction and even modest success and they give up the struggle. Many more who are less handicapped educationally than the obvious failures, nevertheless turn completely away in adolescence and young adulthood from all that education appears to imply. They become antagonistic not only to the formal learning for which in their eyes school stands but their conviction of inadequacy inhibits even the re-learning and training which industrial change implies, and such alienation spreads easily to a rejection of any positive social involvement Groups such as these represent not only a great waste of human potential in the present; they provide the climate of frustration and inadequacy in which their own children will subsequently grow pre-doomed to failure.

INDEPENDENCE AND AUTONOMY

Many children, however, accomplish all that the school seems to ask of them and by fairly simple and conventional standards are successful—

certainly in terms of the older conceptions of an elementary or primary education. They emerge with a standard equipment of general information, some instrumental skills and a learning style which depends upon authority, but they have not achieved any real measure of autonomy. Morally, socially and intellectually they are still, by the end of their primary schooling, not weaned even partially from dependence upon others for incentives and control. Yet, unless within the limits of their imperfect and still for the most part very concrete thought they are capable of judging and deciding for themselves and motivated to learn, with support and help from adults of course, but without coercion or the utter dependence upon approval which marks so many 'good' pupils, they are ill-prepared indeed to meet the drive towards independence which comes with adolescence. They are capable of rejecting and revolting against adult authority, but may be incapable of developing a genuine autonomy.

It is also of the utmost importance at the secondary stage, that pupils have already had an introduction to the differing kinds or modes of thought and knowledge which will subtend not only their ability to profit from secondary education but the whole way in which they are able to view their world. For those whose education in the primary or elementary school is all the formal education which they are likely to get, this training in at least the mathematical-logical, empirical-scientific, aesthetic and moral-personal modes of thinking is even more essential than it is for those who have the chance—through extended exposure to learning in adolescence—perhaps to find their way through for themselves.

This should not be taken to mean that any stage of education is to be considered and planned solely or even mainly in terms of preparation for a subsequent stage. The criterion that 'it may be necessary later' leads to authoritarian methods and provides the excuse for cramming into unwilling heads knowledge or experience which is beyond the immediate grasp or interest. Such a now or never mood in the teacher easily results in the pupils forgetting rapidly the knowledge proffered or in the building up of an accumulating and pervasive disgust for anything of the kind. This is particularly apt to happen with a precocious presentation of masterpieces of literature which in their emotional assumptions go far beyond the maturity of experience of the pupils. But it can occur with almost any aspect of the curriculum which makes demands upon understanding outside the reach of the child.

THE INTEGRITY OF THE PRIMARY STAGE

Like the nursery or infant school, the junior school should look to itself and to the needs and growth of its pupils, adapting its broad aims to the specific stage of development of the children for whom it is responsible. This must mean variety of expectations and approaches to different individuals in the same school or class and considerable differences between schools catering for groups of differing backgrounds. It must, in the light of the cultural and social differences which we know to exist, mean some positive discrimination in favour of the least fortunate groups. But it does not mean that normative demands are to be totally abandoned; only that the broad objectives are sought by appropriate although different routes and probably we have to be content with variable levels in their attainment. There is a strong case for ensuring minimum standards of competence in the instrumental skills and for an early and persistent effort at remedial work where any child appears to be lagging too far behind. There is, however, very little case for uniformity in knowledge or in syllabus, provided that the experiences to which the children are exposed have value and interest for them and in some effective way provide for the development of all the various ways of thinking that they can acquire and will need.

This is particularly important when we consider the other responsibility of those who educate pre-adolescent children—that of assisting their emotional education and building up a realistic albeit optimistic image of themselves. The obviously instrumental skills—the three Rs—are crucial in this for two reasons. Much store is set by parents and teachers on formal attainments and to the child the results of his efforts are readily perceived. The skills are of intrinsic importance too since so much else of later independent mastery depends upon them. But, important though these are, they are rather necessary than sufficient. Social skills, understanding of others, moral knowledge and insight, a trained ability to identify the nature of a problem and the appropriate ways of setting out to solve it are equally essential. The criticism which can legitimately be made of many syllabuses is that they provide a standard package of knowledge which may or may not be relevant (and be perceived by the child to be so) to the mass of other real experiences which dominate life outside the classroom. Such curriculum material may be well conceived in that it provides opportunities for developing and practising some at least of the ways of knowing which we have seen to be essential: but for the children exposed to it, the actual material may be in itself beyond their grasp, or not intrinsically relevant because it does not link with their life or their interests. If this is so they may tend to reject the material or find themselves unable to comprehend it: in fact in doing this they refuse the form of thinking which the material embodies. This is most easily seen in the teaching of mathematics in the old style with problems concerning taps flowing at different rates to fill or empty tanks; but it may equally occur with material thought to be apposite and 'modern' by the teacher. Any child is most likely to fail when he has little or no intrinsic interest in solving the problem with which he is presented, or if it appears grossly unfamiliar or contains concepts or expectations of knowledge or experience which he lacks. And failure teaches the expectation of failure. On the other hand, if a child experiences a deep interest in and need to solve a problem, he will tend to work away at it and may surmount apparently impossible obstacles to achieve his aim. The pedagogic art is to seize upon this kind of motivation and, judiciously, to support the child in his striving, to help him avoid as many as possible of the blind alleys and to assist—through questions, through reformulations of discoveries and through correlating other material—the process of generalization of concepts and the transfer of effective strategies of learning or problem solving to other and different areas of interest.

EMOTIONAL AND SOCIAL EDUCATION

School programmes and curricula rarely provide explicitly for the education of the emotional and social life, for the understanding of the self and others. This very important aspect of education tends to go forward, if at all, in more or less accidental and incidental ways. It seems to be assumed that the homes will in general do it or that children will pick it up as they go along. In school certain habits are enforced and rules have to be obeyed; occasionally or regularly, inside religious or civic instruction, moral precepts are given; and from time to time in an *ad hoc* sort of way children are rebuked or praised. The hope, too, is that through exposure to literature, art, music, drama and such like, the emotional life will be shaped and sensibility refined. Perhaps, provided the offering is rich enough, the general climate of the school is on the whole fostering and unaggressive and the adults are sufficiently mature and in accord with a general ethos, some children will profit in a diffused way from such an unplanned situation. But we now know that many do not, especially those who bring with them all kinds of difficulties of development, attitudes and serious misadjustments arising in their lives outside the school. If social and personal education is left to hazard, there is for all children a very serious risk that their understanding of themselves and others will be imperfect. This will be a poor preparation for that restructuring of the personality which takes place under the impact of the changes of adolescence and the generally increased introspection which accompanies it.

Again it should be unnecessary to emphasize that we are not suggesting that emotional and personal education should be a formal subject in the time-table or that teachers should be encouraged to think of themselves as psycho-therapists.[1] But it does mean that matters of feeling and behaviour, moral problems and dilemmas, notions about prejudices and their origins, the way in which others think and feel and the reasons why they do so. the encouragement of empathy and the like are as legitimate for discussion in schools by teachers and pupils as are history, geography and science. Children under ten are interested in animals and in babies; they do ask themselves questions about the behaviour of others towards them; they are moved by the feelings and situations described in books; and they do puzzle about sex, and about emotional incidents in their own lives and those of their friends. They can discover for themselves, with profit, how their pets learn, how babies grow, why they cry or smile; they can discuss among themselves, with the occasional intervention of a trusted adult, the ways humans behave and why they behave as they do; and they can seek models in life or in books to imitate and, by imitating, understand. There is little or no reason why their spontaneous drama should not deal with real or imaginary situations related to problems with which they are coping and why the mature adult should not contribute—as an adult—his or her understanding of meanings and moral frameworks. encouraging children to question these and to find out why he or she takes the position that he does. If the teacher is perceptive, such interpretive interventions will not be confined to lessons in literature, history, drama or what ever; they will occur as occasions prompt; and, particularly at times when the child is emotionally stirred, the sensitive adult will re-spond to the question which the child cannot or dare not ask.

A CONSTRUCTIVE ROLE FOR THE TEACHER

More perhaps than any other suggestion made in the course of this volume, this notion of a deliberately constructive role for the teacher in the personal development of his pupils is a departure from the tradi-tional perception of the pedagogue—though in one form or another it has been advocated (usually for adolescents) at least from the day of Plato. Moreover, it is a major part of what nursery and infant school teachers do, often unconsciously, as a matter of course since their per-ceptions of their role are more akin to those of an enlightened mother than are the ways in which many teachers of older children still see themselves. It is a preparedness to interact with children and to accept as valid any experience, any question, any feeling they may offer in terms of a common human equality and entitlement to respect. At the same time, the teacher is not a child: he or she is an authority by virtue of greater maturity, greater knowledge and responsibility both to the child and to the community. Thus, while only rarely imposing views, interpretations or rules, it is part of a teacher's professional obligation to explain, to direct attention to the values which he or she believes in, to give reasons for value judgements which are made and to help the child to make choices which will carry him further in knowledge, in insight and in the understanding of others as well as himself. Where the questions or needs do not spontaneously arise in the child's mind or are not prompted by his experience, it is a task of teachers—in terms of what they know to be important to the subsequent growth of their pupils—to bring into their pupils' field of attention provocative experiences, to ask provocative questions, and to ensure that whatever is missing from the environment is made present in the school. In this sense, what we are proposing is that education should be deliberately constructive, within a minimally uniform set of basic social and cognitive demands.

But for many, one might even say for most or all, children it has also to be remedial in the sense that large numbers of children are deprived and, for many more, modern environments do not provide all that an individual needs emotionally and cognitively, to be able to venture into the unknown with confidence. Such remedial action, as we have seen, is likely to be less effective if it is confined to what goes on in school, and does not bring home, school and community into participation, from the earliest stages of education. This is what 'en-schooling' society means—a restoration to all adults of their responsibility for the shaping of the next generation, and the emergence of the teacher from his role of the isolated and conservative guardian of sometimes irrelevant standards, to that of the expert educator who catalyses, refines and directs a learning-teaching team of adults and children learning together.

In spite of what we have said earlier about the importance of each stage of education conducting its affairs without specifically preparing for the next, it should nonetheless be prospective. We can no longer provide children in our schools with a map—moral, philosophical, religious or cognitive—by which they can guide themselves into a known future; we have in fact to equip them with a compass and the ability and confidence to use it to find their own way in a world the nature of which we cannot predict. Learned answers to problems become dysfunctional when the problems change; what we are asking for is that education should produce the ability to pose the right questions and equip children with the means of finding their own answers.

CREATIVITY AND DYNAMIC ADJUSTABILITY

It is here that a theme, latent in all the discussion so far, emerges as perhaps the dominant one; and certainly as a critical aspect of education in childhood prior to its extension in adolescence. The power to adjust and to change, to find new solutions to novel problems implies perceiving situations as they are rather than forcing them into habitual moulds, being able to create for oneself ways of interacting with them which are effective and apposite; and a developed ability to summon up trial solutions or hypotheses and to test them for fit. In fact, whatever the area of life with which we are concerned, it means a creative form of thinking rather than a fixed set of habitual responses. In this sense we are looking to education for the development of a high degree of intelligence of a specially adaptive kind.

In our present systems, intelligence tends to be equated with conventional academic success: with the learning and understanding of systematic knowledge and the acquisition of instrumental skills. It is true that people who are judged highly intelligent by these kinds of criteria, tend also to be those able to cope more readily and effectively than the rest of us with novelty. But this is not necessarily and always so.

It has been pointed out[2] that most intelligence tests, tests of attainment and traditional examinations measure the capacity to reproduce items of acquired knowledge and to apply conventional strategies of problem solving, the faultless application of a set of learned rules leading to a unique solution. This kind of thinking is often called 'linear' and tests of it (and curricula which imply it) tend to favour those whose intelligence runs along conventional lines—the 'convergers'. Many highly intelligent convergers while they do very well in formal academic work, find it difficult if they are asked to innovate or to undertake original research: they may lack originality and the ability to develop new and effective syntheses.

Among the gifted and probably at all levels there are those whose thinking is at least in some areas more 'lateral' and 'divergent' than others; instead of producing the learned response or the one determined by convention, or proceeding logically from 'a' to 'b', they possess the ability to produce a variety of responses educed by a variety of less orthodox criteria and from other than straightforwardly or logically associative processes. In some responses this form of thinking resembles the way that young children associate items of experience before they have developed the styles of thought, perception and attention which formal education fosters. For example, a two-year old having acquired (imperfect) concepts of a bee and of a motor car and seeing a snail said: 'Look—a bee in a car.' Similarly children's drawings and paintings sometimes exhibit an apparent freshness of vision and sincerity of execution, which though not intentional, makes them seem creative and original art works to the adult beholder. Much, however, of this freshness is due to imperfections of thought, perception or expressive skill rather than to a deliberately different way of going about viewing and presenting experience: there is in fact a very wide gulf between the naive child or the primitive 'artist' and the highly self-conscious creator like Picasso.

The ability to recombine experience in new ways is obviously a fundamental element in true creativity of any kind in any field, from the use of words to the eduction of scientific hypotheses. But it is not the only one. It is clearly important to be able to entertain a rich variety of associations and possible hypotheses not all of them logically linked in the same way; but equally it is important to have the capacity to reject those which are in appropriately bizarre or banal and to choose the one or those most effective for the purpose in hand. Similarly, since associations and ideas can only arise from the mind, the quality and richness of experience and prior thinking is an important determinant of the value of what will be available for choice and creative resynthesis.

Research with tests of 'creativity'[3] tends to show that the more intelligent children, adolescents and adults tend to produce more, and more original, responses: they seem to be generally more fluent and flexible in their thinking. But, and this is important, the correlation between the kind of high ability shown on 'convergent' intelligence or attainment measures and high scores on tests of 'divergent thinking' is not absolute. There may in fact be two broadly different but over-lapping groups at least of children: those comparatively low on divergence and high on convergence and those markedly the other way.[4] The first group tends to be more or less conformist, successful in school and consequently appreciated and valued by their teachers; the second may be less successful academically, more likely to be undervalued or indeed rejected by their teachers, and sometimes to become maladjusted, particularly if their teachers are of a markedly 'convergent' type of thinking. It seems probable that differences are at least fostered by education and vary with education systems, even with particular schools and teachers; although so far as individuals are concerned within any system or school much depends upon factors in their personality as well as upon the circumstances of the particular task with which they are faced.

It is likely too that creative work of any level achieved by adults in different fields of human activity requires qualitatively very different kinds of intelligent thought and that certain kinds of divergent thinking, particularly if not critically controlled, would be a positive disadvantage in many situations. Affective and personality correlates—particularly degrees of inhibition which control the accessibility of more or less unconscious material, rigidity or flexibility of thought, levels of anxiety, susceptibility to excitement in the face of a problem, dispositions to attend and powers of concentration—play a very important part too in determining whether and how ability will declare itself in original achievement. They may well be determinant in the relation of intellectual power or talent to what we would recognize as genius.[5]

GENIUS

This is a matter of central importance to education which we should pursue since exceptional genius is not a thing apart but the culmination of a continuum on which education should help to place each child. It is, however, doubtful whether creative genius of a high order is possible without a level of general ability well above the average. In certain fields this is self-evident: for example, it is difficult to conceive of creative genius in science without there being the ability intellectually to master a demanding intellectual discipline. On the other hand, while conventional academic abilities may not be essential to painting, there is more to a work of visual art than formal skills of colour or design; an organizing, problem solving sensitivity is required and for the very greatest work, a power of reflective comment. Even the physical gifts and skills of the ballerina will not bring success unless they are accompanied by a high general ability to learn. In some fields, high intelligence and determination will bring about the necessary level of executive skill to subtend the expression of creative thought. Indeed in any creative field—the arts, the sciences, literature, human relations, administration, scholarship—outstanding individuals will exhibit very different combinations of high intelligence and special aptitudes.

Moreover, there are degrees of precocity with which genius reveals itself. The more productivity depends upon experience, learning and knowledge of life, the later genius or a high degree of special ability tends to declare itself or develop. Mathematical genius can, and often does, appear very early;[6] so do certain forms of musical ability.[7] On the other hand the juvenilia of even the greatest poets are no clear indication of what is to be;[8] and many highly intelligent children and adolescents produce juvenilia of high quality but subsequently have no flash of genius.[9]

As in many other areas of development, what we call intelligence and special ability tend to operate as threshold variables: they are necessary but not sufficient to very high achievement which depends upon a complex galaxy of environmental and personal factors. Musical families for example, like the Bachs, provide the environment within which musical skill and marked musical ability can emerge; a probably higher degree of motivation and ability would be necessary for musical genius to emerge from a family or school system providing little opportunity or encouragement. It may well have been the circumstances and bent of the time that made Shakespeare express himself through drama rather than in politics or science. Leonardo da Vinci found and profited from a situation in which he could be scientist, architect, engineer, politician and painter—a combination of circumstances which has

hardly arisen in Europe since the end of the seventeenth century. Again,
however, we are dealing with necessary rather than sufficient conditions.
Genius implies the creation of something new, some major expansion of
knowledge or of human sensitivity, something which is not merely
highly competent achievement along conventional lines. For this, as the
accounts given of discoveries—from the ringing cry of 'Eureka',[10] down
to the casual observation of penicillin mould—show that three conditions appear to be necessary. The first of these is that, consciously or
unconsciously the individual must have been 'aware' of a problem, have
'worked' hard at it and enriched the content of his mind with a vast
amount of information, experience and sensation. This may be the hard
and systematic amassing of facts and the results of experiments by the
scientist which enables him to attend selectively to what he is interested
in and to be aware of whether it fits or does not fit; or the sensitivity
to sights, sounds and words of a poet like Keats or Coleridge.[11] The
quality of this 'compost' will obviously be determined by the intellectual
quality of the individual's mind and by his trained sensitivity. The second
factor of crucial importance is a high degree of mastery of the appropriate means of expression: and again this is something which is
acquired by continuous application.

Almost all accounts of 'inspiration' or 'discovery' emphasize the
sudden flash of insight, the moment or the period where ideas, impressions, items of knowledge 'magically' fall into new and significant
combinations by some process which appears to be outside the normal.
Keats talks of the 'magic hand of chance', others of solutions that come
in sleep, others like Handel or Blake of visions. There are two characteristic features, intense excitement and concentration and, at least momen-
tarily, a dissociation of the rational, critical mind[12] which allows material
from the unconscious or subconscious mind to emerge in relationships
not dictated by conventional rationality.[13]

It will be noted that this process, as described above, is not
apparently greatly different in its mechanisms from that which leads to
psychotic art or indeed to much of the creative work of children: the
contents of the unconscious mind emerge in relationships determined by
unconscious associations and uninhibited by rational thought or experience. But there are differences: in pathological cases, the subject does
not subsequently critically accept or reject and choose among the
offerings of the unconscious. What he produces tends to be bizarre
rather than significantly original or, if it is original in any true sense, it
is not distinguishable from merely heteroclite conjunctions of odd
symbolisms. Nor, usually, is the unconscious material particularly rich,
at least not in the same sense as that gathered by the sensitivity and
intelligence of genius.[14] Finally the psychotic does not master the means
of expression and the ability to relate the valuably novel to what exists

already, eliminating the commonplace or merely odd. Similarly the creative products of children owe a good deal to their lack of experience, imperfect command of the medium and relatively undeveloped conceptualization. Some of their 'freshness' too is due to their not having trained themselves in the repression of interfering associations which is the result of the disciplining of attention. Finally they may not have acquired standards of relevance and originality by which to judge their own productions.

There are, one must repeat, considerable differences among forms of human activity and between individuals in the ways in which 'insight' and 'inspiration' will pierce the commonplace. In some cases, the sensation of inspiration is minimal and the result is obtained by hard, sustained and concentrated work. In others imagination is so fluid, powerful and yet disciplined that the excitement of production is itself enough to spark off the effective new juxtaposition—leading to such compact statements as:

> '. . . let the candied tongue lick absurd pomp;
> And crook the pregnant hinges of the knee
> Where thrift may follow fawning. . . .'[15]

in which a great deal of experience, observation and feeling come together in a characteristic utterance not so much of the author, Shakespeare, as of his intensely felt characterization of Hamlet.

FOSTERING CREATIVENESS

All this may seem something of an excursion away from the education of children in their primary schools but as has been said, what we call genius is only the extreme and striking example of a form of thinking of vital importance in the life of all adults, particularly in changing times when the supports of traditions are withdrawn. Young children have more curiosity, a more fluid approach to reality, but in our sense they are not truly 'creative', though the experiences to which their naive interests lead may well be for the child himself in terms of excitement and expression. However, even in reasonably free and open education systems, the process of socialization tends to impel children to surrender even this form of creativity and to conform to group activities, to rules and regulations.[16] The problem is in fact so to educate all children that, in the process of acquiring the knowledge, skills and the convergent kinds of thinking of which they also have need, they do not lose the ability to recombine their experiences in novel ways.[17]

True creativeness involves qualities of mind which must be cultivated, and cannot be left to chance. There must be exposure to a rich and varied experience which is both cognitively and emotionally stimulating and which provides the 'compost' from which to recombine experience in new ways.

There must also be a degree of mastery of the relevant modes of thinking and knowing as well as a sufficient command of the means of expression. The lateral or associative thinking, the hypothesis-making or the bringing up of unusual or 'original' combinations of ideas depend upon a certain fluency of thought, upon the ability to be excited or to concentrate attention on what the mind brings forth without, initially, being too self-critical. It is, too, of almost equal importance that the judgement should be trained to choose among the material produced that which is efficient for its purpose, that which is truly original, rejecting the merely bizarre or banal.

Looked at in this way, the fostering of creative thought certainly calls in question, even if it is not diametrically opposed to, the assumptions which underlie the heavily normative functions of traditional education. The tendency of most of our schools is to provide a lock-step kind of curriculum in which all pupils are taught the same general body of information, provided with a similar set of experiences and expected, by and large, to reproduce the predetermined (and unique) answer. Stress is laid upon the identification of errors and upon their correction and the objectives of whatever is done are set by the curriculum or by the teacher rather than by the pupils themselves. In the best schools of this type, the mastery of some relevant modes of thinking and knowing, of formal means of expression and a fairly narrowly conceived ability to criticize a production according to restricted criteria of correctness, are well developed.

It is also true that many creative geniuses have emerged from or at least survived schooling of this kind, though if it is very restrictive and formal it may create problems for the very gifted and creative child, particularly in his 'teens.

The kind of solid achievement which is the mark of formal schooling should not be despised or underrated and teaching which insists on systematic learning and linear thinking is not inimical to or even incompatible with a much fuller development of creativeness. Nor conversely does the development of creativeness imply that all the values, methods and intellectual discipline of the traditional school should be thrown out of the window—as some of the more arrogant reformers would have us think. Children in their primary schools enjoy and need formal masteries and the security of getting something clearly right or wrong, of knowing what is expected, of developing standards of judgement which they can apply in almost mathematical ways. They need the assurance that the teacher knows where he is going and wishes them to go, just as they need a calculable discipline and authority as the basis from which they can develop an ability to tolerate freedom and self-determination. No service is done to the young by the attitude that the only standards of behaviour or of intellectual production are highly relative, centred upon the sacredness of the self, or simply being different or on 'doing one's own thing'. Nor is it helpful to praise any piece of expressive work without discrimination and without an appeal to the child's own judgement and awareness of his own objectives.

On the other hand, few pupils by the age of 11 will have reached the stage of 'formal' thinking as outlined by Piaget—the final stage of cognitive development characterized by abstract thinking, the capacity to make true hypotheses, to verify them in a structured combinatorial way, and the ability to distinguish between lawful and probable events.[18] Hence both their creativeness and their powers of judgement will be imperfect by adult standards. Too much, and particularly too authoritarian, intervention by adults imposing standards of 'rightness' seems likely both to repress creativity altogether or by confronting children with criteria which are literally incomprehensible, to induce a rigid and parrot-like conformity.

As in almost every other aspect of the early education of children, what is needed is a nice balance between authority and self-determination, between linear and lateral thinking, between reproductive and creative activity, and a developed capacity to choose appropriately between them for the purpose in hand.

In terms of fostering in all children—dull, average or bright—the joy of breaking new ground, the feeling of excited satisfaction that comes from creating for oneself, and the flexibility of mind that makes new adjustments possible without undue stress, school work has to be planned with a clear idea that creativeness should be not only acceptable when it occurs (even if it is initially shocking) but stimulated and fostered; and this in a context in which the formal attainments and masteries of the vehicles of expression are seen by the children themselves as also a necessary part of the whole. It seems reasonable, for example, that there should be times when children are encouraged — freely and without the inhibitions which attention to an imperfect command of formal skills so often means—to produce as many and as many kinds of ideas as possible. The teacher will deliberately and intentionally excite his class and use the state of excitement to help them develop, as it were, a heap of material without thought initially for its quality. But such brain-storming sessions should be followed by others where the aim is to eliminate the banal and to test the relevance of what remains against criteria which children have themselves evolved in discussion with their teacher. Finally they should see that the working up of an original set of ideas, of visual form, of sounds, phrases or of hypotheses involves the formal skills and the hard work of applying them. The vehicle is thus to be seen as an important part of what they want to achieve. The teacher should, of course, lend his help where the technique required is beyond their present mastery or where the need is felt by the child for something which he has not yet learned.[19]

It must be emphasized that such an approach should not be confined to the conventional 'expressive' subjects, like art or spontaneous drama. It can and should be used in work in the mother tongue, written as well as spoken, in the study of the environment, in simple science.[20] The important aspects are those of encouragement, free excited expression and discovery without too much critical inhibition, and the subsequent attempt to get the children to educe their own objectives, their own criteria of judgement—always in a context which implies that standards are really determined not by arbitrary decision of adults, but by factors inherent in the situation itself—by whether a piece of painting or a poem communicates to another what its author felt, by whether a hypothesis stands up to a rigorous test and so on. The judgement, support and praise of the teacher are important, particularly the degree to which children can be made to feel that originality and creativeness are welcomed, even if they challenge the teacher's own orthodoxy. The teacher will, justly, be regarded as an authority by the pupils and he or she is the guide. Pedagogic skill lies in directing and sharpening attention by question and remark, by pointing out successes and asking why, in helping children to surmount the technical difficulties which beset their expression, and in providing increasingly subtly analysed 'models' from the adult world, not so much to be imitated as to be understood and evaluated in the same kind of terms as children try to understand and evaluate their own work.

We must not forget that other, vitally important aspect of creativeness—the component of rich and varied experience which forms the very basis on which new combinations can arise. Nor must we overlook that the form in which ability of any kind or level declares itself is to some extent a function of the stimulation and possibilities provided by the environment. It seems unlikely, for example, that musical talent will declare itself effectively in an unmusical environment or that scientific insight will grow where the child has little contact with the kind of thinking and knowledge which it implies. Creativeness in human relations, too, implies an affective and moral environment where behaviour and motive can be spontaneously discussed, where different solutions to personal problems can at least be played out in dramatic form.

SCHOOL AS A PROVOCATIVE ENVIRONMENT

This must lead us to plan the school as what might be called a provocative environment, a place where the child is solicited by the possibility of many kinds of activity—musical, dramatic, scientific, artistic —and where the world is brought into the classroom and the children sally forth in search of experience, sensation and knowledge. Children are deeply influenced by the enthusiasms of adults whom they like and respect and who make direct contact with them. One cannot expect even a team of teachers to have knowledge of and enthusiasm for all the exciting kinds of experience which the world has to offer; but one can reasonably ask that they have some enthusiasms to share and that they will provide the means whereby their pupils can meet and talk with many sorts and varieties of people in the world outside. One can, too, ask that they are watchful for the least sign of talent, that they foster and nourish it and seek others who can take the child further along any line for which he shows interest and aptitude.

For all children and particularly for the talented or the very intelligent, the five or six years of the primary school are likely to be critical in determining whether their cognitive style is limited to one mode— usually that of linear or convergent thinking—or whether they have at their command different styles of thinking and are aware of their differing appropriateness to various situations. It is of the utmost importance, too, that the technical means of expression are mastered not with an attempt at blind perfection but as a flexible basis for the embodiment of thinking and problem solving, and in a way which permits the child to change and adapt his techniques to novel situations. Creativity implies confidence in the worthwhileness of the activity and of one's own responses and a certain daring in rejecting the safe and known solutions, a certain openness to associations and ideas which are not sanctioned by familiarity or by authority; but if it is to be of real service to the individual, it also implies the ability to appraise one's work with a degree of objectivity and by means of clear criteria and not to accept an idea merely because it is unusual.

The outcome of much primary schooling is a certain rigidity of thought coupled with an unwillingness to move outside the accepted forms of expression. What is known is believed to be absolute and is seen as a closed system rather than an open-ended one which will change with extending experience. This tends to mean that school knowledge is regarded as something apart from life and what goes on outside the classroom: it is a series of tricks which one learns to master for no particular reason and more or less well.

The change one would wish to see—and which seems essential in preparing children for adolescence and for the world of rapid transformations in which they will live—is one which emphasizes openendedness, which sees the skills which we must all command as instrumental and not as ends in themselves and which regards knowledge not as the purpose of education but as the essential raw material of experience from which new combinations arise to meet new circumstances.

NOTES

1. But schools have much to learn from therapeutic communities. For a detailed analysis of the concepts and structures involved see: Sugarman, B. The therapeutic community and the school. *Interchange (Canada)* (Toronto), vol. 1, no. 2, 1970.

2. For the best general review and bibliography on the topic see: Freeman, F.; Butcher, H. J.; Christie, T. *Creativity.* 2nd ed. London, Society for Research into Higher Education Ltd., 1971.

3. Basically, tests, success in which is determined by the number, originality or sometimes the quality of responses to a stimulus rather than by the obvious and received response—e.g., 'How many uses can you find for a brick?' as distinct from 'What is the purpose for which bricks are used?' These tests are better described as tests of 'divergent thinking' than of creativity since they do not include other aspects which are important for productive creativity. (Butcher, H. J. Divergent thinking and creativity. In: Wall, W. D.; Varma, V., eds. *Advances in educational psychology. I.* London, University of London Press, 1972.)

4. But they are only *broadly* different and younger children may not exhibit such a difference at all (Hasan, P.; Butcher, H. J. Creativity and intelligence: a partial replication with Scottish children of Getzel and Jackson's Study. *British journal of educational psychology* (London), vol. 57, pt. 2, 1966). As Butcher (Op. cit.) points out, the solution of a difficult 'convergent' problem involves the production of a considerable number of hypotheses before the right one is found. L. Hudson (*Contrary imaginations.* London, Methuen, 1966. / *Frames of mind: ability, perception and self-perception.* London, Methuen, 1968) suggests plausibly that scientists are predominantly convergent thinkers (and none the less creative) and arts specialists predominantly divergers. This may well be because the verbal content of many tests favours the arts speciaist. Cronbach 1968 (cited by Butcher. Op. cit. 1968) argues that the less divergent thinkers impose a higher standard of control on the quality and relevance of the ideas which they produce. One should also be reminded that in 'divergent production' there are probably many independent functions and that each individual shows an uneven pattern of these. Guilford's model of intelligence is a 4 x 4 x 6 cube, providing some 96 functions of which about 24 are related to divergent production (Guilford, J. P. Creativity: retrospect and prospect. *Journal of creative behaviour* (Buffalo, N.Y.), vol. 4, no. 3, 1970).

5. See the summary of researchers bearing upon this compiled by F. Freeman and his colleagues (*Creativity*, Op. cit., p. 99ff); and particularly those of H. M. Parlo and others (personality characteristics which differentiate creative male adolescents and adults. *Journal of personality* (Durham, N.C.), vol. 36, pt. 4, 1968).

6. Newton corrected errors in his father's accounts at the age of eight.

7. The classical case is the young Mozart.

8. See, for example, the early poems of Shelley (*The poetical works of Percy Bysshe Shelley*. Edited by E. Dowden. London, Macmillan, 1891. p. 611ff). Pope, it is true, claimed that he '. . . lisped in numbers for the numbers came' but we have nothing left to judge by!

9. Terman, L., *et al. Genetic studies of genius*. Vol. I: *Mental and physical traits of a thousand gifted children*. Stanford, Stanford University Press, 1926.

10. See the detailed treatment of Archimedes 'Eureka' experience in: Koestler, A. *The act of creation*. London, Hutchinson, 1962.

11. It has been shown (Livington Lowes. *The road to Xanadu*. London, Constable, 1966) that Coleridge's reading in a great variety of books of travel is directly reflected in the most strikingly original passages of the 'Ancient Mariner' and 'Kubla Khan'. Keats acknowledges his debt to Chapman's 'Homer'.

12. Blake was very aware of this. He speaks of the 'meddling intellect' as the great inhibitor of the imagination and the instinctual life.

13. For example, Poincaré's account of his discovery of Fuchsian functions (Koestler, A. Op. cit.).

14. The productions of genius in psychotic episodes tend to have a much higher quality and in some forms of dissociation—for example, under the influence of drugs as in the case of Coleridge and de Quincy, or schizoid episodes, as with Blake—the quality, originality and creativeness are higher than that produced in normal circumstances. Another example is the famous drawings of a cat produced by Louis Wain during a psychotic episode. See also: Prinzhorn, H. *Bildnerei der Geisteskranken*. Berlin, Springer, 1970.

15. *Hamlet*, act III, sc. ii.

16. Pulsifer, S. N. *Children are poets*. Cambridge, Mass., Dresser Chapman & Grimes, 1963.

17. Of recent years, proposals have been made (for example: De Bono, E. *Lateral thinking*. London, Ward Lock, 1970) for research into the ways in which children may be trained in 'lateral' thinking. However, the suggestion that 'thinking' should be a subject on the time-table (rather than a matter for attention in any learning situation) seems likely to be counterproductive in the same way that setting moral education up as a separate subject so often is.

18. Piaget, J.; Inhelder, Bärbel. *La psychologie de l'enfant*. Paris, Presses universitaires de France, 1947. Idem. *The growth of logical thinking from childhood to adolescence*. New York, Basic Books, 1958.

19. E. P. Torrance (Achieving socialisation without sacrificing creativity. *Journal of creative behaviour* (Buffalo, N.Y.), vol. 4, no. 3, 1970) details a series of researches and experiments involving mainly five-year-old children. See also his *Rewarding creative behavior* (Englewood Cliffs, N.J., Prentice Hall, 1965), and *Encouraging creativity in the classroom* (Dubuque, Iowa, Brown, 1970).

20. The sort of work that can be done with primary school children in the mother tongue is described by A. B. Clegg (*The excitement of writing*. London, Chatto & Windus, 1964) and in a work edited by T. Blackburn (*Presenting poetry*. London, Methuen, 1966). Much more wide-ranging suggestions of a practical kind covering all the forms of knowledge for children up to 8 or 9 years old are made in: Brearley, M., ed. *Fundamentals in the first school*. Oxford, Blackwell, 1969. Corresponding attempts have been conducted in the U.S.S.R. (Kel', O. S.; Čerepašenec, G. R., eds.

Razvitie samostojateľ nostri i tvorčeskoj aktivnosti škoľnikov. Moskva, Prosceščenie, 1964); the work describes experiments in the development of spontaneity and creative action by school children through work in the classroom, in study circles and in a variety of out-of-school activities. For work with rather older children (11–13) see: *Polyphème* (Genève), vol. 19 and 20, 1971–73.

21. Though, just as children learn by playing out roles in an imitative way, many creative artists also apprentice themselves to an imitation of the great masters of their art. Robert Louis Stevenson acquired his mastery of English prose by 'playing the sedulous ape' to his great predecessors; Beethoven learned from Mozart.

FURTHER READING

Avaster, A. *Creativity in the life cycle.* I—Annotated bibliography; II—An interpretive account of creativity in childhood, adolescence and adulthood. Leiden, Brill, 1968.

Beaudot, A. *La créativité à l'école.* Paris, Presses universitaires de France, 1969.

Freeman, F.; Butcher, H. J.; Christie, T. *Creativity.* 2nd edition. London, Society for Research into Higher Education Ltd., 1971.

Graton, R.; Clere, V. *L'activité créatrice chez l'enfant.* Tournai, Casterman, 1971.

Gowan, J. C.; Demos, G. D.; Torrance, E. P. *Creativity: its educational implications.* New York, London; Wiley, 1967.

Guilford, J. P. *Intelligence, creativity and their educational implications.* San Diego, Calif., Knapp, 1968.

Kel', O. S.; Čerepašenec, G. R., eds. *Razvitie samostojateľnosti i tvor-českoj aktivnosti škoľnikov* [Development of independent and creative activities of school children]. Moskva, Prosveščenie, 1964.

Koestler, A. *The act of creation.* London, Hutchinson, 1962.

Landau, E. *Psychologie der kreativität* [Psychology of creativity]. München, Reinhardt, 1969.

Lytton, H. *Creativity and education.* London, Routledge & Kegan Paul, 1971.

Stern, A. *Initiation à l'activité créatrice.* Montreal, Education Nouvelle, 1970.

Taylor, C. W., ed. *Widening horizons in creativity.* New York, Wiley, 1964. (The proceedings of the Fifth Utah Creativity Research Conference).

Torrance, E. P. *Encouraging creativity in the classroom.* Dubuque, Iowa, Brown, 1970.

———. *Rewarding creative behaviour.* Englewood Cliffs, N.J., Prentice-Hall, 1965.

Subject Index

335

Authors Index